THE GUINNESS BOOK OF WINNERS AND CHAMPIONS

SECOND EDITION

CHRIS COOK
ANNE MARSHALL

SPORTS EDITOR
PETER MATTHEWS

Guinness Superlatives Limited
2 Cecil Court, London Road, Enfield, Middlesex EN2 6DJ

British Library Cataloguing in Publication Data
Cook, Chris
  The Guinness book of winners and champions.
  2nd ed.
  I. Title   II. Marshall, Anne
  790. 1'34
  ISBN 0–85112–218–3

Published by Guinness Superlatives Limited
2 Cecil Court, London Road, Enfield, Middlesex EN2 6DJ

Guinness is a registered trademark of
Guinness Superlatives Limited

Designer: Jean Whitcombe
Layout: David Roberts

Photoset, printed and bound in Great Britain
by Redwood Burn Ltd, Trowbridge, Wiltshire

Front cover
Design and artwork: Robert Heesom
Photography: Vernon Morgan/Rapier Arts

The editor would like to thank the following for providing items for inclusion in the photograph: Egon Ronay Organisation – 'Hotel of the Year' gold plate; Royal Smithfield Club – rosette from Royal Smithfield Show; John Player & Sons – John Player League Trophy; The Muppet Show – Kermit; The Glenfyne Distillery Co. Ltd – Langs Supreme *Times* Crossword trophy.

PREFACE

This new edition of *The Guinness Book of Winners and Champions* provides a wide-ranging, authoritative and yet often amusing book of equal value for reference and for pleasure. As with the first edition, the aim has been to include as many varied and interesting events, both national and international, as possible that will appeal to all members of the family. The entries range from such long-established contests as Miss Universe, the Eurovision Song Contest and Mastermind, to such newer contests as Musician of the Year, or the CAMRA Beer of the Year award. All entries have been updated to include the latest results at the time of going to press. Sports enthusiasts will find comprehensive results of the 1980 Moscow Olympics, pop music fans the latest rock and pop awards. Each competition is arranged under a main heading (eg all the film awards are under Cinema) but the comprehensive index at the end of the book should be consulted if in any doubt. Nationalities of individuals are included, where appropriate, in brackets after the name, using a system of the first three letters of the country.

The editors would welcome suggestions for additional entries and would be grateful for any information concerning updated entries to include in the next edition of this book.

ACKNOWLEDGEMENTS

The second edition of this new work of reference would never have appeared without the help and co-operation of many scores of people. Countless information officers and secretaries of a host of organisations, many of them replying voluntarily in their spare time, provided much of the information contained in this book. A special debt is due to the staffs of the BBC and ITV for many hours of research.

Among the colleagues and friends who have provided ideas and inspiration are Stephen Brooks, Richard Clayton, Mark Donachy, Margaret Kennard, Peter Morgan, Keith Reader, Will Richardson, Hilary Rubinstein, Pat Smith and John Stevenson. Richard Gordon, Graham Hatton and Peter Humphries also provided convivial support and equally convivial company. Both Philip Jones and Ian Wheeler have played a considerable part in the revisions necessary for this second edition.

For secretarial help the largest debt is due to Jean Ali and Shirley Sheppard who have undertaken research and the burden of typing the revised manuscript with unfailing good humour.

CONTENTS

Advertising

Full lists of award winners are published each year in *Campaign* magazine, and the following are just several of the main awards.

CAMPAIGN PRESS ADVERTISING AWARDS

These awards are made annually by *Campaign*. The winning advertisements are selected by a jury consisting of individuals who work for, or clients who employ, advertising agencies.

GOLD AWARDS 1981

Best Individual Advertisement: Death. Creative dir: Frank Lowe; Art dir: Neil Godfrey; Copywriter: Tony Brignull; Typo: Nigel Dawson; Photo: James Wormser; Accounting dir: Michelle Adruab; Agency: Advertising and Marketing Services; Client: Albany Life Assurance.

Best Individual Advertisement: Sitting Art dir: Ron Collins; Copywriter: Andrew Rutherford; Typo: Mike Rix; Photo: Terry Donovan; Agency: Wight Collins Rutherford Scott Ltd; Chefaro Properietaries Ltd.

Best Campaign of Colour Advertisements: Christmas Pyramids, Artist's Easel, Umbrellas, Integrated Circuit: Creative dir: Tony Brignull; Art dirs: David Horry, Alan Waldie, Neil Godfrey, Nigel Rose; Copywriter: Alfredo Marcantonio; Photo: Alan Brooking, Brian Duffy, Neil Godfrey, Ed White; Agency: Collett Dickenson Pearce & Partners Ltd; Client: Gallaher Ltd.

Best Campaign of Black and White Advertisements: Safety cell, Save your life, Ditto, Be on the safe side, Crunchy on the outside. Creative dir: Dawson Yeoman; Art dir: Max Henry; Copywriter: Stuart Blake; Typo: Jeff Jessop; Agency: Doyle Dane Bernbach Ltd; Client: Volkswagen (GB) Ltd.

D&AD AWARDS

The Designers and Art Directors Association Awards are given each year by the charity of that name for the best of British Graphics, Advertising, Television and Editorial Design.

GOLD AWARDS 1981

For Film Advertising: 'Kipper'/Lego. Dir: Ken Turner; Copywriter: Mike Cozens; Art Dir: Graham Watson; Agency Prod: Jane Bearman; Ed: Patrick Udale; Lighting Cameraman: Tom Harrison; Agency: TBWA Ltd; Producer: David Mitten; Production Co: Clearwater Films; Advertising Man: Clive Nicholls; Animator: Denis Russo; Model Maker: David Lyall; Client: Lego (UK) Ltd.

Answer these ten questions and work out the date of your own death.

Entitled 'Death' a Gold Award was given for this 'Best Individual Advertisement' in the 1981 Campaign *Press Advertising Awards*

For Design for Television: 'Thérèse Raquin' – 3 part serial. Dir: Simon Langton; Graphic Designer: Stefan Pstrowski; Set Designer: David Myerscough-Jones; Lighting: Howard King; Prod. Co: BBC Television; Costume Designer: Reg Samuel; Make-Up: Jean Speak; Prod: Jonathan Powell; Music Composer/Arranger: Patrick Gower; Programme Co: BBC Television.

For a Poster: 'This much lead in this much pencil'/Parker Continuous Feed Pencils. Art Dir: John Horton; Copywriter: Richard Foster; Photo: Graham Ford; Typo: Maggie Lewis; Agency: Collett Dickenson Pearce & Partners Ltd; Marketing Services: Phillip Blowfield; Marketing Dir: Jack Margry; Client: Parker Pen Co. Ltd.

For Sales Promotion: Slumberdown (FIOS) Padded Quilt. Art Dir: John McConnell; Designers: John McConnell, Keren House, Mark Biley; Illus: Dan Fern; Design Group: Pentagram; Marketing Dir: Mr T. L. Kay; Client: FIOS Ltd.

American Football

The American Professional Football Association was formed in 1920. Its name was changed in 1922 to the National Football League (NFL).

In 1933 the National Football League was divided into two divisions – Eastern and Western, with the winners of each division meeting in the championship play-off. From

1950 to 1952 the two divisions were named American and National, before reverting to Eastern and Western from 1953 to 1970.

Meanwhile in 1960 the American Football League (AFL) was formed and from 1970 under the umbrella of the National Football League there was a re-organisation of teams. From then there were two conferences, the National Conference and the American Conference, each containing three divisions.

SUPER BOWL WINNERS

At the end of each season the winners of each Conference meet in the Super Bowl. The game is played in mid-January. Results have been:

1967	Green Bay (NFL)	35
	Kansas City (AFL)	10
1968	Green Bay (NFL)	33
	Oakland (AFL)	14
1969	New York (AFL)	16
	Baltimore (NFL)	7
1970	Kansas City (AFL)	23
	Minnesota (NFL)	7
1971	Baltimore (AFC)	16
	Dallas (NFC)	13
1972	Dallas (NFC)	24
	Miami (AFC)	3
1973	Miami (AFC)	14
	Washington (NFC)	7
1974	Miami (AFC)	24
	Minnesota (NFC)	7
1975	Pittsburgh (AFC)	16
	Minnesota (NFC)	6
1976	Pittsburgh (AFC)	21
	Dallas (NFC)	17
1977	Oakland (AFC)	32
	Minnesota (NFC)	14
1978	Dallas (NFC)	27
	Denver (AFC)	10
1979	Pittsburgh (AFC)	35
	Dallas (NFC)	31
1980	Pittsburgh (AFC)	31
	Los Angeles (NFC)	19
1981	Oakland (AFC)	27
	Philadelphia (NFC)	10

HEISMAN MEMORIAL TROPHY

Awarded annually since 1935 by the Downtown Athletic Club of New York City to the top college footballer of the year as determined by a poll of journalists.

The only man to win the trophy twice is Archie Griffin of Ohio State (1974 and 1975). Recent winners:

1976 Tony Dorsett (Pittsburgh)
1977 Earl Campbell (Texas)
1978 Billy Sims (Oklahoma)
1979 Charles White (Southern California)
1980 George Rogers (South Carolina)

O. J. (Orenthal James) Simpson in action for the Buffalo Bills. In 1967 he ran on the University of Southern California world record sprint relay team

Angling

WORLD CHAMPIONSHIPS

World championships have been held annually since 1957, following European championships which started in 1953. Winners:

TEAM

1957 Italy	1966 France
1958 Belgium	1967 Belgium
1959 France	1968 France
1960 Belgium	1969 Holland
1961 GDR	1970 Belgium
1962 Italy	1971 Italy
1963 France	1972 France
1964 France	1973 Belgium
1965 Romania	1974 France

1975 France	1978 France
1976 Italy	1979 France
1977 Luxembourg	1980 W. Germany

INDIVIDUAL

1957 Mandeli (Ita)
1958 Garroit (Bel)
1959 Robert Tesse (Fra)
1960 Robert Tesse (Fra)
1961 Ramon Legogue (Fra)
1962 Raimondo Tedesco (Ita)
1963 Billy Lane (Eng)
1964 Joseph Fontanet (Fra)
1965 Robert Tesse (Fra)

1966 Henri Guiheneuf (Fra)
1967 Jacques Isenbaert (Bel)
1968 Gunter Grebenstein (Ger)
1969 Robin Harris (Eng)
1970 Marcel van den Eynde (Bel)
1971 Dino Bassi (Ita)
1972 Hubert Levels (Hol)
1973 Pierre Michiels (Bel)
1974 Aribert Richter (Ger)
1975 Ian Heaps (Eng)
1976 Dino Bassi (Ita)
1977 Jean Mainil (Bel)
1978 Jean-Pierre Fougeat (Fra)
1979 Gerard Heulard (Fra)
1980 Wolfgang Kremkus (Ger)

Dave Burr (centre) *of Rugby poses with one of two keepnets of bream which, in the 1965 National, gave him the record individual weight* (Colin W. Graham)

ENGLISH NATIONAL FEDERATION OF ANGLERS' CHAMPIONSHIP

First held in 1906. Team winner on most occasions has been Leeds with 7 wins (1909, 1910, 1914, 1928, 1948, 1949, 1952). The only man to win two individual titles is James Bazley (Leeds) in 1909 and 1927.

The record catch is 76 lb 9 oz by David Burr (Rugby) in the Huntspill, Somerset in 1965.

Winners since 1960 (note that from 1972 the NFA introduced Divisions, and the winners given are those of Division One):

Year	Venue	Team	Weight			Individual	Weight		
			lb	oz	dr		lb	oz	dr
1960	Ant, Bure and Thurne	King's Lynn	81	15	4	K. Smith (Norwich)	50	14	8
1961	Trent	Coventry	77	4	4	J. Blakey (Saltaire)	23	12	12
1962	Welland	Lincoln	56	2	12	V. Baker (Derby)	13	11	0
1963	Gloucester Canal	Northampton Nene	18	11	8	R. Sims (N. Somerset)	14	15	8
1964	Severn	Kidderminster	50	13	8	C. Burch (Essex County)	32	3	0
1965	Huntspill	Rugby	93	7	4	D. Burr (Rugby)	76	9	0
1966	Witham	Boston	75	1	4	R. Jarvis (Boston)	29	1	8
1967	Relief Channel	Derby Railway	83	4	4	E. Townsin (Cambridge)	40	6	2
1968	Ant, Bure and Thurne	Leighton Buzzard	74	0	8	D. Groom (Leighton Buzzard)	37	6	4
1969	Trent	Stoke	32	8	8	R. Else (Lincoln)	9	7	12
1970	Middle Level Drain	Cambridge FPS	97	2	0	B. Lakey (Cambridge)	35	4	2
1971	Severn	Leicester AS	124	8	8	R. Harris (Peterborough)	40	5	0
1972	Bristol Avon	Birmingham AA	51	1	12	P. Coles (Leicester)	33	8	0
1973	Witham	Grimsby ASA	92	10	4	A. Wright (Derby Railway)	41	10	8
1974	Welland	Leicester AS	25	9	4	P. Anderson (Cambridge)	40	2	8
1975	Nene	Birmingham AA	43	15	12	M. Hoad-Reddick (Rotherham)	63	7	0
1976	Trent	Birmingham AA	50	0	4	N. Wells (Newark)	28	0	8
1977	Welland	Coventry AA	33	15	8	R. Foster (Rotherham)	39	10	4
1978	Bristol Avon	Coleshill AS	85	1	8	D. Harris (Bradford)	48	13	0
1979	Great Ouse and Cam	Barnsley ASA	10	15	4	M. Cullen (Oxford)	11	8	0
1980	Trent	Nottingham Fed	93	5	12	P. Burrell (Essex County)	27	8	0

Apples

THE FINEST APPLE COMPETITION

This is held by the fruit distributors, The Mack Organisation. The judges sample Britain's premier apples, and each is marked for appearance, aroma, flavour, texture and juiciness. Winners:

1978 Flandres Cox, grown by L. J. Fermor at Perry Court, Biltin, nr. Ashford
1979 Flandres Cox, grown by G. W. Breach & Sons at the Chittenden Orchards, Staplehurst, Kent
1980 Spartan, grown by Paul Jenkins at Yopps Green Farm, Plaxtol, nr. Tonbridge

Spartans took the first, second and third prize in the 1980 Most Eatable Apple Contest. Below: *Panellists during the judging*

Archaeology

RESCUE: BRITISH ARCHAEOLOGICAL TRUST AWARDS

The *Illustrated London News* sponsor an award for the best presentation to the public of an archaeological excavation or fieldwork. The Duke of Gloucester awarded a cheque for £250 to the 1980 winner.

1978 Dover Roman Painted House and Norton Priory Museum, Runcorn
1979 York Archaeological Trust, for the display on its Coppergate excavation
1980 Bede Monastery Museum, Jarrow

THE BBC 'CHRONICLE' ARCHAEOLOGICAL AWARDS

These have been given since 1977 for the best 'rescue' by a group of amateur archaeologists.

In effect, this means digs of archaeological sites or the recording of above-ground remains that are unlikely to be dealt with by professionals and which are threatened with destruction. Three prizes are awarded, the first prize being a crystal goblet and a cheque for £250. Winners of the first prize:

1977

Manchester University Extramural Group for their survey of the major Anglo-Saxon monument of Offa's Dyke. This revealed the fact that, despite it being scheduled as an Ancient Monument, several miles of the length had already been recently destroyed or was still under threat.

1978

The Alice Holt Survey Group for their total historical and archaeological survey of the ancient forest of Alice Holt, near Farnham in Hampshire, which uncovered one of the largest Roman pottery industries in Britain.

1979
Henry Wills of Wilton, Salisbury, who spent five years recording and analysing the remains of wartime pill boxes. He located 5000 mini-forts and

searched Home Office manuals and War Office records.

1980
Derrick Riley, Sheffield, for his work on mapping crop marks on land near his home.

Archery

WORLD CHAMPIONSHIPS
World championships were first held in 1931, and were held annually from 1931 to 1939 and 1946 to 1950. From 1959 they have been held every other year, while they were also held in 1952, 1953, 1955, 1957 and 1958. Since 1957 both team and individual competitions have been held with competitors shooting Double FITA (Fédération Internationale de Tir à l'Arc) rounds. That is 72 arrows each, at four different distances.

Winners since 1957 of Target Archery championships:

Men's individual
1957 O. K. Smathers (USA) 2231
1958 S. Thysell (Swe) 2101
1959 James Caspers (USA) 2247
1961 Joseph Thornton (USA) 2310
1963 Charles Sandlin (USA) 2332
1965 Matti Haikonen (Fin) 2313
1967 Ray Rogers (USA) 2298
1969 Hardy Ward (USA) 2423
1971 John Williams (USA) 2445
1973 Viktor Sidoruk (USSR) 2185
1975 Darrell Pace (USA) 2548
1977 Richard McKinney (USA) 2501
1979 Darrell Pace (USA) 2474
1981 Kyosti Laasonen (Fin) 2541

Women's individual
1957 Carole Meinhart (USA) 2120
1958 Sigrid Johansson (Swe) 2053
1959 Ann Weber Corby (USA) 2023
1961 Nancy Vonderheide (USA) 2173
1963 Victoria Cook (USA) 2253
1965 Maire Lindholm (Fin) 2214
1967 Maria Mazynska (Pol) 2240
1969 Dorothy Lidstone (Can) 2361
1971 Emma Gapchenko (USSR) 2380
1973 Linda Myers (USA) 2204
1975 Zebiniso Rustamova (USSR) 2465
1977 Luann Ryon (USA) 2515
1979 Jin-Ho Kim (SK) 2507
1981 Natalya Butusova (USSR) 2514

Team competitions

	MEN	WOMEN
1957	USA 6591	USA 6187
1958	Not held	
1959	USA 6634	USA 5847
1961	USA 6601	USA 6376
1963	USA 6887	USA 6508
1965	USA 6792	USA 6358
1967	USA 6816	Poland 6686

Darrell Pace, world champion and record holder (All-Sport)

MEN	WOMEN
1969 USA 7194	USSR 6897
1971 USA 7050	Poland 6907
1973 USA 6400	USSR 6389
1975 USA 7444	USSR 7252
1977 USA 7444	USA 7379
1979 USA 7409	S Korea 7314
1981 USA 7547	USSR 7455

OLYMPIC CHAMPIONSHIPS
Archery was included in the Olympic Games of 1900, 1904, 1908 and 1920 and re-introduced in 1972, since when the winners have been:

MEN
1972 John Williams (USA) 2528
1976 Darrell Pace (USA) 2571
1980 Tomi Poikolainen (Fin) 2455

WOMEN
1972 Doreen Wilbur (USA) 2424
1976 Luann Ryon (USA) 2499
1980 Keto Losaberidze (USSR) 2491

Architecture

THE *FINANCIAL TIMES* INDUSTRIAL ARCHITECTURE AWARD

The award is open to all, both architects and engineers, concerned with the design of industrial works which can bring to either town or country an outstanding contribution in encouraging a better industrial environment. The award has been presented to the following:

1967 Reliance Controls Ltd, Swindon
Architects: N. Foster, W. Foster and R. Rogers (Foster Associates)
1968 Engineering Research Station for the Northern Gas Board, Killingworth, Newcastle upon Tyne
Architects: Ryder and Yates and Partners
1969 Wallace Arnold Quality Tested Used Car Factory, York Road, Leeds
Architects: Derek Walker and Partners
1970 Chemical and Administration Building, Treatment Plant for Bradford Water Supply, Chellow Heights, Bradford
Architects: Whicheloe and Macfarlane
1971 Lee Abbey Farm, Lynton, North Devon
Architect: John Burkett (Scarlett Burkett Associates)
1972 IBM Havant Plant for IBM United Kingdom
Architects: Arup Associates
1973 Horizon Project, Nottingham for John Player and Sons
Architects: Arup Associates
1974 Warehouse and office for Modern Art Glass Company, Thamesmead Industrial Estate
Architects: N. Foster, W. Foster and R. Rogers (Foster Associates)
1975 Carlsberg Brewery, Northampton
Architect: Knud Munk
1976 PATS Centre, Industrial Research Laboratory, Melbourn, Herts

Architects: Piano and Rogers
1977 Furniture Factory for Herman Miller Ltd, Bath, Avon
Architects: Farrell/Grimshaw Partnership
1978 Solid Wastes Rail Transfer Station, Brentford
Architects: GLC Department of Architects and Civil Design
1979 St. Sergus North Sea Gas Terminal
Architects: Area Design Group
1980 Greene King and Sons Brewery (Cask Department), Bury St. Edmunds
Architects: Michael Hopkins Architects

ROYAL GOLD MEDALLISTS OF THE ROYAL INSTITUTE OF BRITISH ARCHITECTS

The Royal Gold Medal for the promotion of architecture, instituted by Her Majesty Queen Victoria in 1848, is conferred annually by the Sovereign on some distinguished architect, or group of architects, for work of high merit, or on some distinguished person or group whose work has promoted either directly or indirectly the advancement of architecture. The following have been the recipients since 1970:

1970 Professor Sir Robert Matthew, CBE, ARSA, LLD, MA
1971 Hubert de Cronin Hastings
1972 Louis I. Kahn
1973 Sir Leslie Martin, MA, PhD, LLD
1974 Powell and Moya
1975 Michael Scott
1976 Sir John Summerson, CBE, FBA, FSA
1977 Sir Denys Lasdun, CBE
1978 John Utzon (Aus and Den)
1979 Charles and Ray Eames Office
1980 James Stirling
1981 Sir Philip Dowson

Art

ROYAL ACADEMY OF ARTS 'PICK OF THE SUMMER SHOW'
Instituted at the Academy in 1977, and now a

regular event, members of the public are asked to vote for their favourite work in the Summer Exhibition, and the prize is presented to the exhibit which receives the most votes. Sponsorship was first introduced in 1979, the prize being presented by the *Daily Mirror*. In 1980 BP took over sponsorship of the event, and a £1200 prize was awarded.

1977 Anthony Green, 'A Hall of Mirrors' (oil painting)
1978 Sydney Harpley, 'Girl on a Bicycle' (bronze sculpture)
1979 Sydney Harpley, 'Girl on a Swing' (bronze sculpture)
1980 William P. Mundy, 'Early Apples' (oil painting)

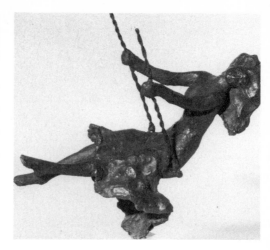

'Girl on a Swing', the bronze sculpture that was voted 'Pick of the Summer Show' in 1979

Association Football

WORLD CUP
First held in 1930 in Uruguay. Held every four years.

1930	Uruguay	1962	Brazil
1934	Italy	1966	England
1938	Italy	1970	Brazil
1950	Uruguay	1974	West Germany
1954	West Germany	1978	Argentina
1958	Brazil		

EUROPEAN FOOTBALL CHAMPIONSHIP
First contested as the Nations Cup between 1958 and 1960, the European Football Championship is played every four years over a two-year period.

1960	USSR	1972	West Germany
1964	Spain	1976	Czechoslovakia
1968	Italy	1980	West Germany

EUROPEAN CHAMPION CLUBS CUP (European Cup)
Contested annually since the 1955–56 season by the champion clubs of each member of the European Union (UEFA) together with the previous winner.

1955–56 Real Madrid
1956–57 Real Madrid
1957–58 Real Madrid
1958–59 Real Madrid
1959–60 Real Madrid
1960–61 Benfica
1961–62 Benfica
1962–63 A C Milan
1963–64 Inter Milan
1964–65 Inter Milan
1965–66 Real Madrid
1966–67 Celtic (Glasgow)
1967–68 Manchester United
1968–69 A C Milan
1969–70 Feyenoord
1970–71 Ajax (Amsterdam)
1971–72 Ajax (Amsterdam)
1972–73 Ajax (Amsterdam)
1973–74 Bayern Munich
1974–75 Bayern Munich
1975–76 Bayern Munich
1976–77 Liverpool
1977–78 Liverpool
1978–79 Nottingham Forest
1979–80 Nottingham Forest
1980–81 Liverpool

EUROPEAN CUP WINNERS CUP
Contested annually since the 1960–61 season by the winners of national cup competitions (or the runners-up, if the winners contest the European Cup).

1960–61 Florentina
1961–62 Atletico Madrid
1962–63 Tottenham Hotspur
1963–64 Sporting Lisbon
1964–65 West Ham United
1965–66 Borussia Dortmund
1966–67 Bayern Munich
1967–68 A C Milan
1968–69 Slovan Bratislava
1969–70 Manchester City
1970–71 Chelsea
1971–72 Rangers (Glasgow)
1972–73 A C Milan
1973–74 Magdeburg
1974–75 Dynamo Kiev
1975–76 Anderlecht
1976–77 SV Hamburg
1977–78 Anderlecht
1978–79 Barcelona

Steve Heighway, Ray Kennedy, Emlyn Hughes, Terry McDermott, Jimmy Case and Tommy Smith (left to right) *celebrate Liverpool's 1977 European Cup win* (Syndication International)

1979–80 Valencia
1980–81 Dinamo Tbilisi

UEFA CUP (Fairs Cup)

First contested over a three year period 1955–58 as the Inter-City Fairs Cup. Now held annually and known since the 1971–72 season as the UEFA (Union of European Football Associations) Cup.

1955–58 Barcelona
1958–60 Barcelona
1960–61 A S Roma
1961–62 Valencia
1962–63 Valencia
1963–64 Real Zaragossa
1964–65 Ferencvaros
1965–66 Barcelona
1966–67 Dynamo Zagreb
1967–68 Leeds United
1968–69 Newcastle United
1969–70 Arsenal
1970–71 Leeds United
1971–72 Tottenham Hotspur
1972–73 Liverpool
1973–74 Feyenoord
1974–75 Borussia Mönchengladbach
1975–76 Liverpool
1976–77 Juventus
1977–78 PSV Eindhoven
1978–79 Borussia Mönchengladbach
1979–80 Eintracht Frankfurt
1980–81 Ipswich Town

EUROPEAN SUPER CUP

Held annually since 1972 between the winners of the European Champion Clubs Cup and the European Cup Winners Cup.

1972 Ajax (Amsterdam)
1973 Ajax (Amsterdam)
1974 Not contested
1975 Dynamo Kiev
1976 Anderlecht
1977 Liverpool
1978 Anderlecht
1979 Nottingham Forest (played 1980)
1980 Valencia

OLYMPIC CHAMPIONS

1908	Great Britain	1952	Hungary
1912	Great Britain	1956	USSR
1920	Belgium	1960	Yugoslavia
1924	Uruguay	1964	Hungary
1928	Uruguay	1968	Hungary
1932	Not held	1972	Poland
1936	Italy	1976	GDR
1948	Sweden	1980	Czechoslovakia

FOOTBALLER OF THE YEAR

Elected annually since 1947–48 by the Football Writers' Association.

1947–48 Stanley Matthews
1948–49 Johnny Carey
1949–50 Joe Mercer
1950–51 Harry Johnston
1951–52 Billy Wright
1952–53 Nat Lofthouse
1953–54 Tom Finney
1954–55 Don Revie
1955–56 Bert Trautmann
1956–57 Tom Finney
1957–58 Danny Blanchflower
1958–59 Sid Owens
1959–60 Bill Slater
1960–61 Danny Blanchflower
1961–62 Jimmy Adamson
1962–63 Stanley Matthews
1963–64 Bobby Moore
1964–65 Bobby Collins
1965–66 Bobby Charlton
1966–67 Jackie Charlton
1967–68 George Best
1968–69 Dave Mackay and Tony Book
1969–70 Billy Bremner
1970–71 Frank McLintock
1971–72 Gordon Banks
1972–73 Pat Jennings
1973–74 Ian Callaghan
1974–75 Alan Mullery
1975–76 Kevin Keegan
1976–77 Emlyn Hughes
1977–78 Kenny Burns
1978–79 Kenny Dalglish

1979–80 Terry McDermott
1980–81 Frans Thijssen

EUROPEAN FOOTBALLER OF THE YEAR

Elected annually since 1956 in a poll organised by *France Football* by journalists from all over Europe.

1956 Stanley Matthews (Blackpool and England)
1957 Alfredo Di Stefano (Real Madrid and Spain)
1958 Raymond Kopa (Real Madrid and France)
1959 Alfredo Di Stefano (Real Madrid and Spain)
1960 Luis Suarez (Barcelona and Spain)
1961 Omar Sivori (Juventus and Italy)
1962 Josef Masopust (Dukla, Prague and Czechoslovakia)
1963 Lev Yashin (Moscow Dynamo and USSR)
1964 Denis Law (Manchester Utd and Scotland)
1965 Eusebio (Benfica and Portugal)
1966 Bobby Charlton (Manchester Utd and England)
1967 Florian Albert (Ferencvaros and Hungary)
1968 George Best (Manchester Utd and N. Ireland)
1969 Gianni Rivera (A C Milan and Italy)
1970 Gerd Müller (Bayern Munich and W. Germany)
1971 Johann Cruyff (Ajax and Holland)
1972 Franz Beckenbauer (Bayern Munich and W. Germany)
1973 Johann Cruyff (Barcelona and Holland)
1974 Johann Cruyff (Barcelona and Holland)
1975 Oleg Blokhin (Dynamo Kiev and USSR)
1976 Franz Beckenbauer (Bayern Munich and W. Germany)
1977 Allan Simonsen (Borussia Mönchengladbach and Denmark)
1978 Kevin Keegan (SV Hamburg and England)
1979 Kevin Keegan (SV Hamburg and England)
1980 Karl-Heinz Rummenigge (Bayern Munich and W. Germany)

PFA PLAYER OF THE YEAR

The Professional Footballers' Association (PFA) vote annually for their player of the year, young player of the year, and for teams representing each of the four divisions of the Football League. They also present a merit award annually for outstanding service to the game. Winners have been:

PLAYER OF THE YEAR

1973–74 Norman Hunter (Leeds Utd)
1974–75 Colin Todd (Derby Co)
1975–76 Pat Jennings (Tottenham H)
1976–77 Andy Gray (Aston Villa)
1977–78 Peter Shilton (Nottingham F)
1978–79 Liam Brady (Arsenal)
1979–80 Terry McDermott (Liverpool)
1980–81 John Wark (Ipswich)

YOUNG PLAYER OF THE YEAR

1973–74 Kevin Beattie (Ipswich T)
1974–75 Mervyn Day (West Ham Utd)
1975–76 Peter Barnes (Manchester C)
1976–77 Andy Gray (Aston Villa)
1977–78 Tony Woodcock (Nottingham F)

Franz Beckenbauer, who made 103 appearances for West Germany, whom he captained from 1972 to 1977 (Colorsport)

1978–79 Cyrille Regis (West Bromwich A)
1979–80 Glen Hoddle (Tottenham H)
1980–81 Gary Shaw (Aston Villa)

PFA MERIT AWARD

1973–74 Bobby Charlton
1974–75 Denis Law
1975–76 George Eastham
1976–77 Jack Taylor
1977–78 Bill Shankly
1978–79 Tom Finney
1979–80 Matt Busby
1980–81 John Trollope

BELL'S SCOTCH WHISKY FOOTBALL MANAGER OF THE YEAR

Voted annually since 1966 by a panel of 25 leading soccer writers and commentators.

1965–66 Jock Stein (Celtic)
1966–67 Jock Stein (Celtic)

1967–68 Matt Busby (Manchester Utd)
1968–69 Don Revie (Leeds Utd)
1969–70 Don Revie (Leeds Utd)
1970–71 Bertie Mee (Arsenal)
1971–72 Don Revie (Leeds Utd)
1972–73 Bill Shankly (Liverpool)
1973–74 Jack Charlton (Middlesbrough)
1974–75 Ron Saunders (Aston Villa)
1975–76 Bob Paisley (Liverpool)
1976–77 Bob Paisley (Liverpool)
1977–78 Brian Clough (Nottingham F)
1978–79 Bob Paisley (Liverpool)
1979–80 Bob Paisley (Liverpool)
1980–81 Ron Saunders (Aston Villa)

Brian Clough, leading goal scorer for Middlesbrough in the late 1950s, before he started his managing career at Hartlepool (Press Association)

F.A. CUP

First held in the 1871–72 season. Finals since 1923 have been held at Wembley.

1872	Wanderers
1873	Wanderers
1874	Oxford University
1875	Royal Engineers
1876	Wanderers
1877	Wanderers
1878	Wanderers
1879	Old Etonians
1880	Clapham Rovers
1881	Old Carthusians
1882	Old Etonians
1883	Blackburn Olympic
1884	Blackburn Rovers
1885	Blackburn Rovers
1886	Blackburn Rovers
1887	Aston Villa
1888	West Bromwich Albion
1889	Preston North End
1890	Blackburn Rovers
1891	Blackburn Rovers
1892	West Bromwich Albion
1893	Wolverhampton Wanderers
1894	Notts County
1895	Aston Villa
1896	Sheffield Wednesday
1897	Aston Villa
1898	Nottingham Forest
1899	Sheffield United
1900	Bury
1901	Tottenham Hotspur
1902	Sheffield United
1903	Bury
1904	Manchester City
1905	Aston Villa
1906	Everton
1907	Sheffield Wednesday
1908	Wolverhampton Wanderers
1909	Manchester United
1910	Newcastle United
1911	Bradford City
1912	Barnsley
1913	Aston Villa
1914	Burnley
1915	Sheffield United
1920	Aston Villa
1921	Tottenham Hotspur
1922	Huddersfield Town
1923	Bolton Wanderers
1924	Newcastle United
1925	Sheffield United
1926	Bolton Wanderers
1927	Cardiff City
1928	Blackburn Rovers
1929	Bolton Wanderers
1930	Arsenal
1931	West Bromwich Albion
1932	Newcastle United
1933	Everton
1934	Manchester City
1935	Sheffield Wednesday
1936	Arsenal
1937	Sunderland
1938	Preston North End
1939	Portsmouth
1946	Derby County
1947	Charlton Athletic
1948	Manchester United
1949	Wolverhampton Wanderers
1950	Arsenal
1951	Newcastle United
1952	Newcastle United
1953	Blackpool
1954	West Bromwich Albion
1955	Newcastle United
1956	Manchester City
1957	Aston Villa
1958	Bolton Wanderers
1959	Nottingham Forest
1960	Wolverhampton Wanderers
1961	Tottenham Hotspur
1962	Tottenham Hotspur
1963	Manchester United
1964	West Ham United
1965	Liverpool
1966	Everton
1967	Tottenham Hotspur
1968	West Bromwich Albion
1969	Manchester City
1970	Chelsea
1971	Arsenal
1972	Leeds United
1973	Sunderland
1974	Liverpool
1975	West Ham United
1976	Southampton
1977	Manchester United
1978	Ipswich Town
1979	Arsenal
1980	West Ham United
1981	Tottenham Hotspur

FOOTBALL LEAGUE CHAMPIONS

1888–89	Preston North End
1889–90	Preston North End
1890–91	Everton
1891–92	Sunderland
1892–93	Sunderland
1893–94	Aston Villa
1894–95	Sunderland
1895–96	Aston Villa
1896–97	Aston Villa
1897–98	Sheffield United
1898–99	Aston Villa
1899–1900	Aston Villa
1900–01	Liverpool
1901–02	Sunderland
1902–03	Sheffield Wednesday
1903–04	Sheffield Wednesday
1904–05	Newcastle United
1905–06	Liverpool
1906–07	Newcastle United
1907–08	Manchester United
1908–09	Newcastle United
1909–10	Aston Villa
1910–11	Manchester United
1911–12	Blackburn Rovers
1912–13	Sunderland
1913–14	Blackburn Rovers
1914–15	Everton
1919–20	West Bromwich Albion
1920–21	Burnley
1921–22	Liverpool
1922–23	Liverpool
1923–24	Huddersfield Town
1924–25	Huddersfield Town
1925–26	Huddersfield Town
1926–27	Newcastle United
1927–28	Everton
1928–29	Sheffield Wednesday
1929–30	Sheffield Wednesday
1930–31	Arsenal
1931–32	Everton
1932–33	Arsenal
1933–34	Arsenal
1934–35	Arsenal
1935–36	Sunderland
1936–37	Manchester City
1937–38	Arsenal
1938–39	Everton
1946–47	Liverpool
1947–48	Arsenal
1948–49	Portsmouth
1949–50	Portsmouth
1950–51	Tottenham Hotspur
1951–52	Manchester United
1952–53	Arsenal
1953–54	Wolverhampton Wanderers
1954–55	Chelsea
1955–56	Manchester United
1956–57	Manchester United
1957–58	Wolverhampton Wanderers
1958–59	Wolverhampton Wanderers
1959–60	Burnley
1960–61	Tottenham Hotspur
1961–62	Ipswich Town
1962–63	Everton
1963–64	Liverpool
1964–65	Manchester United
1965–66	Liverpool
1966–67	Manchester United
1967–68	Manchester City
1968–69	Leeds United
1969–70	Everton
1970–71	Arsenal
1971–72	Derby County
1972–73	Liverpool
1973–74	Leeds United
1974–75	Derby County
1975–76	Liverpool
1976–77	Liverpool
1977–78	Nottingham Forest
1978–79	Liverpool
1979–80	Liverpool
1980–81	Aston Villa

FOOTBALL LEAGUE CUP

First contested in the 1960–61 season. Winners (year shown is that of second half of each season):

1961 Aston Villa
1962 Norwich City
1963 Birmingham City
1964 Leicester City
1965 Chelsea
1966 West Bromwich Albion
1967 Queen's Park Rangers
1968 Leeds United
1969 Swindon Town
1970 Manchester City
1971 Tottenham Hotspur
1972 Stoke City
1973 Tottenham Hotspur
1974 Wolverhampton Wanderers
1975 Aston Villa
1976 Manchester City
1977 Aston Villa
1978 Nottingham Forest
1979 Nottingham Forest
1980 Wolverhampton Wanderers
1981 Liverpool

SCOTTISH CUP
First contested in the 1873–74 season. Held on a knock-out basis. Summarised table of winners (year shown is that of second half of each season):

Queens Park 1874, 1875, 1876, 1880, 1881, 1882, 1884, 1886, 1890, 1893
Vale of Leven 1877, 1878, 1879
Dumbarton 1883
Renton 1885, 1888
Hibernian 1887, 1902
Third Lanark 1889, 1905
Heart of Midlothian 1891, 1896, 1901, 1906, 1956
Celtic 1892, 1899, 1900, 1904, 1907, 1908, 1911, 1912, 1914, 1923, 1925, 1927, 1931, 1933, 1937, 1951, 1954, 1965, 1967, 1969, 1971, 1972, 1974, 1975, 1977, 1980
Rangers 1894, 1897, 1898, 1903, 1928, 1930, 1932, 1934, 1935, 1936, 1948, 1949, 1950, 1953, 1960, 1962, 1963, 1964, 1966, 1973, 1976, 1978, 1979, 1981

St Bernards 1895
Dundee 1910
Falkirk 1913, 1957
Kilmarnock 1920, 1929
Partick Thistle 1921
Morton 1922
Airdrieonians 1924
St Mirren 1926, 1959
East Fife 1938
Clyde 1939, 1955, 1958
Aberdeen 1947, 1970
Motherwell 1952
Dunfermline 1961, 1968
Cup withheld in 1909 after two drawn games between Celtic and Rangers

SCOTTISH LEAGUE
Formed in the 1890–91 season. The second division was formed in 1893, but was suspended from 1915 to 1921. A third division was included from 1925–27 and 1946–55. In 1975 the League was reformed into Premier, First and Second Divisions. Summarised winners of the First Division from 1891 to 1975 (year shown is that of second half of each season):

Dumbarton 1891 (shared), 1892
Rangers 1891 (shared), 1899, 1900, 1901, 1902, 1911, 1912, 1913, 1918, 1920, 1921, 1923, 1924, 1925, 1927, 1928, 1929, 1930, 1931, 1933, 1934, 1935, 1937, 1939, 1947, 1949, 1950, 1953, 1956, 1957, 1959, 1961, 1963, 1964, 1975
Celtic 1893, 1894, 1896, 1898, 1905, 1906, 1907, 1908, 1909, 1910, 1914, 1915, 1916, 1917, 1919, 1922, 1926, 1936, 1938, 1954, 1966, 1967, 1968, 1969, 1970, 1971, 1972, 1973, 1974
Heart of Midlothian 1895, 1897, 1958, 1960
Hibernian 1903, 1948, 1951, 1952
Third Lanark 1904
Motherwell 1932
Aberdeen 1955
Dundee 1962
Kilmarnock 1965

PREMIER DIVISION CHAMPIONS
1976 Rangers
1977 Celtic
1978 Rangers
1979 Celtic
1980 Aberdeen
1981 Celtic

SCOTTISH LEAGUE CUP
First contested in the 1945–46 season. Summarised list of winners:

Aberdeen 1946, 1956, 1977
Rangers 1947, 1949, 1961, 1962, 1964, 1965, 1971, 1976, 1978, 1979
East Fife 1948, 1950, 1954
Motherwell 1951
Dundee 1952, 1953, 1974
Heart of Midlothian 1955, 1959, 1960, 1963
Celtic 1957, 1958, 1966, 1967, 1968, 1969, 1970, 1975
Partick Thistle 1972
Hibernian 1973
Dundee United 1980

Athletics

OLYMPIC CHAMPIONSHIPS

The first Olympics of the modern age were held in 1896 in Athens. They are still very much the pinnacle of athletics success, although world championships have been announced by the International Amateur Athletic Federation (IAAF) for 1983 and for certain non-Olympic events at earlier dates. Olympic champions since 1948 have been:

MEN
100 metres
1948 Harrison Dillard (USA) 10·3
1952 Lindy Remigino (USA) 10·4
1956 Bobby-Joe Morrow (USA) 10·5
1960 Armin Hary (Ger) 10·2
1964 Robert Hayes (USA) 10·05
1968 James Hines (USA) 9·95
1972 Valeriy Borzov (USSR) 10·14
1976 Hasely Crawford (Tri) 10·06
1980 Allan Wells (GB) 10·25

200 metres
1948 Melvin Patton (USA) 21·1
1952 Andrew Stanfield (USA) 20·7
1956 Bobby-Joe Morrow (USA) 20·6
1960 Livio Berrutti (Ita) 20·5
1964 Henry Carr (USA) 20·36
1968 Tommie Smith (USA) 19·83
1972 Valeriy Borzov (USSR) 20·00
1976 Donald Quarrie (Jam) 20·23
1980 Pietro Mennea (Ita) 20·19

Jim Hines won the 1968 Olympic 100 metres title in a time of 9.95 sec, which still stands as a world record 13 years later

400 metres
1948 Arthur Wint (Jam) 46·2
1952 George Rhoden (Jam) 45·9
1956 Charles Jenkins (USA) 46·7
1960 Otis Davis (USA) 44·9
1964 Michael Larrabee (USA) 45·15
1968 Lee Evans (USA) 43·86
1972 Vincent Matthews (USA) 44·66
1976 Alberto Juantorena (Cub) 44·26
1980 Viktor Markin (USSR) 44·60

800 metres
1948 Malvin Whitfield (USA) 1:49·2
1952 Malvin Whitfield (USA) 1:49·2
1956 Thomas Courtney (USA) 1:47·7
1960 Peter Snell (NZ) 1:46·3
1964 Peter Snell (NZ) 1:45·1
1968 Ralph Doubell (Aus) 1:44·3
1972 David Wottle (USA) 1:44·9
1976 Alberto Juantorena (Cub) 1:43·5
1980 Steven Ovett (GB) 1:45·4

1500 metres
1948 Henry Eriksson (Swe) 3:49·8
1952 Josef Barthel (Lux) 3:45·1
1956 Ron Delany (Ire) 3:41·2
1960 Herbert Elliott (Aus) 3:35·6
1964 Peter Snell (NZ) 3:38·1
1968 Kipchoge Keino (Ken) 3:34·9
1972 Pekka Vasala (Fin) 3:36·3
1976 John Walker (NZ) 3:39·2
1980 Sebastian Coe (GB) 3:38·4

5000 metres
1948 Gaston Reiff (Bel) 14:17·6
1952 Emil Zatopek (Cze) 14:06·6
1956 Vladimir Kuts (USSR) 13:39·6
1960 Murray Halberg (NZ) 13:43·4
1964 Robert Schul (USA) 13:48·8

1968 Mohamed Gammoudi (Tun) 14:05·0
1972 Lasse Viren (Fin) 13:26·4
1976 Lasse Viren (Fin) 13:24·8
1980 Miruts Yifter (Eth) 13:21·0

10 000 metres
1948 Emil Zatopek (Cze) 29:59·6
1952 Emil Zatopek (Cze) 29:17·0
1956 Vladimir Kuts (USSR) 28:45·6
1960 Pyotr Bolotnikov (USSR) 28:32·2
1964 William Mills (USA) 28:24·4
1968 Naftali Temu (Ken) 29:27·4
1972 Lasse Viren (Fin) 27:38·4
1976 Lasse Viren (Fin) 27:40·4
1980 Miruts Yifter (Eth) 27:42·7

Marathon
1948 Delfo Cabrera (Arg) 2:34:51·6
1952 Emil Zatopek (Cze) 2:23:03·2
1956 Alain Mimoun (Fra) 2:25:00·0
1960 Abebe Bikila (Eth) 2:15:16·2
1964 Abebe Bikila (Eth) 2:12:11·2
1968 Mamo Wolde (Eth) 2:20:26·4
1972 Frank Shorter (USA) 2:12:19·8
1976 Waldemar Cierpinski (GDR) 2:09:55·0
1980 Waldemar Cierpinski (GDR) 2:11:03·0

4 × 100 metres relay
1948 USA 40·6
1952 USA 40·1
1956 USA 39·5
1960 Germany 39·5
1964 USA 39·06
1968 USA 38·23
1972 USA 38·19
1976 USA 38·33
1980 USSR 38·26

4 × 400 metres relay
1948 USA 3:10·4
1952 Jamaica 3:03·9
1956 USA 3:04·8
1960 USA 3:02·2
1964 USA 3:00·7
1968 USA 2:56·1
1972 Kenya 2:59·8
1976 USA 2:58·7
1980 USSR 3:01·1

110 metres hurdles
1948 William Porter (USA) 13·9
1952 Harrison Dillard (USA) 13·7
1956 Lee Calhoun (USA) 13·5
1960 Lee Calhoun (USA) 13·8
1964 Hayes Jones (USA) 13·67
1968 Willie Davenport (USA) 13·33
1972 Rodney Milburn (USA) 13·24
1976 Guy Drut (Fra) 13·30
1980 Thomas Munkelt (GDR) 13·39

400 metres hurdles
1948 Roy Cochran (USA) 51·1
1952 Charles Moore (USA) 50·8
1956 Glenn Davis (USA) 50·1
1960 Glenn Davis (USA) 49·3
1964 Warren 'Rex' Cawley (USA) 49·69
1968 David Hemery (GB) 48·12
1972 John Akii-Bua (Uga) 47·82
1976 Edwin Moses (USA) 47·64
1980 Volker Beck (GDR) 48·70

3000 metres steeplechase
1948 Tore Sjöstrand (Swe) 9:04·6
1952 Horace Ashenfelter (USA) 8:45·4
1956 Christopher Brasher (GB) 8:41·2
1960 Zdzislaw Krzyszkowiak (Pol) 8:34·2
1964 Gaston Roelants (Bel) 8:30·8
1968 Amos Biwott (Ken) 8:51·0
1972 Kipchoge Keino (Ken) 8:23·6
1976 Anders Garderud (Swe) 8:08·0
1980 Bronislaw Malinowski (Pol) 8:09·7

10 000 metres walk
1948 John Mikaelsson (Swe) 45:13·2
1952 John Mikaelsson (Swe) 45:02·8

20 000 metres walk
1956 Leonid Spirin (USSR) 1:31:27·4
1960 Vladimir Golubnichiy (USSR) 1:34:07·2
1964 Kenneth Matthews (GB) 1:29:34·0
1968 Vladimir Golubnichiy (USSR) 1:33:58·4
1972 Peter Frenkel (GDR) 1:26:42·4
1976 Daniel Bautista (Mex) 1:24:40·6
1980 Maurizio DaMilano (Ita) 1:23:35·5

50 000 metres walk
1948 John Ljunggren (Swe) 4:41:52·0
1952 Giuseppe Dordoni (Ita) 4:28:07·8
1956 Norman Read (NZ) 4:30:42·8
1960 Don Thompson (GB) 4:25:30·0
1964 Abdon Pamich (Ita) 4:11:12·4
1968 Christophe Höhne (GDR) 4:20:13·6
1972 Bernd Kannenberg (GDR) 3:56:11·6
1976 Not held
1980 Hartwig Gauder (GDR) 3:49:24·0

High jump
1948 John Winter (Aus) 1·98
1952 Walter Davis (USA) 2·04
1956 Charles Dumas (USA) 2·12
1960 Robert Shavlakadze (USSR) 2·16
1964 Valeriy Brumel (USSR) 2·18
1968 Richard Fosbury (USA) 2·24
1972 Yuriy Tarmak (USSR) 2·23
1976 Jacek Wszola (Pol) 2·25
1980 Gerd Wessig (GDR) 2·36

Pole vault
1948 Guinn Smith (USA) 4·30
1952 Robert Richards (USA) 4·55
1956 Robert Richards (USA) 4·56
1960 Donald Bragg (USA) 4·70
1964 Frederick Hansen (USA) 5·10
1968 Robert Seagren (USA) 5·40
1972 Wolfgang Nordwig (GDR) 5·50

Jesse Owens, winner of four gold medals at the 1936 Olympic Games. His 1935 long jump world record of 8.13 m (26 ft 8¼ in) stood for 25 years

1976 Tadeusz Slusarski (Pol) 5·50
1980 Wladyslaw Kozakiewicz (Pol) 5·78

Long jump
1948 William Steele (USA) 7·82
1952 Jerome Biffle (USA) 7·57
1956 Gregory Bell (USA) 7·83
1960 Ralph Boston (USA) 8·12
1964 Lynn Davies (GB) 8·07
1968 Robert Beamon (USA) 8·90
1972 Randy Williams (USA) 8·24
1976 Arnie Robinson (USA) 8·35
1980 Lutz Dombrowski (GDR) 8·54

Triple jump
1948 Arne Ahman (Swe) 15·40
1952 Adhemar Ferreira da Silva (Bra) 16·22
1956 Adhemar Ferreira da Silva (Bra) 16·35
1960 Jozef Schmidt (Pol) 16·81
1964 Jozef Schmidt (Pol) 16·85
1968 Viktor Saneyev (USSR) 17·39
1972 Viktor Saneyev (USSR) 17·35
1976 Viktor Saneyev (USSR) 17·29
1980 Jaak Uudmae (USSR) 17·35

Shot
1948 Wilbur Thompson (USA) 17·12
1952 Parry O'Brien (USA) 17·41
1956 Parry O'Brien (USA) 18·57
1960 William Nieder (USA) 19·68
1964 Dallas Long (USA) 20·33
1968 Randel Matson (USA) 20·54
1972 Wladyslaw Komar (Pol) 21·18
1976 Udo Beyer (GDR) 21·05
1980 Vladimir Kiselyov (USSR) 21·35

Discus
1948 Adolfo Consolini (Ita) 52·78
1952 Sim Iness (USA) 55·03
1956 Alfred Oerter (USA) 56·36
1960 Alfred Oerter (USA) 59·18
1964 Alfred Oerter (USA) 61·00
1968 Alfred Oerter (USA) 64·78
1972 Ludvik Danek (Cze) 64·40
1976 Mac Wilkins (USA) 67·50
1980 Viktor Rasschupkin (USSR) 66·64

Hammer
1948 Imre Nemeth (Hun) 56·07
1952 Jozsef Csermak (Hun) 60·34
1956 Harold Connolly (USA) 63·19
1960 Vasiliy Rudenkov (USSR) 67·10
1964 Romuald Klim (USSR) 69·74
1968 Gyula Zsivotzky (Hun) 73·36
1972 Anatoliy Bondarchuk (USSR) 75·50
1976 Yuriy Syedikh (USSR) 77·52
1980 Yuriy Syedikh (USSR) 81·80

Javelin
1948 Tapio Rautavaara (Fin) 69·77
1952 Cyrus Young (USA) 73·78
1956 Egil Danielsen (Nor) 85·71
1960 Viktor Tsibulenko (USSR) 84·64
1964 Pauli Nevala (Fin) 82·66
1968 Janis Lusis (USSR) 90·10
1972 Klaus Wolfermann (Ger) 90·48
1976 Miklos Nemeth (Hun) 94·58
1980 Dainis Kula (USSR) 91·20

Decathlon
1948 Robert Mathias (USA) 6825
1952 Robert Mathias (USA) 7731

Irena Szewinska (left) *and Marita Koch*

1956 Milton Campbell (USA) 7708
1960 Rafer Johnson (USA) 8001
1964 Willi Holdorf (Ger) 7887
1968 William Toomey (USA) 8193
1972 Nikolai Avilov (USSR) 8454
1976 Bruce Jenner (USA) 8618
1980 Daley Thompson (GB) 8495

WOMEN
100 metres
1948 Fanny Blankers-Koen (Hol) 11·9
1952 Marjorie Jackson (Aus) 11·5
1956 Betty Cuthbert (Aus) 11·5
1960 Wilma Rudolph (USA) 11·0
1964 Wyomia Tyus (USA) 11·49
1968 Wyomia Tyus (USA) 11·07
1972 Renate Stecher (GDR) 11·07
1976 Annegret Richter (Ger) 11·08
1980 Lyudmila Kondratyeva (USSR) 11·06

200 metres
1948 Fanny Blankers-Koen (Hol) 24·4
1952 Marjorie Jackson (Aus) 23·7
1956 Betty Cuthbert (Aus) 23·4
1960 Wilma Rudolph (USA) 24·0
1964 Edith Maguire (USA) 23·05
1968 Irena Szewinska (Pol) 22·58
1972 Renate Stecher (GDR) 22·40
1976 Barbel Eckert (GDR) 22·37
1980 Barbel Wöckel (née Eckert) (GDR) 22·03

400 metres
1964 Betty Cuthbert (Aus) 52·01
1968 Colette Besson (Fra) 52·03
1972 Monika Zehrt (GDR) 51·08
1976 Irena Szewinska (Pol) 49·29
1980 Marita Koch (GDR) 48·88

800 metres
1960 Lyudmila Shevtsova (USSR) 2:04·3
1964 Ann Packer (GB) 2:01·1
1968 Madeline Manning (USA) 2:00·9
1972 Hildegard Falck (Ger) 1:58·6
1976 Tatyana Kazankina (USSR) 1:54·9
1980 Nadyezhda Olizarenko (USSR) 1:53·5

1500 metres
1972 Lyudmila Bragina (USSR) 4:01·4
1976 Tatyana Kazankina (USSR) 4:05·5
1980 Tatyana Kazankina (USSR) 3:56·6

4 × 100 metres relay
1948 Netherlands 47·5
1952 USA 45·9
1956 Australia 44·5
1960 USA 44·5
1964 Poland 43·69
1968 USA 42·87
1972 W. Germany 42·81
1976 GDR 42·55
1980 GDR 41·60

4 × 400 metres relay
1972 GDR 3:23·0
1976 GDR 3:19·2
1980 USSR 3:20·2

80 metres hurdles
1948 Fanny Blankers-Koen (Hol) 11·2
1952 Shirley Strickland (Aus) 10·9
1956 Shirley Strickland (Aus) 10·7
1960 Irina Press (USSR) 10·8
1964 Karin Balzer (GDR) 10·5
1968 Maureen Caird (Aus) 10·3

100 metres hurdles
1972 Annelie Ehrhardt (GDR) 12·59
1976 Johanna Schaller (GDR) 12·77
1980 Vera Komisova (USSR) 12·56

High jump
1948 Alice Coachman (USA) 1·68
1952 Esther Brand (SA) 1·67
1956 Mildred McDaniel (USA) 1·76
1960 Iolanda Balas (Rom) 1·85
1964 Iolanda Balas (Rom) 1·90
1968 Miloslava Rezkova (Cze) 1·82
1972 Ulrike Meyfarth (Ger) 1·92
1976 Rosi Ackermann (GDR) 1·93
1980 Sara Simeoni (Ita) 1·97

Sara Simeoni always rose to the big occasion, setting a world record of 2.01 m (6 ft 7 in) twice in 1978, and winning an Olympic gold medal in 1980 (All Sport)

Long jump
1948 Olga Gyarmati (Hun) 5·69
1952 Yvette Williams (NZ) 6·24
1956 Elzbieta Krzesinska (Pol) 6·35
1960 Vyera Krepkina (USSR) 6·37
1964 Mary Rand (GB) 6·76
1968 Viorica Viscopoleanu (Rom) 6·82
1972 Heide Rosendahl (Ger) 6·78
1976 Angela Voigt (GDR) 6·72
1980 Tatyana Kolpakova (USSR) 7·06

Shot
1948 Micheline Ostermeyer (Fra) 13·75
1952 Galina Zybina (USSR) 15·28
1956 Tamara Tishkyevich (USSR) 16·59
1960 Tamara Press (USSR) 17·32
1964 Tamara Press (USSR) 18·14
1968 Margitta Gummel (GDR) 19·61
1972 Nadyezhda Chizhova (USSR) 21·03
1976 Ivanka Khristova (Bul) 21·16
1980 Ilona Slupianek (GDR) 22·41

Discus
1948 Micheline Ostermeyer (Fra) 41·92
1952 Nina Ponomaryeva (USSR) 51·42
1956 Olga Fikotova (Cze) 53·69
1960 Nina Ponomaryeva (USSR) 55·10
1964 Tamara Press (USSR) 57·27
1968 Lia Manoliu (Rom) 58·28
1972 Faina Melnik (USSR) 66·62
1976 Evelin Schlaak (GDR) 69·00
1980 Evelin Jahl (née Schlaak) (GDR) 69·96

Javelin
1948 Herma Bouma (Aut) 45·57
1952 Dana Zatopkova (Cze) 50·47
1956 Inese Jaunzeme (USSR) 53·86
1960 Elvira Ozolina (USSR) 55·98
1964 Mihaela Penes (Rom) 60·54
1968 Angela Nemeth (Hun) 60·36
1972 Ruth Fuchs (GDR) 63·88
1976 Ruth Fuchs (GDR) 65·94
1980 Maria Colon (Cub) 68·40

Pentathlon
80 m hurdles, Shot, High jump, Long jump, 200 m
1964–68: 100 m hurdles replaced 80 mh from 1972 and 800 m replaced 200 m from 1976.

1964 Irina Press (USSR) 4702
1968 Ingrid Becker (Ger) 4559
1972 Mary Peters (GB) 4801
1976 Sigrun Siegl (GDR) 4745
1980 Nadyezhda Tkachenko (USSR) 5083
(1964 and 1968 scores re-totalled on current scoring tables)
Most Olympic titles: 10 Ray Ewry (standing high, long and triple jumps 1900–1908

WORLD CHAMPIONSHIPS
Announced by the IAAF as due to be held for all regular events in 1983, the first official world championship was held for 50 000 metres walk in 1976, when that event was omitted from the Olympic programme. Winner: Venyamin Soldatenko (USSR) 3:54:40.

In 1980 women's world championships were held at two events. Winners 3000 metres:

Birgit Friedmann (Ger) 8:48·1; 400 metres hurdles: Bärbel Broschat (GDR) 54·55.

WORLD CUP
First contested by eight men's and eight women's teams in 1977.

MEN	WOMEN
1977 GDR	1977 Europe select
1979 USA	1979 GDR

EUROPEAN CUP
First held in 1965, the European Cup is now contested biennially.

MEN	WOMEN
1965 USSR	1965 USSR
1967 USSR	1967 USSR
1970 GDR	1970 GDR
1973 USSR	1973 GDR
1975 GDR	1975 GDR
1977 GDR	1977 GDR
1979 GDR	1979 GDR

EUROPEAN CHAMPIONSHIPS
First held in 1934 (men) and 1938 (women). The European championships are now contested over a full range of events every four years. Winners of three or more gold medals at one event:

4 Janis Lusis (USSR): javelin 1962, 1966, 1969, 1971
4 Nadyezhda Chizhova (USSR): women's shot 1966, 1969, 1971, 1974
3 Adolfo Consolini (Ita): discus 1946, 1950, 1954
3 Vasiliy Kuznyetsov (USSR): decathlon 1954, 1958, 1962
3 Igor Ter-Ovanesyan (USSR): long jump 1958, 1962, 1969
3 Karin Balzer (GDR): women's 80 mh 1966: 100 mh 1969, 1971
3 Wolfgang Nordwig (GDR): pole vault 1966, 1969, 1971
3 Valeriy Borzov (USSR): 100 m 1969, 1971, 1974

Most gold medals in all: 5 Fanny Blankers-Koen (Hol) – women's 80 mh and 4 × 100 m relay 1946, 100 m, 200 m, 80 mh 1950

COMMONWEALTH GAMES
First held in 1930. Athletics events are contested over a full range of events every four years. Winners in 1978 at Edmonton:

MEN
100 metres Don Quarrie (Jam) 10·03
200 metres Allan Wells (Sco) 20·12
400 metres Rick Mitchell (Aus) 46·34
800 metres Mike Boit (Ken) 1:46·4
1500 metres Dave Moorcroft (Eng) 3:35·5
5000 metres Henry Rono (Ken) 13:23·0
10 000 metres Brendan Foster (Eng) 28:13·7
Marathon Gidemas Shahanga (Tan) 2:15:39·8
4 × 100 m relay Scotland 39·24
4 × 400 m relay Kenya 3:03·5
110 m hurdles Berwyn Price (Wal) 13·70
400 m hurdles Daniel Kimaiyo (Ken) 49·48
3000 m steeplechase Henry Rono (Ken) 8:26·5

30 km walk Olly Flynn (Eng) 2:22:03·7
High jump Claude Ferragne (Can) 2·20 m
Pole vault Bruce Simpson (Can) 5·10 m
Long jump Roy Mitchell (Aus) 8·06 m
Triple jump Keith Connor (Eng) 17·21 m
Shot Geoff Capes (Eng) 19·77 m
Discus Borys Chambul (Can) 59·70 m
Hammer Peter Farmer (Aus) 71·10 m
Javelin Phil Olsen (Can) 84·00 m
Decathlon Daley Thompson (Eng) 8467 pts

WOMEN
100 metres Sonia Lannaman (Eng) 11·27
200 metres Denise Boyd (Aus) 22·82
400 metres Donna Hartley (Eng) 51·69
800 metres Judy Peckham (Aus) 2:02·8
1500 metres Mary Stewart (Eng) 4:06·3
3000 metres Paula Fudge (Eng) 9:13·0
4 × 100 m relay England 43·70
4 × 400 m relay England 3:27·2
100 m hurdles Lorna Boothe (Eng) 12·98
High jump Katrina Gibbs (Aus) 1·93 m
Long jump Sue Reeve (Eng) 6·59 m
Shot Gael Mulhall (Aus) 17·31 m
Discus Carmen Ionescu (Can) 62·16 m
Javelin Tessa Sanderson (Eng) 61·34 m
Pentathlon Diane Konihowski (Can) 4768 pts

Winners of three or more gold medals at one event:
3 Valerie Sloper/Young (NZ): women's shot 1958, 1962, 1966
3 Pam Kilborn/Ryan (Aus): women's 80 mh 1962, 1966; 100 mh 1970
3 Howard Payne (Eng): hammer 1962, 1966, 1970
3 Don Quarrie (Jam): 100 m 1970, 1974, 1978

Most gold medals in all: 7 Marjorie Jackson/Nelson (Aus) – 4 in 1950 and 3 in 1954. 6 Pam Kilborn, Don Quarrie, Raelene Boyle

BRITISH ATHLETICS LEAGUE
First held in 1969. Contested by British men's teams.

1969 Birchfield Harriers
1970–71 Thames Valley Harriers
1972–74 Cardiff AAC
1975–80 Wolverhampton & Bilston AC

BRITISH ATHLETICS CUPS
Knock-out inter-club competitions for both men and women. The Men's Cup was first contested in 1973, from 1974 to 1976 it was the Pye Gold Cup and from 1977 to date the GRE Gold-Cup. The Women's Cup was first contested in 1974 and from 1977 has been the GRE Jubilee Cup. Winners:

MEN
1973 Wolverhampton & Bilston AC
1974 Cardiff AAC
1975 Edinburgh Southern Harriers
1976–77 Wolverhampton & Bilston AC
1978 Shaftesbury Harriers
1979–80 Wolverhampton & Bilston AC

WOMEN
1974 Mitcham AC
1975 Edinburgh Southern Harriers
1976–80 Stretford AC

AAA CHAMPIONSHIPS

The AAA (Amateur Athletic Association) championships were first held in 1880. Although, strictly speaking, they are the national championships for England, for many years they have been a major international event on the athletics calendar, and indeed in the early part of the century were regarded as virtually world championships. Most individual titles have been won by:

14 McDonald Bailey: 100 y 1946–47, 1949–53; 220 y 1946–47, 1949–53
13 Dennis Horgan: shot 1893–99, 1904–05, 1908–10, 1912
11 Harry Whittle: 220 yh 1953; 440 yh 1947–53; long jump 1947, 1949; decathlon 1950
10 Alfred Shrubb: 1 mile 1903–04; 4 miles 1901–04; 10 miles 1901–04
10 Ken Matthews: 2 miles walk 1959, 1961–64; 7 miles walk 1959–61, 1963–64
10 Roger Mills: 3000 m walk 1969, 1972–74, 1976–79; 10 000 m walk 1973, 1980

In addition, winners 7 or more times at one event have been:

8 Donald Finlay: 120 yh 1932–38, 1949
8 Maurice Herriott: 3000 m steeplechase 1959, 1961–67
7 Albert Cooper: 2 miles walk 1932–38
7 Bill Tancred: discus 1966–70, 1972–73
7 David Travis: javelin 1965, 1968, 1970–74
7 Tom Ray: pole vault 1881–82, 1884–88
7 Geoff Capes: shot 1972–73, 1975–79

WORLD ATHLETE OF THE YEAR

The American magazine *Track and Field News*, one of the most respected authorities on athletics, annually selects, by a poll of international experts, its world athlete of the year. Male athlete of the year has been selected since 1959 and woman athlete since 1976. For the years 1967 to 1975 the woman athlete of the year was similarly selected by *Women's Track and Field World*.

MALE ATHLETE OF THE YEAR

1959 Martin Lauer (Ger)
1960 Rafer Johnson (USA)
1961 Ralph Boston (USA)
1962 Peter Snell (NZ)
1963 C. K. Yang (Tai)
1964 Peter Snell (NZ)
1965 Ron Clarke (Aus)
1966 Jim Ryun (USA)
1967 Jim Ryun (USA)
1968 Bob Beamon (USA)
1969 Bill Toomey (USA)
1970 Randy Matson (USA)
1971 Rod Milburn (USA)
1972 Lasse Viren (Fin)
1973 Ben Jipcho (Ken)
1974 Rick Wohlhuter (USA)
1975 John Walker (NZ)
1976 Alberto Juantorena (Cub)
1977 Alberto Juantorena (Cub)
1978 Henry Rono (Ken)
1979 Sebastian Coe (GB)
1980 Edwin Moses (USA)

WOMAN ATHLETE OF THE YEAR

1967 Liesl Westermann (Ger)
1968 Margitta Gummel (GDR)
1969 Chi Cheng (Tai)
1970 Chi Cheng (Tai)
1971 Ilona Gusenbauer (Aut)
1972 Heide Rosendahl (Ger)
1973 Renate Stecher (GDR)
1974 Irena Szewinska (Pol)
1975 Faina Veleva (née Melnik) (USSR)
1976 Tatyana Kazankina (USSR)
1977 Rosemarie Ackermann (GDR)
1978 Marita Koch (GDR)
1979 Marita Koch (GDR)
1980 Ilona Slupianek (GDR)

Track and Field News also named athletes of the decade as follows:
MEN 1960s: Peter Snell (NZ); 1970s Viktor Saneyev (USSR)
WOMEN 1970s: Ruth Fuchs (GDR)

Babies

KODAK ROBINSON'S BABY FOOD PHOTOGRAPHIC COMPETITION

This is arranged annually by Kodak Limited and Robinson's Baby Foods to find the best 'candid camera' shot of a baby born since 1 October of the previous year. The competition aims to find the happiest baby under one year old.

Winners:

1975 Andrew Boothman, Goole, N. Humberside
1976 Lyndsey Heys, Blackpool
1977 Joanne Astrup, Moorland, Somerset
1978 Jonathan Rodgers, Lancaster
1979 Victoria Swan, Cleveland
1980 Kathryn Lougheed, Bishop's Stortford, Herts

The 1980 winning photograph of Kathryn Lougheed

Badminton

THOMAS CUP

First held in 1948–49, the Thomas Cup is the international men's team championship, and is contested every three years.

1948–49 Malaya
1951–52 Malaya
1954–55 Malaya
1957–58 Indonesia
1960–61 Indonesia
1963–64 Indonesia
1966–67 Malaysia
1969–70 Indonesia
1972–73 Indonesia
1975–76 Indonesia
1978–79 Indonesia

UBER CUP

First held in 1956–57, the Uber Cup is the international women's team championship, and is held every three years.

1956–57 USA
1959–60 USA
1962–63 USA
1965–66 Japan
1968–69 Japan
1971–72 Japan
1974–75 Indonesia
1977–78 Japan
1980–81 Japan

WORLD CHAMPIONSHIPS

The first-ever world championships were held in 1977 and are to be held every three years. Winners:

1977

Men's singles: Flemming Delfs (Den)
Women's singles: Lene Köppen (Den)
Men's doubles: Johan Wahjudi and Tjun-Tjun (Ind)
Women's doubles: Etsuko Tuganoo and Emiko Veno (Jap)
Mixed doubles: Steen Skovgaard and Lene Köppen (Den)

1980

Men's singles: Rudy Hartono (Ind)
Women's singles: Wiharjo Verawaty (Ind)
Men's doubles: Ade Chandra and Hadinata Christian (Ind)
Women's doubles: Nora Perry and Jane Webster (Eng)
Mixed doubles: Hadinata Christian and Imelda Wigoeno (Ind)

ALL-ENGLAND CHAMPIONSHIPS

First held in 1899 and, until the advent of the world championships, the premier tournament in the world.

MEN'S SINGLES
Winners since 1970:

1970 Rudy Hartono (Ind)
1971 Rudy Hartono (Ind)

Judy Hashman won a record 10 All-England badminton titles and shares the record for the total number of championships (including doubles) at 17

1972 Rudy Hartono (Ind)
1973 Rudy Hartono (Ind)
1974 Rudy Hartono (Ind)
1975 Svend Pri (Den)
1976 Rudy Hartono (Ind)
1977 Flemming Delfs (Den)
1978 Liem Swie King (Ind)
1979 Liem Swie King (Ind)
1980 Prakash Padukone (Ind)
1981 Liem Swie King (Ind)

Most wins: 8 Rudy Hartono (Ind) 1968–74, 1976; 7 Erland Kops (Den) 1958, 1960–63, 1965, 1967; 6 Frank Devlin (Ire) 1925–29, 1931

WOMEN'S SINGLES
Winners since 1970:

1970 Etsuko Takenaka (Jap)
1971 Eva Twedberg (Swe)
1972 Noriko Nakayama (Jap)
1973 Margaret Beck (Eng)
1974 Hiroe Yuki (Jap)
1975 Hiroe Yuki (Jap)
1976 Gillian Gilks (Eng)
1977 Hiroe Yuki (Jap)
1978 Gillian Gilks (Eng)
1979 Lene Köppen (Den)
1980 Lene Köppen (Den)
1981 Sun Ai Hwang (Kor)

Most wins: 10 Judy Devlin/Hashman (USA) 1954, 1957–58, 1960–64, 1966–67; 6 Mary Lucas (Eng) 1902, 1905, 1907–10

MEN'S DOUBLES

Winners since 1970:

1970 Tom Backer and Paul Petersen (Den)
1971 Ng Boon Bee and Punch Gunalan (Mal)
1972 Hadinata Christian and Ade Chandra (Ind)
1973 Hadinata Christian and Ade Chandra (Ind)
1974 Tjun Tjun and Johan Wahjudi (Ind)
1975 Tjun Tjun and Johan Wahjudi (Ind)
1976 Bengt Froman and Thomas Kihlstrom (Swe)
1977 Tjun Tjun and Johan Wahjudi (Ind)
1978 Tjun Tjun and Johan Wahjudi (Ind)
1979 Tjun Tjun and Johan Wahjudi (Ind)
1980 Tjun Tjun and Johan Wahjudi (Ind)
1981 Rudy Kartono and Rudy Heryanto (Ind)

Most wins: 6 Frank Devlin and Gordon Mack (Ire) 1923, 1926–27, 1929–31; 6 Finn Kobberö and Jorgen Hammergaard Hansen (Den) 1955–56, 1961–64; 6 Tjun Tjun and Johan Wahjudi (Ind) 1974–75, 1977–80

WOMEN'S DOUBLES

Winners since 1970:

1970 Margaret Boxall and Sue Whetnall (Eng)
1971 Noriko Takagi and Hiroe Yuki (Jap)
1972 Machiko Aizawa and Etsuko Takenaka (Jap)
1973 Machiko Aizawa and Etsuko Takenaka (Jap)
1974 Margaret Beck and Gillian Gilks (Eng)
1975 Machiko Aizawa and Etsuko Takenaka (Jap)
1976 Gillian Gilks and Sue Whetnall (Eng)

1977 Etsuko Toganoo (née Takenaka) and Emiko Ueno (Jap)
1978 Atsuko Tokuda and Mikiko Takada (Jap)
1979 Wiharjo Verawaty and Imelda Wigoeno (Ind)
1980 Gillian Gilks and Nora Perry (Eng)
1981 Nora Perry and Jane Webster (Eng)

Most wins: 6 Sue Devlin/Peard and Judy Devlin/Hashman (USA) 1954, 1956, 1960–61, 1963, 1966

MIXED DOUBLES

Winners since 1970:

1970 Per Walsöe and Pernille Mölgaard Hansen (Den)
1971 Svend Pri and Ulla Strand (Den)
1972 Svend Pri and Ulla Strand (Den)
1973 Derek Talbot and Gillian Gilks (Eng)
1974 David Eddy and Sue Whetnall (Eng)
1975 Elliott Stuart and Nora Gardner (Eng)
1976 Derek Talbot and Gillian Gilks (Eng)
1977 Derek Talbot and Gillian Gilks (Eng)
1978 Mike Tredgett and Nora Perry (née Gardner) (Eng)
1979 Hadinata Christian and Imelda Wigoeno (Ind)
1980 Mike Tredgett and Nora Perry (Eng)
1981 Mike Tredgett and Nora Perry (Eng)

Most wins: 4 George Thomas and Hazel Hogarth (Eng) 1914, 1920–22; Donald Hume and Betty Uber (Eng) 1933–36; Poul Holm and Tonny Ahm/Olsen (Den) 1947, 1950–52; Finn Kobberö and Ulla Rasmussen/Strand (Den) 1962–63, 1965–66

Ballet

THE NEW STANDARD BALLET AWARD

Instituted in 1973 by the London *Evening Standard*, this award for the 'Most Outstanding Achievement in Ballet' aims to promote the arts in London. The winner is chosen by a panel of judges composed of critics from London newspapers. Winners:

1973 Christopher Bruce
1974 Corps de Ballet of the Royal Ballet
1975 London Contemporary Dance Theatre
1976 Lynn Seymour
1977 David Wall
1978 Kenneth MacMillan
1979 Peter Schaufuss
1980 Jennifer Penney

THE QUEEN ELIZABETH II CORONATION AWARD

This is presented annually in recognition of outstanding services to the art of Ballet by the Royal Academy of Dancing.

1954 Dame Ninette de Valois, DBE, DMus, FRAD
1955 Madame Tamara Karsavina
1956 Dame Marie Rambert, DBE, FRAD
1957 Phyllis Bedells, FRAD
1958 Anton Dolin
1959 Sir Frederick Ashton, OM, CH, CBE
1960 Sir Robert Helpman, CBE
1961 Ursula Moreton

1962 Cyril Beaumont, CBE
1963 P. J. S. Richardson, OBE (deceased)
      Dame Alicia Markova, DBE, DMus
1964 Kathleen Gordon
1965 Dame Peggy Van Praagh, DBE
1966 Serge Grigorieff and Lubov Tchernicheva
1967 Madame Lydia Sokolova
1968 Stanislas Idzikowski
1969 John Hart
1970 John Gilpin
1971 Louise Browne, OBE, FRAD
1972 Ruth French, FRAD
1973 Norman Morrice
1974 Brian Shaw
1975 Robin Howard
1976 Pamela May
1977 Winifred Edwards
1978 Kenneth MacMillan
1979 Arnold Haskell
1980 Glen Tetley

THE ROYAL ACADEMY OF DANCING ADELINE GENÉE MEDAL AWARDS

This is a competition for ballet dancers, initiated by Dame Adeline Genée (founder and president of the Royal Academy of Dancing) in 1931. It is designed to test the professional potential of young dancers.

Over the years many distinguished dancers have won gold medals – Bryan Ashbridge,

David Drew, John Gilpin, Maria Guerrero, John Hart, Rowena Jackson, Brenda Last, Diana Vere and Doreen Wells, to name but a few. Winners since 1973:

1973 Jane Devine
1974 Nicola Katrak
     Nigel Jones
1975 Summer Rhatigan
1976 Jill Taylor
1977 Sharon McGorian
1978 Ravenna Tucker
     Roland Price
1979 Madonna Benjamin
1980 No award

Balloons

BEEFEATER GIN BALLOON RACE

Entry is by means of a crowner available from a bottle of Beefeater Gin which is on sale over the Christmas period in the UK. A gas-filled balloon is released for each successful entrant and the one that travels furthest is the winner. The 1980/81 winner received a cash prize of £2000 and the ten runners-up received solid-silver salvers. Winners and distances balloon travelled:

1968–69 W. Shelton, 1370 km (Perugia, Italy)
1969–70 No race
1970–71 Mr. Perryman, 1040 km (Helsinge, Denmark)
1971–72 J. Hartly, 1420 km (Elblag, Poland)
1972–73 Mr. Ripley, 3505 km (Happut, Turkey)
1973–74 B. Tucker, 1190 km (Modena, Italy)
1974–75 No race
1975–76 A. Woodroofe, 950 km (Alzonne, France)
1976–77 G. Vann, 810 km (Félines, France)
1977–78 H. Cross, 1050 km (Genoa, Italy)
1978–79 D. Davis, 1910 km (Lempäälä, Finland)
1979–80 A. P. Fielding, 1750 km (Arad, Romania)
1980–81 J. A. Welford, 2150 km (La Chebba, Tunisia)

UK HOT AIR BALLOON CHAMPIONSHIPS

These are held annually over a week-long period when various flying contests test the pilot's ability to fly a balloon accurately, and to make full use of the wind currents available. Winners and location of event since first championships in 1976:

1976 Richard Worth, London (Castle Howard, Yorks)
1977 Crispin Williams, Doncaster (Castle Howard, Yorks)
1978 Alan Dorman, Surrey (Stanford Hall, Rugby)
1979 Crispin Williams, Doncaster (Wollaton Park, Nottingham)
1980 Ian Jacobs, London (Stanford Hall, Rugby)

Bands

'FANFARE': BBC RADIO SCOTLAND'S BRASS BAND CONTEST

Winners of this annual contest are as follows:

1974 Whitburn Burgh Band
     Conductor: George Thomson
1975 Kirkintilloch Silver Band
     Conductor: David James
1976 Kirkintilloch Silver Band
     Conductor: David James
1977 CWS (Glasgow) Band
     Conductor: Nigel Boddice
1978 CWS (Glasgow) Band
     Conductor: Nigel Boddice
1979 Kilmarnock Concert Brass
     Conductor: Andrew Keachie
1980 Whitburn Burgh Band
     Conductor: Ray Stuttard

ROTHMANS BRASS IN CONCERT CHAMPIONSHIP

Now an annual event, held at Darlington, the Championship is established as one of the major brass band competitions to take place in

Grimethorpe Colliery Band in action during the 1979 Rothmans Brass in Concert Championship

the UK. The bands compete for a first prize of £2000. Winners.

1977 Grimethorpe Colliery Band, Yorks
1978 Hammonds Sauce Works Band, Shipley, Yorks

1979 Grimethorpe Colliery Band, Yorks.
1980 Grimethorpe Colliery Band, Yorks.

TOBACCO WORKERS' UNION TROPHY
Presented to the best featured soloist in the Rothmans Brass In Concert Championship.

1978 Bobby Millar (Wingates Temperance Band), for his euphonium performance of Bladon Races
1979 Stan Priestley (trombone), Grimethorpe Colliery Band
1980 Jim Shepherd (cornet), Ever Ready Band

WORLD PIPE BAND CHAMPIONSHIPS
Bands from around the world compete annually and each year sees representatives from Canada, USA, Australia, New Zealand, Eire, Scandinavia, Netherlands, Denmark, France and bands from HM and Commonwealth Forces.

	Band	Venue	Pipe-Major
1947	Bowhill Colliery	Edinburgh	C. Sutherland
1948	Shotts and Dykehead Caledonia	Glasgow	T. McAllister, Sen., BEM
1949	Glasgow Police	Edinburgh	J. MacDonald
1950	Edinburgh Police	Dundee	D. S. Ramsay
1951	Glasgow Police	Edinburgh	J. MacDonald
1952	Shotts and Dykehead Caledonia	Ayr	T. McAllister, Sen., BEM
1953	Clan MacRae	Edinburgh	A. MacLeod
1954	Edinburgh Police	Aberdeen	D. S. Ramsay
1955	Muirhead and Sons	Stirling	J. Smith
1956	Muirhead and Sons	Belfast	J. Smith
1957	Shotts and Dykehead Caledonia	Paisley	J. K. MacAllister
1958	Shotts and Dykehead Caledonia	Aberdeen	J. K. MacAllister
1959	Shotts and Dykehead Caledonia	Kirkcaldy	J. K. MacAllister
1960	Shotts and Dykehead Caledonia	Inverness	J. K. MacAllister
1961	Muirhead and Sons	Edinburgh	J. Smith
1962	277 (A & SH), Regt., RA(TA)	Belfast	J. Weatherstone, MBE, BEM
1963	Edinburgh Police	Dumfries	I. McLeod
1964	Edinburgh Police	Ayr	I. McLeod
1965	Muirhead and Sons	Forfar	R. Hardie
1966	Muirhead and Sons	Inverness	R. Hardie
1967	Muirhead and Sons	Oban	R. Hardie
1968	Muirhead and Sons	Grangemouth	R. Hardie
1969	Muirhead and Sons	Perth	R. Hardie
1970	Shotts and Dykehead Caledonia	Aberdeen	T. McAllister, Jr
1971	Edinburgh Police	Lanark	I. McLeod
1972	Edinburgh Police	Hawick	I. McLeod
1973	Shotts and Dykehead Caledonia	Ayr	T. McAllister, Jr
1974	Shotts and Dykehead Caledonia	Stirling	T. McAllister, Jr
1975	Edinburgh City Police	Corby	I. McLeod
1976	Strathclyde Police	Hawick	I. McLellan
1977	Dysart and Dundonald	Aberdeen	R. Shepherd
1978	Dysart and Dundonald	Lanark	R. Shepherd
1979	Strathclyde Police	Nottingham	I. McLellan
1980	Shotts and Dykehead Caledonia	Glasgow	T. McAllister, Jr

Baseball

MAJOR LEAGUES IN THE USA
The National League was founded in 1876 and the American League in 1901. In 1903 and each season since 1905 the winners of these two leagues have met in the World Series.

Winners of these major leagues since 1901, with the World Series winners identified by (WS) have been:

National League

1901 Pittsburgh Pirates
1902 Pittsburgh Pirates
1903 Pittsburgh Pirates
1904 New York Giants
1905 New York Giants (WS)
1906 Chicago Cubs
1907 Chicago Cubs (WS)
1908 Chicago Cubs (WS)
1909 Pittsburgh Pirates (WS)
1910 Chicago Cubs
1911 New York Giants
1912 New York Giants
1913 New York Giants
1914 Boston (WS)
1915 Philadelphia
1916 Brooklyn
1917 New York Giants
1918 Chicago Cubs
1919 Cincinnati (WS)
1920 Brooklyn
1921 New York Giants (WS)
1922 New York Giants (WS)
1923 New York Giants
1924 New York Giants
1925 Pittsburgh Pirates (WS)
1926 St Louis Cardinals (WS)
1927 Pittsburgh Pirates
1928 St Louis Cardinals
1929 Chicago Cubs
1930 St Louis Cardinals
1931 St Louis Cardinals (WS)
1932 Chicago Cubs
1933 New York Giants (WS)
1934 St Louis Cardinals (WS)
1935 Chicago Cubs
1936 New York Giants
1937 New York Giants
1938 Chicago Cubs
1939 Cincinnati Reds
1940 Cincinnati Reds (WS)
1941 Brooklyn Dodgers
1942 St Louis Cardinals (WS)
1943 St Louis Cardinals
1944 St Louis Cardinals (WS)
1945 Chicago Cubs
1946 St Louis Cardinals (WS)
1947 Brooklyn Dodgers
1948 Boston Braves
1949 Brooklyn Dodgers
1950 Philadelphia Phillies
1951 New York Giants
1952 Brooklyn Dodgers
1953 Brooklyn Dodgers
1954 New York Giants (WS)
1955 Brooklyn Dodgers (WS)
1956 Brooklyn Dodgers
1957 Milwaukee Braves (WS)
1958 Milwaukee Braves
1959 Los Angeles Dodgers (WS)
1960 Pittsburgh Pirates (WS)
1961 Cincinnati Reds
1962 San Francisco Giants
1963 Los Angeles Dodgers (WS)
1964 St Louis Cardinals (WS)
1965 Los Angeles Dodgers (WS)
1966 Los Angeles Dodgers
1967 St Louis Cardinals (WS)
1968 St Louis Cardinals

Reggie Jackson of the New York Yankees hit most runs and home runs in the 1977 World Series

1969 New York Mets (WS)
1970 Cincinnati Reds
1971 Pittsburgh Pirates (WS)
1972 Cincinnati Reds
1973 New York Mets
1974 Los Angeles Dodgers
1975 Cincinnati Reds (WS)
1976 Cincinnati Reds (WS)
1977 Los Angeles Dodgers
1978 Los Angeles Dodgers
1979 Pittsburgh Pirates (WS)
1980 Philadelphia Phillies (WS)

American League

1901 Chicago White Sox
1902 Philadelphia Athletics
1903 Boston Red Sox (WS)
1904 Boston Red Sox
1905 Philadelphia Athletics
1906 Chicago White Sox (WS)
1907 Detroit Tigers
1908 Detroit Tigers (WS)
1909 Detroit Tigers
1910 Philadelphia Athletics (WS)
1911 Philadelphia Athletics (WS)
1912 Boston Red Sox (WS)
1913 Philadelphia Athletics (WS)
1914 Philadelphia Athletics
1915 Boston Red Sox (WS)
1916 Boston Red Sox (WS)
1917 Chicago White Sox (WS)
1918 Boston Red Sox (WS)
1919 Chicago White Sox
1920 Cleveland Indians (WS)
1921 New York Yankees
1922 New York Yankees
1923 New York Yankees (WS)
1924 Washington (WS)
1925 Washington
1926 New York Yankees
1927 New York Yankees (WS)
1928 New York Yankees (WS)
1929 Philadelphia Athletics (WS)
1930 Philadelphia Athletics (WS)
1931 Philadelphia Athletics
1932 New York Yankees (WS)
1933 Washington

1934 Detroit Tigers
1935 Detroit Tigers (WS)
1936 New York Yankees (WS)
1937 New York Yankees (WS)
1938 New York Yankees (WS)
1939 New York Yankees (WS)
1940 Detroit Tigers
1941 New York Yankees (WS)
1942 New York Yankees
1943 New York Yankees (WS)
1944 St Louis Browns
1945 Detroit Tigers
1946 Boston Red Sox
1947 New York Yankees (WS)
1948 Cleveland Indians (WS)
1949 New York Yankees (WS)
1950 New York Yankees (WS)
1951 New York Yankees (WS)
1952 New York Yankees (WS)
1953 New York Yankees (WS)
1954 Cleveland Indians
1955 New York Yankees
1956 New York Yankees (WS)
1957 New York Yankees
1958 New York Yankees (WS)
1959 Chicago White Sox
1960 New York Yankees
1961 New York Yankees (WS)
1962 New York Yankees (WS)
1963 New York Yankees
1964 New York Yankees
1965 Minnesota Twins
1966 Baltimore Orioles (WS)
1967 Boston Red Sox
1968 Detroit Tigers (WS)
1969 Baltimore Orioles
1970 Baltimore Orioles (WS)
1971 Baltimore Orioles
1972 Oakland Athletics (WS)
1973 Oakland Athletics (WS)
1974 Oakland Athletics (WS)
1975 Boston Red Sox
1976 New York Yankees
1977 New York Yankees (WS)
1978 New York Yankees (WS)
1979 Baltimore Orioles
1980 Kansas City Royals

MOST VALUABLE PLAYER

Each season the 'most valuable player' in each of the major leagues is elected by the Baseball Writers' Association of America. Four men have won three awards: Jimmy Foxx, Stan Musial, Roy Campanella, and Mickey Mantle. Winners since 1970:

National League
1970 Johnny Bench (Cincinnati)
1971 Joseph Torre (St Louis)
1972 Johnny Bench (Cincinnati)
1973 Pete Rose (Cincinnati)
1974 Steve Garvey (Los Angeles)
1975 Joe Morgan (Cincinnati)
1976 Joe Morgan (Cincinnati)
1977 George Foster (Cincinnati)
1978 Dave Parker (Pittsburgh)
1979 { Willie Stargell (Pittsburgh)
        Keith Hernandez (St Louis)
1980 Mike Schmidt (Philadelphia)

American League
1970 John Powell (Baltimore)
1971 Vida Blue (Oakland)
1972 Richard Allen (Chicago)
1973 Reggie Jackson (Oakland)
1974 Jeff Burroughs (Texas)
1975 Fred Lynn (Boston)
1976 Thurman Munson (New York)
1977 Rod Carew (Minnesota)
1978 Jim Rice (Boston)
1979 Don Baylor (California)
1980 George Brett (Kansas City)

Basketball

WORLD CHAMPIONSHIPS

First held in 1950, the World Championships for men are held between Olympic Games. Contested by amateur teams.

1950	Argentina	1967	USSR
1954	USA	1970	Yugoslavia
1959	Brazil	1974	USSR
1963	Brazil	1978	Yugoslavia

Women's World Championships were first held in 1953.

1953	USA	1967	USSR
1957	USA	1971	USSR
1959	USSR	1975	USSR
1964	USSR	1979	USA

OLYMPIC CHAMPIONS

First held in 1936 for men and 1976 for women.

MEN
1936	USA	1964	USA
1948	USA	1968	USA
1952	USA	1972	USSR
1956	USA	1976	USA
1960	USA	1980	Yugoslavia

WOMEN
1976	USSR	1980	USSR

ENGLISH NATIONAL CHAMPIONSHIPS

Held annually from 1936 to 1940 and since 1947, winners of national finals since 1970 have been:

MEN
1970 Liverpool Police
1971 Manchester University
1972 Avenue (Leyton)
1973 London Latvian SK
1974 Sutton and Crystal Palace
1975 Embassy All Stars*
1976 Crystal Palace
1977 Crystal Palace
1978 Crystal Palace
1979 Crystal Palace
1980 Crystal Palace
1981 Sunderland

*Formerly London Latvian SK

NATIONAL CUP WINNERS (separate from National Championships since 1979):

MEN
1979 Team Ziebart Doncaster
1980 Crystal Palace
1981 Crystal Palace

ENGLISH NATIONAL LEAGUE WINNERS

MEN
1972–73 Avenue (Leyton)
1973–74 Crystal Palace
1974–75 Embassy All Stars*
1975–76 Crystal Palace
1976–77 Crystal Palace
1977–78 Crystal Palace
1978–79 Doncaster
1979–80 Crystal Palace
1980–81 Team Fiat Birmingham

*Formerly London Latvian SK

ENGLISH NATIONAL CUP

Held annually since 1965. Winners since 1970:

WOMEN
1970 Abbey Wood
1971 Abbey Wood
1972 Turnford Tigers
1973 Turnford Tigers
1974 Eston Eagles
1975 Cleveland Eagles*
1976 Turnford Tigers
1977 Tigers
1978 Tigers

1979 Tigers
1980 Tigers
1981 Southgate

*Formerly Eston Eagles

ENGLISH NATIONAL LEAGUE WINNERS

WOMEN

1975–76 Tigers (Herts)
1976–77 Tigers (Herts)
1977–78 Cleveland Eagles*
1978–79 Cleveland Eagles*
1979–80 Tigers (Herts)
1980–81 Southgate

*Formerly Eston Eagles

ENGLISH BASKETBALL ASSOCIATION PLAYER OF THE YEAR

MEN

1971 Bill McInnes
1972 Vic Collins
1973 Peter Sprogis
1974 Jim Guymon
1975 Steve Latham
1976 Carl Olssen
1977 Ian Day
1978 Steve Assinder
1979 Dan Lloyd
1980 Alton Byrd
1981 Alton Byrd

Wilt 'The Stilt' Chamberlain (no. 13) and Bill Russell respectively 7 ft 1 in and 6 ft 9 in tall, battle it out at the Boston Garden. Both useful high jumpers at college, they were the top basketball stars of the 1960s. Russell played on 11 championship teams with the Boston Celtics, and Chamberlain, playing here for Philadelphia, dominates the record books

Beauty

MISS BRITAIN

This contest began in 1961 and is held to choose a representative to compete in Miss International held in Tokyo. A Mecca contest organised by JEM International Ltd, the winners have twice won the Miss International title (in 1969 and 1972). The first Miss Britain in 1961 was Nicky Allen and winners since 1970 have been:

1970 Jackie Molloy
1971 Christine Owen
1972 Linda Hooks
1973 Zoe Spink
1974 Joanna Booth
1975 Sharon Jermyn
1976 Janet Withey
1977 Sian Adey-Jones
1978 Sarah Long
1979 Beverley Isherwood
1980 Lorraine Davidson

Lorraine Davidson, Miss Britain 1980

'MISS GREAT BRITAIN' NATIONAL BATHING BEAUTY CONTEST

This was inaugurated in 1945 by the then Morecambe and Heysham Borough Council, and since local government reorganisation in 1974 Lancaster City Council promotes the contest in association with Pontin's holidays. National heats throughout the country are followed by regional finals which produce contestants for the semi-final. During the summer, seasonal heats are held in Morecambe and the winners also qualify for the semi-final, which takes place in September. The winners from this stage are then joined by the winners of various television heats, sponsored by the ITV regional companies, for the grand final. Previous winners are:

1945 Lydia Reed, Morecambe and Heysham
1946 June Rivers, Manchester
1947 June Mitchel, Birmingham
1948 Pamela Bayliss, Northern Ireland
1949 Elaine Price, Bolton
1950 Anne Heywood, Birmingham
1951 Marlene Dee, Henley on Thames
1952 Doreen Dawne, London
1953 Brenda Mee, Derby
1954 Patricia Butler, Hoylake
1955 Jennifer Chimes, Royal Leamington Spa
1956 Iris Waller, Gateshead
1957 Leila Williams, Walsall
1958 Christina Mayo, Abergele
1959 Valerie Martin, Blackburn
1960 Eileen Sheridan, Walton on Thames
1961 Libby Walker, Blackpool
1962 Joy Black, Dumfries
1963 Gillian Taylor, Cheadle
1964 Carol Redhead, Poulton le Fylde
1965 Diane Westbury, Altrincham
1966 Carole Fletcher, Southport
1967 Jennifer Gurley, Sale
1968 Yvonne Ormes, Nantwich
1969 Wendy Ann George, Derby
1970 Kathleen Winstanley, Wigan
1971 Carolyn Moore, Nantwich
1972 Elizabeth Robinson, Nottingham
1973 Gay Spink, Halifax
1974 Marilyn Ward, New Milton
1975 Susan Anne Cuff, Manchester
1976 Dinah May, Little Neston, Wirral
1977 Susan Marcelle Hempel, Bispham
1978 Patricia Morgan, Whitley Bay
1979 Not held
1980 Susan Berger, Hale Barns, Cheshire
1981 Michele Hobson, Kirkby-in-Ashfield

Michele Hobson voted the 1981 Miss Great Britain in the National Bathing Beauty Contest

MISS UNITED KINGDOM

This competition has been held annually since 1958 in Blackpool with the winner gaining automatic entry into the Miss World contest. Miss United Kingdom is a Mecca contest organised by JEM International Ltd.

1958 Eileen Sheridan, Walton-on-Thames
1959 Anne Thelwell, Heswall

1960 Hilda Fairclough, Lancaster
1961 Rosemarie Frankland, Lancaster
1962 Jackie White, Alvaston
1963 Diane Westbury, Ilkeston
1964 Ann Sidney, Parkstone
1965 Lesley Langley, London
1966 Jennifer Lowe, Warrington
1967 Jennifer Lewis, Leicester

1968 Kathleen Winstanley, Wigan
1969 Sheena Drummond, Tullibody
1970 Yvonne Ormes, Nantwich
1971 Marilyn Ward, New Milton
1972 Jenny McAdam, London
1973 Veronica Cross, London
1974 Helen Morgan, Barry
1975 Vicki Harris, London
1976 Carol Grant, Glasgow
1977 Madeleine Stringer, North Shields
1978 Ann Jones, Welshpool
1979 Carolyn Seaward, Yelverton
1980 Kim Ashfield, Buckley, N. Wales

MISS WORLD

Founded in 1951 by Eric D. Morley and sponsored by the Mecca Organisation, the contest is held annually in London. Originally a 'one off' event to publicise the Festival of Britain, it has become an annual fund-raising charitable event, with the entire proceeds going to the Variety Club of Great Britain's children's charities.

1951 Kiki Haakonson (Sweden)
1952 May Louise Flodin (Sweden)
1953 Denise Perrier (France)
1954 Antigone Costanda (Egypt)
1955 Carmen Susana Duijm (Venezuela)
1956 Petra Schurmann (W. Germany)
1957 Marita Lindahl (Finland)
1958 Penny Coelen (South Africa)
1959 Corine Rottschafer (Holland)
1960 Norma Cappegli (Argentina)
1961 Rosemarie Frankland (UK)
1962 Rina Lodders (Holland)
1963 Carole Crawford (Jamaica)
1964 Ann Sidney (UK)
1965 Lesley Langley (UK)
1966 Reita Faria (India)
1967 Madeleine Hartog-Bel (Peru)

Above: *Kim Ashfield, Miss United Kingdom 1980.* Below: *Kimberly Santos (Guam) who became Miss World 1980 after the resignation of Gabriella Brum (W. Germany)*

The final line-up for the 1952 Miss World contest (Popperfoto)

1968 Penny Plummer (Australia)
1969 Eva Rueber-Staier (Austria)
1970 Jennifer Hosten (Grenada)
1971 Lucia Petterle (Brazil)
1972 Belinda Green (Australia)
1973 Marji Wallace (USA)
1974 Helen Morgan (UK) (resigned)
      Anneline Kriel (South Africa)
1975 Wilnelia Merced (Puerto Rico)
1976 Cindy Breakspeare (Jamaica)
1977 Mary Stavin (Sweden)
1978 Silvana Suarez (Argentina)
1979 Gina Swainson (Bermuda)
1980 Gabriella Brum (W. Germany) (resigned)
      Kimberly Santos (Guam)

MISS ENGLAND, MISS SCOTLAND AND MISS WALES

These national competitions are held annually to choose representatives from the three countries to compete in the Miss Universe Beauty Pageant which originated in Long Beach, California, in 1952, and is now held in different parts of the world each year. All of the contests are sponsored by Mecca and organised by JEM International Ltd. Winners since 1970:

Miss England
1970 Yvonne Ormes
1971 Marilyn Ward
1972 Jenny McAdam
1973 Veronica Cross
1974 Kathy Anders
1975 Vicki Harris
1976 Pauline Davies
1977 Sarah Long
1978 Beverley Isherwood
1979 Carolyn Seaward
1980 Julie Duckworth
1981 Suzanne Hughes

Miss Scotland
1970 Lee Hamilton-Marshall
1971 Libus Montgomery
1972 Liz Stevely
1973 Caroline Meade
1974 Catherine Robertson
1975 Marie Kirkwood
1976 Carol Grant
1977 Sandra Bell
1978 Angela MacLeod
1979 Lorraine Davidson
1980 Linda Gallagher
1981 Georgina Kearney

Miss Wales
1970 Sandra Cater
1971 Dawn Cater
1972 Eileen Darroch
1973 Deirdre Greenland
1974 Helen Morgan
1975 Gina Kerler
1976 Sian Adey-Jones
1977 Christine Murphy
1978 Ann Jones
1979 Beverley Neils
1980 Kim Ashfield
1981 Sally Douglas Williams

A group of some of the finalists for the Miss England 1958. The winner, 16-year-old June Cooper is on the left in the front row (Popperfoto)

MISS UNIVERSE

The pre-eminent international beauty competition held in America, and founded in 1952. Miss Universe receives a cash award, a scholarship, a film contract, a personal appearance contract and various prizes – principally clothing, a fur coat and a car.

1952 Armi Kuusela, Finland
1953 Christiane Martel, France
1954 Miriam Stevenson, USA
1955 Hellevi Rombin, Sweden
1956 Carol Morris, USA
1957 Gladys Zender, Peru
1958 Luz Marina Zuluaga, Colombia
1959 Akiko Kojima, Japan
1960 Linda Bement, USA

Maritza Sayalero (Miss Venezuela), aged 20, won the 1979 Miss Universe title (Popperfoto)

1961 Marlene Schmidt, Federal Republic of Germany
1962 Norma Nolan, Argentina
1963 Ieda Maria Vargas, Brazil
1964 Corinna Tsopei, Greece
1965 Apasra Hongsakula, Thailand
1966 Margareta Arvidsson, Sweden
1967 Sylvia Hitchcock, USA
1968 Martha Vasconellos, Brazil
1969 Gloria Diaz, Philippines
1970 Marisol Malaret, Puerto Rico

1971 Georgina Risk, Lebanon
1972 Kerry Anne Wells, Australia
1973 Margarita Morgan, Philippines
1974 Amparo Munoz, Spain
1975 Anne Marie Pohtamo, Finland
1976 Rina Messinger, Israel
1977 Janelle Commissiong, Trinidad and Tobago
1978 Margaret Gardiner, South Africa
1979 Maritza Sayalero, Venezuela
1980 Shawn Nichols Weatherly, USA

Beer

BEER OF THE YEAR COMPETITION

This competition is organised by the Campaign for Real Ale (CAMRA) at the annual Great British Beer Festival, held at Alexandra Palace. It is judged by the general public, within the following categories:

'Judging' at the 1980 Great British Beer Festival

Overall winner
1978 Fullers ESB
     Thwaites Best Mild
1979 Fullers London Pride
1980 Thwaites Best Mild

Strong Bitter Class
1978 Fullers ESB
1979 Fullers ESB
1980 Youngs Special

Ordinary Bitter Class
1978 Ridleys Bitter
1979 Fullers London Pride
1980 Exmoor Ale

Mild Class
1978 Thwaites Best Mild
1979 Hanson's Mild
1980 Thwaites Best Mild

Billiards and Snooker

WORLD PROFESSIONAL BILLIARDS CHAMPIONSHIP

The first world champion to be recognised was William Cook in 1870. The championship has changed hands as follows:

1870 William Cook (Eng)
1870 John Roberts, Jnr (Eng)
1870 John Bennett (Eng)
1871 John Roberts, Jnr (Eng)
1871 William Cook (Eng)
1875 John Roberts, Jnr (Eng)
1880 John Bennett (Eng)
1885 John Roberts, Jnr (Eng)
1889 Charles Dawson (Eng)
1901 H. W. Stevenson (Eng)
1901 Charles Dawson (Eng)
1901 H. W. Stevenson (Eng)
1903 Charles Dawson (Eng)
1908 Melbourne Inman (USA)

(Under Billiards Control Club rules)
1909 H.W. Stephenson (Eng)
1912 Melbourne Inman (USA)
1920 Willie Smith (Eng)
1921 Tom Newman (Eng)
1923 Willie Smith (Eng)
1924 Tom Newman (Eng)
1928 Joe Davis (Eng)
1933 Walter Lindrum (Aus)
1951 Clark McConachy (NZ)
1968 Rex Williams (Eng)
1971 Leslie Driffield (Eng)
*WPBSA Championship**
1971 Rex Williams (Eng) (retained title in 1973, 1974, and 1976)
1980 Fred Davis (Eng)

*World Professional Billiards and Snooker Association

The first two world billiards champions, William Cook and John Roberts Jnr (Mary Evans)

WORLD PROFESSIONAL SNOOKER CHAMPIONSHIP

The championship was held annually from 1927 to 1940 and 1946 to 1957, when the winners were:

1927–40, 1946	Joe Davis (Eng) (15 contests)
1947	Walter Donaldson (Sco)
1948, 1949	Fred Davis (Eng)
1950	Walter Donaldson (Sco)
1951–56	Fred Davis (Eng)
1957	John Pulman (Eng)

The championship was resumed in 1964 on a challenge basis after the Professional Billiard Players' Association and the Billiards Association and Control Council had reconciled their differences. The championship reverted to an open tournament in 1969. Champions:

1964–68	John Pulman (Eng) (7 wins)
1969	John Spencer (Eng)
1970	Ray Reardon (Wal)
1971	John Spencer (Eng)
1972	Alex Higgins (NI)
1973	Ray Reardon (Wal)
1974	Ray Reardon (Wal)
1975	Ray Reardon (Wal)
1976	Ray Reardon (Wal)
1977	John Spencer (Eng)
1978	Ray Reardon (Wal)
1979	Terry Griffiths (Wal)
1980	Cliff Thorburn (Can)
1981	Steve Davis (Eng)

WORLD AMATEUR BILLIARDS CHAMPIONSHIP

First held in 1926 and now contested biennially. Winners:

1926	Joe Earlham (Eng)
1927	Allan Prior (SA)
1929	Leslie Hayes (Aus)
1931	Laurie Steeples (Eng)
1933	Sydney Lee (Eng)
1935	Horace Coles (Wal)
1936	Robert Marshall (Aus)
1938	Robert Marshall (Aus)
1951	Robert Marshall (Aus)
1952	Leslie Driffield (Eng)
1954	Tom Cleary (Aus)
1958	Wilson Jones (Ind)
1960	Herbery Beetham (Eng)
1962	Robert Marshall (Aus)
1964	Wilson Jones (Ind)
1967	Leslie Driffield (Eng)
1969	Jack Karnehm (Eng)
1971	Norman Dagley (Eng)
1973	Mohammed Lafir (Sri)
1975	Norman Dagley (Eng)
1977	Michael Ferreira (Ind)
1979	Paul Mifsud (Malta)

WORLD AMATEUR SNOOKER CHAMPIONSHIP

First held 1963. Winners:

1963	Gary Owen (Eng)
1966	Gary Owen (Eng)
1968	David Taylor (Eng)
1970	Jonathan Barron (Eng)
1972	Ray Edmonds (Eng)

1974 Ray Edmonds (Eng)
1976 Doug Mountjoy (Wal)
1978 Cliff Wilson (Wal)
1980 Jimmy White (Eng)

UK PROFESSIONAL SNOOKER CHAMPIONSHIP
First held 1977. Winners:

1977 Patsy Fagan (Ire)
1978 Doug Mountjoy (Wal)
1979 John Virgo (Eng)
1980 Steve Davis (Eng)

BENSON & HEDGES MASTERS SNOOKER CHAMPIONSHIP
First held 1975. Winners:

1975 John Spencer (Eng)
1976 Ray Reardon (Eng)
1977 Doug Mountjoy (Wal)
1978 Alex Higgins (NI)
1979 Perrie Mans (SA)
1980 Terry Griffiths (Wal)
1981 Alex Higgins (NI)

POT BLACK SNOOKER CHAMPIONSHIP
This competition is shown on BBC Television, the first event being held in 1969. Winners:

1969 Ray Reardon (Wal)
1970 John Spencer (Eng)
1971 John Spencer (Eng)
1972 Eddie Charlton (Aus)
1973 Eddie Charlton (Aus)
1974 Graham Miles (Eng)
1975 Graham Miles (Eng)
1976 John Spencer (Eng)

Fred Davis, doyen of the world billiards and snooker scene (David Muscroft)

1977 Perrie Mans (SA)
1978 Doug Mountjoy (Wal)
1979 Ray Reardon (Wal)
1980 Eddie Charlton (Aus)
1981 Cliff Thorburn (Can)

Birds

NATIONAL EXHIBITION OF CAGE AND AVIARY BIRDS ANNUAL AWARDS
The first 'National' was staged in February 1940 in aid of the Lord Mayor's Red Cross and St. John Fund Appeal This first event attracted 5400 entries. Later the show transferred to Olympia where huge exhibitions attracted up to 10 000 birds with gates of 30 000. Alexandra Palace has been used recently, and the Bingley Hall, Birmingham in 1980. The premier award is the Sir Richard Haddon Challenge Trophy for best bird at the National Exhibition. Winners since 1970:

1970 Reed and Holmes (Wednesbury), Paradise Flycatcher

1971 R.C.J. Sawyer (London), Yellow-headed Gouldian Finch
1972 L. Harris (Birmingham), White Zebra Finches
1973 Mr and Mrs R.E. Oxley (Hornchurch, Essex), Spangled Tanager
1974 C.H. Clark (Swaffham, Norfolk), Canary x Bullfinch
1975 E.C. Lewis (London), Sun Angel Humming Bird
1976 H. Bryan (Lilliput, Dorset), Grey Budgerigar cock
1977 R.S. Fletton (Polebrook, Peterborough), Canary x Bullfinch
1978 C.H. Smith (Sidcup, Kent), Siberian Thrushes
1979 J.P. Broadbent (Stanford-le-Hope, Essex), Canary x Bullfinch Hybrid
1980 Mrs G. Sharratt (Chellaston, Derby), Royal Starling

Bobsleigh and Tobogganing

WORLD AND OLYMPIC CHAMPIONSHIPS

World championships were first held for 4-man bobs in 1924 and for 2-man bobs in 1931. In Olympic years* the Olympic champions are recognised as world champions.

BOBSLEIGH

2-Man

First held 1931. Winners since 1972:

1972* W.Germany (Wolfgang Zimmerer and Peter Utzschneider)
1973 W.Germany (Wolfgang Zimmerer and Peter Utzschneider)
1974 W.Germany (Wolfgang Zimmerer and Peter Utzschneider)
1975 Italy (Giorgio Alvera and Franco Perrugat)
1976* GDR (Meinhard Nehmer and Bernhard Germeshausen)
1977 Switzerland (Hans Hiltebrand and Heinz Meier)
1978 Switzerland (Erich Schärer and Josef Benz)
1979 Switzerland (Erich Schärer and Josef Benz)
1980* Switzerland (Erich Schärer and Josef Benz)
1981 GDR (Bernhard Germeshausen and Hans-Jürgen Gerhardt)

Most wins: 14 Italy (1954, 1956–63, 1966, 1968–69, 1971, 1975) (Eugenio Monti was on 8 of these teams)

4-Man

First held 1924. Winners since 1972:

1972* Switzerland (J. Wicki, E. Hubacher, H. Leutenegger, W. Camichel)
1973 Switzerland (R. Stadler, W. Camichel, K. Schärer, P. Schärer)
1974 W. Germany (W. Zimmerer, A. Wurzer, P. Utzschneider, M. Schumann)
1975 Switzerland (E. Schärer, M. Camichel, J. Benz, P. Schärer)
1976* GDR (M. Nehmer, J. Babok, B. Germeshausen, B. Lehmann)
1977 GDR (M. Nehmer, H. Gerhardt, B. Germeshausen, R. Bethge)
1978 GDR (H. Schönau, H. Bernhardt, B. Musiol, H. Seifert)
1979 W.Germany (S. Galsreiter, H. Wagner, H. Bosche, D. Gebhard)
1980* GDR (M. Nehmer, B. Musiol, B. Germeshausen, H. Gerhardt)
1981 GDR (B. Germeshausen, H. Gerlach, M. Trübner, H. Gerhardt)

Most wins: 12 Switzerland (1924, 1936, 1939, 1947, 1954–57, 1971–73, 1975)

LUGE TOBOGGANING

Women

First held 1955. Winners since 1972:

1972* Anna-Maria Muller (GDR)
1973 Margit Schumann (GDR)
1974 Margit Schumann (GDR)
1975 Margit Schumann (GDR)
1976* Margit Schumann (GDR)
1977 Margit Schumann (GDR)

Italy's world champion 2-man bob team of 1958, Eugenio Monti and Renzo Alvera (Associated Press)

1978 Vera Sosulya (USSR)
1979 Melitta Sollmann (GDR)
1980* Vera Sosulya (USSR)

Most wins: 5 Margit Schumann (GDR) 1973–77

Men

First held 1955. Winners since 1972:

1972* Wolfgang Scheidel (GDR)
1973 Hans Rinn (GDR)
1974 Josef Fendt (Ger)
1975 Wolfram Fielder (GDR)
1976* Detlef Günther (GDR)
1977 Hans Rinn (GDR)
1978 Paul Hildgartner (Ita)
1979 Detlef Günther (GDR)
1980* Bernhard Glans (GDR)

Most wins: 4 Thomas Köhler (GDR) (1962, 1964*, 1966, 1967)

Men's Two-seater

First held 1955. Winners since 1972:

1972* Italy (Paul Hildgartner and Walter Plaikner) and GDR (Horst Hornlein and Reinhard Bredow)
1973 GDR (Horst Hornlein and Reinhard Bredow)
1974 GDR (Bernd Hahn and Ulli Hahn)
1975 GDR (Bernd Hahn and Ulli Hahn)
1976* GDR (Hans Rinn and Norbert Hahn)

1977 GDR (Hans Rinn and Norbert Hahn)
1978 USSR (Dainis Bremze and Aigars Krikis)
1979 GDR (Hans Brandner and Balthasar Schwarm)

1980* GDR (Hans Rinn and Norbert Hahn)

Most wins: 10 GDR (1965, 1967–68, 1973–77, 1979–80)

Body Building

MR UNIVERSE

In 1948 the *Health and Strength* magazine sponsored the first Mr Universe contest as a contribution to the Olympic Games held in London.

In 1950 the National Amateur Body Builders' Association was born and so started the unbroken sequence of Mr Universe contests, which are now recognised throughout the world as the greatest annual event of the year. The winners are as follows:

1948 John Grimek (USA)
1949 No contest
1950 Steve Reeves (USA)
1951 Reg Park (GB)

From 1952 the contest was divided into separate classes: Amateur and Professional

Amateur

1952 Mohamed Nasr (Egy)
1953 Bill Pearl (USA)
1954 Enrico Tomas (USA)
1955 Mickey Hargitay (USA)
1956 Ray Schaeffer (USA)
1957 John Lees (GB)
1958 Earl Clark (USA)
1959 Len Sell (GB)
1960 Henry Downs (GB)
1961 Ray Routledge (USA)
1962 Joe Abbenda (USA)
1963 Tom Sansone (USA)
1964 John Hewlett (GB)
1965 Elmo Santiago (USA)
1966 Chester Yorton (USA)
1967 Arnold Schwarzenegger (Aut)
1968 Dennis Tinerino (USA)
1969 Boyer Coe (USA)
1970 Frank Zane (USA)
1971 Ken Waller (USA)
1972 Elias Petsas (SA)
1973 Chris Dickerson (USA)
1974 Roy Duval (GB)
1975 Ian Lawrence (Sco)
1976 Sigeru Sugita (Jap)
1977 Bertil Fox (St. Kitts)
1978 Dave Johns (USA)
1979 Ahmet Enunlu (Tur)
1980 Bill Richardson (GB)

Professional

1952 Juan Ferrero (Spa)
1953 Arnold Dyson (GB)
1954 Jim Park (USA)
1955 Leo Robert (Can)
1956 Jack Dillenger (USA)
1957 Arthur Robin (Fra)
1958 Reg Park (GB)
1959 Bruce Randall (USA)

Bill Richardson (left) and Tony Pearson, winners of the Amateur and Professional 1980 Mr Universe titles (Edward Hankey MMPA)

1960 Paul Wynter (Ant)
1961 Bill Pearl (USA)
1962 Len Sell (GB)
1963 Joe Abbenda (USA)
1964 Earl Maynard (W. Ind)
1965 Reg Park (GB)
1966 Paul Wynter (Ant)
1967 Bill Pearl (USA)
1968 Arnold Schwarzenegger (Aut)
1969 Arnold Schwarzenegger (Aut)
1970 Arnold Schwarzenegger (Aut)
1971 Bill Pearl (USA)
1972 Frank Zane (USA)
1973 Boyer Coe (USA)
1974 Chris Dickerson (USA)
1975 Boyer Coe (USA)
1976 Serge Nubret (Fra)
1977 Tony Emmot (GB)
1978 Bertil Fox (St. Kitts)
1979 Bertil Fox (GB)
1980 Tony Pearson (USA)

MR AND MISS BRITAIN

These contests have been run by The National Amateur Body-Builders' Association's journal, *Health and Strength* since 1930. The competition is held annually and aims to find the best developed man and woman. Winners since 1970:

	Mr	*Miss*
1970	Albert Beckles	Pat Wheeldon
1971	Albert Beckles	Lynda Thomas
1972	Paul Grant	Marylyn Roberson
1973	Roy Duval	Christine Charles
1974	Eddie McDonough	Linda Cheeseman
1975	Ian Lawrence	Pauline Davies
1976	Bertil Fox	Anne Arthur
1977	Eddie McDonough	Bridget Gibbons
1978	Bill Richardson	Bridget Pasquil (née Gibbons)
1979	Terry Phillips	Carol Thatcher
1980	Graham Brogden	Karen Griffiths
1981	Eddie Millar	Mary Scott

Mr and Miss Britain 1980 receiving their awards (Edward Hankey MMPA)

Bowling (Tenpin)

WORLD CHAMPIONSHIPS

World championships sponsored by the FIQ, the International Bowling Federation, were first held in 1967. They are now held every four years. Singles winners:

MEN
1967	David Pond (GB)
1971	Ed Luther (USA)
1975	Marvin Stoudt (USA)
1979	Oliver Ongtawco (Phi)

WOMEN
1967	Helen Weston (USA)
1971	Ashie Gonzales (PR)
1975	Annedore Haefker (Ger)
1979	Lita de la Rose (Phi)

Bowls

MEN'S WORLD CHAMPIONSHIPS

The first world championships for lawn bowls were held in 1966 in Sydney, Australia and have subsequently been held in 1972, 1976 and 1980. Winners:

Singles
1966	David Bryant (Eng)
1972	Malwyn Evans (Wal)
1976	Doug Watson (SA)
1980	David Bryant (Eng)

Pairs
1966	Geoff Kelley and Bert Palm (Aus)
1972	Cecekio Delgado and Eric Liddell (HK)
1976	Doug Watson and William Moseley (SA)
1980	Alf Sandercock and Peter Rheuber (Aus)

Triples
1966	John Dobbie, Athol Johnson, Don Collins (Aus)
1972	Richard Folkins, Clive Forrester, William Miller (USA)
1976	Kelvin Lightfoot, Nando Gatti, Kevin Campbell (SA)
1980	Jim Hobday, Tony Alcock, David Bryant (Eng)

Fours
1966	Bill O'Neill, Gordon Jolly, Ron Buchan, Norman Lash (NZ)
1972	Norman King, Cliff Stroud, Ted Hayward, Peter Line (Eng)
1976	Kelvin Lightfoot, William Moseley, Nando Gatti, Kevin Campbell (SA)

David Bryant (centre) beat Philip Chok (HK) (right) 21–15 in the final of the 1980 Embassy World Indoor Bowls Championship

1980 Omar Dallah, Eric Liddell, Philip Chok, George Souza (HK)

Leonard Trophy (Team title all-round)
1966 Australia
1972 Scotland
1976 South Africa
1980 England

EMBASSY WORLD INDOOR CHAMPIONSHIP
First held in 1979. Winners:

1979 David Bryant (Eng)
1980 David Bryant (Eng)
1981 David Bryant (Eng)

WOMEN'S WORLD CHAMPIONSHIPS
First held in 1969 at Rockdale, NSW, Australia.

Singles
1969   Gladys Doyle (Pap-NG)
1973–4 Elsie Wilkie (NZ)
1977   Elsie Wilkie (NZ)

Pairs
1969   S. Africa
1973–4 Australia
1977   Hong Kong

Triples
1969   S. Africa
1973–4 New Zealand
1977   Wales

Fours
1969   S. Africa
1973–4 New Zealand
1977   Australia

Overall team
1969   S. Africa
1973–4 New Zealand
1977   Australia

ENGLISH BOWLS ASSOCIATION CHAMPIONSHIPS
First held in 1903. Championships are annually contested at Singles, Doubles, Triples and Pairs.

Most titles have been won by David Bryant with 15 between 1960 and 1977. He won the Singles title in 1960, 1966, 1971, 1972, 1973 and 1975.

The only other man to win more than three Singles titles has been Percy Baker, who won in 1932, 1946, 1952 and 1955. Singles winners since 1970:

1970 Harry Kershaw
1971 David Bryant
1972 David Bryant
1973 David Bryant
1974 Bill Irish
1975 David Bryant
1976 Anthony O'Connell
1977 Chris Ward
1978 Charles Burch
1979 David Cutler
1980 Tom Buller

Boxing

WORLD CHAMPIONSHIPS
There are now two governing bodies that recognise world champions, the World Boxing Council (WBC) and the World Boxing Association (WBA). In the lists that follow, all Heavyweight world champions are shown and for the other weights the longest reign as title-holder (for those weights which have been contested for many years) and winners since 1970 are detailed, with (WBC) or (WBA) in brackets where the champion is recognised by one of these bodies only.

HEAVYWEIGHT
1882 John L. Sullivan
1892 James J. Corbett
1897 Bob Fitzsimmons
1899 James J. Jeffries
1905 Marvin Hart
1906 Tommy Burns
1908 Jack Johnson
1915 Jess Willard
1919 Jack Dempsey
1926 Gene Tunney
1930 Max Schmeling
1932 Jack Sharkey

John L. Sullivan was the first modern heavyweight champion and the first boxer to earn a million dollars

1933 Primo Carnera
1934 Max Baer
1935 James J. Braddock
1937 Joe Louis
1949 Ezzard Charles
1951 Jersey Joe Walcott
1952 Rocky Marciano
1956 Floyd Patterson
1959 Ingemar Johansson
1960 Floyd Patterson
1962 Sonny Liston
1964 Cassius Clay/Muhammad Ali
1965 Ernie Terrell (WBA to 1967)
1968 Joe Frazier (New York State)
      Jimmy Ellis (WBA)
1970 Joe Frazier (undisputed)
1973 George Foreman
1974 Muhammad Ali
1978 Leon Spinks
      Ken Norton (WBC)
      Muhammad Ali (WBA)
      Larry Holmes (WBC)
1979 John Tate (WBA)
1980 Mike Weaver (WBA)

CRUISERWEIGHT (190 lb)
First contested 1980 (WBC only)
1980 Marvin Camel (WBC)

LIGHT-HEAVYWEIGHT (175 lb)
Champion first recognised 1903. Longest: Archie Moore 1952–62.
1968 Bob Foster
1971 Vicente Rondon (WBA)
1972 Bob Foster (undisputed again)
1974 John Conteh (WBC)
      Victor Galindez (WBA)
1977 Miguel Cuello (WBC)
1978 Mate Parlov (WBC)
      Mike Rossman (WBA)
      Marvin Johnson (WBC)
1979 Matthew Saad Muhammad (WBC)
      Victor Galindez (WBA)
      Marvin Johnson (WBA)
1980 Eddie Mustafa Muhammad (WBA)

MIDDLEWEIGHT (160 lb)
Champion first recognised 1884. Longest: Tommy Ryan 1898–1907.
1970 Carlos Monzon
1974 Rodrigo Valdes (WBC)
1976 Carlos Monzon (undisputed)
1977 Rodrigo Valdes
1978 Hugo Corro
1979 Vito Antuofermo
1980 Alan Minter
      Marvin Hagler

LIGHT MIDDLEWEIGHT
(or Super Welterweight) (153½ lb)
First contested 1962. Longest: Koichi Wajima 1971-74.
1970 Carmelo Bossi
1971 Koichi Wajima
1974 Oscar Albarado
1975 Koichi Wajima
      Miguel De Oliveira (WBC)
      Jae Do Yuh (WBA)
      Elisha Obed (WBC)
1976 Koichi Wajima (WBA)
      Jose Duran (WBA)
      Eckhard Dagge (WBC)
      Miguel Castellini (WBA)
1977 Eddie Gazo (WBA)
      Rocky Mattioli (WBC)
1978 Masashi Kudo (WBA
1979 Maurice Hope (WBC)
1980 Ayub Kalule (WBA)
1981 Wilfred Benitez (WBC)

WELTERWEIGHT (147 lb)
Champion first recognised 1890. Longest: Freddie Cochrane 1941–46.
1970 Billy Backus
1971 Jose Napoles
1975 Angel Espada (WBA)
      John H. Stracey (WBC)
1976 Carlos Palomino (WBC)
      Jose Cuevas (WBA)
1979 Wilfredo Benitez (WBC)
      Sugar Ray Leonard (WBC)
1980 Roberto Duran (WBC)
      Thomas Hearns (WBA)
      Sugar Ray Leonard (WBC)

LIGHT WELTERWEIGHT
(or Super Lightweight) (140 lb)
Recognised 1926–33, 1946, since 1959. Longest: Antonio Cervantes 1972–76.
1968 Nicolino Loche (WBA)
1970 Bruno Arcari (WBC)
1972 Alfonso Frazer (WBA)
      Antonio Cervantes (WBA)
1974 Perico Fernandez (WBC)
1975 Saensak Muangsurin (WBC)
1976 Wilfredo Benitez (WBA)
      Miguel Velasquez (WBC)
      Saensak Muangsurin (WBC)
1977 Antonio Cervantes (WBA)
1978 Kim Sang-Hyun (WBC)
1980 Saoul Mamby (WBC)
      Aaron Pryor (WBA)

LIGHTWEIGHT (135 lb)
Champion first recognised 1872. Longest: Jack

McAuliffe 1886–93; Roberto Duran 1972–79.
1970 Ismael Laguna
     Ken Buchanan (WBA)
1971 Ken Buchanan (undisputed)
     Pedro Carrasco (WBC)
1972 Mando Ramos (WBC)
     Roberto Duran (WBA)
     Chango Carmona (WBC)
     Rodolfo Gonzalez (WBC)
1974 Guts Ishimatsu (WBC)
1976 Esteban de Jesus (WBC)
1978 Roberto Duran (undisputed)
1979 Ernesto Espana (WBA)
     Jim Watt (WBC)
1980 Hilmer Kenty (WBA)
1981 Sean O'Grady (WBA)
     Alexis Arguello (WBC)

JUNIOR LIGHTWEIGHT (130 lb)
Contested 1921–33, since 1959. Longest: Flash
Elorde 1960–67.
1970 Yoshiaki Numata (WBC)
1971 Ricardo Arredondo (WBC)
     Alfredo Marcano (WBA)
1972 Ben Villaflor (WBA)
1973 Kuniaki Shibata (WBA)
     Ben Villaflor (WBA)
1974 Kuniaki Shibata (WBA)
1975 Alfredo Escalera (WBC)
1976 Sam Serrano (WBA)
1978 Alexis Arguello (WBC)
1980 Yasastune Uehara (WBA)
     Rafael Limon (WBC)
1981 Cornelius Boza-Edwards (WBC)

FEATHERWEIGHT (136 lb)
Champion first recognised 1889. Longest: Johnny
Kilbane 1912–23.
1970 Vicente Saldivar (WBC)
     Kuniaki Shibata (WBC)

1971 Antonio Gomez (WBA)
1972 Clemente Sanchez (WBC)
     Ernesto Marcel (WBA)
     Jose Legra (WBC)
1973 Eder Joffre (WBC)
1974 Ruben Olivares (WBA)
     Bobby Chacon (WBC)
     Alexis Arguello (WBA)
1975 Ruben Olivares (WBC)
     David Kotey (WBC)
1976 Danny Lopez (WBC)
1977 Rafael Ortega (WBA)
     Cecilio Lastra (WBA)
1978 Eusebio Pedrosa (WBA)
1980 Salvador Sanchez (WBC)

LIGHT FEATHERWEIGHT
(or Super Bantamweight) (122 lb)
First contested 1976.
1976 Rigoberto Riasco (WBC)
     Royal Kobayashi (WBC)
     Dong Kyun Yum (WBC)
1977 Wilfredo Gomez (WBC)
1978 Soo Hwan-Hong (WBA)
     Ricardo Cardona (WBA)
1980 Sergio Palma (WBA)

BANTAMWEIGHT (118 lb)
Champion first recognised 1888. Longest: Panama
Al Brown 1929–35.
1970 Jesus Castillo
1971 Ruben Olivares
1972 Rafael Herrera
     Enrique Pinder

*Cornelius Boza-Edwards, the Ugandan who
lives at Harrow, winner of the world Junior
Lightweight title in 1981* (Sporting Pictures)

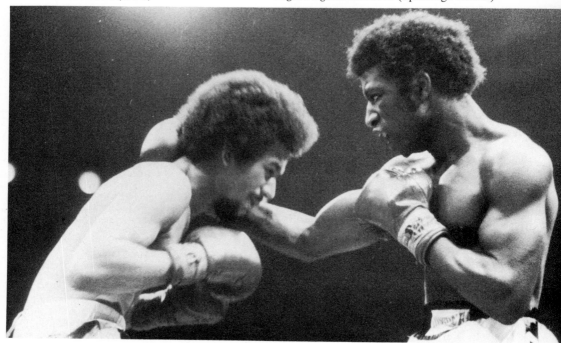

1973 Romeo Anaya (WBA)
     Rafael Herrera (WBC)
     Arnold Taylor (WBA)
1974 Soo Hwan-Hong (WBA)
     Rodolfo Martinez (WBC)
1975 Alfonso Zamora (WBA)
1976 Carlos Zarate (WBC)
1977 Jorge Lujan (WBA)
1979 Guadalupe Pintor (WBC)
1980 Julian Solis (WBA)
     Jeff Chandler (WBA)

SUPER FLYWEIGHT (115 lb)
First contested 1980 (WBC only)
1980 Rafael Orono (WBC)
1981 Chul-Mo Kin (WBC)

FLYWEIGHT (112 lb)
Champion first recognised 1912. Longest: Jimmy
Wilde 1916–23.
1970 Chartchai Chionoi (WBC)
     Berkrerk Chartvanchai (WBA)
     Masao Ohba (WBA)
     Erbito Salavarria (WBC)
1971 Betulio Gonzalez (WBC)
1972 Venice Berksorkor (WBC)
1973 Chartchai Chionoi (WBA)
     Betulio Gonzalez (WBC)
1974 Shoji Oguma (WBC)
     Susumu Hanagata (WBA)
1975 Niguel Canto (WBC)
     Erbito Salavarria (WBA)
1976 Alfonso Lopez (WBA)
     Gustavo Espadas (WBA)
1978 Betulio Gonzalez (WBA)
1979 Chan Hee Park (WBC)
     Luis Ibarra (WBA)
1980 Kim Tae Shik (WBA)
     Shoji Oguma (WBC)
     Peter Mathebula (WBA)
1981 Santos Laciar (WBA)

*Teofilio Stephenson on his way to ending the
hopes of Duane Bobick (USA) at the 1972
Olympic Games*

LIGHT FLYWEIGHT (108 lb)
First contested 1975.
1975 Franco Udella (WBC)
     Jaime Rios (WBC)
     Luis Esteba (WBC)
1976 Juan Guzman (WBA)
     Yoko Gushiken (WBA)
1978 Netranoi Vorasingh (WBC)
1979 Kim Sung-Jun (WBC)
1980 Shigeo Nakejima (WBC)
     Hilario Zapata (WBC)
1981 Pedro Flores (WBA)

**WORLD AMATEUR BOXING
CHAMPIONSHIPS**
First held at Havana in 1974, the world
amateur championships are held every four
years, the second being held at Belgrade in
1978. Winners:

1974
Heavy Teofilio Stevenson (Cub)
Light-heavy Mate Parlov (Yug)
Middle Rufat Riskiev (USSR)
Light-middle Rolando Garbey (Cub)
Welter Emilio Correa (Cub)
Light-welter Ayub Kalule (Uga)
Light Vasiliy Solomin (USSR)
Feather Howard Davis (USA)
Bantam Wilfredo Gomez (PR)
Fly Douglas Rodriguez (Cub)
Light-fly Jorge Hernandez (Cub)

1978
Heavy Teofilio Stevenson (Cub)
Light-heavy Sixto Soria (Cub)
Middle Jose Gomez (Cub)
Light-middle Viktor Savchenko (USSR)
Welter Valeriy Rachkov (USSR)
Light-welter Valeriy Lvov (USSR)
Light Andeh Davison (Nig)
Feather Angel Herrera (Cub)
Bantam Adolfo Horta (Cub)
Fly Henryk Srednicki (Pol)
Light-fly Stephen Muchoki (Ken)

OLYMPIC CHAMPIONSHIPS
Boxing has been included at each Olympic
Games since 1904. Winners of two or more
gold medals have been:

3 Lazlo Papp (Hun): middle 1948, light-middle 1952
  and 1956
3 Teofilio Stevenson (Cub): heavy 1972, 1976 and
  1980
2 Oliver Kirk (USA): feather and bantam 1904
2 Harry Mallin (GB): middle 1920 and 1924
2 Boris Lagutin (USSR): light-middle 1964 and 1968
2 Jerzy Kulej (Pol): light-welter 1964 and 1968

1980 winners:
Heavy (over 81 kg)	Teofilio Stevenson (Cub)
Light-heavy (81 kg)	Slobodan Kacar (Yug)
Middle (75 kg)	Jose Gomez (Cub)
Light-middle (71 kg)	Armando Martinez (Cub)
Welter (67 kg)	Andres Aldama (Cub)
Light-welter (63½ kg)	Patrizio Olivia (Ita)
Light (60 kg)	Angel Herrera (Cub)

| *Feather* (57 kg) | Rudi Fink (GDR) | *Fly* (51 kg) | Petar Lessov (Bul) |
| *Bantam* (54 kg) | Juan Hernandez (Cub) | *Light-fly* (48 kg) | Shamil Sabryov (USSR) |

Brides

THE KODAK BRIDE OF THE YEAR

This competition gives every bride using a professional photographer a chance of becoming a 'Kodak Bride of the Month'. Six 'Bride of the Month' prizes of £100 each are awarded from March to December. Each winner then enters the 'Kodak Bride of the Year' competition which, in 1981, offered a cash prize of £1000 and a second honeymoon for two weeks from Olympic Holidays. Winners:

1972 Gail Mitchelson, Airdrie, Strathclyde
1973 Sharon Blackgrove, London
1974 Helen Ward, St Helens, Lancs
1975 Rhiannan McNicholls, London
1976 No event
1977 Not available
1978 Julia Phillips, Manchester
1979 Susan Rhodes, Eldwick, Yorks
1980 Lyn Wallace, Marple, Cheshire

Lyn Wallace, 1980 Bride of the Year

Bridge

WORLD CHAMPIONSHIPS

World championships for the Bermuda Bowl were first held in 1951. Winners:

1951 USA	1961 Italy	1971 USA
1952 USA	1962 Italy	1972 Not held
1953 USA	1963 Italy	1973 Italy
1954 USA	1964 Not held	1974 Italy
1955 Great	1965 Italy	1975 Italy
Britain	1966 Italy	1976 USA
1956 France	1967 Italy	1977 USA
1957 Italy	1968 Not held	1978 Not held
1958 Italy	1969 Italy	1979 USA
1959 Italy	1970 North	1980 Not held
1960 Not held	America	

TEAM (FOUR) OLYMPIAD

MEN

1960 France	1972 Italy
1964 Italy	1976 Brazil
1968 Italy	1980 France

WOMEN

1960 United Arab Republic	1972 Italy
1964 Great Britain	1976 USA
1968 Sweden	1980 USA

OLYMPIC PAIRS COMPETITION (OPEN)

MEN

1962 France	1974 USA
1966 Holland	1978 Brazil
1970 Austria	

Bubble Gum

The Bubble Yum UK Championships for the largest bubble blown are held annually and are sponsored by Bubble Yum. The current champion is Nigel Fell who blew a bubble of 16½ ins diameter.

The Bubble Yum UK Championship trophy

Business

BUSINESS WOMAN OF THE YEAR

This award, founded in 1973, is sponsored by The Times Newspaper Ltd and Veuve Clicquot Champagne as an accolade for those, often unknown, women who have reached the top in British business. Until 1978 the award was entitled The Times Veuve Clicquot Champagne Award for A Woman in a Man's World. Winners:

1973 Stella Brumell, Managing Director, Benford Ltd, manufacturers of concrete mixers
1974 Alice Coleman, King's College, London, Director of the Land Utilisation Survey of Great Britain
1975 Zofia Sas, Founder and Chairman of SAS Group of Companies – worldwide exporter
1976 Audrey Head, Managing Director, Hill Samuel Unit Trust Managers Ltd
1977 Gillian Lewis, European General Manager, Green Giant Company. A large American concern specialising in canned vegetables – especially sweetcorn
1978 Andree Grenfell, President Glemby International Europe and Senior Vice-President Glemby International (USA), an international franchise hairdressing organisation
1979 Ann Burdus, Chairman, McCann and Co., and of each of the three advertising agencies which form part of that group – McCann Erickson, Harrison McCann, and Universal McCann
1980 Jean Tyrrell, Chairman, Sirdar Limited, textile industry.

THE GUARDIAN YOUNG BUSINESSMAN OF THE YEAR

This award, which began in 1970, is made for a significant contribution to business, not only at a personal and company level but also in the national context. The judges are usually the Directors General of The British Institute of Management, The Institute of Directors, The Confederation of British Industry and the chairman of *The Guardian*. Winners to date:

1970 Colin Chapman, age 41, chairman of Group Lotus
1971 No award
1972 James Gulliver, age 41, chairman of the Fine Fare Group
1973 Sir Hugh Fraser, age 36, chairman of House of Fraser
1974 John Apthorpe, age 38, founder, chairman, and joint managing director of Bejam
1975 Michael Edwardes, age 44, chief executive of the Chloride Group
1976 David Plastow, age 43, group managing director of Rolls Royce Holdings Ltd
1977 Geoffrey Cross, age 43, managing director of International Computers Ltd
1978 Nigel Broackes, age 43, chairman of Trafalgar House Ltd
1979 Anthony Bamford, age 33, chairman and managing director of J. C. Bamford Excavators Ltd
1980 Roger Hurn, age 41, managing director of Smiths Industries Ltd
1981 John Gardiner, age 44, chief executive of the Laird Group

THE NATIONAL MANAGEMENT GAME

Organised since 1970 by the Institute of Chartered Accountants in England and Wales, the *Financial Times* and International Computers Ltd in association with the Confederation of British Industry and the Institute of Directors. Each team, consisting of a minimum of three people, is, in effect, a company making decisions on the deployment of its resources in manufacturing and marketing a product over a number of trading periods. The winning team is the one generating the largest profit at the end of the game. The prizes in 1981 totalled £7500. Winners:

1970 Industrial and Commercial Finance Corporation
1971 Rolls-Royce (1971) Ltd
1972 Essex County Council (Treasurer's Department)
1973 The Norwich Union Insurance Group
1974 'Honeylips' (private entry)
1975 The Littlewoods Organisation
1976 Rank Xerox Ltd
1977 Rank Xerox Ltd
1978 Shell UK
1979 Rank Xerox Ltd
1980 Shell UK

Neil Tomkin, one-man winner of the National Management Game in 1979

INSTITUTE OF CHARTERED ACCOUNTANTS BUSINESS GAME FOR SIXTH FORMERS

Launched in 1967 with the co-operation of International Computers Ltd, the competition is run on identical lines to the National Management Game. The competition involves over 300 schools each year. The winners are as follows:

1968 Downside School, Stratton on the Fosse, Somerset
1969 Cheltenham College, Cheltenham, Glous
1970 Cranbrook School, Cranbrook, Kent
1971 Stowe School, Stowe, Bucks
1972 The King's School, Canterbury, Kent
1973 St Edmund's College, Ware, Herts
1974 Taunton School, Taunton, Somerset
1975 The John Fisher School, Purley, Surrey
1976 Sir John Leman High School, Beccles, Suffolk
1977 South East Essex Sixth Form College, Benfleet, Essex
1978 South East Essex Sixth Form College, Benfleet, Essex
1979 Simon Laughton Grammar School for Boys, Canterbury, Kent
1980 Denstone College, Uttoxeter, Staffs

Canoeing

WORLD CHAMPIONSHIPS

Winners at each event at the 1979 world championships were:

MEN
Kayak singles
500 m   Vladimir Parfenovich (USSR) 1:49·65
1000 m   Rüdiger Helm (GDR) 3:58·62
10 000 m Milan Janic (Yug) 46:01·85

Kayak pairs
500 m   Vladimir Parfenovich and Sergei Chukhrai (USSR) 1:37·58
1000 m   Einar Rasmussen and Olaf Soyland (Nor) 3:36·19
10 000 m Ion Barladeanu and Nicusor Eseanu (Rom) 41:27·81

Kayak fours
500 m   GDR 1:30·03
1000 m   GDR 3:14·44
10 000 m USSR 36:05·47

Canadian singles
500 m   Sergei Postrekhin (USSR) 2:03·33
1000 m   Tamas Wichmann (Hun) 4:22·10
10 000 m Tamas Wichmann (Hun) 49:08·42

Canadian pairs
500 m   Ivan Patzaichin and Petre Capusta (Rom) 1:50·20
1000 m   Vasiliy Urchenko and Uri Lobanov (USSR) 3:54·04
10 000 m Vasiliy Urchenko and Uri Lobanov (USSR) 43:53·66

WOMEN
Kayak singles
500 m Roswitha Eberl (GDR) 2:04·48

Kayak pairs
500 m Natalia Kalashnikova and Nina Dorokh (USSR) 1:54·20

Kayak fours
500 m GDR 1:42·61

OLYMPIC CHAMPIONSHIPS

First held in the Olympic Games in 1936. Winners at each event in 1980 were:

MEN
Kayak singles
500 m   Vladimir Parfenovich (USSR) 1:43·43
1000 m Rüdiger Helm (GDR) 3:48·77

Kayak pairs
500 m   Vladimir Parfenovich and Sergei Chukhrai (USSR) 1:32·38
1000 m Vladimir Parfenovich and Sergei Chukhrai (USSR) 3:26·72

Kayak fours
1000 m Rüdiger Helm, Bernd Olbricht, Harald Marg, Bernd Duvigneau (GDR) 3:13·76

Canadian singles
500 m   Sergei Postrekhin (USSR) 1:53·37
1000 m Lubomir Lubenov (Bul) 4:12·38

Canadian pairs
500 m   Laszlo Foltan and Istvan Vaskuti (Hun) 1:43·39
1000 m Ivan Potzaichin and Toma Simionov (Rom) 3:47·65

WOMEN
Kayak singles
500 m Birgit Fischer (GDR) 1:57·96

Kayak pairs
500 m Carsta Genauss and Martina Bischof (GDR) 1:43·88

Most gold medals in all have been won by Gert Fredriksson (Swe) with six: 1000 m kayak singles in 1948, 1952, 1956; 10 000 m kayak singles in 1948, 1956; 1000 m kayak doubles in 1960.

Most gold medals by a woman: three by Lyudmila Pinayeva (née Khvedosyuk) (USSR): 500 m kayak singles in 1964, 1968; 500 m kayak doubles in 1972.

Carols

THE NATIONWIDE CAROL COMPETITION

Christmas carols are sung each year on BBC Television's Nationwide by choirs and school parties, who either write and present new works or update traditional material.

1976 Mary Hoare, Ann Gray, Julia Andrews, Jacqueline Lashley, Deborah Longstaffe, Caroline Holloway, Jacqueline McGreggar from Southlands School, Reading, Berks, with *The Changing Face of Christmas*

1977 Duncan Lamont of Salesian College, London, with *Three Wise Men*

1978 *Junior Section*; Anita Damianos of Brimsdown Junior School, Enfield, Middx, with *The Innkeepers Song*

Senior Section: Deborah Hyde of Ellen Wilkinson High School, Ealing, with *The Dream of Christmas*

1979 *Junior Section*: Jenny Smith of Bushey Hall School, Bushey Heath, Herts, with *Ding-a, Ding-a, Dong Down*

Senior Section: Christa Moule, Dorothy Mankelow, Kirsa Alberts and Gary Sanctuary of Ridgewaye Secondary School, Southborough, Kent, with *Go After That Star*

1980 *Junior Section*: music classes (9-year-olds) from Manor Hill First School, Stone, Staffs, with *Can You Hear A Baby Cry?*

Senior Section: Rosemary Whitaker, Bryn Halfren Comprehensive School, Barry, S. Glam, with *Peace Child*

Cars

CAR OF THE YEAR

Sponsored since 1973 by the *Sunday Telegraph* (prior to this date, various international magazines made a similar award) and five other European publications, the award is given for general design, comfort, handling and general road-worthiness, safety, driver satisfaction, performance, functionalism and value for money.

1981 Car of the Year – the Ford Escort

1963 Rover 2000	1968 Peugeot 504	1973 Mercedes 450	1978 Porsche 928
1964 Austin 1800	1969 Fiat 128	1974 Citroën CX	1979 Chrysler Horizon
1965 Renault 16	1970 Citroën GS	1975 Not held	1980 Lancia Delta
1966 Fiat 124	1971 Fiat 127	1976 Chrysler Alpine	1981 Ford Escort
1967 NSU Ro 80	1972 Audi 80	1977 Rover 3500	

Cartoons

ALLY SLOPER AWARD

Founded in 1977, this award is presented by the Association of Comics Enthusiasts at the annual convention of British strip/comic artists. It is given to strip cartoonists only, for a lifetime's work in newspapers and comics. The judges are Denis Gifford and advisers from the Cartoonists Club and the Society of Strip Illustration. Winners of the Gold Award:

1977 Terry Wakefield for 'Laurel and Hardy'
1978 Doris White, Link Studios for 'Toby', etc.
1979 Hugh McNeill for 'Our Ernie' and 'Deed-a-Day Danny' in *The Knockout Comic*, 'Harold Hare', etc.
1980 *Children's Comics*: Wally Robertson for 'Marmy and his Ma' in *Funny Wonder*, and 'Waddles the Waiter' in *Comic Cuts*, etc.
Newspaper Strips: Alfred Bestall who took over 'Rupert Bear' in The *Daily Express*

THE GLEN GRANT CARTOONIST OF THE YEAR AWARD

This award is sponsored by Glen Grant 12 Year Old Malt Whisky and has been held since 1979 in association with the Society of Industrial Artists and Designers. The scheme is open to all cartoonists who have had their work published in any British publication and various categories are included.

Overall
1979 Clive Collins, work in *Punch*
Caricature
1979 Wally Fawkes (TROG), front cover of *Punch*, 1979 Christmas issue
1980 Marc Boxer, caricature of William Rees-Mogg, *Now* magazine
Political
1979 Wally Fawkes, 'Top People tell the Times', *The Observer*, 25 Nov 1979
1980 Marc Boxer, cartoon in *The Times*
Social Comment
1979 Clive Collins, 'Burial at Sea', *Punch*, October 1979
1980 Marc Boxer, 'Docherty Assault – £250 fine', *Private Eye*
Royal
1980 Raymond Jackson, cartoon in *Evening Standard*
Strip
1980 John Glashan, cartoon in *Observer* Colour Supplement
Sports
1980 Raymond Jackson, cartoon in *Evening Standard*

Overall winner of the 1979 Glen Grant Cartoonist of the Year award, Clive Collins also won first prize in the Social Comment category with this cartoon

"ERNEST, I'VE SAID IT BEFORE AND I'LL SAY IT AGAIN — THE ANTARCTIC IS NO PLACE FOR A BURIAL AT SEA"

Above: *Hercules the bear receiving the 1980 Gold Joker Award for the cartoons he inspired.* Right: *Brian Bolland won a Society of Strip Illustration award in 1979 for 'Judge Dredd'*

GOLD JOKER OF THE YEAR

The Cartoonists' Club of Great Britain makes this award to those who it feels have best kept cartoonists in good supply for gags during the year. The recipient receives a small tie-tack in gold and in the form of the club motif – jesters heads with paint brush in mouth – rampant, of course! Golden Joker awarded to:

1974 Enoch Powell	1978 Sir Freddie Laker
1975 Margaret Thatcher	1979 Tony Benn
1976 Brian Clough	1980 Hercules (the bear)
1977 Richard Ingrams	

'Willy the Kid' by Leo Baxendale won a 1979 Society of Strip Illustration award

THE SOCIETY OF STRIP ILLUSTRATION AWARDS

The first annual awards of the Society were presented in 1978 by Michael Bentine. Winners:

Category One: Humour
Best artist in comics
1978 Ken Reid 'Faceache'
1979 Leo Baxendale, 'Willy the Kid'
1980 Reg Parlett, 'Busters Diary'

Best artist in newspapers and magazines
1978 Posy Simmonds, 'The Silent Three'
Reg Smythe, 'Andy Capp', *Daily Mirror*
1979 Ron Embleton 'Wicked Wanda'
1980 Bill Tidy, 'Fosdyke Saga'

Category Two: Adventure
Best artist in comics
1978 Brian Lewis, 'Seven Golden Vampires'
1979 Brian Bolland, 'Judge Dredd'
1980 Dave Gibbons, 'Dr. Who'

Best artist in newspapers and magazines
1978 Tony Weare, 'Matt Marriott'
1979 Enrique Romero, 'Axa'
1980 Harry Bishop, 'Slade'

Category Three: Scriptwriters
Best writer in comics
1978 Angus Allen, 'The Bionic Woman' (Adventure)
Ken Reid, 'Faceache' (Humorous)
1979 Roy Davis in IPC comics
1980 John Howard Wagner, IPC (2000 AD comic)

Best writer in newspapers and magazines
1978 Peter O'Donnell 'Modesty Blaise' (Adventure)
Reg Smythe, 'Andy Capp' (Humorous)
1979 Sydney Jorden 'Lance Maclain'
1980 Wally Fawkes and Peter Lewis, 'Flook'

The Frank Bellamy Award
For an outstanding contribution to strip illustration
1978 Mike McMahon, 'Judge Dredd'
1979 Dragons Dream – Publisher
1980 Don Lawrence – Artist

Chemistry

Chess

WORLD CHAMPIONS
The first officially recognised match was won by Wilhelm Steinitz in 1886, but included in this list are unofficially recognised champions before that date.

MEN
1851–58 Adolph Anderssen (Ger)
1858–62 Paul Morphy (USA)

1862–66 Adolph Anderssen (Ger)
1866–94 Wilhelm Steinitz (Aut)
1894–1921 Emanuel Lasker (Ger)
1921–27 José Capablanca (Cub)
1927–35 Alexandre Alekhine (Fra)
1935–37 Max Euwe (Hol)
1937–47 Alexandre Alekhine (Fra)
1948–57 Mikhail Botvinnik (USSR)

Karpov defends his title against Soviet defender Korchnoi in the 1978 world championship (Popperfoto)

1952 USSR	1968 USSR
1954 USSR	1970 USSR
1956 USSR	1972 USSR
1958 USSR	1974 USSR
1960 USSR	1976 USA
1962 USSR	1978 Hungary
1964 USSR	1980 USSR
1966 USSR	

WOMEN	1972 USSR
1957 USSR	1974 USSR
1963 USSR	1976 Israel
1966 USSR	1978 USSR
1969 USSR	1980 USSR

1957–58 Vassiliy Smyslov (USSR)
1958–60 Mikhail Botvinnik (USSR)
1960–61 Mikhail Tal (USSR)
1961–63 Mikhail Botvinnik (USSR)
1963–69 Tigran Petrosian (USSR)
1969–72 Boris Spassky (USSR)
1972–75 Robert Fischer (USA)
1975–   Anatoliy Karpov (USSR)

WOMEN
1927–44 Vera Menchik (GB)
1950–53 Lyudmila Rudenko (USSR)
1953–56 Elizaveta Bykova (USSR)
1956–58 Olga Rubtsova (USSR)
1958–62 Elizaveta Bykova (USSR)
1962–79 Nona Gaprindashvili (USSR)
1979–   Maya Chiburdanidze (USSR)

WORLD TEAM CHAMPIONSHIPS (CHESS OLYMPIAD)
First held in 1927, and now held every two years. Winners:

MEN		
1927 Hungary	1933 USA
1928 Hungary	1935 USA
1930 Poland	1937 USA
1931 USA	1939 Germany
	1950 Yugoslavia

BRITISH CHAMPIONSHIPS
The first British championships were held in 1866 under the auspices of the British Chess Federation. They were held every two years until 1872, were not held between 1872 and 1904, and have been held annually ever since apart from the war years. Winners since 1970:

1970 Robert Wade
1971 Raymond Keene
1972 Brian Eley
1973 William Hartston
1974 George Botterill
1975 William Hartston
1976 Jonathan Mestel
1977 George Botterill
1978 Jonathan Speelman
1979 Robert Bellin
1980 John Nunn

Most wins: 10 Jonathan Penrose 1958–63, 1966–69

BRITISH LADIES CHAMPIONSHIPS
Ladies championships have, like the men's, been held annually since 1904. Winners since 1970:

1970–74 Jana Hartston
1975   Sheila Jackson
1976–77 Jana Hartston
1978   Sheila Jackson
1979   Jana Miles
1980   Sheila Jackson

Most wins: 11 Mrs Rowena Bruce 1937, 1950, 1951, 1954, 1955(=), 1956, 1960, 1962, 1963, 1967(=), 1969(=)

Children

CHAMPION CHILDREN OF THE YEAR
The *Daily Mirror* in association with Dr Barnardo's and C. & A., sponsor this competition, the first year being 1979, to find Britain's 'Champion children'. Readers are asked to nominate a child who does something well, whether sports, dancing, painting, music, drama or literature, and there is a special section for children who have overcome a handicap. Winners:

Superkid
1979 Mark Weeks (15), Bournemouth. Karate club organiser
1980 Michelle Danion (18), Blackpool.

Sport
1979 Sandra Arthurton (16), Leeds. Cross-country runner
1980 Jason Stuart Lawrence (13), London. Modern pentathlon

Mastermind
1979 Peter Swabey (14), Worthing. Zulu War of 1879; Roy Collins (9), Co. Durham. Astronomy
1980 James Taylor (11), W. Midlands. History

Special interests
1979 Nick Stevenson (16) and Mark Wilson (14), Derbyshire. Film makers
1980 Matthew Simmonds (8), Sussex. Hon. Sec. of British Butterfly Conservation Society

Triumph over adversity
1979 Terry Wiles (17), Huntingdon; John Elcock (16), Sheffield; Simon Butterworth (11), Bolton
1980 Debra Hilton (17), Rochdale, Lancs

Painting
1979 Paul Russell (11), London
1980 Paul Isaacs (16), Chigwell, Essex

Dancing
1979 Gary Edwards (12) and Fiona Bunce (12), Romford, Essex; Tracey Fitzgerald (9) and Stephen Quarterly (9), Newport, Wales
1980 Kerry Foster (12), Humberside

Music
1979 Tina Jones (14), Reading, Berks
1980 Amanda Woodford (9), Swindon, Wilts

MINI MISS UK COMPETITION

This competition is sponsored and organised annually by Harringtons (London) Ltd, the baby wear and children's wear manufacturers.

It is open to girls between the ages of three and six years who are invited to enter through entry forms at Harringtons retail stockists throughout the country. Five judges award five points in each of three categories for confidence, personality and grooming and the winner receives a full selection of Harringtons children's wear, a contract with the Tiny Tots to Teens model agency and many other prizes. Past winners are:

1972 Jeanette Kenny, Coventry
1973 Elizabeth Seal, Herts.
1974 Karen Young, Herts.
1975 Justine Hayles, Middx
1976 Shona Glover, Surrey

Kerry Foster, winner in the dancing section of the 1980 Barnardo Champion Children of the Year competition receives her award from Susan Hampshire and Valerie Singleton

1977 Rowena Cockayne, London
1978 Yvette Cowherd, Herts.
1979 Jemma Bagshaw, Coventry
1980 Sarah Davis, London

MISS PEARS

The 'Preparing to be a Beautiful Lady' series of advertisements were first created in 1932, but 1958 was the first year that the 'Miss Pears' competition was run on an area basis (before that time there were no area heats). A panel judges solely from photographs looking for qualities such as a good complexion, and an attractive face, the entrants being between the ages of 3 and 9. The winner receives a cheque for £1000, the six area finalists each receive £200. Winners:

1958 Susan Cadge, 3, Bristol
1959 Susan Fowler, 3, Harrow
1960 Suzanne Lowndes, 4, Carmarthen
1961 Julie Williams, 3, Newport Pagnell
1962 Peggy Ross, 5, London
1963 Elizabeth MacFarlane, 4, Tarbert, Loch Fyne
1964 Corrienne Robb, 4, Belfast
1965 Catherine Hancock, 4, Whitefield, Manchester
1966 Tessa Roberts, 4, Teddington, Middlesex
1967 Deborah Perryman, 4, Wembley, Middlesex
1968 Susan Wood, 3, Leek, Staffs

1969 Justine Hornby, 3, Formby, Liverpool
1970 Belinda-Jane Anderson, 7, Rosneath, Dunbartonshire
1971 Louise Stewart, 2½, Cullercoats, Northumberland
1972 Louise Payne, 3½, Walton-on-Thames, Surrey
1973 Natalie Clark, 5, Loughton, Essex
1974 Katie Goodwin, 4½, Stalybridge, Cheshire
1975 Sharon Fitton, 5, Horncastle, Lincs
1976 Sarah Coombs, 2, Hayling Island, Hants
1977 Sarah Worth, 4, Timperley, Cheshire
1978 Kirsty Leighton, 6, Wylam, Northumberland
1979 Christine Cashman, 5, South Croydon, Surrey
1980 Natalie Norgrove, 5, Kidderminster, Hereford and Worcester

Suzie Lowndes, Miss Pears 1960, meets the new Miss Pears 1980 – Natalie Norgrove

Choirboys

CHORISTER OF THE YEAR
The Rediffusion Award for Chorister of the Year is promoted by Rediffusion Ltd, in association with the Royal School of Church Music, and was inaugurated in 1975. The finalists are selected from courses held by the Royal School of Church Music in various parts of the country. The winner is judged by a panel of three judges.

1975 Matthew Billsborough (High Wycombe, All Saints)
1976 Stephen Drummond (Cookridge, Leeds, Holy Trinity)
1977 Andrew March (Tunbridge Wells, Holy Trinity with Christ Church)
1978 Simon Carney (Stockton-on-Tees, St Peter)
1979 Simon Minns (Bath, Bath Abbey)
1980 Timothy Attree (Bexleyheath, Kent, Christ Church)

Cinema

TOP MONEY-MAKING WOMEN OF THE MOVIES
The *Motion Picture Almanac* publishes an annual poll conducted by exhibitors in the United States to determine the top ten money-making stars of the year.

1932–33	Marie Dressler
1934	Janet Gaynor
1935–39	Shirley Temple
1940–41	Bette Davis
1942–44	Betty Grable
1945	Greer Garson
1946	Ingrid Bergman
1947–51	Betty Grable
1952	Doris Day
1953–54	Marilyn Monroe
1955	Grace Kelly
1956	Marilyn Monroe
1957	none
1958	Elizabeth Taylor
1959–60	Doris Day
1961	Elizabeth Taylor
1962–65	Doris Day
1966–68	Julie Andrews
1969	Katharine Hepburn
1970	Barbra Streisand
1971	Ali MacGraw
1972–75	Barbra Streisand
1976	Tatum O'Neal
1977	Barbra Streisand
1978	Diane Keaton
1979–80	Jane Fonda

TOP MONEY-MAKING MEN OF THE MOVIES

1932	Charles Farrell
1933–35	Will Rogers
1936–38	Clark Gable
1939–41	Mickey Rooney
1942	Abbott and Costello
1943	Bob Hope
1944–48	Bing Crosby
1949	Bob Hope
1950–51	John Wayne
1952	Martin and Lewis

1953	Gary Cooper
1954	John Wayne
1955	James Stewart
1956	William Holden
1957	Rock Hudson
1958	Glenn Ford
1959–62	Rock Hudson
1963	John Wayne
1964	Jack Lemmon
1965–66	Sean Connery
1967	Lee Marvin
1968	Sidney Poitier
1969–70	Paul Newman
1971	John Wayne
1972–73	Clint Eastwood
1974–76	Robert Redford
1977	Sylvester Stallone
1978–80	Burt Reynolds

THE BERLIN FILM FESTIVAL

The Berlin Film Festival was established in 1951. From 1952–55 the films were voted for by the audience. The Golden Bear award for Best Picture was inaugurated in 1956. Winners:

1951 *Without Leaving an Address* (Fra)
   Justice is Done (Fra)
1952 *She Danced for the Summer* (Swe)
1953 *The Wages of Fear* (Fra)
1954 *Hobson's Choice* (GB)
1955 *The Rats* (Ger)
1956 *Invitation to the Dance* (GB)
1957 *Twelve Angry Men* (USA)
1958 *The End of the Day* (Swe)
1959 *The Cousins* (Fra)
1960 *Lazarillo de Tormes* (Spa)
1961 *La Notte* (Ita)
1962 *A Kind of Loving* (GB)
1963 *Oath of Obedience* (Ger)
   The Devil (Ita)
1964 *Dry Summer* (Tur)
1965 *Alphaville* (Fra)
1966 *Cul de Sac* (GB)
1967 *Le Depart* (Bel)
1968 *Ole Dole Doff* (Swe)
1969 *Early Years* (Yug)
1970 No award
1971 *The Garden of the Finzi-Continis* (Ita)
1972 *The Canterbury Tales* (Ita)
1973 *Distant Thunder* (Ind)
1974 *The Apprenticeship of Duddy Kravitz* (Can)
1975 *Okrobefogadas* (Hun)
1976 *Buffalo Bill and the Indians or Sitting Bull's History Lesson* (USA) – award declined
1977 *The Ascent* (USSR)
1978 *The Trouts* (Spa)
   The Words of Max (Spa)
1979 *David* (Ger)
1980 *Heartland* (USA)
   Palermo oder Wolfsberg (Ger)
1981 *Los Tempo* (Spa)

BRITISH ACADEMY OF FILM AND TELEVISION ARTS AWARDS

The major annual awards from the British

Top: *Jane Fonda, top money-making woman of the movies for 1979 and 1980, and* above *Burt Reynolds, top money-making man for 1978, 1979 and 1980*

cinema and TV industries. The Academy was renamed in 1975, formerly being known as the Society of Film and Television Arts from 1967. Prior to this date two societies were in existence which were merged in 1967. These two were the British Film Academy (founded 1947) and the Guild of Television Producers and Directors (founded 1954).

BEST FILM
1947 *The Best Years of Our Lives*
1948 *Hamlet*
1949 *Bicycle Thieves*

Hamlet *won the BAFTA 'Best Film' award in 1948, and Laurence Olivier, for his part, won an Oscar for 'Best Actor'*

1950 All About Eve
1951 La Ronde
1952 The Sound Barrier
1953 Jeux Interdits
1954 Le Salaire de la Peur
1955 Richard III
1956 Gervaise
1957 The Bridge on the River Kwai
1958 Room at the Top
1959 Ben-Hur
1960 The Apartment
1961 Ballad of a Soldier
        The Hustler
1962 Lawrence of Arabia
1963 Tom Jones
1964 Dr Strangelove
1965 My Fair Lady
1966 Who's Afraid of Virginia Woolf?

1967 A Man for all Seasons
1968 The Graduate
1969 Midnight Cowboy
1970 Butch Cassidy and the Sundance Kid
1971 Sunday, Bloody Sunday
1972 Cabaret
1973 Day for Night
1974 Lacombe Lucien
1975 Alice Doesn't Live Here Anymore
1976 One Flew Over the Cuckoo's Nest
1977 Annie Hall
1978 Julia
1979 Manhattan
1980 The Elephant Man

THE BEST BRITISH FILM OF THE YEAR
1947 Odd Man Out
1948 The Fallen Idol
1949 The Third Man
1950 The Blue Lamp
1951 The Lavender Hill Mob
1952 The Sound Barrier
1953 Genevieve
1954 Hobson's Choice
1955 Richard III
1956 Reach for the Sky
1957 The Bridge on the River Kwai
1958 Room at the Top
1959 Sapphire
1960 Saturday Night and Sunday Morning
1961 A Taste of Honey
1962 Lawrence of Arabia
1963 Tom Jones
1964 Dr Strangelove
1965 The Ipcress File
1966 The Spy Who Came in from the Cold
1967 A Man for all Seasons
Discontinued

Midnight Express *won several awards in 1978 including the BAFTA 'Best Direction' award*

BEST DIRECTION
1968 Mike Nichols, *The Graduate*
1969 John Schlesinger, *Midnight Cowboy*
1970 George Roy Hill, *Butch Cassidy and the Sundance Kid*
1971 John Schlesinger, *Sunday, Bloody Sunday*
1972 Bob Fosse, *Cabaret*
1973 Francois Truffaut, *Day for Night*
1974 Roman Polanski, *Chinatown*
1975 Stanley Kubrick, *Barry Lyndon*
1976 Milos Forman, *One Flew Over the Cuckoo's Nest*
1977 Woody Allen, *Annie Hall.*
1978 Alan Parker, *Midnight Express*
1979 Francis Ford Coppola, *Apocalypse Now*
1980 Akira Kurosawa, *Kagemusha*

THE BEST SHORT FILM
(Before 1959: Award for the Best Documentary Film)
1947 *The World is Rich*
1948 *The Louisiana Story*
1949 *Daybreak in Udi*
1950 *The Undefeated*
1951 *Beaver Valley*
1952 *Royal Journey*
1953 *The Conquest of Everest*
1954 *The Great Adventure*
1955 *The Vanishing Prairie*
1956 *On the Bowery*
1957 *Journey into Spring*
1958 *Glass*
1959 *Seven Cities of Antarctica*
1960 *High Journey*
1961 *Terminus*
1962 *Incident at Owl Creek*
1963 *Happy Anniversary*
1964 *Kenojuak*
1965 *Rig Move*
1966 *The War Game*
1967 *Indus Waters*
Discontinued

THE JOHN GRIERSON AWARD
1968 No Award
1969 *Picture to Post*
1970 *Shadow of Progress*
1971 *Alaska – The Great Land*
1972 *Memorial*
1973 *Caring for History*
1974 *Location North Sea*
1975 *Sea Area Forties*
1976 No award
1977 No award
Discontinued

BEST SHORT FILM
1976 *The End of the Road*
1977 *The Living City*
1978 *Hokusia – An Animated Sketch book*
1979 *Butch Minds The Baby*
1980 *Sredni Vashtar*

BEST SHORT FICTIONAL FILM
1976 No Award
1977 *The Bead Game*
Discontinued

The BAFTA 'Best Short Film' for 1979 was Butch Minds The Baby

THE BEST SPECIALISED FILM
(Before 1959: Special Award for work lying outside the feature and documentary fields)
1948 *Atomic Physics*
1949 *La Famille Martin*
1950 *The True Face of Japan*
1951 *Gerald McBoing Boing*
1952 *Animated Genesis*
1953 *The Romance of Transportation*
1954 *Time Out of War*
1955 *The Bespoke Overcoat*
1956 *The Red Balloon*
1957 *A Chairy Tale*
1958 *The Children's Film Foundation*
1959 *This is the BBC*
1960 *Dispute*
1961 No award
1962 *Four Line Conics*
1963 No award
1964 *Driving Technique – Passenger Trains*
1965 *I Do – And I Understand*
1966 *Exploring Chemistry*
1967 *Energy and Matter*
1968 *The Threat in the Water*
1969 *Let There be Light*
1970 *The Rise and Fall of the Great Lakes*
1971 *The Savage Voyage*
1972 *Cutting Oils and Fluids*
1973 *A Man's World*
1974 *Monet in London*
1975 *The Curiosity that Kills the Cat*
1976 *Hydraulics*
1977 *Path of Paddle*
1978 *Twenty Times More Likely*
1979 No award
1980 No award

THE BEST ANIMATED FILM
1954 *Song of the Prairie*
1955 *Blinkity Blank*
1956 *Gerald McBoing Boing on Planet Moo*
1957 *Pan-Tele-Tron*
1958 *The Little Island*
1959 *The Violinist*
1960 *Universe*

55

The BAFTA 'Best Animated Film' award for 1961 was Walt Disney's One Hundred and One Dalmations

1961 *One Hundred and One Dalmatians*
1962 *The Apple*
1963 *Automania 2000; The Critic*
1964 *The Insects*
1965 *Be Careful Boys*
1966 Not Awarded
1967 *Notes on a Triangle*
1968 *Pas de Deux*
1969 No award
1970 *Henry Nine 'Til Five*
1971 No award
1972 No award
1973 *Tchou Tchou*
1974 *La Faim/Hunger*
1975 *Great*
1976–79 No award
1980 *The Three Inventors*

THE ROBERT FLAHERTY AWARD
For the best feature-length film, documentary in content
1959 *The Savage Eye*
1960 No award
1961 *Volcano*
1962 No award
1963 No award
1964 *Nobody Waved Goodbye*
1965 *Tokyo Olympiad*
1966 *Goal! The World Cup*
1967 *To Die in Madrid*
1968 *In Need of Special Care*
1969 *Prologue*
1970 *Sad Song of Yellow Skin*

1971 *The Hellstrom Chronicle*
1972 No award
1973 *Grierson*
1974 *Cree Hunters of Mistassini*
1975 *The Early Americans*
1976 *Los Canadienses*
1977 No award
1978 *The Silent Witness*
1979 *The Tree of Wooden Clogs*
1980 No award

BEST ACTRESS
1952 Vivien Leigh, *A Streetcar Named Desire*
1953 Audrey Hepburn, *Roman Holiday*
1954 Yvonne Mitchell, *The Divided Heart*
1955 Katie Johnson, *The Ladykillers*
1956 Virginia McKenna, *A Town Like Alice*
1957 Heather Sears, *The Story of Esther Costello*
1958 Irene Worth, *Orders to Kill*
1959 Audrey Hepburn, *The Nun's Story*
1960 Rachel Roberts, *Saturday Night and Sunday Morning*
1961 Dora Bryan, *A Taste of Honey*
1962 Leslie Caron, *The L-Shaped Room*
1963 *Rachel Roberts, This Sporting Life*
1964 Audrey Hepburn, *Charade*
1965 Julie christie, *Darling*
1966 Elizabeth Taylor, *Who's Afraid of Virginia Woolf?*
1967 Edith Evans, *The Whisperers*
1968 Katharine Hepburn, *Guess Who's Coming to Dinner* and *Lion in Winter*
1969 Maggie Smith, *The Prime of Miss Jean Brodie*
1970 Katharine Ross, *Butch Cassidy and the Sundance Kid*
1971 Glenda Jackson, *Sunday, Bloody Sunday*
1972 Liza Minnelli, *Cabaret*

1973 Stephanie Audran, *The Discreet Charm of the Bourgeoisie* and *Just before Nightfall*
1974 Joanne Woodward, *Summer Wishes, Winter Dreams*
1975 Ellen Burstyn, *Alice Doesn't Live Here Anymore*
1976 Louise Fletcher, *One Flew Over the Cuckoo's Nest*
1977 Diane Keaton, *Annie Hall*
1978 Jane Fonda, *Julia*
1979 Jane Fonda, *The China Syndrome*
1980 Judy Davis, *My Brilliant Career*

BEST ACTOR
Until 1967, Best British Actor.
1952 Ralph Richardson, *The Sound Barrier*
1953 John Gielgud, *Julius Caesar*
1954 Kenneth More, *Doctor in the House*
1955 Laurence Olivier, *Richard III*
1956 Peter Finch, *A Town Like Alice*
1957 Alec Guinness, *The Bridge on the River Kwai*
1958 Trevor Howard, *The Key*
1959 Peter Sellers, *I'm All Right Jack*
1960 Peter Finch, *The Trials of Oscar Wilde*
1961 Peter Finch, *No Love for Johnny*
1962 Peter O'Toole, *Lawrence of Arabia*
1963 Dirk Bogarde, *The Servant*
1964 Richard Attenborough, *Guns at Batasi* and *Seance on a Wet Afternoon*
1965 Dirk Bogarde, *Darling*
1966 Richard Burton, *Who's Afraid of Virginia Woolf?*
1967 Paul Scofield, *A Man For All Seasons*
1968 Spencer Tracy, *Guess Who's Coming to Dinner*
1969 Dustin Hoffman, *Midnight Cowboy*
1970 Robert Redford, *Butch Cassidy and the Sundance Kid*
1971 Peter Finch, *Sunday, Bloody Sunday*
1972 Gene Hackman, *The French Connection*
1973 Walter Matthau, *Pete 'n Tillie* and *Charley Varrick*
1974 Jack Nicholson, *Chinatown* and *The Last Detail*
1975 Al Pacino, *Dog Day Afternoon* and *Godfather II*
1976 Jack Nicholson, *One Flee Over the Cuckoo's Nest*
1977 Peter Finch, *Network*
1978 Richard Dreyfuss, *The Goodbye Girl*
1979 Jack Lemmon, *The China Syndrome*
1980 John Hurt, *The Elephant Man*

BEST FOREIGN ACTRESS
1952 Simone Signoret, *Casque d'Or*
1953 Leslie Caron, *Lili*
1954 Cornell Borchers, *The Divided Heart*
1955 Betsy Blair, *Marty*
1956 Anna Magnani, *The Rose Tattoo*
1957 Simone Signoret, *The Witches of Salem*
1958 Simone Signoret, *Room at the Top*
1959 Shirley MacLaine, *Ask Any Girl*
1960 Shirley MacLaine, *The Apartment*
1961 Sophia Loren, *Two Women*
1962 Anne Bancroft, *The Miracle Worker*
1963 Patricial Neal, *Hud*
1964 Anne Bancroft, *The Pumpkin Eater*
1965 Patricia Neal, *In Harm's Way*

Katharine Hepburn (seen above in Lion in Winter) *won the 1968 'Best Actress' BAFTA award*

1966 Jeanne Moreau, *Viva Maria*
1967 Anouk Aimee, *Un Homme et Une Femme*
Discontinued

BEST FOREIGN ACTOR
1952 Marlon Brando, *Viva Zapala!*
1953 Marlon Brando, *Julius Caesar*
1954 Marlon Brando, *On the Waterfront*
1955 Ernest Borgnine, *Marty*
1956 Francois Perier, *Gervaise*
1957 Henry Fonda, *Twelve Angry Men*
1958 Sidney Poitier, *The Defiant Ones*
1959 Jack Lemmon, *Some Like it Hot*
1960 Jack Lemmon, *The Apartment*
1961 Paul Newman, *The Hustler*
1962 Burt Lancaster, *Birdman of Alcatraz*
1963 Marcello Mastroianni, *Divorce, Italian Style*
1964 Marcello Mastroianni, *Yesterday, Today and Tomorrow*
1965 Lee Marvin, *The Killers* and *Cat Ballou*
1966 Rod Steiger, *The Pawnbroker*
1967 Rod Steiger, *In the Heat of the Night*
Discontinued

Six BAFTA awards were given in 1969 to Midnight Cowboy, *starring Dustin Hoffman (right)*

THE MOST PROMISING NEWCOMER TO LEADING FILM ROLES

1952 Clair Bloom, *Limelight*
1953 David Kossoff, *The Young Lovers*
1954 Norman Wisdom, *Trouble in Store*
1955 Paul Scofield, *That Lady*
1956 Eli Wallach, *Baby Doll*
1957 Eric Barker, *Brothers in Law*
1958 Paul Massie, *Orders to Kill*
1959 Hayley Mills, *Tiger Bay*
1960 Albert Finney, *Saturday Night and Sunday Morning*
1961 Rita Tushingham, *A Taste of Honey*
1962 Tom Courtenay, *The Loneliness of the Long Distance Runner*
1963 James Fox, *The Servant*
1964 Julie Andrews, *Mary Poppins*
1965 Judi Dench, *Four in the Morning*
1966 Vivien Merchant, *Alfie*
1967 Faye Dunaway, *Bonnie and Clyde*
1968 Dustin Hoffman, *The Graduate*
1969 Jon Voight, *Midnight Cowboy*
1970 David Bradley, *Kes*
1971 Dominic Guard, *The Go-Between*
1972 Joel Grey, *Cabaret*
1973 Peter Egan, *The Hireling*
1974 Georgina Hale, *Mahler*
1975 Valerie Perrine, *Lennie*
1976 Jodie Foster, *Taxi Driver*
1977 Isabelle Huppert, *The Lacemaker*
1978 Christopher Reeve, *Superman*
1979 Dennis Christopher, *Breaking Away*
1980 Judy Davis, *My Brilliant Career*

BEST SUPPORTING ACTRESS

1968 Billie Whitelaw, *The Twisted Nerve* and *Charlie Bubbles*
1969 Celia Johnson, *The Prime of Miss Jean Brodie*
1970 Susannah York, *They Shoot Horses, Don't They?*
1971 Margaret Leighton, *The Go-Between*
1972 Cloris Leachman, *The Last Picture Show*
1973 Valentine Cortese, *Day for Night*

A scene from Apocalypse Now, *award-winning film in 1979*

Woody Allen (right), *seen with Diane Keaton, received a BAFTA award for 'Best Screenplay' in 1979 for* Manhattan

1974 Ingrid Bergman, *Murder on the Orient Express*
1975 Diane Ladd, *Alice Doesn't Live Here Anymore*
1976 Jodie Foster, *Bugsy Malone* and *Taxi Driver*
1977 Jenny Agutter, *Equus*
1978 Geraldine Page, *Interiors*
1979 Rachel Roberts, *Yanks*
1980 No award

BEST SUPPORTING ACTOR

1968 Ian Holm, *The Bofors Gun*
1969 Laurence Olivier, *Oh, What a Lovely War*
1970 Colin Welland, *Kes*
1971 Edward Fox, *The Go-Between*
1972 Ben Johnson, *The Last Picture Show*
1973 Arthur Lowe, *O Lucky Man!*
1974 John Gielgud, *Murder on the Orient Express*
1975 Fred Astaire, *The Towering Inferno*
1976 Brad Dourif, *One Flew Over the Cuckoo's Nest*
1977 Edward Fox, *A Bridge Too Far*
1978 John Hurt, *Midnight Express*
1979 Robert Duvall, *Apocalypse Now*
1980 No award

BEST SCREENPLAY

Until 1967, Best Screenplay of a British film
1954 George Tabori and Robin Estridge, *The Young Lovers*
1955 William Rose, *The Ladykillers*
1956 Nigel Balchin, *The Man Who Never Was*
1957 Pierre Boulle, *The Bridge on the River Kwai*
1958 Paul Dehn, *Orders to Kill*
1959 Frank Harvey, John Boulting and Alan Hackney, *I'm All Right, Jack*
1960 Bryan Forbes, *The Angry Silence*
1961 Val Guest and Wolf Mankowitz, *The Day the Earth Caught Fire*; Shelagh Delaney and Tony Richardson, *A Taste of Honey*
1962 Robert Bolt, *Lawrence of Arabia*
1963 John Osborne, *Tom Jones*
1964 Harold Pinter, *The Pumpkin Eater*
1965 Frederic Raphael, *Darling*
1966 David Mercer, *Morgan – A Suitable Case for Treatment*
1967 Robert Bolt, *A Man for All Seasons*
1968 Calder Willingham and Buck Henry, *The Graduate*
1969 Waldo Salt, *Midnight Cowboy*

1970 William Goldman, *Butch Cassidy and the Sundance Kid*
1971 Harold Pinter, *The Go-Between*
1972 Paddy Chayefsky, *The Hospital*; Larry McMurtry and Peter Bogdanovich, *The Last Picture Show*
1973 Luis Bunuel and Jean-Claude Carrière, *The Discreet Charm of the Bourgeoisie*
1974 Robert Towne, *Chinatown* and *The Last Detail*
1975 Robert Getchell, *Alice Doesn't Live Here Anymore*
1976 Alan Parker, *Bugsy Malone*
1977 Woody Allen and Marshall Brickman, *Annie Hall*
1978 Alvin Sargent, *Julia*
1979 Woody Allen and Marshall Brickman, *Manhattan*
1980 Jerzy Kosinski, *Being There*

BEST CINEMATOGRAPHY IN A BRITISH FILM
Colour
1963 Ted Moore, *From Russia with Love*
1964 Geoffrey Unsworth, *Becket*
1965 Otto Heller, *The Ipcress File*
1966 Christopher Challis, *Arabesque*
1967 Ted Moore, *A Man for All Seasons*
Discontinued
Black and white
1963 Douglas Slocombe, *The Servant*
1964 Oswald Morris, *The Pumpkin Eater*
1965 Oswald Morris, *The Hill*
1966 Oswald Morris, *The Spy Who Came in From the Cold*
1967 Gerry Turpin, *The Whisperers*
Discontinued

BEST CINEMATOGRAPHY
1968 Geoffrey Unsworth, *2001: A Space Odyssey*
1969 Gerry Turpin, *Oh! What a Lovely War*
1970 Conrad Hall, *Butch Cassidy and the Sundance Kid*
1971 Pasquale de Santis, *Death in Venice*
1972 Geoffrey Unsworth, *Cabaret* and *Alice's Adventures in Wonderland*
1973 Anthony Richmond, *Don't Look Now*
1974 Douglas Slocombe, *The Great Gatsby*
1975 John Alcott, *Barry Lyndon*
1976 Russell Boyd, *Picnic at Hanging Rock*
1977 Geoffrey Unsworth, *A Bridge Too Far*
1978 Douglas Slocombe, *Julia*
1979 Vilmas Zsigmond, *The Deer Hunter*
1980 Giuseppe Rotunno, *All That Jazz*

BEST ART DIRECTION IN A BRITISH FILM
Colour
1964 John Bryan, *Becket*
1965 Ken Adam, *The Ipcress File*
1966 Wilfrid Shingleton, *The Blue Max*
1967 John Box, *A Man for All Seasons*
Discontinued
Black and white
1964 Ken Adam, *Dr Strangelove*
1965 Ray Simm, *Darling*
1966 Tambi Larsen, *The Spy Who Came in From the Cold*
1967 No award
Discontinued

A scene from the climax of Close Encounters of the Third Kind *for which Joe Alves received the 1978 BAFTA 'Best Production' award*

BEST PRODUCTION DESIGN/ART DIRECTION
1968 Tony Masters, Harry Lange and Ernie Archer, *2001: A Space Odyssey*
1969 Don Ashton, *Oh! What a Lovely War*
1970 Mario Garbuglia, *Waterloo*
1971 Ferdinando Scarfiotti, *Death in Venice*
1972 Rolf Zehetbaur, *Cabaret*
1973 Natasha Kroll, *The Hireling*
1974 John Box, *The Great Gatsby*
1975 John Box, *Rollerball*
1976 Geoffrey Kirkland, *Bugsy Malone*
1977 Danilo Donati, *Fellini's Casanova*
1978 Joe Alves, *Close Encounters of the Third Kind*
1979 Michael Seymour, *Alien*
1980 Stuart Craig, *The Elephant Man*

BEST FILM EDITING
Until 1967, Best Editing of a British Film
1966 Tom Priestley, *Morgan – A Suitable Case for Treatment*
1967 No award
1968 Sam O'Steen, *The Graduate*
1969 Hugh A. Robertson, *Midnight Cowboy*
1970 John C. Howard and Richard C. Meyer, *Butch Cassidy and the Sundance Kid*
1971 Richard Marden, *Sunday, Bloody Sunday*
1972 Gerry Greenberg, *The French Connection*
1973 Ralph Kemplen, *The Day of the Jackal*
1974 Walter Murch and Richard Chew, *The Conversation*
1975 Dede Allen, *Dog Day Afternoon*
1976 Richard Chew, Lynzee Klingman and Sheldon Kahn, *One Flew Over the Cuckoo's Nest*
1977 Ralph Rosenblum and Wendy Greene Bricmont, *Annie Hall*
1978 Gerry Hambling, *Midnight Express*
1979 Peter Zinner, *The Deer Hunter*
1980 Alan Heim, *All That Jazz*

BEST COSTUME DESIGN
Until 1967, Best Costume Design in a British Film.
After 1967 'Colour' and 'Black and white' categories discontinued
Colour
1964 Margaret Furse, *Becket*

Shirley Russell received the 1979 BAFTA 'Best Costume Design' award for Yanks

1965 Osbert Lancaster and Dinah Greet, *Those Magnificent Men in Their Flying Machines*
1966 Julie Harris, *The Wrong Box*
1967 Elizabeth Haffenden and Joan Bridge, *A Man For All Seasons*
Discontinued
Black and white
1964 Motley, *The Pumpkin Eater*
1965 No award
1966 No award
1967 Jocelyn Rickards, *Mademoiselle*
Discontinued

1968 Danilo Donati, *Romeo and Juliet*
1969 Anthony Mendleson, *Oh! What a Lovely War*
1970 Maria de Matteis and Ugo Pericoli, *Waterloo*
1971 Piero Tosi, *Death in Venice*
1972 Anthony Mendleson, *Young Winston*, *Macbeth* and *Alice's Adventures in Wonderland*
1973 Phyllis Dalton, *The Hireling*
1974 Theoni V. Aldredge, *The Great Gatsby*
1975 Ann Roth, *Day of the Locust*
1976 Moidele Bickel, *Die Marquise von O*
1977 Danilo Donati, *Fellini's Casanova*
1978 Anthony Powell, *Death on the Nile*
1979 Shirley Russell, *Yanks*
1980 Seiichiro Momosawa, *Kagemosha*

BEST SOUNDTRACK
1968 Winston Ryder, *2001: A Space Odyssey*
1969 Don Challis and Simon Kaye, *Oh! What a Lovely War*
1970 Don Hall, David Dockendorf and William Edmundson, *Butch Cassidy and the Sundance Kid*

1971 Vittorio Trenting and Giuseppe Muratori, *Death in Venice*
1972 David Hildyard, Robert Knudson and Arthur Piantadosi, *Cabaret*
1973 Les Wiggins, Gordon K. McCallum and Keith Grant, *Jesus Christ Superstar*
1974 Art Rochester, Nat Boxer, Mike Evje and Walter Murch, *The Conversation*
1975 William A. Sawyer, Jim Webb, Chris McLaughlin and Richard Portman, *Nashville*
1976 Les Wiggins, Clive Winter and Ken Barker, *Bugsy Malone*
1977 Peter Horrocks, Gerry Humphreys, Simon Kaye, Robin O'Donoghue and Les Wiggins, *A Bridge Too Far*
1978 Team of twelve for *Star Wars*
1979 Derrick Leather, Jim Shields and Bill Bowe, *Alien*
1980 Chris Newman, Les Wiggins and Michael J. Kohut, *Fame*

THE ANTHONY ASQUITH MEMORIAL AWARD FOR ORIGINAL FILM MUSIC
1968 John Barry, *The Lion in Winter*
1969 Mikos Theodorakis, *Z*
1970 Burt Bacharach, *Butch Cassidy and the Sundance Kid*
1971 Michel Legrand, *Summer of '42*
1972 Nino Rota, *The Godfather*
1973 Alan Price, *O Lucky Man!*
1974 Richard Rodney Bennett, *Murder on the Orient Express*
1975 John Williams, *Jaws* and *The Towering Inferno*
1976 Bernard Herrmann, *Taxi Driver*
1977 John Addison, *A Bridge Too Far*
1978 John Williams, *Star Wars*
1979 Ernio Morricone, *Days of Heaven*
1980 John Williams, *The Empire Strikes Back*

BRITISH FILM INSTITUTE'S AWARD
This irregular award (first called the Sutherland Trophy) is made for a film (shown at the National Film Theatre) which is considered outstanding in originality and imaginativeness. The awards made so far have been:

SUTHERLAND TROPHY
1958 *Tokyo Story*, Yasujiro Ozu
1959 *World of Apu*, Satyajit Ray
1960 *L'Avventura*, Michelangelo Antonioni
1961 *Il Posto*, Ermanno Olmi
1962 *Paris Nous Appartient*, Jacques Rivette

BRITISH FILM INSTITUTE AWARD
1963 *Muriel*, Alain Resnais
1964 *Hamlet*, Grigori Kozintsev
1965 *Pierrot Le Fou*, Jean-Luc Godard
1966 *Man Who Had His Hair Cut Short*, André Delvaux
1967 *Rebellion*, Masaki Kobayashi
1968 *Chronicle of Anna Magdalen Bach*, Jean-Marie Straub
1969 *L'Amour Fou,* Jacques Rivette
1970 *The Conformist*, Bernardo Bertolucci
1971 *Four Nights of a Dreamer*, Robert Bresson

Two Stage Sisters *jointly won the 1980 British Film Institute Award*

1972 *The Hour of the Furnaces*, Octavio Getino and Fernando E. Solanas
1973 *Pirosmani*, Georgy Shengelaya
1974 *Martha*, Rainer Werner Fassbinder
1975 *The Travelling Players*, Theodor Angelopoulos
1976 No award
1977 *Hitler – A Film from Germany*, Hans-Jurgen Syberberg
1978 *The Scenic Route*, Mark Rapaport
1979 *The Herd*, Yilmaz Güney
1980 *Two Stage Sisters,* Xie Jin
      The Falls, Peter Greenaway

CANNES FILM FESTIVAL

Founded in 1946, the Festival gives the Palme d'Or to the Best Film. In 1946 there was no overall award, but one was made to each country. Winners:

1947 *Antoine et Antoinette* (Fra)
1948 No festival
1949 *The Third Man* (GB)
1950 No festival
1951 *Miracle in Milan* (Ita)
     Miss Julie (Swe)
1952 *Othello* (Mor)
     Two Cents Worth of Hope (Ita)
1953 *Wages of Fear* (Fra)
1954 *Gate of Hell* (Jap)
1955 *Marty* (USA)
1956 *World of Silence* (Fra)
1957 *Friendly Persuasion* (USA)
1958 *The Cranes are Flying* (USSR)
1959 *Black Orpheus* (Fra)
1960 *La Dolce Vita* (Ita)
1961 *Viridiana* (Spa)
     Une aussi longue absence (Fra)
1962 *The Given Word* (Bra)
1963 *The Leopard* (Ita)
1964 *The Umbrellas of Cherbourg* (Fra)
1965 *The Knack* (GB)
1966 *A Man and a Woman* (Fra)
     Signore e Signori (Ita)
1967 *Blow-Up* (GB)
1968 Festival disrupted; no awards

1969 *If* (GB)
1970 *M*A*S*H* (USA)
1971 *The Go-Between* (GB)
1972 *The Working Class Goes to Paradise* (Ita)
     The Mattei Affair (Ita)
1973 *Scarecrow* (USA)
     The Hireling (GB)
1974 *The Conversation* (USA)
1975 *Chronicle of the Burning Years* (Alg)
1976 *Taxi Driver* (USA)
1977 *Padre Padrone* (Ita)
1978 *L'Albero Degli Zoccoli* (Ita)
1979 *The Tin Drum* (Ger)
     Apocalypse Now (USA)
1980 *All That Jazz* (USA)
     Kagemusha (Jap)
1981 *Man of Iron* (Pol)

FILMS ANNUAL AWARDS

These London-based awards were first given in 1950 by *Films and Filming* and were taken over in 1979 by *Films*. A selection of award winners since 1974:

BEST FILM
1974 *Badlands*, Terence Malick; *Amarcord*, Federico Fellini (Best foreign film)
1975 *Lenny*, Bob Fosse; *The Mattei Affair*, Francesco Rosi (Best foreign film)
1976 *Network*, Sidney Lumet
1977 *Illustrious Corpses*, Francesco Rosi
1978 *Interiors*, Woody Allen
1979 *Days of Heaven*, Terence Malick
1980 *All That Jazz*, Bob Fosse

BEST ACTOR
1974 Martin Sheen, *Badlands*
1975 Dustin Hoffman, *Lenny*
1976 Dustin Hoffman, *Marathon Man*
1977 Richard Burton, *Equus*
1978 Jon Voight, *Coming Home*
1979 Martin Sheen, *Apocalypse Now*
1980 Peter Sellers, *Being There*

BEST ACTRESS
1974 Goldie Hawn, *Sugarland Express*
1975 Ann-Margret, *Tommy*
1976 Audrey Hepburn, *Robin and Marian*
1977 Diane Keaton, *Annie Hall*
1978 Geraldine Page, *Interiors*
1979 Sally Field, *Norma Rae*
1980 Bette Midler, *The Rose*

BEST DIRECTOR
1974 Richard Lester, *The Three Musketeers*
1975 Michelangelo Antonioni, *The Passenger*
1976 Milos Forman, *One Flew Over the Cuckoo's Nest*
1977 Martin Ritt, *The Front*
1978 Hal Ashby, *Coming Home*
1979 Peter Yates, *Breaking Away*
1980 Nicolas Roeg, *Bad Timing*

BEST BRITISH FILM
1974 No award
1975 *Tommy*, Ken Russell
1976 *The Man Who Fell to Earth*, Nicholas Roeg
1977 *Jabberwocky*, Terry Gilliam

Ken Russell's film Tommy *received the 'Best British Film' award for 1975 in the* Films Annual Awards

1978 *Midnight Express*, Alan Parker
1979 *Scum*, Alan Clark
1980 No award

The 'novelty' awards include:

MOST DISAPPOINTING FILM
1974 *Stardust*, Michael Apted
1975 *Rocky Horror Picture Show*, Jill Sharman
1976 *The Tenant*, Roman Polanski
1977 *Une Partie de Plaisir*, Claud Chabrol
1978 *An Unmarried Woman*, Paul Mazursky
1979 *Alien*, Ridley Scott
1980 *The Shining*, Stanley Kubrick

MOST DISTASTEFUL FILM
1974 *The Exorcist*, W. Friedkin
1975 *Funny Lady*, Herbert Ross
1976 *Taxi Driver*, Martin Scorcese
1977 *Salon Kitty*, Tinto Brass
1978 *The Greek Tycoon*, J. Lee Thompson
1979 *Quadrophenia*, Franc Roddam
1980 *Cruising*, William Friedkin

MOST UNDERRATED FILM
1974 *Turkish Delight*, Paul Verhoeven
1975 *The Great Waldo Pepper*, George Roy Hill
1976 *Robin and Marian*, Richard Lester
1977 *The Last Tycoon*, Elia Kazan
1978 *Straight Time*, Ulu Grosbard
1979 *Slow Dancing in the Big City*, John G. Adildsen
1980 *Broncho Billy*, Clint Eastwood

EMBARRASSMENT OF THE YEAR
1974 *Confessions of a Window Cleaner*

1975 *Confessions of a Pop Performer* and *Three For All*
1976 *Goodbye, Norma Jean*
1977 *The Prince and the Pauper*
1978 *Oh God*! Carl Reiner
1979 *The Music Machine*
1980 '*10*'

MOST OVERRATED FILM
1974 *Chinatown*, Roman Polanski
1975 *Shampoo*, Hal Ashby
1976 *Taxi Driver*, Martin Scorcese
1977 *Star Wars*, George Lucas
1978 *Driver*, Walter Hill
1979 *The In-Laws*, Arthur Hiller
1980 *Fame*, Alan Parker

MOTION PICTURE ACADEMY AWARDS (OSCARS)
Given by the Academy of Motion Picture Arts and Sciences, the 'Oscar' statuettes were introduced in 1928 and are the highest accolade of the Hollywood film industry. There are some 25 awards each year, for performances and technical achievements. The main categories of winners are as follows:

BEST ACTOR
1927–28 Emil Jannings, *The Way of All Flesh*
1928–29 Warner Baxter, *In Old Arizona*
1929–30 George Arliss, *Disraeli*
1930–31 Lionel Barrymore, *Free Soul*
1931–32 Fredric March, *Dr Jekyll and Mr Hyde;* Wallace Beery, *The Champ*
1932–33 Charles Laughton, *Private Life of Henry VIII*
1934 Clark Gable, *It Happened One Night*
1935 Victor McLaglen, *The Informer*
1936 Paul Muni, *Story of Louis Pasteur*
1937 Spencer Tracy, *Captain Courageous*
1938 Spencer Tracy, *Boys Town*
1939 Robert Donat, *Goodbye Mr Chips*
1940 James Stewart, *The Philadelphia Story*
1941 Gary Cooper, *Sergeant York*
1942 James Cagney, *Yankee Doodle Dandy*
1943 Paul Lukas, *Watch on the Rhine*
1944 Bing Crosby, *Going My Way*
1945 Ray Milland, *The Lost Weekend*
1946 Fredric March, *The Best Years of Our Lives*
1947 Ronald Colman, *A Double Life*
1948 Laurence Olivier, *Hamlet*
1949 Broderick Crawford, *All the King's Men*
1950 José Ferrer, *Cyrano de Bergerac*
1951 Humphrey Bogart, *The African Queen*
1952 Gary Cooper, *High Noon*
1953 William Holden, *Stalag 17*
1954 Marlon Brando, *On the Waterfront*
1955 Ernest Borgnine, *Marty*
1956 Yul Brynner, *The King and I*
1957 Alec Guinness, *The Bridge on the River Kwai*
1958 David Niven, *Separate Tables*
1959 Charlton Heston, *Ben Hur*
1960 Burt Lancaster, *Elmer Gantry*
1961 Maximilian Schell, *Judgment at Nuremberg*
1962 Gregory Peck, *To Kill a Mockingbird*
1963 Sidney Poitier, *Lilies of the Field*

1964 Rex Harrison, *My Fair Lady*
1965 Lee Marvin, *Cat Ballou*
1966 Paul Scofield, *A Man for All Seasons*
1967 Rod Steiger, *In the Heat of the Night*
1968 Cliff Robertson, *Charly*
1969 John Wayne, *True Grit*
1970 George C. Scott, *Patton* (refused)
1971 Gene Hackman, *The French Connection*
1972 Marlon Brando, *The Godfather* (refused)
1973 Jack Lemmon, *Save the Tiger*
1974 Art Carney, *Harry and Tonto*
1975 Jack Nicholson, *One Flew Over the Cuckoo's Nest*
1976 Peter Finch, *Network*
1977 Richard Dreyfuss, *The Goodbye Girl*
1978 Jon Voight, *Coming Home*
1979 Dustin Hoffman, *Kramer vs Kramer*
1980 Robert De Niro, *Raging Bull*

BEST ACTRESS
1927–28 Janet Gaynor, *Seventh Heaven*
1928–29 Mary Pickford, *Coquette*
1929–30 Norma Shearer, *The Divorcee*
1930–31 Marie Dressler, *Min and Bill*
1931–32 Helen Hayes, *Sin of Madelon Claudet*
1932–33 Katharine Hepburn, *Morning Glory*
1934 Claudette Colbert, *It Happened One Night*
1935 Bette Davis, *Dangerous*
1936 Luise Rainer, *The Great Ziegfeld*
1937 Luise Rainer, *The Good Earth*
1938 Bette Davis, *Jezebel*
1939 Vivien Leigh, *Gone With the Wind*
1940 Ginger Rogers, *Kitty Foyle*
1941 Joan Fontaine, *Suspicion*
1942 Greer Garson, *Mrs Miniver*
1943 Jennifer Jones, *The Song of Bernadette*
1944 Ingrid Bergman, *Gaslight*
1945 Joan Crawford, *Mildred Pierce*
1946 Olivia de Havilland, *To Each His Own*
1947 Loretta Young, *The Farmer's Daughter*
1948 Jane Wyman, *Johnny Belinda*

Ginger Rogers in Kitty Foyle *won an Oscar for 'Best Actress' in 1940*

1949 Olivia de Havilland, *The Heiress*
1950 Judy Holliday, *Born Yesterday*
1951 Vivien Leigh, *A Streetcar Named Desire*
1952 Shirley Booth, *Come Back, Little Sheba*
1953 Audrey Hepburn, *Roman Holiday*
1954 Grace Kelly, *The Country Girl*
1955 Anna Magnani, *The Rose Tattoo*
1956 Ingrid Bergman, *Anastasia*
1957 Joanne Woodward, *The Three Faces of Eve*
1958 Susan Hayward, *I Want to Live*
1959 Simone Signoret, *Room at the Top*
1960 Elizabeth Taylor, *Butterfield 8*
1961 Sophia Loren, *Two Women*
1962 Anne Bancroft, *The Miracle Worker*
1963 Patricia Neal, *Hud*

Dustin Hoffman won an Oscar for 'Best Actor' in 1979 for his part in Kramer vs Kramer

1964 Julie Andrews, *Mary Poppins*
1965 Julie Christie, *Darling*
1966 Elizabeth Taylor, *Who's Afraid of Virginia Woolf?*
1967 Katharine Hepburn, *Guess Who's Coming to Dinner*
1968 Katharine Hepburn, *The Lion in Winter;* Barbra Streisand, *Funny Girl*
1969 Maggie Smith, *The Prime of Miss Jean Brodie*
1970 Glenda Jackson, *Women in Love*
1971 Jane Fonda, *Klute*
1972 Liza Minnelli, *Cabaret*
1973 Glenda Jackson, *A Touch of Class*
1974 Ellen Burstyn, *Alice Doesn't Live Here Anymore*
1975 Louise Fletcher, *One Flew Over the Cuckoo's Nest*
1976 Faye Dunaway, *Network*
1977 Diane Keaton, *Annie Hall*
1978 Jane Fonda, *Coming Home*
1979 Sally Field, *Norma Rae*
1980 Sissy Spacek, *Coal Miner's Daughter*

BEST PICTURE
1927–28 *Wings,* Paramount
1928–29 *Broadway Melody,* MGM
1929–30 *All Quiet on the Western Front,* Universal
1930–31 *Cimarron,* RKO
1931–32 *Grand Hotel,* MGM
Special: *Mickey Mouse,* Walt Disney
1932–33 *Cavalcade,* 20th Century-Fox
1934 *It Happened One Night,* Columbia
1935 *Mutiny on the Bounty,* MGM
1936 *The Great Ziegfeld,* MGM
1937 *Life of Emile Zola,* Warner
1938 *You Can't Take It With You,* Columbia
1939 *Gone With the Wind,* Selznick International
1940 *Rebecca,* Selznick International
1941 *How Green Was My Valley,* 20th Century-Fox
1942 *Mrs Miniver,* MGM
1943 *Casablanca,* Warner
1944 *Going My Way,* Paramount
1945 *The Lost Weekend,* Paramount
1946 *The Best Years of Our Lives,* Goldwyn, RKO
1947 *Gentleman's Agreement,* 20th Century-Fox
1948 *Hamlet,* Two Cities Film, Universal International
1949 *All the King's Men,* Columbia
1950 *All About Eve,* 20th Century-Fox
1951 *An American in Paris,* MGM
1952 *The Greatest Show on Earth,* Cecil B. DeMille, Paramount
1953 *From Here to Eternity,* Columbia
1954 *On the Waterfront,* Horizon-American Corp. Columbia
1955 *Marty,* Hecht and Lancaster's Steven Productions UA
1956 *Around the World in 80 Days,* Michael Todd Co. UA
1957 *The Bridge on the River Kwai,* Columbia
1958 *Gigi,* Arthur Freed Production, MGM
1959 *Ben-Hur,* MGM
1960 *The Apartment,* Mirisch Co, UA
1961 *West Side Story,* United Artists
1962 *Lawrence of Arabia,* Columbia
1963 *Tom Jones,* Woodfall Prod. UA-Lopert Pictures
1964 *My Fair Lady,* Warner Bros.

Rocky, *Oscar winning 'Best Picture' in 1976*

1965 *The Sound of Music,* 20th Century-Fox
1966 *A Man for All Seasons,* Columbia
1967 *In the Heat of the Night,* United Artists
1968 *Oliver,* Columbia
1969 *Midnight Cowboy,* United Artists
1970 *Patton,* 20th Century-Fox
1971 *The French Connection,* 20th Century-Fox
1972 *The Godfather,* Paramount
1973 *The Sting,* Universal
1974 *The Godfather, Part II,* Paramount
1975 *One Flew Over the Cuckoo's Nest,* United Artists
1976 *Rocky,* United Artists
1977 *Annie Hall,* United Artists
1978 *The Deer Hunter,* EMI
1979 *Kramer vs Kramer,* Columbia
1980 *Ordinary People,* Paramount

BEST DIRECTOR
1927–28 Frank Borzage, *Seventh Heaven,* Lewis Milestone, *Two Arabian Knights*
1928–29 Frank Lloyd, *The Divine Lady*
1929–30 Lewis Milestone, *All Quiet on the Western Front*
1930–31 Norman Taurog, *Skippy*
1931–32 Frank Borzage, *Bad Girl*
1932–33 Frank Lloyd, *Cavalcade*
1934 Frank Capra, *It Happened One Night*
1935 John Ford, *The Informer*
1936 Frank Capra, *Mr Deeds Goes to Town*
1937 Leo McCarey, *The Awful Truth*
1938 Frank Capra, *You Can't Take It With You*
1939 Victor Fleming, *Gone with the Wind*
1940 John Ford, *The Grapes of Wrath*
1941 John Ford, *How Green Was My Valley*
1942 William Wyler, *Mrs Miniver*
1943 Michael Curtiz, *Casablanca*
1944 Leo McCarey, *Going My Way*
1945 Billy Wilder, *The Lost Weekend*
1946 William Wyler, *The Best Years of Our Lives*
1947 Elia Kazan, *Gentleman's Agreement*
1948 John Huston, *Treasure of Sierra Madre*

Beauty

Miss Great Britain 1980 – Susan Berger (see p. 30)

Mr Universe

*Mr Universe 1980 (left to right): Tony Pearson (Professional), Erika Mes Dutch (Miss Universe Bikini), Bill Richardson (Amateur) (*Edward Hankey*)* (see p. 36)

Circus

The Flying Terrells in action on the flying trapeze during the 1977 Circus World Championships (Peter Baylis) (see p. 66)

Shepherds

John Read from Hampshire, 1980 Shepherd of the Year in the Livestock Farming *competition, cares for a flock of 3000 ewes* (see p. 202)

1949 Joseph L. Mankiewicz, *A Letter to Three Wives*
1950 Joseph L. Mankiewicz, *All About Eve*
1951 George Stevens, *A Place in the Sun*
1952 John Ford, *The Quiet Man*
1953 Fred Zinnemann, *From Here to Eternity*
1954 Elia Kazan, *On the Waterfront*
1955 Delbert Mann, *Marty*
1956 George Stevens, *Giant*
1957 David Lean, *The Bridge on the River Kwai*
1958 Vincente Minnelli, *Gigi*
1959 William Wyler, *Ben-Hur*
1960 Billy Wilder, *The Apartment*
1961 Jerome Robbins, Robert Wise, *West Side Story*
1962 David Lean, *Lawrence of Arabia*
1963 Tony Richardson, *Tom Jones*
1964 George Cukor, *My Fair Lady*
1965 Robert Wise, *Sound of Music*
1966 Fred Zinnemann, *A Man for All Seasons*
1967 Mike Nichols, *The Graduate*
1968 Sir Carol Reed, *Oliver*
1969 John Schlesinger, *Midnight Cowboy*
1970 Franklin J. Schaffner, *Patton*
1971 William Friedkin, *The French Connection*
1972 Bob Fosse, *Cabaret*
1973 George Roy Hill, *The Sting*
1974 Francis Ford Coppola, *The Godfather, Part II*
1975 Milos Forman, *One Flew Over the Cuckoo's Nest*
1976 John Avildsen, *Rocky*
1977 Woody Allen, *Annie Hall*
1978 Michael Cimino, *The Deer Hunter*
1979 Robert Benton, *Kramer vs Kramer*
1980 Robert Redford, *Ordinary People*

THE NEW STANDARD
BRITISH FILM AWARDS

Founded in 1973 by London's *Evening News*, the event is held each year. Gold medals are awarded to the Best Film Drama, the Best Film Comedy, the Best Actress and the Best Actor. Silver medals are given to the Best Newcomer Actress and the Best Newcomer Actor. Occasionally there is a special award for films or performances of merit that do not fit into any of the six categories. In 1980 *The New Standard* took over the presentations, and a new Peter Sellers Award for the best contribution to film comedy was introduced.

BEST FILM (DRAMA)
1973 *Ryan's Daughter*
1974 *Live and Let Die*
1975 *Murder on the Orient Express*
1976 *Aces High*
1977 *A Bridge Too Far*
1978 *Star Wars*
1979 *Death on the Nile*
1980 *Yanks*

BEST FILM (COMEDY)
1973 *The National Health*
1974 *The Three Musketeers*
1975 *The Four Musketeers*
1976 *Return of the Pink Panther*
1977 *The Pink Panther Strikes Again*
1978 *Revenge of the Pink Panther*

A scene from Rising Damp *in which Frances de la Tour* (right) *won 'Best Actress' award in* The New Standard *film awards*

1979 *Porridge*
1980 *Rising Damp*

BEST ACTRESS
1973 Glenda Jackson, *Mary Queen of Scots* and *Triple Echo*
1974 Glenda Jackson, *A Touch of Class*
1975 Wendy Hiller, *Murder on the Orient Express*
1976 Annette Crosbie, *Slipper and the Rose*
1977 Billie Whitelaw, *The Omen*
1978 Nanette Newman, *International Velvet*
1979 Maggie Smith, *California Suite* and *Death on the Nile*
1980 Frances de la Tour, *Rising Damp*

BEST ACTOR
1973 Keith Michell, *Henry VIII*
1974 Michael Caine, *Sleuth*
1975 Albert Finney, *Murder on the Orient Express*
1976 Peter Sellers, *Return of the Pink Panther*
1977 John Thaw, *Sweeney!*

Peter Sellers in Return of the Pink Panther *which received* The New Standard *'Best Film (Comedy)' award in 1976*

1978 Alec Guinness, *Star Wars*
1979 Peter Ustinov, *Death on the Nile*
1980 Denholm Elliott, *Rising Damp*

MOST PROMISING NEWCOMER ACTRESS
1973 Lynne Frederick, *Henry VIII* and *The Amazing Mr Blunden*
1974 Heather Wright, *The Belstone Fox*
1975 Jill Townsend, *Alfie Darling*
1976 Gemma Craven, *The Slipper and the Rose*
1977 Lesley-Anne Down, *The Pink Panther Strikes Again*
1978 Lea Brodie, *Warlords of Atlantis*
1979 Karen Dotrice, *The Thirty-Nine Steps*
1980 Wendy Morgan, *Yanks*

MOST PROMISING NEWCOMER ACTOR
1973 Simon Ward, *Young Winston*
1974 Edward Fox, *The Day of the Jackal*

1975 Robin Askwith, *Confessions of a Pop Performer*
1976 Peter Firth, *Aces High*
1977 Dennis Waterman, *Sweeney!*
1978 Michael J. Jackson, *Sweeney 2*
1979 Simon MacCorkindale, *Riddle of the Sands* and *Death on the Nile*
1980 Jonathan Pryce, *Breaking Glass*

SPECIAL AWARDS
1975 Peter Hall, for *Akenfield*
1976 Stuart Cooper, for *Overlord*
1977 James Mason
1978 David Puttnam
1979 Sir John Mills
1980 David Niven

THE PETER SELLERS AWARD
1980 Leonard Rossiter

Circus

CIRCUS WORLD CHAMPIONSHIP
Inaugurated in 1976, the competitions are organised by Circus World Championships Ltd. The world's top circus performers compete in various categories to become world champions. Winners:

1976
Flying trapeze: The Rock Smith Fliers (USA)
High wire: Manfred Doval (Ger)
Trick cycling: The Bertini Family (Cze)
Ground acrobatics: Johnny Hutch's Herculeans (GB)
High school riding: Katja Schumann (Den)

1977
Flying trapeze: The Flying Terrells/Cavarettas (USA)
High wire: Manfred Doval (Ger)
Juggling: Kris Kremo (Swi)
Strong men: Samson and Delilah (GB)
Trick riding: Jerry, Jimmy and Jonny (Swe)

1978
Flying trapeze: The Flying Oslers (SA)
Springboard: The Boitchanovi Troupe (Bul)
Tight wire: Jose Luis Munoz (Spa)
Risley: The Rios Brothers (Fra)
Escapology: Alan Alan (GB)

1979
Flying trapeze: The Flying Jimenez (Mex)
Trick riding: The Enrico Caroli Troupe (Ita)
Juggling: Dick Franco (USA)
Trampoline: The Six Fornasari (USA)

1980
Flying trapeze: The Flying Jimenez (Mex)
             The Flying Michaels (USA)
High wire: Manfred Doval (Ger)
Acrobats: Ariz Family (Ita)
Western: Bobby Roberts, Moira & Co. (GB)

Manfred Doval, world champion on the high wire in 1976, 1977 and 1980

Composers

STROUD FESTIVAL INTERNATIONAL COMPOSERS' COMPETITION

This is one of the well-known musical events in Britain, organised by Stroud Festival Ltd. The competition first started in 1968 – both judges and instruments are changed every year. Winners:

1968 Any instrument and/or voices (not more than six independent parts): Alexander Abercrombie, 'Tempgravure II for String Quartet
1969 Not held
1970 Flute, oboe, clarinet, bassoon, horn (three or five): Keith Robert Clarke, 'Variation Solos for Wind Quintet'
1971 Contralto, oboe, violin, viola and cello: Louis Noel Belauare (Fra), 'Le Tombeau de Louisa Paulin'
1972 Piano, violin and horn: John Hall, 'Trio No. 3'
1973 Clarinet, violins, viola and cello: Julia Usher, 'Encounter'; Dieter Acker (Ger), 'Tirades'
1974 Tenor voice and classical guitar: Christopher Bochmann, 'Complainte de la Lune en Provence'
1975 Violoncello and piano: James A. Rich, 'Concert piece for Cello and Piano'
1976 Piano: James Sellars (USA), 'Sonata for Piano'
1977 Violin, horn and piano: David Harold Cox, 'Trio for Violin, Horn and Piano'
1978 Clarinet and piano: Howard A. Watt, 'Scenes and Soliloquies for clarinet and piano'
1979 Violin and piano: Martin Vaughan Davies, 'Duo for Violin and Piano'
1980 Songs for Baritone voice and piano: Paul Parkinson, 'Love Songs' (Four poems by Richard Hawkins)

MENUHIN PRIZE

This triennial prize for composers is organised jointly by the City of Westminster Arts Council and the Ernest Read Music Association. The winner receives a cash prize of £1000 and a public performance of his work. Winners to date:

1975 Michael Blake Watkins, Woodford Green, Essex, for a concerto for guitar, oboe and orchestra
1978 Adrian Williams, Croxley Green, Rickmansworth, Herts, for Explorations and Metamorphoses Op. 13

Conductors

RUPERT FOUNDATION INTERNATIONAL YOUNG CONDUCTORS' COMPETITION

This competition is held approximately every 18 months in association with the BBC. The 1980 winner received a cash prize of £7500 from the Rupert Foundation, and the BBC offers a variety of work with its symphony orchestras during the year of the scholarship. Candidates of any nationality who have not reached their 29th birthday on the first day of the awards are eligible to compete, but must have had practical experience of conducting. The winners are:

March 1973 Guido Ajmone-Marsan (USA)
November 1974 Marc Soustrot (Fra)
October 1976 Ivan Fischer (Hun)
April 1978 Gerard Akoka (Fra)
January 1980 Israel Edelson (Isr)
           Vladimir Ponkin (USSR)

Ivan Fischer from Hungary, winner of the third competition for young conductors

Conservation

J. PAUL GETTY WILDLIFE CONSERVATION PRIZE

This conservation prize of $50 000 is awarded each year for outstanding achievement in wildlife and habitat conservation of international significance. Both individuals and organisations are eligible. The prize is administered by the World Wildlife Fund – US. Prizes awarded:

1974 Felipe Benavides (Per), conservationist
1975 Salim A. Ali (Ind), ornithologist
1976 Ian R. Grimwood (GB, later Ken), Chief Game Warden in Kenya
1977 No award
1978 No award
1979 Dr Boonsong Lekagul (Tha), conservationist and educator
1980 Harold Coolidge (US), retired Hon. President of IUCN

WORLD WILDLIFE FUND GOLD MEDAL

The award was founded in 1970 and is made annually for highly meritorious services to the conservation of wildlife or natural environments. The Medal is minted as a donation to the Fund by the South African Chamber of Mines. Gold medallists:

1970 Prof. Dr Bernhard Grzimek (Ger)
     Sir Julian Huxley (UK)
     Dr Jacques Verschuren (Bel)
1971 Miss Phyllis Barclay-Smith (UK)
     John S. Owen (UK)
     Dr Jose A. Valverde (Spa)
1972 Prof. Dr Andrey G. Bannikov (USSR)
     Maj. Ian R. Grimwood (Ken)
     Dr Roger Tory Peterson (USA)
1973 Prof Archie Carr (USA)
     Dr Jose C. M. Carvalho (Bra)
     Col. Jack Vincent (SA)

Arjan Singh, recipient of the 1976 World Wildlife Fund Gold Medal, in Dudhwa National Park, India, with his pet tiger

1974 Dr Anne LaBastille (USA)
1975 Michel Anna (Fra)
1976 Arjan Singh (Ind)
1977 Prof. Dr Rudolf Schenkel (Swi)
1978 Guy Mountfort (UK)
1979 Dr Sidney Holt (UK)
1980 Dr George Schaller (USA)
1981 Prof. Dr Jean Jacques Petter (Fra)

Cookery

THE NEW STANDARD GREAT GOURMET COMPETITION

This contest, first held in 1976, is organised by *The New Standard* and sponsored by Mouton Cadet. In 1978 competitors had to identify three mystery recipes, and in the second round 25 winners answered questions about their lunch menu at Mayfair's Greenhouse Restaurant. The champion was later chosen at the Miller Howe Hotel in the Lake District from three finalists who had to identify the ingredients of the following meal: (a) Tomato, apple and celery soup, also containing butter, onion, sherry, chicken stock, cream, sugar, salt and freshly-ground black pepper; (b) Duck liver pies, flavoured with onion, fennel, garlic, marjoram and thyme, with a puff pastry topping and served with purée sprouts cooked in a rich egg custard and sprinkled with finely chopped French beans tossed in walnut oil, cheese and breadcrumbs; and (c) Brown bread and rum cream ice. In 1979 the competition rules were changed – competitors cooked certain specified dishes.

1976 Bill Vellutini of London, a teacher of English at Godolphin and Latymer School.

1977 Judith Hitching is the wife of writer and film producer Francis Hitching and the mother of 3 daughters, and lives in Twickenham.
1978 Sue Morgan of Islington.
1979 Bill Vellutini – again.
1980 No event
1981 Katharine Blakemore, housewife with one son, from Wimbledon.

MEAL OF THE YEAR MENU COMPETITION

This has been organised annually since 1977 by *Caterer & Hotelkeeper* in association with the California Wine Importers Association. A five-course meal is planned for a maximum of 70 people and this is judged on practicality, originality, gastronomic excellence and the balance struck in the menu between food and wine. Winners:

1977 W. O. Barry Gray (chef) and Maj. Sidney Denham (manager). Catering branch HQ Scotland (Army)
1978 Paul Rogerson (chef) and Dick Beach (manager). Station Hotel, Inverness
1979 Clifford Burgess (chef) and Frederick Watts (manager). The Anglesea Restaurant, Portsmouth, Hants.
1980 Alain Cahour (chef) and George Jarvis (manager). Stuart Cabeldu Catering, London

Cricket

SCHWEPPES COUNTY CHAMPIONSHIP

The County championship has been contested by 17 counties since 1921. The method of deciding the champion has changed several times since the championship was first recognised as official in 1890. The list of champions can be extended back to 1864.

1864	Surrey	1897	Lancashire
1865	Nottinghamshire	1898	Yorkshire
1866	Middlesex	1899	Surrey
1867	Yorkshire	1900	Yorkshire
1868	Nottinghamshire	1901	Yorkshire
1869	{ Nottinghamshire / Yorkshire	1902	Yorkshire
		1903	Middlesex
1870	Yorkshire	1904	Lancashire
1871	Nottinghamshire	1905	Yorkshire
1872	Nottinghamshire	1906	Kent
1873	{ Gloucestershire / Nottinghamshire	1907	Nottinghamshire
		1908	Yorkshire
1874	Gloucestershire	1909	Kent
1875	Nottinghamshire	1910	Kent
1876	Gloucestershire	1911	Warwickshire
1877	Gloucestershire	1912	Yorkshire
1878	Undecided	1913	Kent
1879	{ Nottinghamshire / Lancashire	1914	Surrey
		1919	Yorkshire
1880	Nottinghamshire	1920	Middlesex
1881	Lancashire	1921	Middlesex
1882	{ Nottinghamshire / Lancashire	1922	Yorkshire
		1923	Yorkshire
1883	Nottinghamshire	1924	Yorkshire
1884	Nottinghamshire	1925	Yorkshire
1885	Nottinghamshire	1926	Lancashire
1886	Nottinghamshire	1927	Lancashire
1887	Surrey	1928	Lancashire
1888	Surrey	1929	Nottinghamshire
1889	{ Surrey / Lancashire / Nottinghamshire	1930	Lancashire
		1931	Yorkshire
		1932	Yorkshire
1890	Surrey	1933	Yorkshire
1891	Surrey	1934	Lancashire
1892	Surrey	1935	Yorkshire
1893	Yorkshire	1936	Derbyshire
1894	Surrey	1937	Yorkshire
1895	Surrey	1938	Yorkshire
1896	Yorkshire	1939	Yorkshire

1946	Yorkshire	1963	Yorkshire
1947	Middlesex	1964	Worcestershire
1948	Glamorgan	1965	Worcestershire
1949	{ Middlesex / Yorkshire	1966	Yorkshire
		1967	Yorkshire
1950	{ Lancashire / Surrey	1968	Yorkshire
		1969	Glamorgan
1951	Warwickshire	1970	Kent
1952	Surrey	1971	Surrey
1953	Surrey	1972	Warwickshire
1954	Surrey	1973	Hampshire
1955	Surrey	1974	Worcestershire
1956	Surrey	1975	Leicestershire
1957	Surrey	1976	Middlesex
1958	Surrey	1977	{ Middlesex / Kent
1959	Yorkshire		
1960	Yorkshire	1978	Kent
1961	Hampshire	1979	Essex
1962	Yorkshire	1980	Middlesex

ONE-DAY COMPETITIONS
GILLETTE CUP

First held 1963, the Gillette Cup was contested on a knock-out basis by the 17 first-class counties and the top five minor counties. Matches are played with 60 overs per side. From 1981 renamed the NatWest Bank Trophy.

1963–64 Sussex
1965 Yorkshire
1966 Warwickshire
1967 Kent
1968 Warwickshire
1969 Yorkshire
1970–72 Lancashire
1973 Gloucestershire
1974 Kent
1975 Lancashire
1976 Northamptonshire
1977 Middlesex
1978 Sussex
1979 Somerset
1980 Middlesex

PRUDENTIAL WORLD CUP

Contested by the leading cricketing nations.

First held 1975.

1975 West Indies
1979 West Indies

JOHN PLAYER LEAGUE
First held in 1969, the John Player League is contested by the 17 first-class counties on an all-play-all basis of 40-over matches.

1969–70 Lancashire
1971 Worcestershire
1972–73 Kent
1974 Leicestershire
1975 Hampshire
1976 Kent
1977 Leicestershire
1978 Hampshire
1979 Somerset
1980 Warwickshire

BENSON & HEDGES CUP
First held in 1972, the Benson & Hedges Cup is contested on a zonal, followed by a knock-out basis by the 17 first-class counties, a combined team from Oxford and Cambridge Universities and by two minor counties representative teams. Matches played at 55 overs.

1972 Leicestershire
1973 Kent
1974 Surrey
1975 Leicestershire
1976 Kent
1977 Gloucestershire
1978 Kent
1979 Essex
1980 Northamptonshire

YOUNG CRICKETER OF THE YEAR
Annual trophy awarded by the Cricket Writers Club.

1950 Roy Tattersall (Lancashire)
1951 Peter May (Surrey)
1952 Freddie Trueman (Yorkshire)
1953 Colin Cowdrey (Kent)

Alan Knott whips off the bails but Zaheer Abbas has made his ground. John Edrich is in the background

1954 Peter Loader (Surrey)
1955 Ken Barrington (Surrey)
1956 Brian Taylor (Essex)
1957 Michael Stewart (Surrey)
1958 Colin Ingleby-Mackenzie (Hampshire)
1959 Geoff Pullar (Lancashire)
1960 David Allen (Gloucestershire)
1961 Peter Parfitt (Middlesex)
1962 Phil Sharpe (Yorkshire)
1963 Geoff Boycott (Yorkshire)
1964 Michael Brearley (Middlesex)
1965 Alan Knott (Kent)
1966 Derek Underwood (Kent)
1967 Tony Greig (Sussex)
1968 Bob Cottam (Hampshire)
1969 Alan Ward (Derbyshire)
1970 Chris Old (Yorkshire)
1971 John Whitehouse (Warwickshire)
1972 Dudley Owen-Thomas (Surrey)
1973 Michael Hendrick (Derbyshire)
1974 Philippe Edmonds (Middlesex)
1975 Andrew Kennedy (Lancashire)
1976 Geoff Miller (Derbyshire)
1977 Ian Botham (Somerset)
1978 David Gower (Leicestershire)
1979 Paul Parker (Sussex)
1980 Graham Dilley (Kent)

SHEFFIELD SHIELD
The Australian state championship for the Sheffield Shield is contested annually. First held in the 1892–93 season following the gift of the trophy by Lord Sheffield to the Australian Cricket Council. Winners (year shown is that of second half of each season):

Victoria
1893, 1895, 1898–99, 1901, 1908, 1915, 1922, 1924–25, 1928, 1930–31, 1934–35, 1937, 1947, 1951, 1963, 1967, 1970, 1974, 1979–80.
South Australia
1894, 1910, 1913, 1927, 1936, 1939, 1953, 1964, 1969, 1971, 1976
New South Wales
1896–97, 1900, 1902–7, 1909, 1911–12, 1914, 1920–21, 1923, 1926, 1929, 1932–33, 1938, 1940, 1949–50, 1952, 1954–62, 1965–66
Western Australia
1948, 1968, 1972–3, 1975, 1977–78, 1981

CURRIE CUP
The Cup was presented by Sir Donald Currie and first contested in 1889–90. Competing teams are from the South African provinces and Rhodesia. In some seasons the event has not been held due to the presence of an overseas touring team. Winners (year shown is that of second half of each season, = tied for championship):

Transvaal
1890, 1895, 1903–05, 1907, 1922(=), 1924, 1926–27, 1930, 1935, 1938(=), 1951, 1959, 1966(=), 1969, 1970(=), 1971–73, 1979–80
Griqualand West
1891

Western Province
1893–94, 1897–98, 1909, 1921, 1922(=), 1932, 1953, 1956, 1970(=), 1975, 1978
Natal
1911, 1913, 1922(=), 1934, 1937, 1938(=), 1947–48, 1952, 1955, 1960–61, 1963–64, 1966(=), 1967–68, 1974, 1976–77, 1981

SHELL SHIELD
The Shell Shield, first held in 1966 and held annually since then except for 1968, is contested by the West Indian nations. Winners (=tied for championship):

Barbados
1966–67, 1972, 1974, 1976(=), 1977–80

Jamaica	*Combined Islands*
1969	1981

Trinidad & Tobago
1970–71, 1976(=)
Guyana
1973, 1975

PLUNKET SHIELD
From the 1906–7 season until 1974–75 the New Zealand provinces contested the Plunket Shield, a trophy presented by Lord Plunket. From 1906 to 1921 the trophy was contested on a challenge basis. Since then winners have been (year shown is that of second half of each season):

Auckland
1922, 1927, 1929, 1934, 1937–40, 1947, 1959, 1964, 1969
Canterbury
1923, 1931, 1935, 1946, 1949, 1952, 1956, 1960, 1965
Wellington
1924, 1926, 1928, 1930, 1932, 1936, 1950, 1955, 1957, 1961–62, 1966, 1973, 1974
Otago
1925, 1933, 1948, 1951, 1953, 1958, 1970, 1972, 1975
Central Districts
1954, 1967–68, 1971
Northern Districts
1963

SHELL TROPHY
From the 1975–76 cricket season in New Zealand, the Shell Series replaced the Plunket Shield. Winners of the Shell trophy (year shown is that of second half of each season):

1976 Canterbury	1979 Otago
1977 Otago	1980 Northern Districts
1978 Auckland	1981 Auckland

RANJI TROPHY
The Ranji Trophy, established in memory of K. S. Ranjitsinhji, is contested by the Indian states and provinces. First held in 1934–35 season. (Year shown is that of second half of each season.)

Most wins have been achieved by Bombay:
1935–36, 1942, 1945, 1949, 1952, 1954, 1956–57, 1959–73, 1975–77, 1981
Other winners in recent years:

1958 Baroda, 1974 Karnataka, 1978 Karnataka, 1979 Delhi, 1980 Delhi

TEST CRICKET
The first Test Match was played between England and Australia in 1876 at Melbourne. Winners of Test series:

ENGLAND v AUSTRALIA

Season	Won by Eng.	Won by Aus.	Drawn
1876–77	1	1	0
1878–79	0	1	0
1880	1	0	0
1881–82	0	2	2
1882	0	1	0
1882–83	2	2	0
1884	1	0	2
1884–85	3	2	0
1886	3	0	0
1886–87	2	0	0
1887–88	1	0	0
1888	2	1	0
1890	2	0	0
1891–92	1	2	0
1893	1	0	2
1894–95	3	2	0
1896	2	1	0
1897–98	1	4	0
1899	0	1	4
1901–02	1	4	0
1902	1	2	2
1903–04	3	2	0
1905	2	0	3
1907–08	1	4	0
1909	1	2	2
1911–12	4	1	0
1912	1	0	2
1920–21	0	5	0
1921	0	3	2
1924–25	1	4	0
1926	1	0	4
1928–29	4	1	0
1930	1	2	2
1932–33	4	1	0
1934	1	2	2
1936–37	2	3	0
1938	1	1	2
1946–47	0	3	2
1948	0	4	1
1950–51	1	4	0
1953	1	0	4
1954–55	3	1	1
1956	2	1	2
1958–59	0	4	1
1961	1	2	2
1962–63	1	1	3
1964	0	1	4
1965–66	1	1	3
1968	1	1	3
1970–71	2	0	4
1972	2	2	1
1974–75	1	4	1
1975	0	1	3
1976–77	0	1	0
1977	3	0	2
1978–79	5	1	0
1979–80	0	3	0
1980	0	1	0
Total	79	93	68

Geoff Boycott, Young Cricketer of 1963, in the England vs *Australia match in August 1980* (Sporting Pictures)

Summary of other Test series showing number of wins to each country and the number of draws:

England 46	South Africa 18	Drawn 38
England 21	West Indies 25	Drawn 34
England 27	New Zealand 1	Drawn 25
England 27	India 7	Drawn 24
England 11	Pakistan 1	Drawn 21
Australia 29	South Africa 11	Drawn 13
Australia 25	West Indies 12	Drawn 11
		Tied 1
Australia 7	New Zealand 1	Drawn 4
Australia 19	India 7	Drawn 6
Australia 7	Pakistan 4	Drawn 6
South Africa 9	New Zealand 2	Drawn 6
West Indies 5	New Zealand 3	Drawn 9
West Indies 17	India 5	Drawn 21
West Indies 7	Pakistan 4	Drawn 8
New Zealand 4	India 10	Drawn 11
New Zealand 1	Pakistan 8	Drawn 12
India 4	Pakistan 3	Drawn 17

(As at 1 July 1981)

WOMEN'S CRICKET

WORLD CUP
First held in 1973. Winners:

1973 England
1978 Australia

SUNDAY TELEGRAPH/VICTORIA WINE CRICKETER OF THE SEASON
Voted by readers of the *Sunday Telegraph*.

1978 Ian Botham (Somerset/England)
1979 Mike Proctor (Gloucester/South Africa)
1980 Vivian Richards (Somerset/West Indies)

CRICKETERS' CRICKETER OF THE YEAR
Voted annually since 1969 by county cricketers as their player of the year, the winners receive the Reg Hayter Cup. Winners:

1969 Mike Proctor (Gloucs)
1970 Jack Bond (Lancs)
1971 Lance Gibbs (Warwicks)
1972 Barry Stead (Notts)
1973 Peter Lee (Lancs)
1974 Andy Roberts (Hants)
1975 Peter Lee (Lancs)

1976 Zaheer Abbas (Gloucs)
1977 Mike Proctor (Gloucs)
1978 John Lever (Essex)
1979 John Lever (Essex)
1980 Robin Jackman (Surrey)

NATIONAL VILLAGE CHAMPIONSHIP

There are about 800 entries per year for this championship which was first held in 1972. For the first six years it was sponsored by John Haig and Co, for the following year *The Cricketer* and then by Whitbread and Co. It is now known as the Samuel Whitbread Village Cricket Championship, and organised by *The Cricketer*. Winners:

1972 Troon
1973 Troon
1974 Bomarsund
1975 Gowerton
1976 Troon
1977 Cookley
1978 Linton Park

1979 East Bierley
1980 Marchwiel

NATIONAL CLUB CRICKET CHAMPIONSHIP

This national competition was first played for the Derrick Robins Trophy in 1969. It is now organised by the National Cricket Association and played for the John Haig Trophy, with an annual entry of over 500 clubs. Winners:

1969 Hampstead
1970 Cheltenham
1971 Blackheath
1972 Scarborough
1973 Wolverhampton
1974 Sunbury
1975 York
1976 Scarborough
1977 Southgate
1978 Cheltenham
1979 Scarborough
1980 Moseley

Croquet

MACROBERTSON INTERNATIONAL SHIELD

Contested periodically by Great Britain, New Zealand and Australia.

1925 Great Britain	1956 Great Britain
1928 Australia	1963 Great Britain
1930 Australia	1969 Great Britain
1935 Australia	1974 Great Britain
1937 Great Britain	1979 New Zealand
1950 New Zealand	

THE OPEN CROQUET CHAMPIONSHIP

First held in 1867. Most wins:

10 John W. Solomon: 1953, 1956, 1959, 1961, 1963–68
7 Humphrey Hicks: 1932, 1939, 1947–50, 1952
5 Cyril Corbally: 1902–3, 1906, 1908, 1913

Most wins by a woman:

4 Dorothy Steel: 1925, 1933, 1935–36

Cross-Country Running

INTERNATIONAL/WORLD CROSS-COUNTRY CHAMPIONSHIP

The International Cross-Country Championship was instituted at Hamilton Park Racecourse, Glasgow, Scotland in 1903. The four British countries competed first, with France competing in 1907 for the first time. Increasingly the event became international, and this process was completed when the IAAF included it in its jurisdiction from 1973.

Individual winners and team winners:

MEN

	Individual	Team
1903	Alfred Shrubb (Eng)	England
1904	Alfred Shrubb (Eng)	England
1905	Albert Aldridge (Eng)	England
1906	Charles Straw (Eng)	England
1907	A. Underwood (Eng)	England
1908	Archie Robertson (Eng)	England
1909	Edward Wood (Eng)	England
1910	Edward Wood (Eng)	England
1911	Jean Bouin (Fra)	England
1912	Jean Bouin (Fra)	England
1913	Jean Bouin (Fra)	England
1914	Arthur Nicholls (Eng)	England
1920	James Wilson (Sco)	England
1921	Walter Freeman (Eng)	England
1922	Joseph Guillemot (Fra)	France
1923	Charles Blewitt (Eng)	France
1924	William Cotterell (Eng)	England
1925	Jack Webster (Eng)	England
1926	Ernest Harper (Eng)	France
1927	L. Payne (Eng)	France
1928	H. Eckersley (Eng)	France
1929	William Cotterell (Eng)	France
1930	Thomas Evenson (Eng)	England
1931	Tim Smythe (Ire)	England
1932	Thomas Evenson (Eng)	England
1933	Jack Holden (Eng)	England
1934	Jack Holden (Eng)	England

73

Alain Mimoun shares most wins in the International Cross-Country Championship. Here he leads Ken Norris in the 1958 race

1935	Jack Holden (Eng)	England
1936	William Eaton (Eng)	England
1937	James Flockhart (Sco)	England
1938	John Emery (Eng)	England
1939	Jack Holden (Eng)	France
1946	Raphael Pujazon (Fra)	France
1947	Raphael Pujazon (Fra)	France
1948	John Doms (Bel)	Belgium
1949	Alain Mimoun (Fra)	France
1950	Lucien Theys (Bel)	France
1951	Geoffrey Saunders (Eng)	England
1952	Alain Mimoun (Fra)	France
1953	Franjo Mihalic (Yug)	England
1954	Alain Mimoun (Fra)	England
1955	Frank Sando (Eng)	England
1956	Alain Mimoun (Fra)	France
1957	Frank Sando (Eng)	Belgium
1958	Stanley Eldon (Eng)	England
1959	Fred Norris (Eng)	England

1960	Abdesselem Rhadi (Fra)	England
1961	Basil Heatley (Eng)	Belgium
1962	Gaston Roelants (Bel)	England
1963	Roy Fowler (Eng)	Belgium
1964	Francesco Arizmendi (Spa)	England
1965	Jean Fayolle (Fra)	England
1966	Ben Assou El Ghazi (Mor)	England
1967	Gaston Roelants (Bel)	England
1968	Mohamed Gammoudi (Tun)	England
1969	Gaston Roelants (Bel)	England
1970	Michael Tagg (Eng)	England
1971	David Bedford (Eng)	England
1972	Gaston Roelants (Bel)	England
1973	Pekka Paivarinta (Fin)	Belgium
1974	Eric De Beck (Bel)	Belgium
1975	Ian Stewart (Sco)	New Zealand
1976	Carlos Lopes (Por)	England
1977	Leon Schots (Bel)	Belgium
1978	John Treacy (Ire)	France
1979	John Treacy (Ire)	England
1980	Craig Virgin (USA)	England
1981	Craig Virgin (USA)	Ethiopia

WOMEN (race first held 1967)

	Individual	*Team*
1967	Doris Brown (USA)	England
1968	Doris Brown (USA)	USA
1969	Doris Brown (USA)	USA
1970	Doris Brown (USA)	England
1971	Doris Brown (USA)	England
1972	Joyce Smith (Eng)	England
1973	Paola Cacchi (Ita)	England
1974	Paola Cacchi (Ita)	England
1975	Julie Brown (USA)	USA
1976	Carmen Valero (Spa)	USSR
1977	Carmen Valero (Spa)	USSR
1978	Grete Waitz (Nor)	Romania
1970	Grete Waitz (Nor)	USA
1980	Grete Waitz (Nor)	USSR
1981	Grete Waitz (Nor)	USSR

Crosswords

LANGS SUPREME *TIMES* NATIONAL CROSSWORD CHAMPIONSHIP

This crossword competition attracts over 3000 entries. After an initial qualifying round, competitors are obliged to complete four puzzles under gruelling examination conditions. Dr Sykes has won the competition six times, having entered it eight times, and in 1980 completed the four *Times* Crosswords in 37½ minutes.

1970	Roy Dean	1976	James Atkins
1971	James Atkins	1977	Dr John Sykes
1972	Dr John Sykes	1978	Eric Rodick
1973	Dr John Sykes	1979	Roy Dean
1974	Dr John Sykes	1980	Dr John Sykes
1975	Dr John Sykes		

The championship trophy

Curling

MEN'S WORLD CHAMPIONSHIPS
Contested for the Scotch Cup from 1959 and
for the Air Canada Silver Broom from 1968.

1959 Canada	1965 USA	1971 Canada	1976 USA
1960 Canada	1966 Canada	1972 Canada	1977 Sweden
1961 Canada	1967 Scotland	1973 Sweden	1978 USA
1962 Canada	1968 Canada	1974 USA	1979 Norway
1963 Canada	1969 Canada	1975 Switzerland	1980 Canada
1964 Canada	1970 Canada		

WOMEN'S WORLD CHAMPIONSHIPS

1980 Canada

Custard Pies

THE WORLD CUSTARD PIE THROWING CHAMPIONSHIP

This event is held annually at the Coxheath
Fete. A number of teams enter, complying
with the strict rules of the game. The target
(face) must be 8 ft 3¼ in from the thrower who
must throw a pie, with his left hand, which is
no more than 10¼ in in diameter. Winners
since inception in 1968:

1968 Custard Kings
1969 Coxheath Men

1970 Coxheath Men
1971 The Birds
1972 The Birds
1973 The Bashers
1974 The Clowns
1975 The Hadlow Haystackers
1976 The Magnificent Seven
1977 The Kent Messenger Girls
1978 Anglian Angels
1979 Anglian Angels
1980 The Flobbs
1981 The Flobbs

A scene from the World Custard Pie Throwing Championship

Cycling

WORLD CHAMPIONSHIPS

The first cycling world championships were held for amateurs in 1893, and the first for professionals in 1895. Champions at each event since 1970 (with the cyclists to have won most titles) have been:

MEN
PROFESSIONAL
Sprint
1970 Gordon Johnson (Aus)
1971 Leijin Loeveseijn (Hol)
1972 Robert van Lancker (Bel)
1973 Robert van Lancker (Bel)
1974 Peder Pedersen (Den)
1975 John Nicholson (Aus)
1976 John Nicholson (Aus)
1977 Koichi Nakano (Jap)
1978 Koichi Nakano (Jap)
1979 Koichi Nakano (Jap)
1980 Koichi Nakano (Jap)

Most wins:
7 Jeff Scherens (Bel) 1932–37, 1947; Antonio Maspes (Ita) 1955–56, 1959–62, 1964

Pursuit
1970 Hugh Porter (GB)
1971 Dirk Baert (Bel)
1972 Hugh Porter (GB)
1973 Hugh Porter (GB)
1974 Roy Schuiten (Hol)
1975 Roy Schuiten (Hol)
1976 Francesco Moser (Ita)
1977 Gregor Braun (Ger)
1978 Gregor Braun (Ger)
1979 'Bert' Oosterbosch (Hol)
1980 Tony Doyle (GB)

Most wins:
4 Hugh Porter (GB) 1968, 1970, 1972–73

Motor paced
1970 Ehrenfried Rudolph (Ger)
1971 Theo Verscheuren (Bel)
1972 Theo Verscheuren (Bel)
1973 Cornelius Stam (Hol)
1974 Cornelius Stam (Hol)
1975 Dieter Kemper (Ger)
1976 Wilfried Peffgen (Ger)
1977 Cees Stam (Hol)
1978 Wilfried Peffgen (Ger)
1979 Martin Venix (Hol)
1980 Wilfried Peffgen (Ger)

Most wins:
6 Guillermo Timoner (Spa) 1955, 1959–60, 1962, 1964–65

Road race
1970 Jean-Pierre Monsere (Bel)
1971 Eddy Merckx (Bel)
1972 Marino Basso (Ita)
1973 Felice Gimondi (Ita)
1974 Eddy Merckx (Bel)
1975 Hennie Kuiper (Hol)
1976 Freddy Maertens (Bel)
1977 Francesco Moser (Ita)
1978 Gerrie Kneteman (Hol)
1979 Jaan Raas (Hol)
1980 Bernard Hinault (Fra)

Most wins:
3 Alfredo Dinda (Ita) 1927, 1930, 1932; Henri van Steenbergen (Bel) 1949, 1956–57; Eddy Merckx (Bel) 1967, 1971, 1974

AMATEUR (*Olympic titles in Olympic years)
Sprint
1970 Daniel Morelon (Fra)
1971 Daniel Morelon (Fra)
1972* Daniel Morelon (Fra)
1973 Daniel Morelon (Fra)
1974 Anton Tkac (Cze)
1975 Daniel Morelon (Fra)
1976* Anton Tkac (Cze)
1977 Hans-Jurgen Geschke (GDR)
1978 Anton Tkac (Cze)
1979 Lutz Hesslich (GDR)
1980* Lutz Hesslich (GDR)

Most wins:
8 Daniel Morelon (Fra) 1966–67, 1969–73, 1975

Pursuit
1970 Xavier Kurmann (Swi)
1971 Martin Rodriguez (Col)
1972* Knut Knudsen (Nor)
1973 Knut Knudsen (Nor)
1974 Hans Lutz (Ger)
1975 Thomas Huschke (GDR)
1976* Gregor Braun (Ger)
1977 Norbert Durpisch (GDR)
1978 Detlef Macha (GDR)
1979 Nikolay Makarov (USSR)
1980* Robert Dill-Bundi (Swi)

Most wins:
3 Guido Messina (Ita) 1947–48, 1953; Tieme Groen (Hol) 1964–66

Team pursuit
1970 W. Germany
1971 Italy
1972* W. Germany
1973 W. Germany
1974 W. Germany
1975 W. Germany
1976* W. Germany
1977 GDR
1978 GDR
1979 GDR
1980* USSR

Most wins:
8 Italy (1920*, 1924*, 1928*, 1932*, 1952*, 1956*, 1960*, 1971)

1000 metres time trial
1970 Niels Fredborg (Den)
1971 Eduard Rapp (USSR)
1972* Niels Fredborg (Den)
1973 Jan Kierzkowski (Pol)

1974 Eduard Rapp (USSR)
1975 Klaus-Jurgen Grünke (GDR)
1976* Klaus-Jurgen Grünke (GDR)
1977 Lothar Thoms (GDR)
1978 Lothar Thoms (GDR)
1979 Lothar Thoms (GDR)
1980* Lothar Thoms (GDR)

Most wins:
4 Niels Fredborg (Den) 1967–68, 1970, 1972; Lothar Thoms (GDR) 1977–80

Team time trial (road)
1970 USSR
1971 Belgium
1972* USSR
1973 Poland
1974 Sweden
1975 Poland
1976* USSR
1977 USSR
1978 Holland
1979 GDR
1980* USSR

Most wins:
5 USSR (as above)

Road race
1970 Joergen Schmidt (Den)
1971 Regis Ovion (Fra)
1972* Hennie Kuiper (Hol)
1973 Ryszard Szurkowski (Pol)
1974 Janusz Kowalski (Pol)
1975 Adrianus Gevers (Hol)
1976* Bernt Johansson (Swe)
1977 Claudio Corti (Ita)
1978 Gilbert Glaus (Swi)
1979 Gianni Giacomini (Ita)
1980* Sergei Sukhorushenkov (USSR)

Most wins:
2 Giuseppe Martano (Ita) 1930, 1932; Gustav Adolf Schur (GDR) 1958–59

Motor paced
1970 Cees Stam (Hol)
1971 Horst Gnas (Ger)
1972 Horst Gnas (Ger)
1973 Horst Gnas (Ger)
1974 Jean Breuer (Ger)
1975 Gaby Minneboo (Hol)
1976 Gaby Minneboo (Hol)
1977 Gaby Minneboo (Hol)
1978 Rainer Podlesch (Ger)
1979 Matthieu Pronk (Hol)
1980 Gaby Minneboo (Hol)

Most wins:
7 Leon Meredith (GB) 1904–5, 1907–9, 1911, 1913

Tandem sprint
1970 Jürgen Barth and Rainer Muller (Ger)
1971 Hans-Jurgen Geschke and Werner Otto (GDR)
1972 Vladimir Sements and Igor Tselovalnikov (USSR)*
1973 Vladimir Vackar and Miroslav Vymazal (Cze)
1974 Vladimir Vackar and Miroslav Vymazal (Cze)
1975 Not held
1976 Benedykt Kokot and Janusz Kotlinski (Pol)

1977 Vladimir Vackar and Miroslav Vymazal (Cze)
1978 Vladimir Vackar and Miroslav Vymazal (Cze)
1979 Yave Cahard and Frank Dépine (Fra)
1980 Ivan Kucirek and Pavel Martinek (Cze)

Most wins:
4 Vladimir Vackar and Miroslav Vymazal (Cze) 1973–74, 1977–78

WOMEN
Sprint
1970 Galina Tsareva (USSR)
1971 Galina Tsareva (USSR)
1972 Galina Yermolayeva (USSR)
1973 Sheila Young (USA)
1974 Tamara Piltsikova (USSR)
1975 Sue Novarra (USA)
1976 Sheila Young (USA)
1977 Galina Tsareva (USSR)
1978 Galina Tsareva (USSR)
1979 Galina Tsareva (USSR)
1980 Sue Novarra/Reber (USA)

Most wins:
6 Galina Yermolayeva (USSR) 1958–61, 1963, 1972; Galina Tsareva (USSR) 1969–71, 1977–79

Pursuit
1970 Tamara Garkushina (USSR)
1971 Tamara Garkushina (USSR)
1972 Tamara Garkushina (USSR)
1973 Tamara Garkushina (USSR)
1974 Tamara Garkushina (USSR)
1975 Keetie van Oosten Hage (Hol)
1976 Keetie van Oosten Hage (Hol)
1977 Vera Kuznyetsova (USSR)
1978 Keetie van Oosten Hage (Hol)
1979 Keetie van Oosten Hage (Hol)
1980 Nadyezhda Kibardina (USSR)

Most wins:
6 Tamara Garkushina (USSR) 1967, 1970–74

Road
1970 Anna Konkina (USSR)
1971 Anna Konkina (USSR)
1972 Genevieve Gambillon (Fra)
1973 Nicole van den Broeck (Bel)
1974 Genevieve Gambillon (Fra)
1975 Trijnte Fopma (Hol)
1976 Keetie van Oosten Hage (Hol)
1977 Josiane Bost (Fra)
1978 Beate Habetz (Ger)
1979 Petra de Bruin (Hol)
1980 Beth Heiden (USA)

Most wins:
4 Yvonne Reynders (Bel) 1959, 1961, 1963, 1966

TOUR DE FRANCE
Perhaps the greatest French sporting event, the Tour de France is a stage race all round France, and in some cases into the surrounding countries. Individual winners since the race's inception in 1903:

1903 Maurice Garin (Fra)
1904 Henri Cornet (Fra)
1905 Louis Trousselier (Fra)
1906 René Pottier (Fra)
1907 Lucien Petit-Breton (Fra)

Jacques Anquetil in the third of his four Tour de France wins (UPI)

1949 Fausto Coppi (Ita)
1950 Ferdinand Kubler (Swi)
1951 Hugo Koblet (Swi)
1952 Fausto Coppi (Ita)
1953 Louison Bobet (Fra)
1954 Louison Bobet (Fra)
1955 Louison Bobet (Fra)
1956 Roger Walkowiak (Fra)
1957 Jacques Anquetil (Fra)
1958 Charly Gaul (Lux)
1959 Federico Bahamontes (Spa)
1960 Gastone Nencini (Ita)
1961 Jacques Anquetil (Fra)
1962 Jacques Anquetil (Fra)
1963 Jacques Anquetil (Fra)
1964 Jacques Anquetil (Fra)
1965 Felice Gimondi (Ita)
1966 Lucien Aimar (Fra)
1967 Roger Pingeon (Fra)
1968 Jan Janssen (Hol)
1969 Eddy Merckx (Bel)
1970 Eddy Merckx (Bel)
1971 Eddy Merckx (Bel)
1972 Eddy Merckx (Bel)
1973 Luis Ocana (Spa)
1974 Eddy Merckx (Bel)
1975 Bernard Thevenet (Fra)
1976 Lucien van Impe (Bel)
1977 Bernard Thevenet (Fra)
1978 Bernard Hinault (Fra)
1979 Bernard Hinault (Fra)
1980 Joop Zoetemilk (Hol)

TOUR OF BRITAIN

The Tour of Britain (best known as the Mil▌ Race), first held in 1951, is a stage race fo▌ amateurs.

1908 Lucien Petit-Breton (Fra)
1909 François Faber (Lux)
1910 Octave Lapize (Fra)
1911 Gustave Garrigou (Fra)
1912 Odile Defraye (Bel)
1913 Philippe Thys (Bel)
1914 Philippe Thys (Bel)
1919 Firmin Lambot (Bel)
1920 Philippe Thys (Bel)
1921 Léon Scieur (Bel)
1922 Firmin Lambot (Bel)
1923 Henri Pelissier (Fra)
1924 Ottavio Bottecchia (Ita)
1925 Ottavio Bottecchia (Ita)
1926 Lucien Buysse (Bel)
1927 Nicholas Frantz (Lux)
1928 Nicholas Frantz (Lux)
1929 Maurice Dewaele (Bel)
1930 André Leducq (Fra)
1931 Antonin Magne (Fra)
1932 André Leducq (Fra)
1933 Georges Speicher (Fra)
1934 Antonin Magne (Fra)
1935 Romain Maes (Bel)
1936 Sylvere Maes (Bel)
1937 Roger Lapebie (Fra)
1938 Gino Bartali (Ita)
1939 Sylvere Maes (Bel)
1947 Jean Robic (Fra)
1948 Gino Bartali (Ita)

	Individual	*Team*
1951	Ian Steel (GB)	Viking
1952	Kenneth Russell (GB)	BSA
1953	Gordon Thomas (GB)	Wearwell
1954	Eugene Tamburlini (Fra)	France
1955	Anthony Hewson (GB)	Viking
1956–57	Not held	
1958	Richard Durlacher (Aut)	Belgium
1959	Bill Bradley (GB)	Belgium
1960	Bill Bradley (GB)	England
1961	Billy Holmes (GB)	Northern
1962	Eugen Pokorny (Pol)	England
1963	Peter Chisman (GB)	Poland
1964	Arthur Metcalfe (GB)	England
1965	Les West (GB)	Poland
1966	Josef Gawliczek (Pol)	USSR
1967	Les West (GB)	USSR
1968	Gosta Pettersson (Swe)	USSR
1969	Fedor Den Hertog (Hol)	Poland
1970	Jiri Mainus (Cze)	Poland
1971	Fedor Den Hertog (Hol)	Holland
1972	Hennie Kuiper (Hol)	Holland
1973	Piet van Katwijk (Hol)	Sweden
1974	Roy Schuiten (Hol)	Holland
1975	Bernt Johansson (Swe)	Czechoslovakia
1976	Bill Nickson (GB)	Great Britain
1977	Said Gusseinov (USSR)	USSR
1978	Jan Brzezny (Pol)	USSR
1979	Yuriy Kachinine (USSR)	USSR
1980	Ivan Mitchtenko (USSR)	USSR
1981	Sergei Krivocheev (USSR)	USSR

Cyclo-Cross

WORLD CHAMPIONSHIPS

The first cross-country world championships were held in 1950 and since 1967 have been divided into amateur and professional categories

OPEN (1950–66)
1950 Jean Robic (Fra)
1951–53 Roger Rondeaux (Fra)
1954–58 André Dufraisse (Fra)
1959 Renato Longo (Ita)
1960–61 Rolf Wolfshohl (Ger)
1962 Renato Longo (Ita)
1963 Rolf Wolfshohl (Ger)
1964–65 Renato Longo (Ita)
1966 Eric de Vlaeminck (Bel)

AMATEUR
1967 Michel Pelchat (Fra)
1968 Roger de Vlaeminck (Bel)
1969 René Declercq (Bel)
1970–71 Robert Vermeier (Bel)
1972 Norbert de Deckere (Bel)
1973 Klaus-Peter Thaler (Ger)
1974–75 Robert Vermeier (Bel)
1976 Klaus-Peter Thaler (Ger)
1977 Robert Vermeier (Bel)
1978 Roland Liboton (Bel)
1979 Vito di Tano (Ita)
1980 Fritz Saladin (Swi)
1981 Milos Fisera (Cze)

PROFESSIONAL
1967 Renato Longo (Ita)
1968–73 Eric de Vlaeminck (Bel)
1974 Albert Van Damme (Bel)
1975 Roger de Vlaeminck (Bel)
1976–79 Albert Zweifel (Swi)
1980 Roland Liboton (Bel)
1981 Johannes Stamsnijder (Hol)

Dancing

CARL ALAN AWARDS

Originated in 1954 by Eric D. Morley, over 300 Carl Alans have been presented to date. The awards cover amateur and professional ballroom dancers, formation team coaches, dance teachers, band leaders, groups, and singers.

BALLROOM DANCING

The following are the major championships and their winners since 1970, organised by Mecca.

WORLD AMATEUR MODERN DANCING CHAMPIONSHIP
Held since 1959
1970 Richard Gleave and Janet Wade
1971 Byron Charlton and Maureen Alexander
1972 Michael Barr and Vicky Green
1973 Michael Barr and Vicky Green
1974 Frank Venables and Linda Horwood
1975 Glen and Lynette Boyce
1976 Bob and Barbara Grover
1977 Greg Smith and Marion Alleyne
1978 Stephen and Lindsay Hillier
1979 Stephen and Lindsay Hillier

Anne and Hans Laxholme from Denmark, winners of the 1980 World Amateur Modern Dancing Championship

1980 Anne and Hans Laxholme
1981 Kenny Welsh and Kathy Gilmartin

WORLD AMATEUR LATIN DANCING CHAMPIONSHIP
Held since 1961
1970 Peter Neubeck and H. Kaufmann
1971 Peter Neubeck and H. Kaufmann
1972 Alan and Hazel Fletcher
1973 Alan and Hazel Fletcher
1974 Peter Maxwell and Lyn Harman
1975 Ian and Ruth Walker
1976 Espen and Kirsten Salberg
1977 Jeffrey Dobbinson and Debbie-Lee London
1978 David Sycamore and Denise Weaver
1979 David Sycamore and Denise Weaver
1980 Raymond Myrenghen and Gunn Bergien
1981 Donnie Burns and Gaynor Fairweather

WORLD PROFESSIONAL MODERN DANCING CHAMPIONSHIP
Held since 1959
1970 Peter Eggleton and Brenda Winslade
1971 Anthony Hurley and Fay Saxton
1972 Anthony Hurley and Fay Saxton
1973 Richard and Janet Gleave
1974 Richard and Janet Gleave
1975 Richard and Janet Gleave
1976 Richard and Janet Gleave
1977 Richard and Janet Gleave
1978 Richard and Janet Gleave
1979 Richard and Janet Gleave
1980 Richard and Janet Gleave
1981 Richard and Janet Gleave

WORLD PROFESSIONAL LATIN DANCING CHAMPIONSHIP
Held since 1959
1970 Rudolf and Mechtild Trautz
1971 Rudolf and Mechtild Trautz
1972 Wolfgang and Evelyn Opitz
1973 Hans Peter and Ingeborg Fischer
1974 Hans Peter and Ingeborg Fischer
1975 Hans Peter and Ingeborg Fischer
1976 Peter Maxwell and Lyn Harman
1977 Alan and Hazel Fletcher
1978 Alan and Hazel Fletcher
1979 Alan and Hazel Fletcher
1980 Alan and Hazel Fletcher
1981 Alan and Hazel Fletcher

MOST OUTSTANDING OLD-TIME PROFESSIONAL PARTNERSHIP
Held since 1953
1970 Glyn and Anne Watkins
1971 Not given
1972 Not given
1973 Jeff and Muriel Aldren
1974 Jim Hall and Denise Mayo
1975 Roy and Linda Muldoon
1976 Wayne and Wendy Packard
1977 Garry Waite and Jennifer Pople
1978 Not given
1979 Susan Earnshaw
1980 Gary and Patricia Waite

PERSON WHO DID MOST FOR BALLROOM DANCING
Held since 1953
1970 Eric Morley

1971 Bob Garganico
1972 Wilfred Orange
1973 Alex Warren, OBE
1974 Eric Morley
1975 Barrie Edgar
1976 Not given
1977 Terry Wogan
1978 Victor Silvester, OBE
1979 Terry Wogan
1980 Wilfred Orange

BBC INTER-REGIONAL 'COME DANCING' CHAMPIONSHIP
This is the final award in the popular television ballroom dancing series which is organised each year by the BBC.

1956 South of England
1957 South of England
1958 Wales
1959 Midlands
1960 South London
1961 West Midlands
1962 North West
1963 North London
1964 South London
1965 Home Counties North
1966 Home Counties North
1967 North West
1968 Home Counties South
1969 Home Counties North
1970 North
1971 Wales
1972 North
1973 South Wales
1974 England
1975 Midlands and West
1976 Midlands and West
1977 Midlands and West
1978 Midlands and West
1979 Midlands and West
1980 Midlands and West

FORMATION TEAM TROPHY WINNERS
1958 Sybil Marks and Phil Williams
1959 Thorpe-Hancock School of Dance
1960 Frank and Peggy Spencer
1961 Laura Dixon School of Dance
1962 Frank and Peggy Spencer
1963 Russell-Vale Team (N. London), and James Stevenson Team (E. Midlands)
1964 Frank and Peggy Spencer
1965 Ada Unsworth
1966 Tony Smith
1967 John Stead, and Frank and Peggy Spencer
1968 Frank and Peggy Spencer
1969 Stanley Jackson
1970 Jack and Joyce Briggs
1971 Sybil Marks
1972 Sybil Marks, and Jack and Joyce Briggs
1973 Jack and Joyce Briggs
1974 Stanley Jackson, and Sybil Marks
1975 Janet and Stanley Jackson
1976 John and Joan Knight
1977 Jack and Joyce Briggs
1978 Ted Burroughs Formation Team
1979 Ted Burroughs Formation Team
1980 Manchester Latin Team

Darts

EMBASSY WORLD PROFESSIONAL CHAMPIONSHIP
First held in 1978 in Stoke-on-Trent. Winners:

1978 Leighton Rees (Wal)
1979 John Lowe (Eng)
1980 Eric Bristow (Eng)
1981 Eric Bristow (Eng)

WORLD CUP
First held in 1977 at the Wembley Conference Centre, London. Winners:

Individual
1977 Leighton Rees (Wal)
1979 Nicky Virachkul (USA)

Team:
1977 Wales (Alan Evans, Leighton Rees, David 'Rocky' Jones, Phil Obbard)
1979 England (John Lowe, Eric Bristow, Tony Brown, Bill Lennard)

WORLD MASTERS INDIVIDUAL
First held at the West Centre Hotel, London, in 1974. Sponsored by Winmau. Winners:

1974 Cliff Inglis (Eng)
1975 Alan Evans (Wal)
1976 John Lowe (Eng)
1977 Eric Bristow (Eng)
1978 Ronnie Davis (Eng)
1979 Eric Bristow (Eng)
1980 John Lowe (Eng)

BRITISH OPEN CHAMPIONSHIP
First held in 1975.

MEN
1975 Alan Evans (Wal)
1976 Jack North (Eng)
1977 John Lowe (Eng)
1978 Eric Bristow (Eng)
1979 Tony Brown (Eng)
1980 Cliff Lazarenko (Eng)
1981 Eric Bristow (Eng)

First held in 1979

WOMEN
1979 Judy Campbell (Eng)
1980 Linda Batten (Eng)
1981 Ann Marie Davies (Wal)

HOME INTERNATIONAL SERIES
First held in Bristol in 1973, contested by England, Scotland, Ireland and Wales.

1973 England
1974 England
1975 Wales
1976 Scotland and England
1977 Wales
1978 England
1979 England
1980 England

The characteristic action of Eric Bristow

Leighton Rees, winner of the Singles and on the winning Welsh team at the first World Cup in 1977 (Daily Mirror)

EUROPE CUP

First held in Copenhagen in 1978. Winners:

Team
1978 England
1980 England

NORTH AMERICAN OPEN CHAMPIONSHIPS

Men's Individual
1970 Vince Lubbering (USA)
1971 Bob Thiede (USA)
1972 Ray Fischer (USA)
1973 Ray Fischer (USA)
1974 Joe Baltadonis (USA)
1975 Conrad Daniels (USA)
1976 Ricky Fusco (Eng)
1977 Alan Glazier (Eng)
1978 Bobby George (Eng)
1979 Eric Bristow (Eng)
1980 Len Heard (USA)

Women's Individual
1970 Robbi Dobbs (USA)
1971 Gerry Dover (USA)
1972 Gerry Dover (USA)
1973 Carol Toulson (USA)
1974 Helen Scheerbaum (USA)
1975 Julie Nicholl (USA)
1976 Donna Dertadian (USA)
1977 Maureen Flowers (Eng)
1978 Kathy Karpowich (USA)
1979 Maureen Flowers (Eng)
1980 Sandra Gibb (Wal)

Doubles
1970 Joe Young and Conrad Daniels (USA)
1971 Frank Blair and Gus Popelier (USA)
1972 Gary Curtaz and Phil Albers (USA)
1973 Butch Wilson and Jack Cantu (USA)
1974 George Murphy and Terry James (USA)
1975 Joe Baltadonis and Nicky Virachkul (USA)

1976 Andy Green and Jody Simkins (USA)
1977 John Lowe and Tony Brown (Eng)
1978 John Lowe and Tony Brown (Eng)
1979 Eric Bristow (Eng) and Leighton Rees (Wal)
1980 Bobby George and Tony Sontag (Eng)

NDA LADIES' CHAMPIONSHIP

Ladies' Champions of the National Darts Association of Great Britain. First held in 1967. Winners:

1967 Marjorie Drabble	1974 Jean Dickinson
1968 Jean Smith	1975 Betty Hughes
1969 Patricia Clifford	1976 May Lynch
1970 Judy Campbell	1977 Sandra Gibb
1971 Anne Westwood	1978 Not held
1972 Jean Smith	1979 Maureen Flowers
1973 Mary Smith	1980 Maureen Flowers

NEWS OF THE WORLD DARTS CHAMPIONSHIP

First held in 1927 as a London area tournament. Re-launched in 1947/48 as a national competition. Winners:

1948 Harry Leadbetter	1965 Tom Barrett
1949 Jackie Boyce	1966 Wilf Ellis
1950 Dixie Newberry	1967 Wally Seaton
1951 Harry Perryman	1968 Bill Duddy
1952 Tommy Gibbons	1969 Barry Twomlow
1953 Jimmy Arr	1970 Henry Barney
1954 Oliver James	1971 Dennis Filkins
1955 Tom Reddington	1972 Brian Netherton
1956 Trevor Peachey	1973 Ivor Hodgkinson
1957 Alwyn Mullins	1974 Peter Chapman
1958 Tommy Gibbons	1975 Derek White
1959 Albert Welch	1976 Bill Lennard
1960 Tom Reddington	1977 Mick Norris
1961 Alec Adamson	1978 Stefan Lord (Swe)
1962 Eddie Brown	1979 Bobby George
1963 Robbie Rumney	1980 Stefan Lord (Swe)
1964 Tom Barrett	

Disco Dancing

THE EMI WORLD DISCO DANCING CHAMPIONSHIP

These championships have been run by EMI since 1978. Local clubs/discotheques hold contests from which 14 finalists are chosen for the UK final. The UK champion then goes on to represent the UK at the world final. The championship is open to single dancers between the ages of 18 and 35. Marks are awarded on creative dance routine, artistic interpretation of the music, personality and visual presentation.

Godfrey Raseroka (SA), EMI world disco dancing champion 1980

The 1980 world champion prize was a TR7 sportscar, a £2000 cash prize and a trophy and medal. Winners:

UK Championship
1978 Grant Santino
1979 Julie Brown
1980 Jean Munroe-Martin

World Championship
1978 Tadaaki Dan (Jap)
1979 Julie Brown (UK)
1980 Godfrey Raseroka (SA)

Jean Munroe-Martin, winner of the 1980 EMI UK Disco Dancing Championship

Dogs

CRUFT'S DOG SHOW

Although the first dog show was held at Newcastle-upon-Tyne in 1859, Cruft's was not started until 1886, but this famous national dog show now enjoys both tremendous popular interest and an international reputation. The first award for Best-in-Show was made in 1928:

Winners:

1928 Greyhound. Primely Sceptre. H. Whitley
1929 Scottish Terrier. Heather Necessity. E. Chapman
1930 Spaniel (Cocker). Luckystar of Ware. H. S. Lloyd
1931 Spaniel (Cocker). Luckystar of Ware. H. S. Lloyd
1932 Retriever (Labrador). Bramshaw Bob. Lorna Countess Howe
1933 Retriever (Labrador). Bramshaw Bob. Lorna Countess Howe
1934 Greyhound. Southball Moonstone. B. Hartland Worden
1935 Pointer. Pennine Prima Donna. A. Eggleston
1936 Chow Chow. Ch Choonam Hung Kwong. Mrs V. A. M. Mannooch
1937 Retriever (Labrador). Ch. Cheveralla Ben of Banchory. Lorna Countess Howe
1938 Spaniel (Cocker). Exquisite Model of Ware. H. S. Lloyd
1939 Spaniel (Cocker). Exquisite Model of Ware. H. S. Lloyd
1948 Spaniel (Cocker). Tracey Witch of Ware. H. S. Lloyd
1949 No Show
1950 Spaniel (Cocker). Tracey Witch of Ware. H. S. Lloyd
1951 Welsh Terrier. Twynstar Dyma-Fi. Fl. Capt. and Mrs I. M. Thomas
1952 Bulldog. Ch. Noways Chuckles. J. T. Barnard
1953 Great Dane. Ch. Elch Elder of Ouborough. W. G. Siggers

1954 (Cancelled)
1955 Poodle (Standard). Ch. Tzigane Aggri of Nashend. Mrs A. Proctor
1956 Greyhound. Treetops Golden Falcon. Mrs W. de Casembroot and Miss H. Greenish
1957 Keeshond. Ch. Volkrijk of Vorden. Mrs I. M. Tucker
1958 Pointer. Ch. Chiming Bells. Mrs W. Parkinson
1959 Welsh Terrier. Ch. Sandstorm Saracen. Mesdames Leach and Thomas
1960 Irish Wolfhound. Sulhamstead Merman. Mrs Nagle and Miss Clark
1961 Airedale Terrier. Ch. Riverina Tweedsbairn. Miss P. Mc Caughey and Mrs D. Schuth
1962 Fox Terrier (Wire). Ch. Crackwyn Cockspur. H. L. Gill
1963 Lakeland Terrier. Rogerholm Recruit. W. Rogers
1964 English Setter. Sh. Ch. Silbury Soames of Madavale. Mrs A. Williams
1965 Alsatian (GSD). Ch. Fenton of Kentwood. Miss S. H. Godden
1966 Poodle (Toy). Oakington Puckshill Amber Sunblush. Mrs C. E. Perry
1967 Lakeland Terrier. Ch. Stingray of Derryabah. Mr and Mrs W. Postlewaite
1968 Dalmatian. Ch. Fanhill Faune. Mrs E. J. Woodyatt
1969 Alsatian (GSD). Ch. Hendrawen's Nibelung of Charavigne Mr and Mrs E. J. White
1970 Pyrenean Mountain Dog. Bergerie Knur. Mr and Mrs F. S. Prince
1971 Alsatian (GSD). Ch. Ramacon Swashbuckler. Prince Ahmed Husain
1972 Bull Terrier. Ch. Abraxas Audacity. Miss V. Drummond-Dick
1973 Cavalier King Charles Spaniel. Alansmere Aquarius. Messrs Hall and Evans
1974 St Bernard. Ch. Burtonswood Bossy Boots. Miss M. Hindes
1975 Fox Terrier (Wire). Ch. Brookewire Brandy of Layven. Messrs Benelli and Dondina

Mr and Mrs Wakefield with their champion
Bulldog being awarded the prize for 1978 Pup
of the Year

1976 West Highland White Terrier. Ch. Dianthus
Buttons. Mrs K. Newstead
1977 English Setter. Bournehouse Dancing Master.
Mr G. F. Williams
1978 Fox Terrier (Wire). Ch. Harrowhill Huntsman. Miss E. Howles
1979 Kerry Blue Terrier. Ch. Callaghan of Leander.
Mrs W. Streatfield
1980 Flatcoat Retriever. Ch. Shargleam Blackcap.
Miss P. Chapman
1981 Irish Setter. Ch. Astley's Portia of Rua. Mrs
M. Tuite

PUP OF THE YEAR

This competition was instigated by the *Daily
Express* in 1971. In 1973 Spillers Foods also
sponsored the event until 1977 when the *Daily
Express* withdrew and *Dog World* took their
place along with Spillers. Eliminating rounds

are held at major championship dog shows
with the ten finalists meeting at London Zoo
for the judging of the overall winner. Winners:

1971 Wire Fox Terrier. Ch. Cripsey Townville
T'other 'un. W. Havenhand
1972 Standard Poodle. Ch. Josato Pink Gin of
Kelramo. Mrs J. Timson
1973 Chow Chow Ch. Edlen Cassandra. Miss C.
Entwisle
1974 German Shepherd Dog (Alsatian). Tracelyn
Enterprise. Messrs Peden and Young.
1975 Pomeranian. Ch. Hadleigh Honey Puff. Mrs
G. Dyke
1976 Bull Terrier. Ch. Kearby's Temptress. Mrs Q.
Yuatt
1977 Scottish Terrier. Ch. Brio Chief Barker. Jane
Miller. '
1978 Bulldog. Ch. Outdoors Jubilant. Mrs D.
Wakefield
1979 Smooth Dachshund. Ch. Turlshill Trouba-
dour. Mr and Mrs R. W. B. Pinches
1980 West Highland White Terrier. Ch. Halfmoon
of Olac. Mr and Mrs D. Tattersall

Drama

PULITZER PRIZE FOR DRAMA

The pre-eminent award for play writers in the
United States. For further details see under
main heading on Pulitzer Prizes.

1918 Jesse Lynch Williams, *Why Marry?*
1919 No award
1920 Eugene O'Neill, *Beyond the Horizon*
1921 Zona Gale, *Miss Lulu Bett*

1922 Eugene O'Neill, *Anna Christie*
1923 Owen Davis, *Icebound*
1924 Hatcher Hughes, *Hell-Bent for Heaven*
1925 Sidney Howard, *They Knew What They
Wanted*
1926 George Kelly, *Craig's Wife*
1927 Paul Green, *In Abraham's Bosom*
1928 Eugene O'Neill, *Strange Interlude*
1929 Elmer Rice, *Street Scene*

1930 Marc Connelly, *The Green Pastures*
1931 Susan Glaspell, *Alison's House*
1932 George S. Kaufman, Morris Ryskind and Ira Gershwin, *Of Thee I Sing*
1933 Maxwell Anderson, *Both Your Houses*
1934 Sidney Kingsley, *Men in White*
1935 Zoe Akins, *The Old Maid*
1936 Robert E. Sherwood, *Idiot's Delight*
1937 George S. Kaufman and Moss Hart, *You Can't Take It With You*
1938 Thornton Wilder, *Our Town*
1939 Robert E. Sherwood, *Abe Lincoln in Illinois*
1940 William Saroyan, *The Time of Your Life*
1941 Robert E. Sherwood, *There Shall Be No Night*
1943 Thornton Wilder, *The Skin of Our Teeth*
1945 Mary Chase, *Harvey*
1946 Russel Crouse and Howard Lindsay, *State of the Union*
1948 Tennessee Williams, *A Streetcar Named Desire*
1949 Arthur Miller, *Death of a Salesman*
1950 Richard Rodgers, Oscar Hammerstein (2nd) and Joshua Logan, *South Pacific*
1952 Joseph Kramm, *The Shrike*
1953 William Inge, *Picnic*
1954 John Patrick, *Teahouse of the August Moon*
1955 Tennessee Williams, *Cat on a Hot Tin Roof*
1956 Frances Goodrich and Albert Hackett, *The Diary of Anne Frank*
1957 Eugene O'Neill, *Long Day's Journey Into Night*
1958 Ketti Frings, *Look Homeward, Angel*
1959 Archibald MacLeish, *J.B.*
1960 George Abbott, Jerome Weidman, Sheldon Harnick and Jerry Bock, *Fiorello*
1961 Tad Mosel, *All the Way Home*
1962 Frank Loesser and Abe Burrows, *How To Succeed In Business Without Really Trying*
1965 Frank D. Gilroy, *The Subject Was Roses*
1967 Edward Albee, *A Delicate Balance*
1969 Howard Sackler, *The Great White Hope*
1970 Charles Gordone, *No Place to Be Somebody*
1971 Paul Zindel, *The Effect of Gamma Rays on Man-in-the Moon Marigolds*
1973 Jason Miller, *That Championship Season*
1975 Edward Albee, *Seascape*
1976 Michael Bennett, James Kirkwood, Nicholas Dante, Marvin Hamlisch, Edward Kleban, *A Chorus Line*
1977 Michael Cristofer, *The Shadow Box*
1978 Donald L. Coburn, *The Gin Game*
1979 Sam Shepard, *Buried Child*
1980 Lanford Wilson, *Talley's Folly*
1981 Beth Henley, *Crimes of the Heart*

Draughts

BRITISH OPEN CHAMPIONSHIP
First held in 1926 and contested biennially.

1926 R. T. Ward
1928 W. Kilgour
1930 S. Cohen
1932 S. Cohen
1934 L. Claxton
1936 S. Levy
1938 S. Cohen
1948 J. Marshall
1950 J. Marshall
1952 J. Marshall
1954 J. Marshall
1956 D. E. Oldbury
1958 Dr. M. Tinsley
1960 A. G. Huggins
1962 D. E. Oldbury
1964 J. McGill
1966 J. Marshall
1968 J. McGill
1970 I. Edwards
1972 G. Davies
1974 J. McGill
1976 A. Huggins
1978 J. McGill

ENGLISH OPEN DRAUGHTS CHAMPIONSHIP
First held in 1886. From 1949 the championship has been contested every other year. Winners since 1965:

1965 J. McGill
1967 A. Huggins
1969 N. Wexler and A. Huggins
1971 F. Bucklow and A. Huggins
1973 A. Huggins
1975 J. Marshall
1977 T. Watson
1979 W. Edwards

Most wins:
6 S. Cohen 1924, 1927, 1929, 1933, 1937, 1939. 4 A. Jordan 1892, 1907, 1908, 1909; D. Oldbury 1953, 1955, 1957, 1963; A. Huggins 1967, 1969 (=1st), 1971 (=1st), 1973

INTERNATIONAL TEAMS TOURNAMENT
First held at Morecambe in 1980, winner – Republic of Ireland.

Economics

NOBEL PRIZE FOR ECONOMICS
For further details see under main heading of Nobel Prizes.

1969 Ragnar Frisch (Nor)
     Jan Tinbergen (Hol)
1970 Paul A. Samuelson (USA)

1971 Simon Kuznets (USA)
1972 Kenneth J. Arrow (USA)
    Sir John R. Hicks (GB)
1973 Vassily Leontief (USA) (Russian-born)
1974 Gunnar Myrdal (Swe)
    Friedrich A. von Hayek (Aut)
1975 Leonid V. Kantorovich (USSR)
    Tjalling C. Koopmans (USA) (Dutch-born)

1976 Milton Friedman (USA)
1977 Bertil Ohlin (Swe)
    James Edward Meade (GB)
1978 Herbert Simon (USA)
1979 Sir Arthur Lewis (GB)
    (St. Lucien-born)
    Theodore W. Schultz (USA)
1980 Lawrence Klein (USA)

Eisteddfod

ROYAL NATIONAL EISTEDDFOD OF WALES

The principal annual event in the cultural life of Wales. Competitions range across a wide field of literature, music and the arts, the medium of communication being Welsh.

WINNERS OF THE BARDIC CHAIR AND CROWN FOR POETRY (since 1945) (founded 1861) (winners of Chair listed first, followed by Crown)

1945 Tom Parri-Jones
1946 Geraint Bowen
    Rev. Rhydwen Williams
1947 John Eilian
    Rev. Griffith John Roberts
1948 Dewi Emrys (Rev. David Emrys Jones)
    Rev. Euros Bowen
1949 Rolant o Fôn (Roland Jones)
    John Eilian
1950 Rev. Gwilym R. Tilsley
    Rev. Euros Bowen
1951 Brinley Richards
    T. Glyn Davies
1952 John Evans
    No award
1953 Rev. Erni Llwyd Williams
    Dilys Cadwaladr
1954 John Evans
    Rev. Erni Llwyd Williams
1955 Rev. Gwilym Ceri Jones
    Rev. W. J. Gruffydd
1956 Mathonwy Hughes
    No award
1957 Rev. Gwilym R. Tilsley
    Dyfnallt Morgan
1958 T. Llew Jones
    Llewelyn Jones
1959 T. Llew Jones
    Tom Huws
1960 No award
    Rev. W. J. Gruffydd

1961 Rev. Emrys Edwards
    Rev. L. Haydn Lewis
1962 Caradog Prichard
    Rev. D. Emlyn Lewis
1963 No award
    Tom Parri-Jones
1964 Rev. R. Bryn Williams
    Rev. Rhydwen Williams
1965 W. D. Williams
    Tom Parri-Jones
1966 Dio Jones
    Dafydd Jones
1967 Emrys Roberts
    Eluned Phillips
1968 Rev. R. Bryn Williams
    Rev. L. Haydn Lewis
1969 James Nicholas
    Rev. Dafydd Rowlands
1970 Tomi Evans
    Bryan Martin Davies
1971 Emrys Roberts
    Bryan Martin Davies
1972 Rev. Dafydd Owen
    Rev. Dafydd Rowlands
1973 Alan Llwyd
    Alan Llwyd
1974 Moses Glyn Jones
    W. R. P. George
1975 Gerallt Lloyd Owen
    Elwyn Roberts
1976 Alan Llwyd
    Alan Llwyd
1977 Donald Evans
    Donald Evans
1978 No award
    Siôn Eirian
1979 No award
    Rev. Meirion Evans
1980 Donald Evans
    Donald Evans

Elections

WINNERS OF GENERAL ELECTIONS IN GREAT BRITAIN (since 1900)

					Turnout (per cent)
28 Sept–24 Oct 1900	*Conservative* 402	Liberal 184	Labour 2	Others 82	74·6
12 Jan–7 Feb 1906	*Liberal* 400	Conservative 157	Labour 30	Others 83	82·6

14 Jan–9 Feb 1910	*Liberal* 275	Conservative 273	Labour 40	Others 82	86·6
2–19 Dec 1910	*Liberal* 272	Conservative 272	Labour 42	Others 84	81·1
14 Dec 1918	*Conservative* 383	Liberal 161	Labour 73	Others 90	58·9
15 Nov 1922	*Conservative* 345	Labour 142	Liberal 116	Others 12	71·3
6 Dec 1923	*Conservative** 258	Labour 191	Liberal 159	Others 7	70·8
29 Oct 1924	*Conservative* 419	Labour 151	Liberal 40	Others 5	76·6
30 May 1929	*Labour* 288	Conservative 260	Liberal 59	Others 8	76·1
27 Oct 1931	*Conservative* 521	Labour 52	Liberal 37	Others 5	76·3
14 Nov 1935	*Conservative* 432	Labour 154	Liberal 20	Others 9	71·2
5 July 1945	*Labour* 393	Conservative 213	Liberal 12	Others 22	72·7
23 Feb 1950	*Labour* 315	Conservative 298	Liberal 9	Others 3	84·0
25 Oct 1951	*Conservative* 321	Labour 295	Liberal 6	Others 3	82·5
25 May 1955	*Conservative* 344	Labour 277	Liberal 6	Others 3	76·7
8 Oct 1959	*Conservative* 365	Labour 258	Liberal 6	Others 1	78·8
15 Oct 1964	*Labour* 317	Conservative 303	Liberal 9	Others 1	77·1
31 Mar 1966	*Labour* 363	Conservative 253	Liberal 12	Others 2	75·9
18 June 1970	*Conservative* 330	Labour 288	Liberal 6	Others 6	72·0
28 Feb 1974	*Labour* 301	Conservative 297	Liberal 14	Others 23	78·8
10 Oct 1974	*Labour* 319	Conservative 277	Liberal 13	Others 26	72·8
3 May 1979	*Conservative* 339	Labour 268	Liberal 11	Others 17	76·0

*Although the Conservatives won the most seats, Labour went on to form a minority government

FAMOUS BY-ELECTION WINNERS (since 1958)

	Party	Constituency	Date	Remarks
Mark Bonham Carter	Liberal	Torrington	27 Mar 1958	First Liberal victory at a by-election since 1929.
Eric Lubbock	Liberal	Orpington	14 Mar 1962	The most sensational Liberal victory of the 1960s. The party swept to victory in a safe Tory seat.
Sir Alec Douglas-Home	Conservative	Kinross and W. Perthshire	7 Nov 1963	The by-election in which the former 14th Earl of Home returned to the Commons as Sir Alec Douglas-Home.
Ronald Buxton	Conservative	Leyton	21 Jan 1965	Defeated Labour's Foreign Secretary, Patrick Gordon Walker, in a normally safe East London Labour stronghold.
David Steel	Liberal	Roxburgh, Selkirk and Peebles	24 Mar 1965	David Steel won a safe Conservative seat to become the 'baby of the House' and eventual Liberal Party leader.
Gwynfor Evans	Plaid Cymru	Carmarthen	14 July 1966	The first – and so far the only – Welsh Nationalist to win a seat in a by-election.
Winifred Ewing	Scottish National Party	Hamilton	2 Nov 1967	The first SNP by-election victory since the party won Motherwell in a wartime by-election in April 1945. Hamilton heralded the revival of the SNP.
Don Williams	Conservative	Dudley	28 Mar 1968	The by-election which saw the largest swing ever recorded to the Conservatives during the 1966–70 Wilson Government.
Cyril Smith	Liberal	Rochdale	26 Oct 1972	First of the famous series of Liberal by-election victories of 1972–73.
Graham Tope	Liberal	Sutton and Cheam	7 Dec 1972	A sensational Liberal victory in one of the safest Tory areas – the London suburbs.
Dick Taverne	Democratic Labour	Lincoln	1 Mar 1973	Dick Taverne won a personal triumph as a Democratic Labour Candidate having previously been the town's Labour MP.
Margo MacDonald	Scottish National Party	Glasgow Govan	Oct 1973	The first SNP by-election victory since Hamilton in 1967.

R. G. Hodgson	Conservative	Walsall North	4 Nov 1976	The safe Labour stronghold formerly held by John Stonehouse fell on a swing of 22.6 per cent to the Conservatives – the largest swing of the 1974–79 Parliament to a Conservative.
Austin Mitchell	Labour	Grimsby	28 Apr 1977	Labour's best result of the 1974–79 Parliament – held the same day that Ashfield fell to the Tories on a 20.8 per cent swing.
David Alton	Liberal	Liverpool Edge Hill	29 Mar 1979	A sweeping Liberal victory by 8133 votes in a hitherto safe Labour seat. The 32 per cent swing to the Liberals was the highest in post war politics.

EUROPEAN PARLIAMENT

The first direct elections to the 410-member European Parliament took place in June 1979. In Great Britain the result was as follows:

Party	Votes	Votes (per cent)	Seats
Conservative	6 504 481	50·6	60
Labour	4 253 210	33·0	17
Liberal	1 690 600	13·1	—
Others	421 553	3·3	1(SNP)

In Northern Ireland, where proportional representation was used, the three MPs elected were: Rev. Ian Paisley (Democratic Unionist), John Hume (SDLP) and John Taylor (Official Unionist).

AMERICAN PRESIDENTIAL ELECTIONS (since 1900)

Presidential Candidates	Party	Electoral Vote	Popular Vote
1900 William McKinley	Republican	292	7 219 530
William J. Bryan	Dem People's	155	6 358 071
Eugene V. Debs	Social Democratic	0	94 768
1904 Theodore Roosevelt	Republican	336	7 628 834
Alton B. Parker	Democratic	140	5 084 491
Eugene V. Debs	Socialist	0	402 400
1908 William H. Taft	Republican	321	7 679 006
William J Bryan	Democratic	162	6 409 106
Eugene V. Debs	Socialist	0	420 820
1912 Woodrow Wilson	Democratic	435	6 286 214
Theodore Roosevelt	Progressive	88	4 126 020
William H. Taft	Republican	8	3 483 922
Eugene V. Debs	Socialist	0	897 011
1916 Woodrow Wilson	Democratic	277	9 129 606
Charles E. Hughes	Republican	254	8 538 221
A. L. Benson	Socialist	0	585 113
1920 Warren G. Harding	Republican	404	16 152 200
James M. Cox	Democratic	127	9 147 353
Eugene V. Debs	Socialist	0	917 799
1924 Calvin Coolidge	Republican	382	15 725 016
John W. Davis	Democratic	136	8 385 586
Robert M. LaFollette	Progressive, Socialist	13	4 822 856
1928 Herbert Hoover	Republican	444	21 392 190
Alfred E. Smith	Democratic	87	15 016 443
Norman Thomas	Socialist	0	267 420
1932 Franklin D. Roosevelt	Democratic	472	22 821 857
Herbert Hoover	Republican	59	15 761 841
Norman Thomas	Socialist	0	884 781
1936 Franklin D. Roosevelt	Democratic	523	27 751 597
Alfred M. Landon	Republican	8	16 679 583
Norman Thomas	Socialist	0	187 720

President Ronald Reagan giving a 'thumbs up' sign after winning the presidency from Jimmy Carter in November 1980 (Popperfoto)

1940	Franklin D. Roosevelt	Democratic	449	27 244 160
	Wendell L. Willkie	Republican	82	22 305 198
	Norman Thomas	Socialist	0	99 557
1944	Franklin D. Roosevelt	Democratic	432	25 602 504
	Thomas E. Dewey	Republican	99	22 006 285
	Norman Thomas	Socialist	0	80 518
1948	Harry S. Truman	Democratic	303	24 179 345
	Thomas S. Dewey	Republican	189	21 991 291
	J. Strom Thurmond	States' Rights Dem	39	1 176 125
	Henry A. Wallace	Progressive	0	1 157 326
	Norman Thomas	Socialist	0	139 572
1952	Dwight D. Eisenhower	Republican	442	33 936 234
	Adlai E. Stevenson	Democratic	89	27 314 992
1956	Dwight D. Eisenhower	Republican	457	35 590 472
	Adlai E. Stevenson	Democratic	73	26 022 752
1960	John F. Kennedy	Democratic	303	34 226 731
	Richard M. Nixon	Republican	219	34 108 157
1964	Lyndon B. Johnson	Democratic	486	43 129 484
	Barry M. Goldwater	Republican	52	27 178 188
1968	Richard M. Nixon	Republican	301	31 785 480
	Hubert H. Humphrey	Democratic	191	31 275 166
	George C. Wallace	American Ind	46	9 906 473
1972	Richard M. Nixon	Republican	520	47 169 911
	George McGovern	Democratic	17	29 170 383
	John G. Schmitz	American	0	1 099 482
1976	Jimmy Carter	Democratic	297	40 828 657
	Gerald R. Ford	Republican	240	39 145 520
	Eugene J. McCarthy	Independent	0	756 605
1980	Ronald Reagan	Republican	489	43 209 016
	Jimmy Carter	Democratic	49	34 921 696
	John Anderson	Independent	0	5 581 710

Environment

BRITAIN IN BLOOM

Sponsored by the British Tourist Authority since 1964, the Britain in Bloom competition is a nationwide campaign aimed at encouraging people to make cities, towns and villages as attractive as possible by the imaginative and decorative use of trees, shrubs and flowers.

National trophies are awarded annually to the winning city, town and village. A 'Keep Britain Tidy' trophy, first awarded in 1973, goes to the Britain in Bloom finalist most active in litter prevention, and the Gordon Ford Trophy, first awarded in 1971, is awarded to the city, town or village where the commercial sector of the community has made the greatest contribution. Winners since 1970:

City
1970 Aberdeen
1971 Aberdeen
1972 Bath
     Hartlepool
1973 Aberdeen
1974 Aberdeen
     City of London
1975 Bath
1976 Bath
1977 Aberdeen
1978 Bath
1979 Aberdeen
1980 Exeter

Town
1970 Falmouth
1971 Falmouth
1972 Ayr
1973 Bridlington
     Falmouth
1974 Shrewsbury
1975 Sidmouth
1976 Harrogate
1977 Harrogate
1978 Douglas (Large town)
     Sidmouth (Small town)
1979 Harrogate, (Large town)
     Falmouth, and St. Andrews,
     (Small town)
1980 Douglas, Isle of Man (Large town)
     Ryton, (Small town)

Village
1970 Abington
1971 Abington
1972 Chagford
1973 Ryton
1974 Clovelly
1975 Clovelly
1976 Bampton
1977 Wolviston
1978 Aberdovey
     Carrington
1979 Holywell
1980 Killingworth

Gordon Ford Trophy
1971 Bath
1972 Bath
1973 Bath
1974 Bath
1975 City of London
1976 Bath
1977 Bath
1978 Swansea
1979 York
1980 Sidmouth

'Keep Britain Tidy' Award
1973 Bridlington
1974 Clovelly
1975 London Borough of Camden
1976 Wolviston
1977 Exeter
1978 Holywell
1979 Douglas, Isle of Man
1980 Forres

Above: *Ryton, winner of the Small town section, and* below *Killingworth, winner of the Village section in the 1980 'Britain in Bloom' competition*

Equestrian Events

SHOW JUMPING

WORLD CHAMPIONSHIPS

MEN
First held 1953.
1953 Francisco Goyoago (Spa) on *Quorum*
1954 Hans Günter Winkler (Ger) on *Halla*
1955 Hans Günter Winkler (Ger) on *Halla*
1956 Raimondo d'Inzeo (Ita) on *Merano*
1960 Raimondo d'Inzeo (Ita) on *Gowran Girl*
1966 Pierre d'Oriola (Fra) on *Pomone*
1970 David Broome (GB) on *Beethoven*
1974 Hartwig Steenken (Ger) on *Simona*
1978 Gerd Wiltfang (Ger) on *Roman*

WOMEN
First held 1965.
1965 Marion Coakes (GB) on *Stroller*
1970 Janou Lefebvre (Fra) on *Rocket*
1974 Janou Tissot (née Lefebvre) (Fra) on *Rocket*
(Women and men now compete on equal terms)

TEAM
First held 1978
1978 Great Britain

Richard Meade, winner of three Olympic gold medals 1968–72 (ED Lacey)

OLYMPIC CHAMPIONSHIPS

First held 1900. Winners since 1948 have been:

	Individual	*Team*
1948	Humberto Mariles Cortés (Mex) on *Arete*	Mexico
1952	Pierre d'Oriola (Fra) on *Ali Baba*	Great Britain
1956	Hans Günter Winkler (Ger) on *Halla*	W. Germany
1960	Raimondo d'Inzeo (Ita) on *Posillippo*	W. Germany
1964	Pierre d'Oriola (Fra) on *Lutteur*	W. Germany
1968	William Steinkraus (USA) on *Snowbound*	Canada
1972	Graziano Mancinelli (Ita) on *Ambassador*	W. Germany
1976	Alwin Schockemöhle (Ger) on *Warwick Rex*	France
1980	Jan Kowalczyk (Pol) on *Artemor*	USSR

PRESIDENT'S CUP

The award for the world team championship, based on each country's best six Nations Cup results in a season.

1965	Great Britain	1973	Great Britain
1966	USA	1974	Great Britain
1967	Great Britain	1975	W. Germany
1968	USA	1976	W. Germany
1969	W. Germany	1977	Great Britain
1970	Great Britain	1978	Great Britain
1971	W. Germany	1979	Great Britain
1972	Great Britain	1980	France

THREE-DAY EVENT

WORLD CHAMPIONSHIPS

First held 1966.

	Individual	*Team*
1966	Carlos Moratorio (Arg) on *Chalon*	Ireland
1970	Mary Gordon-Watson (GB) on *Cornishman V*	Great Britain
1974	Bruce Davidson (USA) on *Irish Cap*	USA
1978	Bruce Davidson (USA) on *Might Tango*	Canada

OLYMPIC CHAMPIONSHIPS

First held 1912. Winners since 1948 have been:

	Individual	*Team*
1948	Bernard Chevallier (Fra) on *Aiglonne*	USA
1952	Hans von Blixen-Finecke (Swe) on *Jubal*	Sweden
1956	Petrus Kastenman (Swe) on *Iluster*	Great Britain
1960	Lawrence Morgan (Aus) on *Salad Days*	Australia
1964	Mauro Checcoli (Ita) on *Surbean*	Italy
1968	Jean-Jacques Guyon (Fra) on *Pitou*	Great Britain
1972	Richard Meade (GB) on *Laurieston*	Great Britain
1976	Edmund Coffin (USA) on *Bally-cor*	USA
1980	Federico Roman (Ita) on *Rossinan*	USSR

DRESSAGE

WORLD CHAMPIONSHIPS
First held 1966.

	Individual	*Team*
1966	Josef Neckermann (Ger) on *Mariano*	W. Germany
1970	Elena Petouchkova (USSR) on *Pepel*	USSR
1974	Reiner Klimke (Ger) on *Mehmed*	W. Germany
1978	Christine Stückelberger (Swi) on *Granat*	W. Germany

OLYMPIC CHAMPIONSHIPS
First held 1912. Winners since 1948 have been:

	Individual	*Team*
1948	Hans Moser (Swi) on *Hummer*	France
1952	Henri St Cyr (Swe) on *Master Rufus*	Sweden
1956	Henri St Cyr (Swe) on *Juli*	Sweden
1960	Sergey Filatov (USSR) on *Absent*	Not held
1964	Henri Chammartin (Swi) on *Woermann*	W. Germany
1968	Ivan Kizimov (USSR) on *Ikhor*	W. Germany
1972	Liselott Linsenhoff (Ger) on *Piaff*	USSR
1976	Christine Stückelberger (Swi) on *Granat*	W. Germany
1980	Elisabeth Thevrer (Aut) on *Mon Cherie*	USSR

BADMINTON THREE-DAY EVENT
Held annually at Badminton House since 1949. Winners (GB except where shown):

1949 John Shedden on *Golden Willow*
1950 Tony Collings on *Remus*
1951 Hans Schwarzenbach (Swi) on *Vae Victus*
1952 Mark Darley (Ire) on *Emily Little*
1953 Lawrence Rook on *Starlight*
1954 Margaret Hough on *Bambi*
1955 Francis Weldon on *Kilbarry*
1956 Francis Weldon on *Kilbarry*
1957 Sheila Wilcox on *High and Mighty*
1958 Sheila Wilcox on *High and Mighty*
1959 Sheila Waddington (née Wilcox) on *Airs and Graces*
1960 William Roycroft (Aus) on *Our Solo*
1961 Lawrence Morgan (Aus) on *Salad Days*
1962 Anneli Drummond-Hay on *Merely-A-Monarch*
1963 Not held
1964 James Templar on *M'Lord Connolly*
1965 Eddie Boylan (Ire) on *Durlas Eile*
1966 Not held
1967 Celia Ross-Taylor on *Jonathan*
1968 Jane Bullen on *Our Nobby*
1969 Richard Walker on *Pasha*
1970 Richard Meade on *The Poacher*
1971 Mark Phillips on *Great Ovation*
1972 Mark Phillips on *Great Ovation*

David Broome on Mister Softee
(ED Lacey)

1973 Lucinda Prior-Palmer on *Be Fair*
1974 Mark Phillips on *Columbus*
1975 Not held
1976 Lucinda Prior-Palmer on *Wideawake*
1977 Lucinda Prior-Palmer on *George*
1978 Jane Holderness-Roddam (née Bullen) on *Warrior*
1979 Lucinda Prior-Palmer on *Killaire*
1980 Mark Todd (NZ) on *Southern Comfort*
1981 Mark Phillips on *Lincoln*

ROYAL INTERNATIONAL HORSE SHOW

This famous show was first staged as the International Horse Show in 1907 at Olympia. It is now held annually at Wembley. The two most famous of the events contested at the show are the King George V Gold Cup, which was first held in 1911, and the Queen Elizabeth II Cup for lady riders, first held in 1949.

KING GEORGE V GOLD CUP

The rider to have won most often is David Broome – four times: 1960 on *Sunsalve*, 1966 on *Mister Softee*, 1972 on *Sportsman* and 1977 on *Philco*. Three wins were achieved by J. A. Talbot-Ponsonby (1930, 1932, 1934), Harry Llewellyn on *Foxhunter* (1948, 1950 and 1953), and Piero d'Inzeo (Ita) (1957, 1961, 1962). Winners since 1970 (GB except where shown):

1970 Harvey Smith on *Mattie Brown*
1971 Gerd Wiltfang (Ger) on *Askan*
1972 David Broome on *Sportsman*
1973 Paddy McMahon on *Penwood Forge Mill*
1974 Frank Chapot (USA) on *Main Spring*
1975 Alwin Schockemöhle (Ger) on *Rex The Robber*
1976 Michael Saywell on *Chain Bridge*
1977 David Broome on *Philco*
1978 Jeff McVean (Aus) on *Claret*
1979 Robert Smith on *Video*
1980 David Bowen on *Scorton*

QUEEN ELIZABETH II CUP

The rider to have won most often is Marion Mould (née Coakes) – 3 times: 1965 and 1971 on *Stroller*, 1976 on *Elizabeth Ann*. Winners since 1970:

1970 Anneli Drummond-Hay on *Merely-A-Monarch*
1971 Marion Mould on *Stroller*
1972 Ann Moore on *Psalm*
1973 Ann Moore on *Psalm* and Alison Dawes on *Mister Banbury*
1974 Jean Davenport on *All Trumps*
1975 Jean Davenport on *Hang On*
1976 Marion Mould on *Elizabeth Ann*
1977 Liz Edgar on *Everest Wallaby*
1978 Caroline Bradley on *Marius*
1979 Liz Edgar on *Forever*
1980 Caroline Bradley on *Tigre*

Eyes

MISS BEAUTIFUL EYES

The aim of this competition, organised since 1968 by the British Safety Council, is to find a girl with beautiful eyes to feature on a British Safety Council eye safety poster and to promote and stimulate interest in safety and the need to wear eye protection where necessary. The entries are judged initially by photograph and then by interview. The 1981 winner won a holiday for two on the Island of Aruba in the Dutch Antilles.
Winners:

1968 Fay Bird, Leicester
1969 Moira-Ann Harley, Glasgow
1970 Linda Cunningham, Ipswich
1971 Penelope Dussek, Bromley, Kent
1972 Teresa Flanagan, Sutton Coldfield
1973 Maralyn Robertson, Chingford, Essex
1974 Jaqui Horgan, Plymouth
1975 Penny Hilditch, Nottingham
1976 Helene Granville, Dorset
1977 Moya Ann Church, Bristol
1978 Suzanne Stead, Tewkesbury
1979 Pauline Hegarty, Liverpool
1980 Ann McFarlane, Glasgow
1981 Alison Chapman, Glooston, Leics

Ann McFarlane, 1980 Miss Beautiful Eyes

Fashion

BRITAIN'S BEST DRESSED MEN

Revived in 1979 by the Menswear Association of Britain, the awards represent the judgement of Britain's fashion experts on men in the public eye. Winners:

1979
Robert Powell
Other finalists: Dave Allen, Roy Castle, John Conteh, Ronnie Corbett, Edward Fox, Mickey Most, Oliver Tobias, Ernie Wise, Mike Yarwood
1980
Kevin Keegan
Other finalists: Michael Aspel, Roy Castle, John Cleese, Bruce Forsyth, Larry Grayson, David Hamilton, Vince Hill, Sir Keith Joseph, Terry Wogan.

WORLD'S WORST DRESSED WOMEN

Mr Blackwell's first 'Worst-Dressed Women' list appeared in the *American Weekly*, Sunday magazine section, in the United States in October 1960. He is one of the leading high fashion designers and a broadcaster in Los Angeles. The lists since 1970 have been:

1970 Sophia Loren, Angie Dickinson, Gloria Vanderbilt Cooper
1971 Ali MacGraw, Jacqueline Onassis, Princess Anne
1972 Racquel Welch, Julie Andrews, Mia Farrow
1973 Bette Midler, Princess Anne, Racquel Welch
1974 Helen Reddy, Princess Elizabeth of Yugoslavia, Fanne Foxe
1975 Caroline Kennedy, Helen Reddy, Nancy Kissinger
1976 Louise Lasser, Maralin Niska, Angie Dickinson
1977 Farrah Fawcett-Majors, Linda Ronstadt, Charo
1978 Dolly Parton, Suzanne Somers, Christina Onassis Kauzov
1979 Bo Derek, Jill Clayburgh, Loni Anderson
1980 Brooke Shields, Elizabeth Taylor, Suzanne Somers

Kevin Keegan, 1980 'Britain's Best Dressed Man'

Fencing

OLYMPIC AND WORLD CHAMPIONSHIPS

Fencing has been included in each of the modern Olympic Games, and Olympic Championships are recognised as world championships in Olympic years.* World championships are held annually, and hav had official status since 1936, but followe European championships which were fir held in 1921. Women's events were first held i 1929.

Winners since 1965:

INDIVIDUAL

Men's Foil
1965 Jean-Claude Magnan (Fra)
1966 Gherman Sveshnikov (USSR)
1967 Viktor Putyatin (USSR)
1968* Ion Drimba (Rom)
1969 Friedrich Wessel (Ger)
1970 Friedrich Wessel (Ger)
1971 Vassily Stankovich (USSR)
1972* Witold Woyda (Pol)
1973 Christian Nöel (Fra)
1974 Aleksandr Romankov (USSR)
1975 Christian Nöel (Fra)
1976* Fabio dal Zotto (Ita)
1977 Aleksandr Romankov (USSR)
1978 Didier Flament (Fra)
1979 Aleksandr Romankov (USSR)
1980* Vladimir Smirnov (USSR)

Most wins:
5 Christian d'Oriola (Fra) 1947, 1949, 1952*, 1953, 1954

Men's Epée
1965 Zoltan Nemere (Hun)
1966 Aleksey Nikanchikov (USSR)
1967 Aleksey Nikanchikov (USSR)
1968* Gyözö Kulcsar (Hun)
1969 Bogdan Andrzejewski (Pol)
1970 Aleksey Nikanchikov (USSR)
1971 Grigory Kriss (USSR)
1972* Csaba Fenyvesi (Hun)
1973 Rolf Edling (Swe)
1974 Rolf Edling (Swe)
1975 Alexander Pusch (Ger)
1976* Alexander Pusch (Ger)
1977 Johan Harmenberg (Swe)
1978 Alexander Pusch (Ger)
1979 Philippe Riboud (Fra)
1980* Johan Harmenberg (Swe)

Most wins:
3 Georges Buchard (Fra) 1927, 1931, 1933, Aleksey Nikanchikov 1966, 1967, 1970; Alexander Pusch 1975, 1976* 1978

Men's Sabre
1965 Jerzy Pawlowski (Pol)
1966 Jerzy Pawlowski (Pol)
1967 Mark Rakita (USSR)
1968*Jerzy Pawlowski (Pol)
1969 Viktor Sidiak (USSR)
1970 Tibor Pezsa (Hun)
1971 Michele Maffei (Ita)
1972* Viktor Sidiak (USSR)
1973 Mario Aldo Montano (Ita)
1974 Mario Aldo Montano (Ita)
1975 Vladimir Nazlimov (USSR)
1976* Viktor Krovopuskov (USSR)
1977 Pal Gerevich (Hun)
1978 Viktor Krovopuskov (USSR)
1979 Vladimir Nazlimov (USSR)
1980* Viktor Krovopuskov (USSR)

Most wins:
4 Rudolf Karpati (Hun) 1954, 1956*, 1959, 1960*, Aladar Gerevich (Hun) 1935, 1948*, 1951, 1955, Jerzy Pawlowski (Pol) 1957, 1965, 1966, 1968*

Christian D'Oriola (left) *against Raymond Paul of Great Britain* (Associated Press)

Women's Foil
1965 Galina Gorokhova (USSR)
1966 Tatyana Samusenko (USSR)
1967 Alexandra Zabelina (USSR)
1968* Elena Novikova (USSR)
1969 Elena Novikova (USSR)
1970 Galina Gorokhova (USSR)
1971 Marie-Chantal Demaille (Fra)
1972* Antonella Ragno-Lonzi (Ita)
1973 Valentina Nikonova (USSR)
1974 Ildiko Bobis (Hun)
1975 Ecaterina Stahl (Rom)
1976* Ildiko Schwarczenberger (Hun)
1977 Valentina Sidorova (USSR)
1978 Valentina Sidorova (USSR)
1979 Cornelia Hanisch (Ger)
1980* Pascale Trinquet (Fra)

Most wins:
5 Ilona Elek (Hun) 1934, 1935, 1936* 1948* 1951; 4 Helene Mayer (Ger) 1928*, 1929, 1931, 1937; Ellen Preis (Aut) 1932*, 1947, 1949, 1950(=)

TEAM

Men's foil

1965 USSR	1974 USSR
1966 USSR	1975 France
1967 Romania	1976* W. Germany
1968* France	1977 W. Germany
1969 USSR	1978 Poland
1970 USSR	1979 USSR
1971 France	1980* France
1972* Poland	Most Wins:
1973 USSR	17 USSR

Men's Epée

1965 France	1974 Sweden
1966 France	1975 Sweden
1967 USSR	1976* Sweden
1968* Hungary	1977 Sweden
1969 USSR	1978 Hungary
1970 Hungary	1979 USSR
1971 Hungary	1980* France
1972* Hungary	Most wins:
1973 W.Germany	16 Italy

Men's Sabre		Women's Foil	
1965 USSR	1974 USSR	1965 USSR	1974 USSR
1966 Hungary	1975 USSR	1966 USSR	1975 USSR
1967 USSR	1976* USSR	1967 Hungary	1976* USSR
1968* USSR	1977 USSR	1968* USSR	1977 USSR
1969 USSR	1978 Hungary	1969 Romania	1978 USSR
1970 USSR	1979 USSR	1970 USSR	1979 USSR
1971* USSR	1980* USSR	1971 USSR	1980* France
1972* Italy	Most wins:	1972* USSR	Most wins:
1973 Hungary	24 Hungary	1973 Hungary	13 USSR

Floristry

THE HUXLEY CUP

This competition for members of the Women's Institute is staged annually by the Royal Agricultural Society of England and judged in the floral arrangement section of the flower show at the Royal Show. The competition aims to find a flower arranger who can create an artistic arrangement at low cost using the most basic materials. The theme changes each year.

The most recent winners were:

1974	'Gardener's Reward'	Kesteven
1975	WI Diamond Jubilee –	
	'60 years Then and Now'	Warwickshire
1976	'Summer Simplicity'	Gwent
1977	'The Crown Jewels'	Avon
1978	'The Village Green'	Gloucester
1979	'The Secret Garden'	East Kent
1980	'Curtain Call'	Surrey

NATIONAL ASSOCIATION OF FLOWER ARRANGEMENT SOCIETIES OF GREAT BRITAIN: ANNUAL FESTIVAL OF FLOWER ARRANGEMENT

This Association has held an annual Festival of Flower Arrangement since 1962, at which the national competitions are held. The national festival and competitions are organised by one of the twenty areas into which the National Association is divided, and is therefore held in a different part of the country each year.

The Julia Clements Challenge Trophy for the Best Exhibit in the national competitions has been awarded to the following members of NAFAS:

1962 Mrs D. Starling, London and Overseas
1963 Mrs P. Mann, Wessex
1964 Mrs K. M. Nicol, North Midlands
1965 Mrs J. Taylor, Mercia and North Wales
1966 Mrs K. Young, London and Overseas
1967 Mrs J. Taylor, Mercia and North Wales
1968 Mrs J. M. Abbott, London and Overseas
1969 Miss E. Tomkinson, Mercia and North Wales
1970 Mrs A. Horsley, South Midlands
1971 Mrs R. Hewitt, Surrey
1972 Mrs C. Jephcott, South-West England
1973 Mr D. Bridges, North-East England
1974 Mrs A. Wiltshire, Wessex
1975 Mrs S. Lewis, Three Counties and South Wales
1976 Mrs D. Da Rosa, Surrey
1977 Mrs N. Hegarty, London and Overseas
1978 Mrs M. MacFarlane, Scotland
1979 Mrs Judy Ward, Kent
1980 Mrs Barbara Rogers, North West

Gaelic Football

ALL-IRELAND CHAMPIONSHIP

First contested in 1887. Winners since 1965:

1965 Galway	1970 Kerry	1975 Kerry	1980 Kerry
1966 Galway	1971 Offaly	1976 Dublin	Most wins:
1967 Meath	1972 Offaly	1977 Dublin	26 Kerry
1968 Down	1973 Cork	1978 Kerry	
1969 Kerry	1974 Dublin	1979 Kerry	

Games

GAME OF THE YEAR AWARD

The *Games & Puzzles* Game of the Year, first given in 1975, is the proprietary indoor game voted best by readers of the magazine. It is awarded to the manufacturer. Traditional games (eg chess), card games with usual

Photography

Niall Sinclair Cotton's winning photograph of an oil rig in the 1980 British Photography Competition (see p. 173)

Custard Pies

Amid the debris of the 1980 World Custard Pie Throwing Championship, the Flobbs hold up their winning trophy (see p. 75)

Gardening

Hilary and Norman Sharp, joint winners of the Gardener of the Year competition, showing off their plot (see p. 98)

Choirboys

Timothy Attree from Bexleyheath who received the 1980 Rediffusion award for Chorister of the Year (see p. 52)

pack(s) and similar are not eligible. Winners are:

1975 Scrabble
1976 Diplomacy
1977 Diplomacy
1978 Kingmaker
1979 Kingmaker
1980 Kingmaker

IT'S A CHAMPIONSHiP KNOCKOUT

The British competition is organised by BBC Television. Teams from various towns take part in a number of events, designed to test skills, ingenuity and speed but above all to provide entertainment for the viewer.

Prior to 1972 no team was designated British champion team. From 1972 to 1975 the *Radio Times* trophy was awarded to the team which gained the highest number of points in the domestic competition. The winners were as follows:

1972 Luton
1973 Ely
1974 Southport
1975 Onchen (Isle of Man)

From 1976 the *Radio Times* trophy was awarded for 'It's a Championship Knockout' which is a competition between the seven

Contestants in action during one of the games in the championship (BBC copyright)

The Radio Times *'It's a Championship Knockout' trophy* (BBC copyright)

teams of 'It's a Knockout' (ie the seven heat winners of the domestic competition). Winners:

1976 Blackpool
1977 Macclesfield
1978 Sandwell
1979 Douglas
1980 Kettering

JEUX SANS FRONTIÈRES

This is the European Competition of 'It's a Knockout'. Since Britain began competing the winners have been as follows:

1967 Bardenberg, West Germany
1968 Osterholz Scharmbeck, West Germany

Gardening

GARDENER OF THE YEAR

This competition, started in 1976, covers Great Britain. The country is divided into regions and a regional winner is selected from each. From this the main top four prize winners are chosen – the 1980 prize being a holiday for two in America worth £2000. Entrants send in 300 words describing their garden plus two or three colour photographs, and each year at the beginning of August the judges visit the gardens shortlisted. They look for people who have made the best use of space available to them. Winners:

1976 George and Freda King, Kendal, Cumbria

1977 Len Lester, Harborne, Birmingham
1978 Bill Bailey, Muswell Hill, London
1979 Ralph Dixon, Doncaster
1980 Hilary and Norman Sharp, West Bretton, W. Yorks

GIANT FRUIT AND VEGETABLE COMPETITION

This competition was started by *Garden News* in 1960 and has been run annually since then. It was launched following the publication of one or two letters from readers claiming to have grown vegetables of record dimensions. The 1980 winners together with the UK standing record are as follows:

	UK Standing record	1980 Winning weight/length	Winner
Beetroot	24 lb 0 oz	9 lb 4 oz	E. A. Smith, Swansea
Broad Bean	23 ⅜ in	22 ⅞ in	A. Adrain, Irvine, Ayrshire
Cabbage	114 lb 3 oz	55 lb 0 oz	G. Garland, Birmingham
Carrot	7 lb 11½ oz	6 lb 5 oz	B. Small, London
Cauliflower	52 lb 11½ oz	24 lb 0 oz	J. Biffen, Cullompton, Devon
Celery	35 lb 0 oz	12 lb 4 oz	K. C. Ayliffe, Brecon, Powys
Cucumber	11 lb 8 oz	9 lb 6 oz	R. A. Butcher, Stockbridge, Hants.
Leek	9 lb 5½ oz (blanch)	8 lb 13 oz (pot)	T. Fenton, Preston, Lancs.
Marrow	69 lb 0 oz	69 lb 0 oz (new record)	D. C. Payne, Forthampton, Glos.
Onion	6 lb 7 ⅛ oz	6 lb 7 ⅛ oz (new record)	R. E. Rodger, Fife, Scotland
Parsnip	10 lb 8½ oz	7 lb 0 oz	E. Stone, East Woodyates, Wilts.
Pea	10 ⅛ in	10 in	W. Stalley, Hartlepool, Cleveland
Potato	7 lb 1 oz	3 lb 0 oz	A. E. Jones, Llanfyllin, Powys.
Pumpkin	229 lb 0 oz	211 lb 8 oz	R. A. Butcher, Stockbridge, Hants.
Radish	17 lb 0 oz	6 lb 9 oz	K. C. Ayliffe, Brecon, Powys.
Runner Bean	39 in	32 ⅝ in	E. C. W. Cooper, Bognor Regis, Sussex
Tomato	4 lb 4 oz	4 lb 3¾ oz	R. A. Butcher, Stockbridge, Hants.
Apple	3 lb 1 oz	1 lb 14 oz	W. A. Wells, Swanley, Kent
Melon	13 lb 4 oz (water)	11 lb ½ oz (water)	M. J. Barling, Southall, Middlesex
Pear	2 lb 10½ oz	1 lb 11¼ oz	F. S. Holmes, London
Rhubarb	5 lb 11 oz	3 lb 7 oz	A. C. Setterfield, Reading, Berks.

1980 Supreme Champion is R. E. Rodger, Fife, Scotland

A selection of winning vegetables from the 'Giant Fruit and Vegetable Competition' run by Garden News. *Top left:* Mr Howcroft with his 7 lb 11½ oz carrot. *Top right:* Mr Payne with his 69 lb marrow which won the 1980 competition and also now holds the record UK weight. *Bottom left:* The UK standing record beetroot weighing in at 24 lb. *Bottom right:* Mr Butcher with his record weight pumpkin of 229 lb

Gliding

WORLD CHAMPIONSHIPS

The first world gliding (or soaring) championships were held in 1937. They are held every two or three years, and there are now three categories – Open, Standard and 15 metres. Winners of each category:

OPEN
1937 Heini Dittmar (Ger)
1948 Per Persson (Swe)
1950 Billy Nilsson (Swe)
1952 Phillip Wills (GB)
1954 Gerard Pierre (Fra)
1956 Paul MacCready (USA)
1958 Ernst Haase (Ger)
1960 Rudolf Hossinger (Arg)
1963 Edward Makula (Pol)
1965 Jan Wroblewski (Pol)
1968 Harro Wodl (Aut)
1970 George Moffat (USA)
1972 Goran Ax (Swe)
1974 George Moffat (USA)
1976 George Lee (GB)
1978 George Lee (GB)
1981 George Lee (GB)

2-Seater
1952 Luis Juez and J. Ara (Spa)
1954 Z. Rain and P. Komac (Yug)
1956 Nick Goodhard and Frank Foster (GB)

STANDARD
1958 Adam Witek (Pol)
1960 Heinz Huth (Ger)
1963 Heinz Huth (Ger)
1965 François Henry (Fra)
1968 A. J. Smith (USA)
1970 Helmut Reichmann (Ger)
1972 Jan Wroblewski (Pol)
1974 Helmut Reichmann (Ger)
1976 Ingo Renner (Aus)
1978 Baer Selen (Hol)

15 METRES
1978 Helmut Reichmann (Ger)

Golf

THE OPEN CHAMPIONSHIP

The first championship was held at Prestwick in 1860. In 1892 the competition was extended from 36 to 72 holes. Winners (GB except where shown):

		Score
1860	Willie Park, Sr	174
1861	Tom Morris, Sr	163
1862	Tom Morris, Sr	163
1863	Willie Park, Sr	168
1864	Tom Morris, Sr	167
1865	Andrew Strath	162
1866	Willie Park, Sr	169
1867	Tom Morris, Sr	170
1868	Tom Morris, Jr	170
1869	Tom Morris, Jr	154
1870	Tom Morris, Jr	149
1871	Not held	
1872	Tom Morris, Jr	166
1873	Tom Kidd	179
1874	Mungo Park	159
1875	Willie Park, Sr	166
1876	Robert Martin	176
1877	Jamie Anderson	160
1878	Jamie Anderson	157
1879	Jamie Anderson	170
1880	Robert Ferguson	162
1881	Robert Ferguson	170
1882	Robert Ferguson	171
1883	Willie Fernie	159
1884	Jack Simpson	160
1885	Bob Martin	171
1886	David Brown	157
1887	Willie Park, Jr	161
1888	Jack Burns	171
1889	Willie Park, Jr	155
1890	John Ball	164
1891	Hugh Kirkaldy	169
1892	Harold H. Hilton	305
1893	William Auchterlonie	322
1894	John H. Taylor	326
1895	John H. Taylor	322
1896	Harry Vardon	316
1897	Harold H. Hilton	314
1898	Harry Vardon	307
1899	Harry Vardon	310
1900	John H. Taylor	309
1901	James Braid	309
1902	Alexander Herd	307
1903	Harry Vardon	300
1904	Jack White	296
1905	James Braid	318
1906	James Braid	300
1907	Arnaud Massy	312
1908	James Braid	291
1909	John H. Taylor	295
1910	James Braid	299
1911	Harry Vardon	303
1912	Edward (Ted) Ray	295
1913	John H. Taylor	304
1914	Harry Vardon	306
1920	George Duncan	303
1921	Jock Hutchison (USA)	296
1922	Walter Hagen (USA)	300
1923	Arthur G. Havers	295
1924	Walter Hagen (USA)	301
1925	James M. Barnes (USA)	300
1926	Robert T. Jones, Jr (USA)	291
1927	Robert T. Jones, Jr (USA)	285
1928	Walter Hagen (USA)	292

	Score
1929 Walter Hagen (USA)	292
1930 Robert T. Jones, Jr (USA)	291
1931 Tommy D. Armour (USA)	296
1932 Gene Sarazen (USA)	283
1933 Denny Shute (USA)	292
1934 Henry Cotton	283
1935 Alfred Perry	283
1936 Alfred Padgham	287
1937 Henry Cotton	290
1938 Reg Whitcombe	295
1939 Richard Burton	290
1946 Sam Snead (USA)	290
1947 Fred Daly	293
1948 Henry Cotton	284
1949 Bobby Locke (SA)	283
1950 Bobby Locke (SA)	279
1951 Max Faulkner	285
1952 Bobby Locke (SA)	287
1953 Ben Hogan (USA)	282
1954 Peter Thomson (Aus)	283
1955 Peter Thomson (Aus)	281
1956 Peter Thomson (Aus)	286
1957 Bobby Locke (SA)	279
1958 Peter Thomson (Aus)	278
1959 Gary Player (SA)	284
1960 Kel Nagle (Aus)	278
1961 Arnold Palmer (USA)	284
1962 Arnold Palmer (USA)	276
1963 Bob Charles (NZ)	277
1964 Tony Lema (USA)	279
1965 Peter Thomson (Aus)	285
1966 Jack Nicklaus (USA)	282
1967 Roberto de Vincenzo (Arg)	278
1968 Gary Player (SA)	299
1969 Tony Jacklin	280
1970 Jack Nicklaus (USA)	283
1971 Lee Trevino (USA)	278
1972 Lee Trevino (USA)	278
1973 Tom Weiskopf (USA)	276
1974 Gary Player (SA)	282
1975 Tom Watson (USA)	279
1976 Johnny Miller (USA)	279
1977 Tom Watson (USA)	268
1978 Jack Nicklaus (USA)	281
1979 Severiano Ballesteros (Spa)	283
1980 Tom Watson (USA)	271

US MASTERS CHAMPIONSHIP

Played each year at the Augusta National Golf Course, Augusta, Georgia. Instituted in 1934. Stroke play over 72 holes. Winners (USA except where shown):

	Score
1934 Horton Smith	284
1935 Gene Sarazen	282
1936 Horton Smith	285
1937 Byron Nelson	283
1938 Henry Picard	285
1939 Ralph Guldahl	279
1940 Jimmy Demaret	280
1941 Craig Wood	280
1942 Byron Nelson	280
1946 Herman Keiser	282
1947 Jimmy Demaret	281
1948 Claude Harmon	279
1949 Sam Snead	282

Ben Hogan at Wentworth in 1956 (Action Photos)

	Score
1950 Jimmy Demaret	283
1951 Ben Hogan	280
1952 Sam Snead	286
1953 Ben Hogan	274
1954 Sam Snead	289
1955 Cary Middlecoff	279
1956 Jack Burke	289
1957 Doug Ford	283
1958 Arnold Palmer	284
1959 Art Wall	284
1960 Arnold Palmer	282
1961 Gary Player (SA)	280
1962 Arnold Palmer	280
1963 Jack Nicklaus	286
1964 Arnold Palmer	276
1965 Jack Nicklaus	271
1966 Jack Nicklaus	288
1967 Gay Brewer	280
1968 Bob Goalby	277
1969 George Archer	281
1970 Billy Casper	279
1971 Charles Coody	279
1972 Jack Nicklaus	286
1973 Tommy Aaron	283
1974 Gary Player (SA)	278
1975 Jack Nicklaus	276
1976 Ray Floyd	271
1977 Tom Watson	276
1978 Gary Player (SA)	277
1979 Fuzzy Zoeller	280
1980 Severiano Ballesteros (Spa)	275
1981 Tom Watson	280

US OPEN CHAMPIONSHIP

First held in 1895. Stroke play over 72 holes. Winners (USA except where shown):

1895 Horace Rawlins	173
1896 James Foulis	152
1897 Joe Lloyd	162
1898 Fred Herd	328

1899	Willie Smith	315	1973	Johnny Miller	279
1900	Harry Vardon (GB)	313	1974	Hale Irwin	287
1901	Willie Anderson	331	1975	Lou Graham	287
1902	Laurie Auchterlonie	307	1976	Jerry Pate	277
1903	Willie Anderson	307	1977	Hubert Green	278
1904	Willie Anderson	303	1978	Andy North	285
1905	Willie Anderson	314	1979	Hale Irwin	284
1906	Alex Smith	295	1980	Jack Nicklaus	272
1907	Alex Ross	302	1981	David Graham (Aus)	273
1908	Fred McLeod	322			
1909	George Sargent	290			

US PROFESSIONAL GOLFERS' ASSOCIATION CHAMPIONSHIP

First played in 1916. From then until 1957 it was a knock-out match play tournament, but since 1958 has been decided over 36 holes of stroke play. Winners (USA except where shown):

1910	Alex Smith	298
1911	John McDermott	307
1912	John McDermott	294
1913	Francis Ouimet	304
1914	Walter Hagen	290
1915	Jerome D. Travers	297
1916	Charles Evans, Jr	286
1919	Walter Hagen	301
1920	Edward Ray (GB)	295
1921	Jim Barnes	289
1922	Gene Sarazen	288
1923	Robert T. Jones, Jr	296
1924	Cyril Walker	297
1925	Willie Macfarlane	291
1926	Robert T. Jones, Jr	293
1927	Tommy Armour	301
1928	Johnny Farrell	294
1929	Robert T. Jones, Jr	294
1930	Robert T. Jones, Jr	287
1931	Billy Burke	292
1932	Gene Sarazen	286
1933	John Goodman	287
1934	Olin Dutra	293
1935	Sam Parks, Jr	299
1936	Tony Manero	282
1937	Ralph Guldahl	281
1938	Ralph Guldahl	284
1939	Byron Nelson	284
1940	Lawson Little	287
1941	Craig Wood	284
1946	Lloyd Mangrum	284
1947	Lew Worsham	282
1948	Ben Hogan	276
1949	Cary Middlecoff	286
1950	Ben Hogan	287
1951	Ben Hogan	287
1952	Julius Boros	281
1953	Ben Hogan	283
1954	Ed Furgol	284
1955	Jack Fleck	287
1956	Gary Middlecoff	281
1957	Dick Mayer	282
1958	Tommy Bolt	283
1959	Billy Casper	282
1960	Arnold Palmer	280
1961	Gene Littler	281
1962	Jack Nicklaus	283
1963	Julius Boros	293
1964	Ken Venturi	278
1965	Gary Player (SA)	282
1966	Billy Casper	278
1967	Jack Nicklaus	275
1968	Lee Trevino	275
1969	Orville Moody	281
1970	Tony Jacklin (GB)	281
1971	Lee Trevino	280
1972	Jack Nicklaus	290

1916	James M. Barnes		
1919	James M. Barnes		
1920	Jock Hutchison		
1921	Walter Hagen		
1922	Gene Sarazen		
1923	Gene Sarazen		
1924	Walter Hagen		
1925	Walter Hagen		
1926	Walter Hagen		
1927	Walter Hagen		
1928	Leo Diegel		
1929	Leo Diegel		
1930	Tommy Armour		
1931	Tom Creavy		
1932	Olin Dutra		
1933	Gene Sarazen		
1934	Paul Runyan		
1935	Johnny Revolta		
1936	Denny Shute		
1937	Denny Shute		
1938	Paul Runyan		
1939	Henry Picard		
1940	Byron Nelson		
1941	Vic Ghezzi		
1942	Sam Snead		
1943	Not held		
1944	Bob Hamilton		
1945	Byron Nelson		
1946	Ben Hogan		
1947	Jim Ferrier		
1948	Ben Hogan		
1949	Sam Snead		
1950	Chandler Harper		
1951	Sam Snead		
1952	Jim Turnesa		
1953	Walter Burkemo		
1954	Chick Harbert		
1955	Doug Ford		
1956	Jack Burke		
1957	Lionel Hebert		*Score*
1958	Dow Finsterwald		276
1959	Bob Rosburg		277
1960	Jay Hebert		281
1961	Jerry Barber		277
1962	Gary Player (SA)		278
1963	Jack Nicklaus		279
1964	Bob Nichols		271
1965	Dave Marr		280
1966	Al Geiberger		280
1967	Don January		281

	Score
1968 Julius Boros	281
1969 Ray Floyd	276
1970 Dave Stockton	279
1971 Jack Nicklaus	281
1972 Gary Player (SA)	281
1973 Jack Nicklaus	277
1974 Lee Trevino	276
1975 Jack Nicklaus	276
1976 Dave Stockton	281
1977 Lanny Wadkins	282
1978 John Mahaffey	276
1979 David Graham (Aus)	272
1980 Jack Nicklaus	274

WORLD MATCH PLAY TOURNAMENT

Sponsored by Piccadilly from 1964 to 1976, and by Colgate from 1977.

1964 Arnold Palmer (USA)
1965 Gary Player (SA)
1966 Gary Player (SA)
1967 Arnold Palmer (USA)
1968 Gary Player (SA)
1969 Bob Charles (NZ)
1970 Jack Nicklaus (USA)
1971 Gary Player (SA)
1972 Tom Weiskopf (USA)
1973 Gary Player (SA)
1974 Hale Irwin (USA)
1975 Hale Irwin (USA)
1976 David Graham (Aus)
1977 Graham Marsh (Aus)
1978 Isao Aoki (Jap)
1979 Bill Rogers (USA)
1980 Greg Norman (Aus)

BRITISH AMATEUR CHAMPIONSHIP

First played in 1885, the Amateur Championship is a knock-out match play event. Winners since 1965:

1965 Michael Bonallack (GB)
1966 Bobby Cole (SA)
1967 Bob Dickson (USA)
1968 Michael Bonallack (GB)
1969 Michael Bonallack (GB)
1970 Michael Bonallack (GB)
1971 Steve Melnyk (USA)
1972 Trevor Homer (GB)
1973 Dick Siderowf (USA)
1974 Trevor Homer (GB)
1975 Marvin Giles (USA)
1976 Dick Siderowf (USA)
1977 Peter McAvoy (GB)
1978 Peter McAvoy (GB)
1979 Jay Sigel (USA)
1980 Duncan Evans (GB)
1981 Philippe Ploujoux (Fra)

Most wins:
8 John Ball (GB) 1888, 1890, 1892, 1894, 1899, 1907, 1910, 1912

US AMATEUR CHAMPIONSHIP

First played in 1893, a match play tournament over 36 holes per round. Winners since 1965:

1965 Bob Murphy

1966 Gary Cowan
1967 Bob Dickson
1968 Bruce Fleisher
1969 Steve Melnyk
1970 Lanny Wadkins
1971 Gary Cowan
1972 Marvin Giles
1973 Craig Stadler
1974 Jerry Pate
1975 Fred Ridley
1976 Bill Sander
1977 John Fought
1978 John Cook
1979 Mark O'Meara
1980 Hal Sutton

Most wins:
5 Robert T. Jones 1924, 1925, 1927, 1928, 1930

US WOMEN'S OPEN CHAMPIONSHIP

First held in 1946 as match play, but since 1947 has been at 72 holes stroke play. Winners since 1965 (all USA except where stated):

1965 Carol Mann 290
1966 Sandra Spuzich 277
1967 Catherine Lacoste (Fra) 294
1968 Sue Maxwell Berning 289
1969 Donna Caponi 294
1970 Donna Caponi 287
1971 JoAnne Carner 288
1972 Sue Maxwell Berning 299
1973 Sue Maxwell Berning 290
1974 Sandra Haynie 295
1975 Sandra Palmer 295
1976 JoAnne Carner 292
1977 Hollis Stacy 292

Joyce Wethered (later Lady Heathcote-Amory) in 1925 (RTHPL)

1978 Hollis Stacy 289
1979 Jerilyn Britz 284
1980 Amy Alcott 280

Most wins:
4 Betsy Rawls 1951, 1953, 1957, 1960; Mickey Wright 1958, 1959, 1961, 1964

BRITISH LADIES' OPEN CHAMPIONSHIP
First held 1976, this tournament succeeded the British Ladies' Amateur Stroke Play Championship which had been inaugurated in 1969

1976 Jennifer Lee Smith (GB) 299
1977 Vivien Saunders (GB) 306
1978 Janet Melville (GB) 310
1979 Alison Sheard (SA) 301
1980 Debbie Massey (USA) 294

BRITISH LADIES' AMATEUR CHAMPIONSHIP
First held in 1893, a knock-out match play event. Winners since 1965:

1965 Brigitte Varangot (Fra)
1966 Elizabeth Chadwick (GB)
1967 Elizabeth Chadwick (GB)
1968 Brigitte Varangot (Fra)
1969 Catherine Lacoste (Fra)
1970 Dinah Oxley (GB)
1971 Michelle Walker (GB)
1972 Michelle Walker (GB)
1973 Ann Irvin (GB)
1974 Carol Semple (USA)
1975 Nancy Syms (USA)
1976 Catherine Panton (GB)
1977 Angela Uzielli (GB)
1978 Edwina Kennedy (Aus)
1979 Maureen Madill (Ire)
1980 Ann Sander (GB)
1981 Belle Robertson (GB)

Most wins:
4 Cecilia Leitch 1914, 1920, 1921, 1926; Joyce Wethered, 1922, 1924, 1925, 1929

WORLD CUP
Contested by 2-man national teams of professionals. Instituted in 1953 as the Canada Cup. Winners (over 72 holes unless otherwise indicated):

	Team	Best Individual
1953	Argentina	Tony Cerda (Arg) 140 (36 holes)
1954	Australia	Stan Leonard (Can) 275
1955	USA	Ed Furgol (USA) 279
1956	USA	Ben Hogan (USA) 277
1957	Japan	Torakichi Nakamura (Jap) 274
1958	Ireland	Angel Miguel (Spa) 286
1959	Australia	Stan Leonard (Can) 275
1960	USA	Flory Van Donck (Bel) 279
1961	USA	Sam Snead (USA) 272
1962	USA	Roberto de Vicenzo (Arg) 276
1963	USA	Jack Nicklaus (USA) 237 (63 holes)
1964	USA	Jack Nicklaus (USA) 276
1965	South Africa	Gary Player (SA) 284
1966	USA	George Knudson (Can) 272
1967	USA	Arnold Palmer (USA) 276

1968	Canada	Al Balding (Can) 274
1969	USA	Lee Trevino (USA) 275
1970	Australia	Roberto de Vicenzo (Arg) 269
1971	USA	Jack Nicklaus (USA) 271
1972	Taiwan	Hsieh Min Nam (Tai) 217 (54 holes)
1973	USA	Johnny Miller (USA) 277
1974	South Africa	Bobby Cole (SA) 271
1975	USA	Johnny Miller (USA) 275
1976	Spain	Ernesto Perez Acosta (Mex) 282
1977	USA	Gary Player (SA) 280
1978	USA	John Mahaffey (USA) 281
1979	USA	Hale Irwin (USA) 285
1980	Canada	Sandy Lyle (Sco) 282
1981	Not held	

RYDER CUP
Contested every two years by professional teams from the United States and Europe (Great Britain up to 1977. First held in 1927. The USA have won on 18 occasions, most recently in 1971, 1973, 1975, 1977 and 1979. Great Britain/British Isles won in 1929, 1933 and 1957 and the 1969 match was halved.

WALKER CUP
Contested every two years by amateur teams from the United States and Great Britain. First held in 1922. The USA have won on 24 occasions, most recently in 1973, 1975, 1977 and 1979. Great Britain won in 1947 and 1971 and the 1965 match was halved.

CURTIS CUP
Contested every two years by teams of lady golfers from the United States and Great Britain. First held in 1932. The USA have won on 17 occasions, most recently in 1970, 1972, 1974, 1976, 1978 and 1980. Great Britain won in 1952 and 1956 and the 1936 and 1958 matches were halved.

EISENHOWER TROPHY
Contested by 4-man amateur national teams. Held biennially since 1958.

1958 Australia
1960 USA
1962 USA
1964 GB and Ireland
1966 Australia
1968 USA
1970 USA
1972 USA
1974 USA
1976 GB and Ireland
1978 USA
1980 USA

WORLD WOMEN'S AMATEUR TEAM CHAMPIONSHIP
Contested every two years for the Espirito Santo Trophy.

1964 France
1966 USA

1968 USA
1970 USA
1972 USA
1974 USA
1976 USA
1978 Australia
1980 USA

US PGA PLAYER-OF-THE-YEAR AWARD

Each year the PGA (Professional Golfers' Association) of America honours the Tour's leading player by presenting him with the PGA Player-of-the-Year Award.

The award now is made on the basis of playing record for the year. Points are awarded on the following basis: 25 points to winner of PGA, World Series of Golf and US Open. 10 points to winners of all other co-sponsored or approved events, including Masters, Canadian and British Opens. Points also awarded to top 10 on the year's money list and top 10 on the year's scoring average list (10 for 1st, 9 for 2nd, 8 for 3rd, etc, down to 1 for 10th). Winners since inception:

1948	Ben Hogan	1963	Julius Boros
1949	Sam Snead	1964	Ken Venturi
1950–51	Ben Hogan	1965	Dave Marr
1952	Julius Boros	1966	Billy Casper
1953	Ben Hogan	1967	Jack Nicklaus
1954	Ed Furgol	1968	No award
1955	Doug Ford	1969	Orville Moody
1956	Jack Burke	1970	Billy Casper
1957	Dick Mayer	1971	Lee Trevino
1958	Dow Finsterwald	1972–73	Jack Nicklaus
1959	Art Wall	1974	Johnny Miller
1960	Arnold Palmer	1975–76	Jack Nicklaus
1961	Jerry Barber	1977–80	Tom Watson
1962	Arnold Palmer		

US LPGA PLAYER-OF-THE-YEAR AWARD

In 1966, the LPGA (Ladies Professional Golf Association) established the Player-of-the-Year Award (sponsored by Chrysler Corporation) to recognise the player who, during a current tour year, had the most consistent and outstanding record. Points are only awarded to those players finishing in the first five positions in official LPGA co-sponsored or approved events. Winners:

1966–69 Kathy Whitworth
1970 Sandra Haynie
1971–73 Kathy Whitworth
1974 JoAnne Carner
1975 Sandra Palmer
1976–77 Judy Rankin
1978–79 Nancy Lopez
1980 Beth Daniel

HARRY VARDON TROPHY (GB)

Currently awarded to the PGA (Professional Golfers Association) member heading the

Tom Watson in unaccustomed trouble during the Piccadilly World Match Play event in 1975 (Action Photos)

order of merit at the end of the season. Winners since inception (GB except where shown):

1937 Charles Whitcombe
1938 Henry Cotton
1939 Reg Whitcombe
1946 Bobby Locke (SA)
1947 Norman Von Nida (Aus)
1948–49 Charles Ward
1950 Bobby Locke (SA)
1951 John Panton
1952 Harry Weetman
1953 Flory van Donck (Bel)
1954 Bobby Locke (SA)
1955 Dai Rees
1956 Harry Weetman
1957 Eric Brown
1958 Bernard Hunt
1959 Dai Rees
1960 Bernard Hunt
1961–62 Christy O'Connor
1963 Neil Coles
1964 Peter Alliss
1965 Bernard Hunt
1966 Peter Alliss
1967 Malcolm Gregson
1968 Brian Huggett
1969 Bernard Gallacher
1970 Neil Coles
1971–74 Peter Oosterhuis
1975 Dale Hayes (SA)
1976–78 Severiano Ballesteros (Spa)
1979–80 Sandy Lyle

Grandmothers

BUTLIN'S GLAMOROUS GRANDMOTHER

There are many competitions at local level throughout Britain to find the most glamorous granny, and, since 1978, BBC Television's Nationwide organises a national award scheme. As well as the silver challenge trophy, the winner receives a cash prize and a holiday for two: Winners:

1978 Pamela Burnell (age 40), Cardiff
1979 Patricia Stables (age 45), Brigg, South Humberside
1980 Verona Sampson (age 54), Coventry
1981 Judith Bardwell (age 43), Chingford

Glamorous grandmother 45-year-old Patricia Stables with Arthur Mullard receiving her trophy (Popperfoto)

Greyhound Racing

GREYHOUND DERBY

Britain's premier race, the Greyhound Derby, is held at the White City Stadium over a distance of 500 metres. It was first held in 1927. Winners have been:

1927 Entry Badge
1928 Boher Ash
1929 Mick The Miller
1930 Mick The Miller
1931 Seldom Lad
1932 Wild Woolley
1933 Future Cutlet
1934 Davesland
1935 Greta Ranee
1936 Fine Jubilee
1937 Wattle Bark
1938 Lone Keel
1939 Highland Rum
1940 G. R. Archduke
1945 Ballyhennessy Seal
1946 Mondays News
1947 Trevs Perfection
1948 Priceless Border
1949 Narrogar Ann
1950 Ballmac Ball
1951 Ballylanigan Tanist
1952 Endless Gossip
1953 Daws Dancer
1954 Pauls Fun
1955 Rushton Mack
1956 Dunmore King
1957 Ford Spartan
1958 Pigalle Wonder
1959 Mile Bush Pride
1960 Duleek Dandy

1961 Palms Printer
1962 The Grand Canal
1963 Lucky Boy Boy
1964 Hack Up Chieftain
1965 Chittering Clapton
1966 Faithful Hope
1967 Tric-Trac
1968 Camira Flash
1969 Sand Star
1970 John Silver
1971 Dolores Rocket
1972 Patricia's Hope
1973 Patricia's Hope
1974 Jimsun
1975 Tartan Khan
1976 Mutts Silver
1977 Balliniska Band
1978 Lacca Champion
1979 Sarah's Bunny
1980 Indian Joe

GREYHOUND GRAND NATIONAL

First held in 1927 and run over 500 metres hurdles at the White City Stadium.

1927 Bonzo
1928 Cormorant
1929 Levator
1930 Stylish Cutlet
1931 Rule the Roost
1932 Long Hop
1933 Scapegoat
1934 Lemonition
1935 Quarter Day
1936 Kilganny Bridge
1937 Flying Wedge

Patricia's Hope, *after winning the 1972 Greyhound Derby at odds of 7–1. His joint owners Basil Marks* (left) *and Brian Stanley* (centre) *look jubilant* (Press Association)

1938 Juvenile Classic
1939 Valiant Bob
1940 Juvenile Classic
1946 Barry from Limerick
1947 Baytown Pigeon
1948 Joves Reason
1949 Blossom of Annagura
1950 Blossom of Annagura
1951 XPDNC
1952 Whistling Laddie
1953 Denver Berwick
1954 Prince Lawrence
1955 Barrowside
1956 Blue Sand
1957 Tanyard Tulip
1958 Fodda Champion
1959 Prince Poppit
1960 Bruff Chariot
1961 Ballinatona Special
1962 Corsican Reward
1963 Indoor Sport
1964 Two Aces
1965 I'm Crazy
1966 Halfpenny King
1967 The Grange Santa
1968 Ballintore Tiger
1969 Tony's Friend
1970 Sherry's Prince
1971 Sherry's Prince

1972 Sherry's Prince
1973 Killone Flash
1974 Shanney's Darkie
1975 Pier Hero
1976 Weston Pete
1977 Salerno
1978 Top O' The Tide
1979 Top O' The Tide
1980 Gilt Edge Flyer

THE LAURELS
First held in 1930 and run over 500 metres at Wimbledon.

1930 Kilbrean Boy
1931 Future Cutlet
1932 Beef Cutlet
1933 Wild Woolley
1934 Brilliant Bob
1935 Kitshine
1936 Top O' The Carlow Road
1937 Ballyhennessy Sandhills
1938 Ballyhennessy Sandhills
1939 Musical Duke
1940 April Burglar
1945 Burhill Moon
1946 Shannon Shore
1947 Rimmells Black
1948 Good Worker
1949 Ballymac Ball
1950 Ballymac Ball
1951 Ballylanigan Tanist
1952 Endless Gossip
1953 Polonius

1954 Coolkill Chieftain	1968 Ambiguous
1955 Duet Leader	1969 Ardine Flame
1956 Duet Leader	1970 Sole Aim
1957 Ford Spartan	1971 Black Andrew
1958 Granthamian	1972 Cricket Bunny
1959 Mighty Hassan	1973 Black Banjo
1960 Dunstown Paddy	1974 Over Protected
1961 Clonalvy Pride	1975 Pineapple Grand
1962 Tuturama	1976 Xmas Holiday
1963 Dalcassion Son	1977 Greenfield Fox
1964 Conna Count	1978 Jet Control
1965 Conna Count	1979 Another Spatter
1966 Super Fame	1980 Flying Pursuit
1967 Carry on Oregon	

Gymnastics

WORLD AND OLYMPIC CHAMPIONSHIPS

Gymnastics have been included in each Olympic Games since 1896. Since the 1948 Games the events have been:

MEN

Floor exercises, side horse, rings, horse vault, parallel bars, horizontal bar.

WOMEN

Horse vault, asymmetrical bars, balance beam, floor exercises.

Competitors compete for medals in both these events and combined events, including all activities. Winners of each event since 1968 and winner of most titles since 1948 (*=Olympic winners):

MEN

TEAM
1968* Japan
1970 Japan
1972* Japan
1974 Japan
1976* Japan
1978 Japan
1980* USSR

Most wins:
10 Japan

COMBINED EXERCISES
1968* Sawao Kato (Jap)
1970 Eizo Kenmotsu (Jap)
1972* Sawao Kato (Jap)
1974 Shigeru Kasamatsu (Jap)
1976* Nikolai Andrianov (USSR)
1978 Nikolai Andrianov (USSR)
1980* Aleksandr Dityatin (USSR)

Most wins:
2 Viktor Chukarin (USSR) 1952*, 1956*; Boris Shakhlin (USSR) 1958, 1960*; and as above

FLOOR EXERCISES
1968* Sawao Kato (Jap)
1970 Akinori Nakayama (Jap)

1972* Nikolai Andrianov (USSR)
1974 Shigeru Kasamatsu (Jap)
1976* Nikolai Andrianov (USSR)
1978 Kurt Thomas (USA)
1980* Roland Bruckner (GDR)

Most wins:
2 Valentin Muratov (USSR) 1954, 1956*; Nobuyaki Aihara (Jap) 1960*, 1962; Akinori Nakayama (Jap) 1966, 1970; and as above

SIDE HORSE
1968* Miroslav Cerar (Yug)
1970 Miroslav Cerar (Yug)
1972* Viktor Klimenko (USSR)
1974 Zoltan Magyar (Hun)
1976* Zoltan Magyar (Hun)
1978 Zoltan Magyar (Hun)
1980* Zoltan Magyar (Hun)

Most wins:
5 Miroslav Cerar (Yug) 1962, 1964*, 1966, 1968*, 1970

RINGS
1968* Akinori Nakayama (Jap)
1970 Akinori Nakayama (Jap)
1972* Akinori Nakayama (Jap)
1974 Nikolai Andrianov (USSR)
    and Danat Grecu (Rom)
1976* Nikolai Andrianov (USSR)
1978 Nikolai Andrianov (USSR)
1980* Aleksandr Dityatin (USSR)

Most wins:
4 Albert Azaryan (USSR) 1954, 1956*, 1958, 1960*

HORSE VAULT
1968* Mikhail Voronin (USSR)
1970 Mitsuo Tsukahara (Jap)
1972* Klaus Köste (GDR)
1974 Shigeru Kasamatsu (Jap)
1976* Nikolai Andrianov (USSR)
1978 Junichi Shimizu (Jap)
1980* Nikolai Andrianov (USSR)

Most wins:
no double winner

PARALLEL BARS
1968* Akinori Nakayama (Jap)

1970 Akinori Nakayama (Jap)
1972* Sawao Kato (Jap)
1974 Eizo Kenmotsu (Jap)
1976* Sawao Kato (Jap)
1978 Eizo Kenmotsu (Jap)
1980* Aleksandr Tkachyov (USSR)

Most wins:
2 Hans Eugster (Swi) 1950, 1952*; Viktor Chukarin (USSR) 1954, 1956*; Boris Shakhlin (USSR) 1958, 1960*; and as above

HORIZONTAL BAR
1968* Akinori Nakayama (Jap)
      and Mikhail Voronin (USSR)
1970 Eizo Kenmotsu (Jap)
1972* Mitsuo Tsukahara (Jap)
1974 Eberhard Gienger (Ger)
1976* Mitsuo Tsukahara (Jap)
1978 Shigeru Kasamatsu (Jap)
1980* Stoyan Deltchev (Bul)

Most wins:
3 Takashi Ono (Jap) 1956*, 1960*, 1962

WOMEN

TEAM
1968* USSR	1976* USSR
1970 USSR	1978 USSR
1972* USSR	1980* USSR
1974 USSR	Most wins:
	13 USSR

Nadia Comaneci at the 1976 Olympic Games (G. Herringshaw)

COMBINED EXERCISES
1968* Vera Caslavska (Cze)
1970 Lyudmila Tourischeva (USSR)
1972* Lyudmila Tourischeva (USSR)
1974 Lyudmila Tourischeva (USSR)
1976* Nadia Comaneci (Rom)
1978 Elena Mukhina (USSR)
1980* Elena Davidova (USSR)

Most wins:
4 Larissa Latynina (USSR) 1956*, 1958, 1962*, 1966

FLOOR EXERCISES
1968* Vera Caslavska (Cze)
      and Larissa Petrik (USSR)
1970 Lyudmila Tourischeva (USSR)
1972* Olga Korbut (USSR)
1974 Lyudmila Tourischeva (USSR)
1976* Nelli Kim (USSR)
1978 Nelli Kim (USSR)
1980* Nelli Kim (USSR)

Most wins:
4 Larissa Latynina (USSR) 1956*, 1960*, 1962, 1964*

Olga Korbut, who charmed millions of TV viewers of the 1972 Olympic Games (ED Lacey)

HORSE VAULT

1968* Vera Caslavska (Cze)
1970 Erika Zuchold (GDR)
1972* Karin Janz (GDR)
1974 Olga Korbut (USSR)
1976* Nelli Kim (USSR)
1978 Nelli Kim (USSR)
1980* Natalya Shaposhnikova (USSR)

Most wins:
4 Vera Caslavska (Cze) 1962, 1964*, 1966, 1968*

ASSYMMETRICAL BARS

1968* Vera Caslavska (Cze)
1970 Karin Janz (GDR)
1972* Karin Janz (GDR)
1974 Annelore Zinke (GDR)
1976* Nadia Comaneci (Rom)

1978 Marcia Frederick (USA)
1980* Maxi Gnauck (GDR)

Most wins:
2 Agnes Keleti (Hun) 1954, 1956*; Polina Astakhova (USSR) 1960*, 1964*; and as above

BALANCE BEAM

1968* Natalia Kuchinskaya (USSR)
1970 Erika Zuchold (GDR)
1972* Olga Korbut (USSR)
1974 Lyudmila Tourischeva (USSR)
1976* Nadia Comaneci (Rom)
1978 Nadia Comaneci (Rom)
1980* Nadia Comaneci (Rom)

Most wins:
3 Nadia Comaneci (Rom) as above

Hairdressing

HEAD OF THE YEAR

This is an annual award given by the National Hairdressers' Federation to men and women in the public eye. Past winners have included Eammon Andrews, Cilla Black, Cliff Richard, Lulu, David Dimbleby and Noel Gordon. Recent winners:

1978 Angela Rippon, BBC TV News
     Peter Shilton, Nottingham Forest Football Club
1979 Isla St. Clair, BBC TV's 'The Generation Game'
     Dave Lee Travis, BBC Radio 1 disc jockey
1980 Felicity Kendall, actress
     Laurie McMenemy, Southampton Football Club manager

1979 winners: Isla St. Clair and Dave Lee Travis after receiving their awards of silver-backed hairbrushes in inscribed cases

Handball

First held in the Olympic Games in 1936, the sport for men was re-introduced in 1972, and is now held indoor.

OLYMPIC CHAMPIONSHIPS

MEN
1936 Germany
1972 Yugoslavia
1976 USSR
1980 GDR

WOMEN
1976 USSR
1980 USSR

WORLD CHAMPIONSHIPS

MEN		*Indoor*
Outdoor		1954 Sweden
1938 Germany		1958 Sweden
1948 Sweden		1961 Romania
1952 West Germany		1964 Romania
1955 West Germany		1967 Czechoslovakia
1959 West Germany		1970 Romania
1963 GDR		1974 Romania
1966 West Germany		1978 West Germany

WOMEN
Outdoor
1949 Hungary
1956 Romania
1960 Romania

Indoor
1957 Czechoslovakia
1962 Romania
1965 Hungary
1971 GDR

1973 Yugoslavia
1975 GDR
1978 GDR

Hockey

OLYMPIC CHAMPIONSHIPS
Winners of the men's hockey title at the Olympic Games – first included in 1908:

1908 England	1956 India
1920 Great Britain	1960 Pakistan
1928 India	1964 India
1932 India	1968 Pakistan
1936 India	1972 West Germany
1948 India	1976 New Zealand
1952 India	1980 India

Winners of the women's hockey title at the Olympic Games – first included in 1980:

1980 Zimbabwe

WORLD CUP
The first men's World Cup was held in 1971. Winners:

1971 Pakistan	1975 India
1973 Holland	1978 Pakistan

The FIH, the international federation governing hockey for both men and women, organised the first official world championship for women – the World Cup – in 1974. Winners:

1974 Holland
1976 W. Germany
1978 Holland

WORLD CHAMPIONSHIPS
The IFWHA (International Federation of Women's Hockey Associations) organised a world championship in 1975, and a second in August 1979. Winners:

1975 England
1979 Holland

EUROPEAN CUP
First men's held in 1970. Winners:

1970 W. Germany
1974 Spain
1978 W. Germany

COUNTY CHAMPIONSHIPS
MEN
First held 1957–58 season:
1958 Lincolnshire
1959 Middlesex
1960 Hertfordshire
1961 Middlesex
1962 Durham
1963 Surrey
1964 Kent
1965 Kent
1966 Cheshire
1967 Wiltshire
1968 Wiltshire
1969 Lancashire
1970 Wiltshire
1971 Staffordshire
1972 Wiltshire
1973 Surrey
1974 Hertfordshire
1975 Kent
1976 Hertfordshire
1977 Middlesex
1978 Lancashire
1979 Kent
1980 Buckinghamshire
1981 Middlesex

WOMEN
First held 1968–69 season:
1969 Hertfordshire & Lancashire
1970 Lancashire
1971 Hertfordshire & Lancashire
1972 Essex
1973 Lancashire
1974 Lancashire
1975 Surrey & Leicestershire
1976 Lancashire
1977 Lancashire
1978 Hertfordshire
1979 Lancashire
1980 Leicestershire & Suffolk
1981 Staffordshire

The winning Indian hockey team at the 1936 Olympic Games. The team scored 39 goals to 1 against in five games, beating Germany 8–1 in the final

Horse Racing

THE CLASSICS

The five English Classics are all for 3-year-old horses. They are the 2000 Guineas, the 1000 Guineas, the Derby, the Oaks, and the St. Leger. The 1000 Guineas and the Oaks are restricted to fillies.

Two horses have won four classics: *Formosa* (1868) and *Sceptre* (1902), each won all bar the Derby. Fifteen horses have won the 2000 Guineas, Derby and St. Leger – the only horse since 1935 being *Nijinsky* in 1970. Six horses have won the 1000 Guineas, Oaks and St. Leger – since 1942 the only one to do so being *Meld* in 1955.

1000 GUINEAS

Run at Newmarket over 1 mile. First run in 1814. Winning horses and jockeys since 1946 have been:

1946 *Hypericum,* Douglas Smith
1947 *Imprudence*, Rae Johnstone
1948 *Queenpot*, Gordon Richards
1949 *Musidora*, Edgar Britt
1950 *Camaree*, Rae Johnstone
1951 *Belle of All*, Gordon Richards
1952 *Zabara*, Ken Gethin
1953 *Happy Laughter*, Manny Mercer
1954 *Festoon*, Scobie Breasley
1955 *Meld*, Harry Carr
1956 *Honeylight*, Edgar Britt
1957 *Rose Royale*, Charlie Smirke
1958 *Bella Paola*, Serge Boullenger
1959 *Petite Etoile*, Douglas Smith
1960 *Never Too Late*, Roger Poincelet
1961 *Sweet Solera*, Bill Rickaby
1962 *Abermaid*, Bill Williamson
1963 *Hula Dancer*, Roger Poincelet
1964 *Pourparler*, Garnie Bougoure
1965 *Night Off*, Bill Williamson
1966 *Glad Rags*, Paul Cook
1967 *Fleet*, George Moore
1968 *Caergwrle*, Sandy Barclay
1969 *Full Dress II*, Ron Hutchinson
1970 *Humble Duty*, Lester Piggott
1971 *Altesse Royale*, Yves Saint-Martin
1972 *Waterloo*, Edward Hide
1973 *Mysterious*, Geoff Lewis
1974 *Highclere*, Joe Mercer
1975 *Nocturnal Spree*, Johnny Roe
1976 *Flying Water*, Yves Saint-Martin
1977 *Mrs McArdy*, Edward Hide
1978 *Enstone Spark*, Ernie Johnson
1979 *One In a Million*, Joe Mercer
1980 *Quick As Lightning,* Brian Rouse
1981 *Fairy Footsteps*, Lester Piggott

2000 GUINEAS

Run at Newmarket over 1 mile. First run in 1809. Winning horses and jockeys since 1946 have been:

1946 *Happy Knight*, Tommy Weston
1947 *Tudor Minstrel*, Gordon Richards
1948 *My Babu*, Charlie Smirke
1949 *Nimbus*, Charlie Elliott
1950 *Palestine*, Charlie Smirke
1951 *Ki Ming*, Scobie Breasley
1952 *Thunderhead II*, Roger Poincelet
1953 *Nearula*, Edgar Britt
1954 *Darius*, Manny Mercer
1955 *Our Babu*, Douglas Smith
1956 *Gilles de Retz*, Frank Barlow
1957 *Crepello*, Lester Piggott
1958 *Pall Mall*, Douglas Smith
1959 *Taboun*, George Moore
1960 *Martial*, Ron Hutchinson
1961 *Rockavon*, Norman Stirk
1962 *Privy Councillor*, Bill Rickaby
1963 *Only For Life*, Jimmy Lindley
1964 *Baldric II*, Bill Pyers
1965 *Niksar*, Duncan Keith
1966 *Kashmir II*, Jimmy Lindley
1967 *Royal Palace*, George Moore
1968 *Sir Ivor*, Lester Piggott
1969 *Right Tack*, Geoff Lewis
1970 *Nijinsky*, Lester Piggott
1971 *Brigadier Gerard*, Joe Mercer
1972 *High Top*, Willie Carson
1973 *Mon Fils*, Frankie Durr
1974 *Nonoalco*, Yves Saint-Martin
1975 *Bolkonski*, Gianfranco Dettori
1976 *Wollow*, Gianfranco Dettori
1977 *Nebbiolo*, Gabriel Curran
1978 *Roland Gardens*, Frankie Durr
1979 *Tap On Wood*, Steve Cauthen
1980 *Known Fact*, Willie Carson
1981 *To-Agori-Mou*, Greville Starkey

THE DERBY

Run at Epsom over 1½ miles. First run in 1780. Winning horses and jockeys since 1946 have been:

1946 *Airborne,* Thomas Lowrey
1947 *Pearl Diver*, George Bridgland
1948 *My Love*, Rae Johnstone
1949 *Nimbus*, Charlie Elliott
1950 *Galcador*, Rae Johnstone
1951 *Arctic Prince*, Charles Spares
1952 *Tulyar*, Charlie Smirke
1953 *Pinza*, Gordon Richards
1954 *Never Say Die*, Lester Piggott
1955 *Phil Drake*, Fred Palmer
1956 *Lavandin*, Rae Johnstone
1957 *Crepello*, Lester Piggott
1958 *Hard Ridden*, Charlie Smirke
1959 *Parthia*, Harry Carr
1960 *St Paddy*, Lester Piggott
1961 *Psidium*, Roger Poincelet
1962 *Larkspur*, Neville Sellwood
1963 *Relko*, Yves Saint-Martin
1964 *Santa Claus*, Scobie Breasley
1965 *Sea Bird II*, Pat Glennon
1966 *Charlottown*, Scobie Breasley
1967 *Royal Palace*, George Moore
1968 *Sir Ivor*, Lester Piggott
1969 *Blakeney*, Ernie Johnson
1970 *Nijinsky*, Lester Piggott
1971 *Mill Reef*, Geoff Lewis
1972 *Roberto*, Lester Piggott
1973 *Morston*, Edward Hide
1974 *Snow Knight*, Brian Taylor
1975 *Grundy*, Pat Eddery

1976 *Empery*, Lester Piggott
1977 *The Minstrel*, Lester Piggott
1978 *Shirley Heights*, Greville Starkey
1979 *Troy*, Willie Carson
1980 *Henbit*, Willie Carson
1981 *Shergar,* Walter Swinburn

THE OAKS
Run at Epsom over 1½ miles. First run in 1779. Winning horses and jockeys since 1946:

1946 *Steady Aim*, Harry Wragg
1947 *Imprudence*, Rae Johnstone
1948 *Masaka*, Willie Nevett
1949 *Musidora*, Edgar Britt
1950 *Asmena*, Rae Johnstone
1951 *Neasham Belle,* Stan Clayton
1952 *Frieze*, Edgar Britt
1953 *Ambiguity*, Joe Mercer
1954 *Sun Cap*, Rae Johnstone
1955 *Meld*, Harry Carr
1956 *Sicarelle*, Fred Palmer
1957 *Carrozza*, Lester Piggott
1958 *Bella Paola*, Max Garcia
1959 *Petite Etoile*, Lester Piggott
1960 *Never Too Late*, Roger Poincelet
1961 *Sweet Solera*, Bill Rickaby
1962 *Monade*, Yves Saint-Martin
1963 *Noblesse*, Garnie Bougoure
1964 *Homeward Bound*, Greville Starkey
1965 *Long Look*, Jack Purtell
1966 *Valoris*, Lester Piggott
1967 *Pia*, Edward Hide
1968 *La Lagune*, Gerard Thiboeuf
1969 *Sleeping Partner*, John Gorton
1970 *Lupe*, Sandy Barclay
1971 *Altesse Royale*, Geoff Lewis
1972 *Ginevra*, Tony Murray
1973 *Mysterious*, Geoff Lewis
1974 *Polygamy*, Pat Eddery
1975 *Juliette Marny*, Lester Piggott
1976 *Pawneese*, Yves Saint-Martin
1977 *Dunfermline*, Willie Carson
1978 *Fair Salinia*, Greville Starkey
1979 *Scintillate*, Pat Eddery
1980 *Bireme*, Willie Carson
1981 *Blue Wind,* Lester Piggott

ST LEGER
Run at Doncaster over 1 mile 6 furlongs 132 yards. First run in 1776. Winning horses and jockeys since 1946:

1946 *Airborne*, Thomas Lowrey
1947 *Sayajirao*, Edgar Britt
1948 *Black Tarquin*, Edgar Britt
1949 *Ridge Wood*, Michael Beary
1950 *Scratch II*, Rae Johnstone
1951 *Talma II*, Rae Johnstone
1952 *Tulyar*, Charlie Smirke
1953 *Premonition*, Eph Smith
1954 *Never Say Die*, Charlie Smirke
1955 *Meld*, Harry Carr
1956 *Cambremer*, Fred Palmer
1957 *Ballymoss*, Thomas Burns
1958 *Alcide*, Harry Carr
1959 *Cantelo*, Edward Hide
1960 *St. Paddy*, Lester Piggott
1961 *Aurelius*, Lester Piggott
1962 *Hethersett*, Harry Carr
1963 *Ragusa*, Garnie Bougoure

1964 *Indiana*, Jimmy Lindley
1965 *Provoke*, Joe Mercer
1966 *Sodium*, Frankie Durr
1967 *Ribocco*, Lester Piggott
1968 *Ribero*, Lester Piggott
1969 *Intermezzo*, Ron Hutchinson
1970 *Nijinsky*, Lester Piggott
1971 *Athens Wood*, Lester Piggott
1972 *Boucher*, Lester Piggott
1973 *Peleid*, Frankie Durr
1974 *Bustino*, Joe Mercer
1975 *Bruni*, Tony Murray
1976 *Crow*, Yves Saint-Martin
1977 *Dunfermline*, Willie Carson
1978 *Julio Mariner*, Edward Hide
1979 *Son of Love*, Alain Lequeux
1980 *Light Cavalry*, Joe Mercer

PRIX DE L'ARC DE TRIOMPHE
Europe's most prestigious race was first run in 1920. It is run at Longchamp, Paris, over 1½ miles and is open to all ages. Winning horses and jockeys since 1946 have been:

1946 *Caracalla*, Charlie Elliott
1947 *Le Paillon*, Fernand Rochetti
1948 *Migole*, Charlie Smirke
1949 *Coronation*, Roger Poincelet
1950 *Tantième*, Jacko Doyasbere
1951 *Tantième*, Jacko Doyasbere
1952 *Nuccio*, Roger Poincelet
1953 *La Sorellina*, Maurice Larraun
1954 *Sica Boy*, Rae Johnstone
1955 *Ribot*, Enrico Camici
1956 *Ribot*, Enrico Camici
1957 *Oroso*, Serge Boullenger
1958 *Ballymoss*, Scobie Breasley
1959 *Saint Crespin*, George Moore
1960 *Puissant Chef*, Max Garcia
1961 *Molvedo*, Enrico Camici
1962 *Soltikoff*, Marcel Depalmas
1963 *Exbury*, Jean Deforge
1964 *Prince Royal II*, Roger Poincelet
1965 *Sea Bird II*, Pat Glennon
1966 *Bon Mot III*, Freddy Head
1967 *Topyo*, Bill Pyers
1968 *Vaguely Noble*, Bill Williamson
1969 *Levmoss*, Bill Williamson
1970 *Sassafras*, Yves Saint-Martin
1971 *Mill Reef*, Geoff Lewis
1972 *San San*, Freddy Head
1973 *Rheingold*, Lester Piggott
1974 *Allez France*, Yves Saint-Martin
1975 *Star Appeal*, Greville Starkey
1976 *Ivanjica*, Freddy Head
1977 *Alleged*, Lester Piggott
1978 *Alleged*, Lester Piggott
1979 *Three Troikas*, Freddy Head
1980 *Detroit*, Pat Eddery

NATIONAL HUNT RACING

GRAND NATIONAL
Held at Aintree, Liverpool – a steeplechase over 4 miles 856 yards. Winning horses and jockeys since 1946 have been:

1946 *Lovely Cottage*, Robert Petre
1947 *Caughoo*, Edward Dempsey

1948 *Sheila's Cottage*, Arthur Thompson
1949 *Russian Hero*, Liam McMorrow
1950 *Freebooter*, Jimmy Power
1951 *Nickel Coin*, Johnny Bullock
1952 *Teal*, Arthur Thompson
1953 *Early Mist*, Bryan Marshall
1954 *Royal Tan*, Bryan Marshall
1955 *Quare Times*, Pat Taaffe
1956 *E.S.B.*, Dave Dick
1957 *Sundew*, Fred Winter
1958 *Mr. What*, Arthur Freeman
1959 *Oxo*, Michael Scudamore
1960 *Merryman II*, Gerald Scott
1961 *Nicolaus Silver*, Bobby Beasley
1962 *Kilmore*, Fred Winter
1963 *Ayala*, Pat Buckley
1964 *Team Spirit*, Willie Robinson
1965 *Jay Trump*, Tommy Smith
1966 *Anglo*, Tim Norman
1967 *Foinavon*, John Buckingham
1968 *Red Alligator*, Brian Fletcher
1969 *Highland Wedding*, Eddie Harty
1970 *Gay Trip*, Pat Taaffe
1971 *Specify*, John Cook
1972 *Well To Do*, Graham Thorner
1973 *Red Rum*, Brian Fletcher
1974 *Red Rum*, Brian Fletcher
1975 *L'Escargot*, Tommy Carberry
1976 *Rag Trade*, John Burke
1977 *Red Rum*, Tommy Stack
1978 *Lucius*, Bob Davies
1979 *Rubstic*, Maurice Barnes
1980 *Ben Nevis*, Charlie Fenwick
1981 *Aldaniti*, Bob Champion

CHELTENHAM GOLD CUP

Held at Cheltenham – a steeplechase run over 3¼ miles. Distance: 1924–28 about 3¼ miles; 1929–35 3 miles and about 3 furlongs; 1936–39 3 miles and about 2 furlongs; 1940–45 3 miles; 1946–57 3 miles and about 2 furlongs; 1958 3¼ miles and 130 yards; from 1965 3 miles 2 furlongs and 76 yards. (All horses now carry 12 st.) Winning horses and jockeys since 1946:

1946 *Prince Regent*, Tim Hyde
1947 *Fortina*, Richard Black
1948 *Cottage Rake*, Aubrey Brabazon
1949 *Cottage Rake*, Aubrey Brabazon
1950 *Cottage Rake*, Aubrey Brabazon
1951 *Silver Fame*, Martin Molony
1952 *Mont Tremblant*, Dave Dick
1953 *Knock Hard*, Tim Molony
1954 *Four Ten*, Tommy Cusack
1955 *Gay Donald*, Tony Grantham
1956 *Limber Hill*, Jimmy Power
1957 *Linwell*, Michael Scudamore
1958 *Kerstin*, Stan Hayhurst
1959 *Roddy Owen*, Bobby Beasley
1960 *Pas Seul*, Bill Rees
1961 *Saffron Tartan*, Fred Winter
1962 *Mandarin*, Fred Winter
1963 *Mill House*, Willie Robinson
1964 *Arkle*, Pat Taaffe
1965 *Arkle*, Pat Taaffe
1966 *Arkle*, Pat Taaffe
1967 *Woodland Venture*, Terry Biddlecombe
1968 *Fort Leney*, Pat Taaffe
1969 *What a Myth*, Paul Kelleway
1970 *L'Escargot*, Tommy Carberry

1971 *L'Escargot*, Tommy Carberry
1972 *Glencaraig Lady*, Frank Berry
1973 *The Dikler*, Ron Barry
1974 *Captain Christy*, Bobby Beasley
1975 *Ten Up*, Tommy Carberry
1976 *Royal Frolic*, John Burke
1977 *Davy Lad*, Dessie Hughes
1978 *Midnight Court*, Johnny Francome
1979 *Alverton*, Jon Jo O'Neill
1980 *Master Smudge*, Richard Hoare
1981 *Little Owl*, Jim Wilson

CHAMPION HURDLE

Held at Cheltenham – a steeplechase over 2 miles. Distance: 1927–28, 2 miles; 1929–57, 2 miles and a few yards; 1958–60, 2 miles; 1961–64, 2 miles 100 yards; 1965–79, 2 miles 200 yards. Winning horses and jockeys since 1946:

1946 *Distel*, Robert O'Ryan
1947 *National Spirit*, Danny Morgan
1948 *National Spirit*, Ron Smyth
1949 *Hatton's Grace*, Aubrey Brabazon
1950 *Hatton's Grace*, Aubrey Brabazon
1951 *Hatton's Grace*, Tim Molony
1952 *Sir Ken*, Tim Molony
1953 *Sir Ken*, Tim Molony
1954 *Sir Ken*, Tim Molony
1955 *Clair Soleil*, Fred Winter
1956 *Doorknocker*, Harry Sprague

Sea Pigeon (left) *and* Monksfield (right) *at the last fence in the 1980 Champion Hurdle. (Sea Pigeon ridden by Jon Jo O'Neill came through to win thus preventing* Monksfield's *bid for a treble.)* (Sporting Pictures)

1957 *Merry Deal*, Granville Underwood
1958 *Bandalore*, George Slack
1959 *Fare Time*, Fred Winter
1960 *Another Flash*, Bobby Beasley
1961 *Eborneezer*, Fred Winter
1962 *Anzio*, Willie Robinson
1963 *Winning Fair,* Alan Lillingston
1964 *Magic Court*, Pat McCarron
1965 *Kirriemuir*, Willie Robinson
1966 *Salmon Spray*, Johnnie Haine
1967 *Saucy Kit*, Roy Edwards
1968 *Persian War*, Jimmy Uttley
1969 *Persian War*, Jimmy Uttley
1970 *Persian War*, Jimmy Uttley
1971 *Bula*, Paul Kelleway
1972 *Bula*, Paul Kelleway
1973 *Comedy of Errors*, Bill Smith
1974 *Lanzarote*, Richard Pitman
1975 *Comedy of Errors*, Ken White
1976 *Night Nurse*, Paddy Broderick
1977 *Night Nurse*, Paddy Broderick
1978 *Monksfield*, Tommy Kinane
1979 *Monksfield*, Dessie Hughes
1980 *Sea Pigeon*, JonJo O'Neill
1981 *Sea Pigeon*, Johnny Francome

AMERICAN TRIPLE CROWN
The American Triple Crown is made up of three races for three-year-olds:

KENTUCKY DERBY
1¼ miles at Churchill Downs, Louisville, Kentucky; first held in 1875.

BELMONT STAKES
1½ miles at Belmont Park, New York; first held in 1867.

PREAKNESS STAKES
1³⁄₁₆ miles at Pimlico, Baltimore, Maryland; first held in 1873.

Horses to have won all three races have been:
1919 *Sir Barton*
1930 *Gallant Fox*
1935 *Omaha*
1937 *War Admiral*
1941 *Whirlaway*
1943 *Count Fleet*
1946 *Assault*
1948 *Citation*
1973 *Secretariat*
1977 *Seattle Slew*
1978 *Affirmed*

BRITISH FLAT RACING – CHAMPION JOCKEYS
The rider of the most winners on the flat each year.

Champions since 1946:
1946 Gordon Richards 212
1947 Gordon Richards 269
1948 Gordon Richards 224
1949 Gordon Richards 261
1950 Gordon Richards 201
1951 Gordon Richards 227
1952 Gordon Richards 231
1953 Gordon Richards 191
1954 Doug Smith 129
1955 Doug Smith 168
1956 Doug Smith 155
1957 Scobie Breasley 173
1958 Doug Smith 165
1959 Doug Smith 157
1960 Lester Piggott 170
1961 Scobie Breasley 171
1962 Scobie Breasley 179
1963 Scobie Breasley 176
1964 Lester Piggott 140
1965 Lester Piggott 166
1966 Lester Piggott 191
1967 Lester Piggott 117
1968 Lester Piggott 139
1969 Lester Piggott 163
1970 Lester Piggott 162
1971 Lester Piggott 162
1972 Willie Carson 132
1973 Willie Carson 163
1974 Pat Eddery 148
1975 Pat Eddery 164
1976 Pat Eddery 162
1977 Pat Eddery 176
1978 Willie Carson 182
1979 Joe Mercer 164
1980 Willie Carson 165

Most years as champion:
26 Gordon Richards 1925, 1927–29, 1931–40, 1942–53; most wins in a year: 269 in 1947, 261 in 1949, 259 in 1933, 231 in 1952, 227 in 1951, 224 in 1948, 214 in 1937, 212 in 1934 and 1946, 210 in 1935, 206 in 1938, 201 in 1950.
14 George Fordham 1855–63, 1865, 1867–69, 1871 (shared); most wins in a year: 166 in 1862.
13 Fred Archer 1874–86; most wins in a year: 246 in 1885, 241 in 1884, 232 in 1883, 229 in 1878, 220 in

Lester Piggott, rider of eight Derby winners (G. Cranham)

1881, 218 in 1887, 210 in 1882, 207 in 1876.
13 Elnathan Flatman 1840–52; most wins in a year:
104 in 1848.
10 Steve Donoghue: 1914–22, 1923 (shared); most
wins in a year: 143 in 1920.

NATIONAL HUNT RACING – CHAMPION JOCKEYS

From 1900 to 1925 champions were listed for
the calendar year, but since 1925–26 they have
been accepted for the season from one year to
another. The years shown below denote the
second half of the season.

Champions since 1946:

1946 Fred Rimell 54
1947 Jack Dowdeswell 58
1948 Bryan Marshall 66
1949 Tim Molony 60
1950 Tim Molony 95
1951 Tim Molony 83
1952 Tim Molony 99
1953 Fred Winter 121
1954 Dick Francis 76
1955 Tim Molony 67
1956 Fred Winter 74
1957 Fred Winter 80
1958 Fred Winter 82
1959 Tim Brookshaw 83
1960 Stan Mellor 68
1961 Stan Mellor 118

1962 Stan Mellor 80
1963 Josh Gifford 70
1964 Josh Gifford 94
1965 Terry Biddlecombe 114
1966 Terry Biddlecombe 102
1967 Josh Gifford 122
1968 Josh Gifford 82
1969 Bob Davies 77
     Terry Biddlecombe 77
1970 Bob Davies 91
1971 Graham Thorner 74
1972 Bob Davies 89
1973 Ron Barry 125
1974 Ron Barry 94
1975 Tommy Stack 82
1976 Johnny Francome 96
1977 Tommy Stack 97
1978 JonJo O'Neill 149
1979 Johnny Francome 95
1980 JonJo O'Neill 117
1981 Johnny Francome 105

Most years as champion:
7 Gerry Wilson 1933–38, 1941; most wins in a year:
73 in 1935
6 'Tich' Mason 1901–2, 1904–7; most wins in a year:
73 in 1905
5 Frederick Rees 1920–21, 1923–24, 1927; most wins
in a year: 108 in 1924
5 Billy Stott 1928–32; most wins in a year: 88 in 1928
5 Tim Molony 1949–52, 1955; most wins in a year: 99
in 1952

Hotels

EGON RONAY HOTEL OF THE YEAR

This annual award in Britain for the best hotel is given by the gourmet and critic, Egon Ronay. The award is made to a hotel whose consistent excellence or enterprise is found to be outstanding. The winner receives and keeps for a year an engraved Gold Plate. Winners since inception:

1969 Lygon Arms, Broadway (Hereford and Worcester)
1970 Inn on the Park, London W1
1971 Inverlochy Castle, Fort William (Highland)
1972 Berkeley Hotel, London SW1
1973 Gleneagles Hotel, Auchterarder (Tayside)
1974 Sharrow Bay Country House Hotel, Ullswater (Cumbria)
1975 Ashford Castle, Cong (Co. Mayo, Eire)
1976 Chewton Glen Hotel, New Milton (Hampshire)
1977 Gravetye Manor, East Grinstead (West Sussex)
1978 The Ritz, London W1
1979 Connaught Hotel, London W1
1980 Royal Crescent Hotel, Bath

Hurling

ALL-IRELAND CHAMPIONSHIP

First contested in 1887. Winners since 1965:

1965 Tipperary
1966 Kilkenny
1967 Kilkenny
1968 Wexford
1969 Tipperary
1970 Cork
1971 Tipperary
1972 Kilkenny
1973 Limerick
1974 Kilkenny
1975 Kilkenny
1976 Cork
1977 Cork
1978 Cork
1979 Kilkenny
1980 Galway

Most wins:
24 Cork

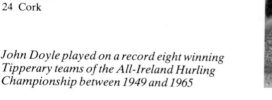

John Doyle played on a record eight winning Tipperary teams of the All-Ireland Hurling Championship between 1949 and 1965

Ice Hockey

STANLEY CUP

The Stanley Cup, the premier trophy in North American ice hockey, is contested by the professional teams in the National Hockey League. It was first competed for in 1893. Winners since 1965:

1964–65 Montreal Canadiens
1965–66 Montreal Canadiens
1966–67 Toronto Maple Leafs
1967–68 Montreal Canadiens
1968–69 Montreal Canadiens
1969–70 Boston Bruins
1970–71 Montreal Canadiens
1971–72 Boston Bruins
1972–73 Montreal Canadiens
1973–74 Philadelphia Flyers
1974–75 Philadelphia Flyers
1975–76 Montreal Canadiens
1976–77 Montreal Canadiens
1977–78 Montreal Canadiens
1978–79 Montreal Canadiens
1979–80 New York Islanders
1980–81 New York Islanders

Most wins:
22 Montreal Canadiens 1916, 1924, 1930–31, 1944,

The Chicago Black Hawks attack the Montreal Canadiens goal in 1973

1946, 1953, 1956–60, 1965–66, 1968–69, 1971, 1973, 1976–79

WORLD CHAMPIONSHIPS
First held in conjunction with the Olympics, and amateur only until 1976, but now held annually. Winners since 1965:

1965 USSR
1966 USSR
1967 USSR
1968 USSR
1969 USSR
1970 USSR
1971 USSR
1972 Czechoslovakia
1973 USSR
1974 USSR
1975 USSR
1976 Czechoslovakia
1977 Czechoslovakia
1978 USSR
1979 USSR
1980 Not held

Most wins:
Canada 19, USSR 15

OLYMPIC CHAMPIONSHIPS
First held 1920.

1920 Canada
1924 Canada
1928 Canada
1932 Canada
1936 Great Britain
1948 Canada
1952 Canada
1956 USSR
1960 USA
1964 USSR
1968 USSR
1972 USSR
1976 USSR
1980 USA

Sports Illustrated *Sports Personalities of 1980, the winning US Olympic ice hockey team after their 4–3 win over the USSR* (United Press International)

Ice Skating

WORLD CHAMPIONSHIPS

World figure skating championships were first held in 1896 for men, and in 1906 for women. Pairs skating titles have been decided since 1908 and ice dancing since 1952.

MEN'S FIGURE SKATING

Winners since 1947:

1947 Hans Gerschwiler (Swi)
1948 Richard Button (USA)
1949 Richard Button (USA)
1950 Richard Button (USA)
1951 Richard Button (USA)
1952 Richard Button (USA)
1953 Hayes Jenkins (USA)
1954 Hayes Jenkins (USA)
1955 Hayes Jenkins (USA)
1956 Hayes Jenkins (USA)
1957 David Jenkins (USA)
1958 David Jenkins (USA)
1959 David Jenkins (USA)
1960 Alain Giletti (Fra)
1961 Not held
1962 Donald Jackson (Can)
1963 Donald McPherson (Can)
1964 Manfred Schnelldorfer (Ger)
1965 Alain Calmat (Fra)
1966 Emmerich Danzer (Aut)
1967 Emmerich Danzer (Aut)
1968 Emmerich Danzer (Aut)
1969 Tim Wood (USA)
1970 Tim Wood (USA)
1971 Ondrej Nepela (Cze)
1972 Ondrej Nepela (Cze)
1973 Ondrej Nepela (Cze)
1974 Jan Hoffmann (GDR)
1975 Sergei Volkov (USSR)
1976 John Curry (GB)
1977 Vladimir Kovalev (USSR)
1978 Charles Tickner (USA)
1979 Vladimir Kovalev (USSR)
1980 Jan Hoffmann (GDR)
1981 Scott Hamilton (USA)

Most wins:
10 Ulrich Salchow (Swe) 1901–5, 1907–11; 7 Karl Schäfer (Aut) 1930–36

WOMEN'S FIGURE SKATING

Winners since 1947:

1947 Barbara Ann Scott (Can)
1948 Barbara Ann Scott (Can)
1949 Aja Vrzanova (Cze)
1950 Aja Vrzanova (Cze)
1951 Jeanette Altwegg (GB)
1952 Jeanette Altwegg (GB)
1953 Tenley Albright (USA)
1954 Gundi Busch (Ger)
1955 Tenley Albright (USA)
1956 Carol Heiss (USA)
1957 Carol Heiss (USA)
1958 Carol Heiss (USA)
1959 Carol Heiss (USA)
1960 Carol Heiss (USA)
1961 Not held
1962 Sjoukje Dijkstra (Hol)
1963 Sjoukje Dijkstra (Hol)
1964 Sjoukje Dijkstra (Hol)
1965 Petra Burka (Can)
1966 Peggy Fleming (USA)
1967 Peggy Fleming (USA)
1968 Peggy Fleming (USA)
1969 Gabriele Seyfert (GDR)
1970 Gabriele Seyfert (GDR)
1971 Beatrix Schuba (Aut)
1972 Beatrix Schuba (Aut)
1973 Karen Magnussen (Can)
1974 Christine Errath (GDR)
1975 Dianne de Leeuw (Hol)
1976 Dorothy Hamill (USA)
1977 Linda Fratianne (USA)
1978 Annette Pötzsch (GDR)
1979 Linda Fratianne (USA)
1980 Annette Pötzsch (GDR)
1981 Denise Beillman (Swi)

Most wins:
10 Sonja Henie (Nor) 1927–36

PAIRS SKATING

1947–48 Pierre Baugniet and Micheline Lannoy (Bel)
1949 Ede Király and Andrea Kékessy (Hun)
1950 Peter Kennedy and Karol Kennedy (USA)
1951–52 Paul Falk and Ria Baran/Falk (Ger)
1953 John Nicks and Jennifer Nicks (GB)
1954–55 Norris Bowden and Frances Dafoe (Can)
1956 Kurt Oppelt and Sissy Schwarz (Aut)
1957–60 Robert Paul and Barbara Wagner (Can)
1961 Not held

Jayne Torvill and Christopher Dean swept to ice dance prominence in 1981, winning both European and world titles (Sporting Pictures)

1962 Otto Jelinek and Maria Jelinek (Can)
1963–64 Hans-Jürgen Bäumler and Marika Kilius (Ger)
1965–68 Oleg Protopopov and Lyudmila Protopopov (USSR)
1969–72 Alexei Ulanov and Irina Rodnina (USSR)
1973–78 Aleksandr Zaitsev and Irina Rodnina (USSR)
1979 Randy Gardner and Tai Babilonia (USA)
1980 Sergei Shakhrai and Marina Chervasova (USSR)
1981 Igor Lisovski and Irina Vorobyeva (USSR)

ICE DANCE SKATING
1952–55 Lawrence Demmy and Jean Westwood (GB)
1956 Paul Thomas and Pamela Weight (GB)
1957–58 Courtney Jones and June Markham (GB)
1959–60 Courtney Jones and Doreen Denny (GB)
1961 Not held
1962–65 Pavel Roman and Eva Romanova (Cze)
1966–69 Bernard Ford and Diane Towler (GB)
1970–74 Aleksandr Gorshkov and Lyudmila Pakhomova (USSR)
1975 Andrei Minenkov and Irina Moiseyeva (USSR)
1976 Aleksandr Gorshkov and Lyudmila Pakhomova (USSR)
1977 Andrei Minenkov and Irina Moiseyeva (USSR)
1978–79 Gennadiy Karponosov and Natalia Linichuk (USSR)
1980 Andras Sallay and Krisztine Regoczy (Hun)
1981 Christopher Dean and Jayne Torvill (GB)

OLYMPIC CHAMPIONSHIPS
Figure skating was first included in the Olympic Games in 1908, and has been included at each celebration since 1920. Winners since 1948:

MEN'S FIGURE SKATING
1948 Richard Button (USA)
1952 Richard Button (USA)
1956 Hayes Jenkins (USA)
1960 David Jenkins (USA)
1964 Manfred Schnelldorfer (Ger)
1968 Wolfgang Schwarz (Aut)
1972 Ondrej Nepela (Cze)
1976 John Curry (GB)
1980 Robin Cousins (GB)

Robin Cousins, BBC Sports Personality of 1980, winner of the Olympic ice-skating title (Sporting Pictures)

WOMEN'S FIGURE SKATING
1948 Barbara Ann Scott (Can)
1952 Jeanette Altwegg (GB)
1956 Tenley Albright (USA)
1960 Carol Heiss (USA)
1964 Sjoukje Dijkstra (Hol)
1968 Peggy Fleming (USA)
1972 Beatrix Schuba (Aut)
1976 Dorothy Hamill (USA)
1980 Annette Pötzsch (GDR)

PAIRS SKATING
1948 Pierre Baugniet and Micheline Lannoy (Bel)
1952 Paul Falk and Ria Falk (Ger)
1956 Kurt Oppelt and Sissy Schwarz (Aut)
1960 Robert Paul and Barbara Wagner (Can)
1964 Oleg Protopopov and Lyudmila Belousova (USSR)
1968 Oleg Protopopov and Lyudmila Belousova (USSR)
1972 Alexei Ulanov and Irina Rodnina (USSR)
1976 Aleksandr Zaitsev and Irina Rodnina (USSR)
1980 Aleksandr Zaitsev and Irina Rodnina (USSR)

ICE DANCE SKATING
First held 1976
1976 Aleksandr Gorshkov and Lyudmila Pakhomova (USSR)
1980 Gennadiy Karponosov and Natalie Linichuk (USSR)

Speed Skating

WORLD CHAMPIONSHIPS
World championships were first held in 1893. For men they are contested at 500, 1500, 5000 and 10 000 metres and for women at 500, 1000, 3000 and 5000 metres. Overall world champions are determined over the four distances. Overall world champions since 1947 have been:

MEN
1947 Lauri Parkkinen (Fin)
1948 Odd Lundberg (Nor)
1949 Kornel Pajor (Hun)
1950 Hjalmar Andersen (Nor)
1951 Hjalmar Andersen (Nor)
1952 Hjalmar Andersen (Nor)
1953 Oleg Goncharenko (USSR)
1954 Boris Schilkov (USSR)

1955 Sigvard Ericsson (Swe)
1956 Oleg Goncharenko (USSR)
1957 Knut Johannesen (Nor)
1958 Oleg Goncharenko (USSR)
1959 Juhani Järvinen (Fin)
1960 Boris Stenin (USSR)
1961 Hendrik van der Grift (Hol)
1962 Viktor Kosichkin (USSR)
1963 Johnny Nilsson (Swe)
1964 Knut Johannesen (Nor)
1965 Per Moe (Nor)
1966 Kees Verkerk (Hol)
1967 Kees Verkerk (Hol)
1968 Anton Maier (Nor)
1969 Dag Fornaess (Nor)
1970 Ard Schenk (Hol)
1971 Ard Schenk (Hol)
1972 Ard Schenk (Hol)
1973 Goran Claesson (Swe)
1974 Sten Stensen (Nor)
1975 Harm Kuipers (Hol)
1976 Piet Kleine (Hol)
1977 Eric Heiden (USA)
1978 Eric Heiden (USA)
1979 Eric Heiden (USA)
1980 Hilber van der Duin (Hol)
1981 Amund Sjoebrend (Nor)

WOMEN
1947 Verne Lesche (Fin)
1948 Maria Isakova (USSR)
1949 Maria Isakova (USSR)
1950 Maria Isakova (USSR)
1951 Eva Huttunen (Fin)
1952 Lydia Selichova (USSR)
1953 Khalida Schegoleyeva (USSR)
1954 Lydia Selichova (USSR)
1955 Rimma Zhukova (USSR)
1956 Sofia Kondakova (USSR)
1957 Inga Artamonova (USSR)
1958 Inga Artamonova (USSR)
1959 Tamara Rylova (USSR)
1960 Valentina Stenina (USSR)
1961 Valentina Stenina (USSR)
1962 Inga Voronina (née Artamonova) (USSR)
1963 Lydia Skoblikova (USSR)
1964 Lydia Skoblikova (USSR)
1965 Inga Voronina (USSR)
1966 Valentina Stenina (USSR)
1967 Stein Kaiser (Hol)
1968 Stein Kaiser (Hol)
1969 Lasma Kauniste (USSR)
1970 Atje Keulen-Deelstra (Hol)
1971 Nina Statkevich (USSR)
1972 Atje Keulen-Deelstra (Hol)
1973 Atje Keulen-Deelstra (Hol)
1974 Atje Keulen-Deelstra (Hol)
1975 Karin Kessow (GDR)
1976 Sylvia Burka (Can)
1977 Vera Bryndzey (USSR)
1978 Tatiana Averina (USSR)
1979 Elizabeth Heiden (USA)
1980 Natalia Petruseva (USSR)
1981 Natalia Petruseva (USSR)

OLYMPIC CHAMPIONSHIPS
Speed skating has been included on the Olympic programme since 1924 for men, and since 1960 for women. Winners since 1948:

MEN
500 metres
1948 Finn Helgesen (Nor) 43·1
1952 Kenneth Henry (USA) 43·2
1956 Yevgeniy Grischin (USSR) 40·2
1960 Yevgeniy Grischin (USSR) 40·2
1964 Richard McDermott (USA) 40·1
1968 Erhard Keller (Ger) 40·3
1972 Erhard Keller (Ger) 39·44
1976 Yevgeniy Kulikov (USSR) 39·17
1980 Eric Heiden (USA) 38·03

1000 metres
1976 Peter Mueller (USA) 1:19·32
1980 Eric Heiden (USA) 1:15·18

1500 metres
1948 Sverre Farstad (Nor) 2:17·6
1952 Hjalmar Andersen (Nor) 2:20·4
1956 Yevgeniy Grischin (USSR) and
      Yuriy Mikhailov (USSR) 2:08·6
1960 Roald Aas (Nor) and Yevgeniy Grischin
      (USSR) 2:10·4
1964 Ants Antson (USSR) 2:10·3
1968 Cornelis Verkerk (Hol) 2:03·4
1972 Ard Schenk (Hol) 2:02·96
1976 Jan Egil Storholt (Nor) 1:59·38
1980 Eric Heiden (USA) 1:55·44

5000 metres
1948 Reidar Liaklev (Nor) 8:29·4
1952 Hjalmar Andersen (Nor) 8:10·6
1956 Boris Schilkov (USSR) 7:48·7
1960 Viktor Kositschkin (USSR) 7:51·3
1964 Knut Johannesen (Nor) 7:38·4
1968 Anton Maier (Nor) 7:22·4
1972 Ard Schenk (Hol) 7:23·61
1976 Sten Stensen (Nor) 7:24·48
1980 Eric Heiden (USA) 7:02·29

10 000 metres
1948 Åke Seyffarth (Swe) 17:26·3
1952 Hjalmar Andersen (Nor) 16:45·8
1956 Sigvard Ericsson (Swe) 16:35·9
1960 Knut Johannesen (Nor) 15:46·6
1964 Johnny Nilsson (Swe) 15:50·1
1968 Johnny Hoeglin (Swe) 15:23·6
1972 Ard Schenk (Hol) 15:01·35
1976 Piet Kleine (Hol) 14:50·59
1980 Eric Heiden (USA) 14:28·13

WOMEN
500 metres
1960 Helga Haase (Ger) 45·9
1964 Lydia Skoblikova (USSR) 45·0
1968 Lyudmila Titova (USSR) 46·1
1972 Anne Henning (USA) 43·33
1976 Sheila Young (USA) 42·76
1980 Karin Enke (GDR) 41·78

1000 metres
1960 Klala Guseva (USSR) 1:34·1
1964 Lydia Skoblikova (USSR) 1:33·2
1968 Cololina Geijssen (Hol) 1:32·6
1972 Monika Pflug (Ger) 1:31·40
1976 Tatyana Averina (USSR) 1:28·43
1980 Natalia Petruseva (USSR) 1:24·10

1500 metres
1960 Lydia Skoblikova (USSR) 2:25·2
1964 Lydia Skoblikova (USSR) 2:22·6

1968 Kaija Mustonen (Fin) 2:22·4	1964 Lydia Skoblikova (USSR) 5:14·9
1972 Dianne Holum (USA) 2:20·85	1968 Johanna Schut (Hol) 4:56·2
1976 Galina Stepanskaya (USSR) 2:16·58	1972 Stein Baas-Kaiser (Hol) 4:52·14
1980 Annie Borckink (Hol) 2:10·95	1976 Tatyana Averina (USSR) 4:45·19
	1980 Eva Jensen (Nor) 4:32·13

3000 metres
1960 Lydia Skoblikova (USSR) 5:14·3

Jai Alai (Pelota)

WORLD AMATEUR JAI ALAI CHAMPIONSHIPS

Under the auspices of the Federación Internacional de Pelota Vasca, which is based in Spain. First held in 1952. Recent winners:

1966 Mexico
1968 Spain

1970 France
1971 Spain
1974 France
1975 United States
1976 France
1978 Spain

Journalism

BRITISH PRESS AWARDS

These began in 1963 as the Hannen Swaffer National Press Awards, sponsored by Odhams Press in memory of Hannen Swaffer. The title was changed to the IPC Press Awards in 1967 when the International Publishing Corporation took over Odhams, and a further change was made in 1975 when the present name was adopted. The *Daily Mirror* gave up its control over the awards, which are now sponsored by several major newspaper groups. In 1976 photographic classes were introduced for the first time. Winners since inception:

JOURNALIST OF THE YEAR
1963 D. H. Hopkinson, *Sheffield Telegraph*
1964 Denis Hamilton, *The Sunday Times*
1965 Michael Randall, *Daily Mail*
1966 Sir Gordon Newton, *Financial Times*
1967 John Pilger, *Daily Mirror*
1968 Victor Zorza, *The Guardian*
1969 Anthony Grey, *Reuter's*
1970 Alastair Hetherington, *The Guardian*
1971 Simon Winchester, *The Guardian*
1972 Harold Evans, *The Sunday Times*
1973 Adam Raphael, *The Guardian*
1974 Harry Longmuir, *Daily Mail*
1975 Jon Swain, *The Sunday Times*
1976 No award
1977 *Lancashire Evening Post* (editor, assistant editor and chief reporter)
1978 Martin Bailey, Bernard Rivers and Peter Kelluer, *The Sunday Times*
1979 John Pilger, *Daily Mirror*
1980 Phillip Knightley, *The Sunday Times*

YOUNG JOURNALIST OF THE YEAR
1967 June Sparey, Reading *Evening Post*
1968 Kevin Rafferty, *The Sun*

1969 Raymond Fitzwalker, Bradford *Telegraph and Argus*
1970 Janice Cave, Southend *Evening Echo*
1971 Yvonne Roberts, Northampton *Chronicle and Echo*
1972 Andrew Kruyer, Southend *Evening Echo*
1973 Roger Beam, Lancs *Evening Post*
1974 Gordon Ogilvie, Aberdeen *Evening Express*
1975 Melanie Phillips, Hemel Hempstead *Evening Post Echo*
1976 Richard Woolveridge, *South London Press*
1977 Tina Brown, *Telegraph Sunday Magazine* and Jad Adams, South East London and Kentish *Mercury*
1978 Andrew Cooper, Walsall *Observer*
1979 Steve Latter, Buckinghamshire *Advertiser*
1980 Lionel Barber, *The Scotsman*

REPORTER OF THE YEAR
1963 Henry Brandon, *The Sunday Times*
1964 Michael Gabbert, *The People*
1965 Anthony Carthew, *The Sun* and *Daily Mail*
1966 Ken Gardner, *The People*
1967 David Farr, *The People*
1968 Harold Jackson, *The Guardian*
1969 Mary Holland, *The Observer*
1970 Monty Meth, *Daily Mail*
1971 John Clare, *The Times*
1972 Peter Harvey, *The Guardian*
1973 John Burns, Belfast *Telegraph*
1974 John Pilger, *Daily Mail*
1975 John Edwards, *Daily Mail*
1976 Geraldine Norman, *The Times*
1977 Richard Stott, *Daily Mirror*
1978 *Daily Mirror:* Team of Roger Beam, Barry Wigmore, Frank Palmer, Kent Gavin
1979 Melanie Phillips, *The Guardian*
1980 *Daily Express*: Team of Robert McGowan, Peter Hardy, Ian Black, Peter Mason

INTERNATIONAL REPORTER OF THE YEAR

1966 Louis Heren, *The Times*
1967 Christopher Dobson, *Daily Mail*
1968 Walter Partington, *Daily Express*
1969 Murray Sayle, *The Sunday Times*
1970 John Pilger, *Daily Mirror*
1971 Peter Hazelhurst, *The Times*, and Gavin Young, *The Observer*
1972 John Fairhall, *The Guardian*
1973 Peter Niesewand, *The Guardian*
1974 Colin Smith, *The Observer*
1975 Martin Wollacott, *The Guardian*
1976 Peter Niesewand, *The Guardian*
1977 Robin Smyth, *The Observer*
1978 Peter Lewis, *Daily Mail*
1979 Robert Fisk, *The Times*
1980 Robert Fisk, *The Times*

PROVINCIAL JOURNALIST OF THE YEAR

1964 Anthony Hancox, *Sunday Mercury*
1965 Frank Laws, *Yorks Evening Post*
1966 Peter Williams, Burnley *Evening Star*
1967 Ernest Moore, Lancs *Evening Post*
1968 Len Doherty, Sheffield *Star*
1969 Eric Forster, Newcastle *Evening Chronicle*
1970 Alfred McCreary, Belfast *Telegraph*
1971 Barry Lloyd Jones, *The Birmingham Post*
1972 Chris Fuller, *The Birmingham Post*
1973 Frank Branston, Bedfordshire *Times*
1974 John Marquis, Watford *Echo*
1975 Carol Robertson, Sunderland *Echo*
1976 Geoffrey Parkhouse, *Glasgow Herald,* and Alan Whitsett, *Belfast News Letter*
1977 Carol Robertson and John Bailey, Sunderland *Echo*
1978 Team at Oldham *Evening Chronicle*
1979 Peter Browne, *Northampton Chronicle and Echo*
1980 Simon Bain, *The Star*

CRITIC OF THE YEAR

1963 Alan Brien, *Sunday Telegraph*
1964 Philip Purser, *Sunday Telegraph*
1965 Michael Foot, *Evening Standard*
1966 Milton Shulman, *Evening Standard*
1967 Alan Brien, *Sunday Telegraph*
1968 Peter Black, *Daily Mail*
1969 Alexander Walker, London *Evening Standard*
1970 George Melly, *The Observer*
1971 Derek Malcolm, *The Guardian*
1972 T. C. Worsley, *Financial Times*
1973 Alexander Walker, *Evening Standard*
1974 Michael Billington, *The Guardian*
1975 Paul Allen, *Sheffield Morning Telegraph*
1976 Chris Dunkley, *Financial Times*
1977 Clive James, *The Observer*
1978 Fay Maschler, *Evening Standard*
1979 Anthony Burgess, *The Observer*
1980 Peter Heyworth, *The Observer*

DESCRIPTIVE WRITER OF THE YEAR

1963 Vincent Mulchrone, *Daily Mail*
1964 Anne Sharpley, *Evening Standard*
1965 James Cameron, *Evening Standard*
1966 John Pilger, *Daily Mirror*

John Pilger, 1979 Journalist of the Year, receives his award from Margaret Thatcher

1967 Donald Zec, *Daily Mirror*
1968 Angus McGill, *Evening Standard*
1969 Michael Frayn, *The Observer*
1970 Vincent Mulchrone, *Daily Mail,* and Keith Waterhouse, *Daily Mirror*
1971 Geoffrey Goodman, *Daily Mirror*
Discontinued

SPORTS JOURNALIST OF THE YEAR

1963 J. L. Manning, *Daily Mail*
1964 George Whiting, *Evening Standard*
1965 Peter Wilson, *Daily Mirror*
1966 Hugh McIlvanney, *The Observer*
1967 Sam Leitch, *Sunday Mirror*
1968 Christopher Brasher, *The Observer*
1969 Hugh McIlvanney, *The Observer*
1970 Frank Butler, *News of the World*
1971 Ian Wooldridge, *Daily Mail*
1972 John Morgan, *Daily Express*
1973 Peter Batt, *The Sun*
1974 Ian Wooldridge, *Daily Mail*
1975 David Gray, *The Guardian*
1976 Chris Brasher, *The Observer*
1977 Hugh McIlvanney, *The Observer*
1978 Hugh McIlvanney, *The Observer*
1979 John Arlott, *The Guardian*
1980 Mike Langley, *The Sunday People*

WOMAN'S PAGE JOURNALIST OF THE YEAR

1967 Christine Galpin, Freelance/*News of the World*
1968 Marjorie Proops, *Daily Mirror*
1969 Felicity Green, *Daily Mirror*
1970 Elizabeth Prosser, *The Sun*

1971 Shirley Kaye, Halifax *Evening Post*, and Jill Tweedie, *The Guardian*
1972 Sue Hercombe, Newcastle *Evening Chronicle*
Discontinued

CAMPAIGNING JOURNALIST OF THE YEAR
1965 R. Stuart Campbell, *The People*
1966 Harold Evans, *Northern Echo*
1967 Colin McGlashan, *The Observer*
1968 Michael Leapman, *The Sun*, and Peter Harland, Bradford *Telegraph and Argus*
1969 Ken Gardner, *The People*
1970 Colin Brannigan, Sheffield *Star*
1971 Barry Askew, Lancs *Evening Post*
1972 Caren Meyer, *Evening News*
1973 Christopher Booker and Benny Gray, freelance
1974 No award
1975 Mary Beith, *Sunday People*, and Angus King, *Yorkshire Post*
1976 Douglas Thain, Alan Hurndall and Graham Hind, *Sheffield Star*
1977 John Pilger, *Daily Mirror*
1978 Team at Liverpool *Echo*
1979 John McCririck, *Sporting Life*
1980 Paul Foot, *Daily Mirror*

SPECIAL AWARD
1966 David Rhys Davies, *Merthyr Express*
1967 Peter Preston, *The Guardian*, Susanne Proudfoot, *The Times*
1968 Henry Longhurst, *The Sunday Times*
1969 Sir Neville Cardus, *The Guardian*
1970 Ken Gardner, *The People*
1971 William Rees-Mogg, *The Times*, and Anthony Mascarenhas, *The Sunday Times*
1972 Laurie Manifold, *Sunday People*, and David Williams, Southend *Evening Echo*
1973 David English, *Daily Mail*
1974 Brian Roberts, *Sunday Telegraph*
1975 No award
1976 Stephen Fay, Hugo Young, *The Sunday Times*
1977 Charles Raw, *The Sunday Times*
1978 Stephen Fay, Hugo Young, *The Sunday Times*
1979 David Leigh, *The Guardian*
1980 Graham Wiles and Chris Bye, *Yorkshire Evening Post*

WOMAN JOURNALIST OF THE YEAR
1962 Clare Hollingworth, *The Guardian*
1963 Anne Sharpley, *Evening Standard*
1964 Joan Seddon, Lancashire *Evening Telegraph*
1965 Wendy Cooper, Birmingham *Post*
1966 Barbara Buchanan, Bristol *Evening Post*
Discontinued

SPECIALIST WRITER OF THE YEAR
1972 John Graham, *Financial Times*
1973 John Davis, *The Observer*
1974 Richard Milner, *The Sunday Times*
1975 Andrew Alexander, *Daily Mail*
1976 Andrew Alexander, *Daily Mail*
1977 Oliver Gillie, *The Sunday Times*
1978 John McCririck, *Sporting Life*
1979 Angus MacPherson, *Daily Mail*
1980 Anatole Kaletsky, *Financial Times*

COLUMNIST OF THE YEAR
1973 Keith Waterhouse, *Daily Mirror*, and Bernard Levin, *The Times*
1974 Bernard Levin, *The Times*
1975 Ian Wooldridge, *Daily Mail*
1976 Ian Wooldridge, *Daily Mail*
1977 Anthony Holden, *The Sunday Times*
1978 Keith Waterhouse, *Daily Mirror*
1979 Sam White, *Evening Standard*
1980 Hugo Young, *The Sunday Times*

CHAIRMAN'S AWARDS
1974 Sydney Jacobson, IPC
1977 David Holden, *The Sunday Times*

PRESS PHOTOGRAPHER OF THE YEAR
1976 David Cairns, *Daily Express*

PHOTOGRAPHER OF THE YEAR
1977 John Downing, *Daily Express*
1978 Mike Lloyd, freelance
1979 Graham Wood, *Daily Mail*
1980 John Downing, *Daily Express*

NEWS PHOTOGRAPHER OF THE YEAR
1977 J. A. Jedrej, Cambridge *Evening News*
1978 Reg Lancaster, *Daily Express*
1979 Kent Gavin, *Daily Mirror*
1980 Frank Barrett, *Daily Star*

DAVID HOLDEN AWARD
1978 Ian Wright and Altaf Gauhar, *The Guardian*
1979 No award
1980 Michael Binyon, *The Times*

CARTOONIST OF THE YEAR
1980 JAK, *The New Standard*

GENERAL FEATURE WRITER OF THE YEAR
1980 Oliver Pritchett, *The Sunday Telegraph*

PULITZER PRIZES
For further details see under main heading of Pulitzer Prizes. The following is a selection of the award winners since 1970.

LOCAL INVESTIGATIVE REPORTING
Founded 1953.
1970 Harold E. Martin, *Montgomery* (Ala.) *Advertiser*
1971 William Hugh Jones, *Chicago Tribune*
1972 Ann De Santis, S. A. Kurkjian, T. Leland, and G. M. O'Neill, *Boston Globe*
1973 *Sun* Newspapers, Omaha, Nebr.
1974 William Sherman, *New York Daily News*
1975 *Indianapolis Star*
1976 Staff of *Chicago Tribune* for exposing conditions in two hospitals that led to their closing and for discovering abuses in federal housing programmes
1977 Acel Moore and Wendell Rawls Jr, *Philadelphia Inquirer*, for investigation of state mental hospital
1978 Anthony R. Dolan, *Stamford* (Conn.) *Advocate*
1979 Gilbert M. Gaul and Elliot G. Jaspin, *Pottsville* (Pa.) *Republican*
1980 Stephen A. Kurkjian, Alexander B. Hawes Jr., Nils Bruzelius, Joan Vennochi and Robert

M. Porterfield, *The Boston Globe* Spotlight Team for articles on Boston's transit system
1981 Clark Hallas and Robert B. Lowe, *Arizona Daily Star*

LOCAL GENERAL REPORTING
Founded 1953.
1970 Thomas Fitzpatrick, *Chicago Sun-Times*
1971 *Akron* (Ohio) *Beacon Journal*
1972 R. I. Cooper and J. W. Machacek, *Rochester* (NY) *Times-Union*
1973 *Chicago Tribune*
1974 Arthur M. Petacque and Hugh F. Hough, *Chicago Sun-Times*
1975 *Xenia* (Ohio) *Daily Gazette*
1976 Gene Miller, *Miami Herald*, who dug up evidence that freed two men convicted of murder. He previously won a Pulitzer Prize in 1967 for uncovering evidence that freed a man and woman convicted of separate murders.
1977 Margo Huston, *Milwaukee Journal*
1978 Richard Whitt, *Louisville* (Ky.) *Courier-Journal*
1979 The San Diego (Calif.) *Evening Tribune*, for its coverage of the collision of a Pacific Southwest airliner with a small plane over its city
1980 The staff of *The Philadelphia Inquirer* for coverage of the nuclear accident at Three Mile Island
1981 *Daily News* staff, *Longview* (Wash.)

NATIONAL REPORTING
Founded 1942.
1970 William J. Eaton, *Chicago Daily News*
1971 Lucinda Franks and Thomas Powers, United Press International
1972 Jack Anderson, syndicated columnist
1973 Robert Boyd and Clark Hoyt, Knight Newspapers
1974 James R. Polk, *Washington Star-News*, and Jack White, *Providence* (RI) *Journal-Bulletin*
1975 Donald L. Barlett and James B. Steel, *Philadelphia Inquirer*
1976 James Risser, *Register*, Des Moines, Iowa, who as Washington correspondent broke story on corruption in American grain export trade
1977 Walter Mears, Associated Press chief political writer.
1978 Gaylord Shaw, *Los Angeles* (Calif.) *Times*
1979 James Risser, *Des Moines Register*
1980 Bette Swenson Orsini and Charles Stafford, *St. Petersburg Times*
1981 John M. Crewdson, *New York Times*

INTERNATIONAL REPORTING
Founded 1942.
1970 Seymour M. Hersh, Dispatch News Service
1971 Jimmie Lee Hoagland, *Washington Post*
1972 Peter R. Kann, *Wall Street Journal*
1973 Max Frankel, *New York Times*
1974 Hedrick Smith, *New York Times*
1975 William Mullen and Ovie Carter, *Chicago Tribune*
1976 Sydney H. Schanberg, *New York Times*, who stayed behind when the Cambodian government was defeated by the communists on 17 April 1975, finally leaving with a convoy on 8 May to send story on the fall of Phnom Penh.
1977 No award

1978 Henry Kamm, *New York Times*
1979 Richard Ben Cramer, *The Philadelphia Inquirer*
1980 Joel Brinkley, reporter, and Jay Mather, photographer, *The Louisville Courier-Journal*
1981 Shirley Christian, *Miami Herald*

EDITORIAL WRITING
Founded 1917.
1970 Philip Geyelin, *Washington Post*
1971 Horance G. Davis Jr, *Gainesville* (Fla.) *Sun*
1972 J. Strohmeyer, *Bethlehem* (Pa.) *Globe-Times*
1973 Roger B. Linscott, *Berkshire Eagle*, Pittsfield, Mass.
1974 F. Gilman Spencer, *Trenton* (N.J.) *Trentonian*
1975 John Daniell Maurice, *Charleston* (W.Va) *Daily Mail*
1976 Philip P. Kerby, *Los Angeles Times*
1977 Warren L. Lerude, Foster Church, Norman F. Cardoza, *Reno Evening Gazette* and *Nevada State Journal*
1978 Meg Greenfield, *The Washington* (D.C.) *Post*
1979 Edwin M. Yoder, Jr., *The Washington Star*
1980 Robert L. Bartley, *The Wall Street Journal*
1981 No award

CARTOON
Founded 1922.
1970 Thomas Darcy, *Newsday*, Garden City, NY
1971 Paul Conrad, *Los Angeles Times*
1972 J. K. MacNelly, *Richmond* (Va.) *News Leader*
1973 No award
1974 Paul Szep, *Boston Globe*
1975 Garry Trudeau, creator of 'Doonesbury' comic strip
1976 Tony Auth, political cartoonist, *Philadelphia Inquirer*
1977 Paul Szep, *Boston Globe*
1978 J. K. McNelly, *Richmond* (Va.) *News Leader*
1979 Herbert L. Block, *The Washington Post*
1980 Don Wright, *The Miami News*
1981 Mike Peters, *Dayton* (Ohio) *Daily News*

NEWS PHOTOGRAPHY
Founded 1942.
1970 Steve Starr, Associated Press
1971 John Paul Filo, amateur photographer
1972 H. Faas, M. Laurent, Associated Press
1973 Huynh Cong Ut, Associated Press
1974 Anthony K. Roberts, freelance
1975 Gerald H. Gay, *Seattle Times*
1976 Stanley Forman, *Boston Herald-American*
1977 Stanley Forman, *Boston Herald-American* and Neal Ulevich, Associated Press
1978 J. Ross Baughman, Associated Press; John W. Blair, freelance; and UPI Indianapolis
1979 Thomas J. Kelly III, *The Pottstown* (Pa.) *Mercury*
1980 Photographer for United Press International, 'Firing Squad in Iran'
1981 Larry C. Price, *Fort Worth* (Tex.) *Star-Telegram*

FEATURE PHOTOGRAPHY
Founded 1968.
1970 Dallas Kinney, *Palm Beach* (Fla.) *Post*
1971 Jack Dykinga, *Chicago Sun-Times*
1972 Dave Kennerly, United Press International

1973 B. Lanker, *Topeka* (Kans.) *Capital-Journal*
1974 Slava Veder, Associated Press
1975 Matthew Lewis, *Washington Post*
1976 Photographic staff of *Louisville Courier-Journal and Times*
1977 Robin Hood, *News-Free Press*. Chattanooga, Tenn.
1978 J. Ross Baughman, Associated Press
1979 Staff photographers of *The Boston Herald American*
1980 Erwin H. Hagler, *Dallas Times Herald*
1981 Taro M. Yamasaki, *Detroit Free Press*

MERITORIOUS PUBLIC SERVICE
Founded 1918.
1970 *Newsday*, Garden City, N.Y.
1971 *Winston-Salem* (N.C.) *Journal and Sentinel*
1972 *New York Times*
1973 *Washington Post*
1974 *Newsday*, Garden City, N.Y.
1975 *Boston Globe*
1976 *Anchorage* (Alaska) *Daily News*
1977 *Lufkin* (Tex) *News,* for inquiry on death of local marine in training camp
1978 *Philadelphia* (Pa.) *Inquirer*
1979 *Point Reyes Light*, a California weekly
1980 Gannett News Service
1981 *Charlotte* (NC) *Observer*

CRITICISM
Founded 1970.
1970 Ada Louise Huxtable, *New York Times*
1971 Harold C. Schonberg, *New York Times*
1972 Frank L. Peters Jr., *St. Louis Post-Dispatch*
1973 Ronald Powers, *Chicago Sun-Times*
1974 Emily Genauer, *Newsday* syndicate
1975 Roger Ebert, *Chicago Sun-Times*
1976 Alan M. Kriegsman, dance critic, *Washington Post*
1977 William McPherson, book critic, *Washington Post*
1978 Walter Kerr, *New York Times*
1979 Paul Gapp, architecture critic of the *Chicago Tribune*
1980 William A. Henry III, *The Boston Globe*
1981 Jonathan Yardley, *Washington Star*

COMMENTARY
Founded 1970.
1970 Marquis Childs, *St. Louis Post-Dispatch*
1971 William A. Caldwell, *Record*, Hackensack, N.J.
1972 Mike Royko, *Chicago Daily News*
1973 David S. Broder, *Washington Post*
1974 Edwin A. Roberts Jr., *National Observer*
1975 Mary McGrory, *Washington Star*
1976 Walter W. (Red) Smith, sports columnist, *New York Times*
1977 George F. Will, syndicated columnist, *Washington Post* Writers Group
1978 Walter Safire, *New York Times*
1979 Russell Baker, *New York Times*
1980 Ellen H. Goodman, *The Boston Globe*
1981 Dave Anderson, *New York Times*

SPECIAL CITATIONS
Founded 1938.
1973 James T. Flexner, for 'George Washington', a four-volume biography.

1976 Scott Joplin (1868–1917), special bicentennial year award for his contributions to American music with such compositions as 'Maple Leaf Rag'.
1976 John Hohenberg, for 22 years of service as administrator of the Pulitzer Prizes.
1977 Alex Haley, for 'Roots', an 'important contribution to the literature of slavery'.
1978 E. B. White, *The New Yorker*
No longer awarded

FEATURE WRITING
Founded 1979.
1979 Jon D. Franklin, science writer for *The Baltimore Evening Sun*
1980 Madeleine Blais, *The Miami Herald*, 'Zepp's Last Stand'
1981 Teresa Carpenter, *The Village Voice*, New York City

'WHAT THE PAPERS SAY' GRANADA TELEVISION PRESS AWARDS
The annual 'What the Papers Say' awards are made by presenters of television's long running late night look at the press.

1957
Editor: Arthur Christiansen, *Daily Express*
Columnist: Cassandra, *Daily Mirror*
Cartoonist: Osbert Lancaster, *Daily Express*

1958
Newspaper: *Daily Mail*
Columnist: Cassandra, *Daily Mirror*
Cartoonist: Osbert Lancaster, *Daily Express*

1959
Newspaper: *The Sunday Times*
Cartoonist: Vicky

1960
Writer: Rebecca West, *The Sunday Times*
Scoop: John Cole, *The Guardian*
Cartoonist: Vicky
Picture: Victor Blackman, *Daily Express*

1961
Newspaper: *Sunday Telegraph*
Columnist: Michael Frayn
Cartoonist: Osbert Lancaster, *Daily Express*

1962
Reporter: Clare Hollingworth, *The Guardian*
Columnist: Peter Simple, *The Daily Telegraph*
Scoop: Walter Terry, *Daily Mail*

1963
Scoop: Peter Jenkins, *The Guardian*
Sports Writer: J. L. Manning, *Daily Mail*
Columnist: Dee Wells, *Daily Herald*
Cartoonist: Osbert Lancaster, *Daily Express*
Strip Cartoon: Dickens, *Evening Standard*
General Pleasure: Beachcomber, *Daily Express*

1964
Reporter: Chapman Pincher
Investigation: *The People*
Cartoonists: Wally Fawkes ('Trog') and George Melly, *Daily Mail*
Picture: Frank Aitken, *Daily Express*

1965
Newspaper: *Daily Mail*
Journalist: James Cameron
Cartoonist: Gerald Scarfe

1966
Reporter: Nicholas Tomalin, *The Sunday Times*
Outstanding Journalist: Bruce Page, *The Sunday Times*
Columnist: Inside Page, *Daily Mirror*
Outstanding Technical Achievement: Derek Marks, *Daily Express*

TENTH ANNIVERSARY AWARDS
Newspaper: *The Sunday Times*
Columnist: Cassandra, *Daily Mirror*
Cartoonist: Vicky
Foreign Correspondent: James Cameron
Reporter: Chapman Pincher

1967
Newspaper: *The Times*
Reporter: John Pilger, *Daily Mirror*
Photographer: Donald McCullin

1968
Newspaper: *Daily Mirror*
Journalist: Brian Priestley
Columnist: Bernard Levin
Sports Reporting: *The Observer*
Irritant: *Private Eye*

1969
Newspaper: *The Guardian*
Best Feature Writer: Vincent Mulchrone
Reporter: Michael Hornsby
Photographer: Donald McCullin

1970
Newspaper: *The Sun*
Columnist: Keith Waterhouse
Reporter: Murray Sayle
Special Award: Sir Gordon Newton
Best Woman's Page: *The Guardian*

1971
Newspaper: *The Guardian*
Columnist: Bernard Levin
For Investigative Journalism: *The Sunday Times*
Best Arts Page: *Financial Times*
The Gerald Barry Award: Anthony Mascarenhas

1972
Newspaper: *Financial Times*
Journalist: Paul Foot
Cartoonist: Marc, *The Times*
Scoop: *Daily Express*
Campaigns and Investigations: *The Sunday Times*

1973
Newspaper: *Washington Post*
British Newspaper: *The Daily Telegraph*
Investigative Reporter: Adam Raphael
Political Columnist: Alan Watkins
Cartoonist: Bill Tidy
The Gerald Barry Award: Sir Hugh Cudlipp 'greatest popular journalist of his time'

1974
Newspaper: *Daily Mail*
Reporter: Robert Fisk
Political Columnist: David Watt

Cartoonist: Nicholas Garland
Scoop: *Peace News*

1975
Campaign: *The Sunday Times*
Reporter: John Edwards, *Daily Mail*
Columnist: Jon Akass, *The Sun*
Journalist: Colin Welch, *The Daily Telegraph*
Scoop: Cyril Byrne Jnr.,

1976
Reporter: Nigel Wade, *The Daily Telegraph*
Journalist: Michael Davie, *The Observer*
Political Columnist: Andrew Alexander, *Daily Mail*
Cartoonist: Wally Fawkes ('Trog')
The Gerald Barry Award: Philip Hope-Wallace, *The Guardian*
Doyen of Directors of the Programme: Peter Mullings

1977
Editor: Donald Woods, *East London Daily Dispatch*
Newspaper: *The Daily Telegraph*
Sketch Writer: Frank Johnson, *The Daily Telegraph*
Special Investigation: Laurie Manifold and Team, *Sunday People*
Investigative Journalist: Charles Raw, *The Sunday Times*
The Gerald Barry Award: Terence Kilmartin, *The Observer*

1978
Journalist: Peter Jenkins, *The Guardian*
Investigative Journalist: Martin Bailey and Bernard Rivers
Columnist: Auberon Waugh, *Spectator*
Sports Writer: Frank Keating, *The Guardian*
Scoop: *Daily Mirror*

1979
Newspaper: *The Guardian*
Editor: Robert Cox, *Buenos Aires Herald*
Columnist: Conor Cruise O'Brien, *The Observer*
Cartoonist: Bryan McAllister, *The Guardian*
Reporter: Rob Rohrer, *The Sunday Times*
The Gerald Barry Award: George Hutchinson, *The Spectator*

1980
Columnist: Peregrine Worsthorne, *The Sunday Telegraph*
Cartoonist: Posy Simmonds, *The Guardian*
Reporter: Phillip Knightley, *The Sunday Times*
The Gerald Barry Award: James Cameron, *The Guardian*
Foreign Correspondent: Andrew Whitley, *Financial Times*

YOUNG JOURNALIST OF THE YEAR AWARD
This prize was first awarded in 1977 in memory of William Hardcastle, editor of the *Daily Mail*. It is organised by *The Northern Echo* and is open to youngsters under 18. The award is made to the best 'story' or feature article of not more than 750 words submitted. Winners:

1977 Simon Ritter, Newcastle-upon-Tyne
1978 Daniel Atkinson, Heathfield, Sussex
1979 Russell Tebbutt, Colne, Lancs
1980 Caroline Storer, Didcot, Oxfordshire

Judo

WORLD AND OLYMPIC CHAMPIONSHIPS

World championships were first held in 1956 and are now held biennially, though they were cancelled in 1977.

Judo was first included in the Olympic Games at Tokyo in 1964, but was not included in 1968.

In the following lists Olympic champions are indicated by an asterisk (*). From 1979 the weight limits were changed.

Open category
1956 Shokichi Natsui (Jap)
1958 Koji Sone (Jap)
1961 Anton Geesink (Hol)
1964* Anton Geesink (Hol)
1965 Isao Inokuma (Jap)
1967 Matsuo Matsunaga (Jap)
1969 Masatoshi Shinomaki (Jap)
1971 Masatoshi Shinomaki (Jap)
1972* Wim Ruska (Hol)
1973 Kazuhiro Ninomiya (Jap)
1975 Haruki Uemura (Jap)
1976* Haruki Uemura (Jap)
1979 Sumio Endo (Jap)
1980* Dietmar Lorenz (GDR)

Heavyweight (Over 93 kg to 1976, over 95 kg from 1979)
1964* Isao Inokuma (Jap)
1965 Anton Geesink (Hol)
1967 Wim Ruska (Hol)
1969 Shuja Suma (Jap)
1971 Wim Ruska (Hol)
1972* Wim Ruska (Hol)
1973 Chonufuhe Tagaki (Jap)
1975 Sumio Endo (Jap)
1976* Sergei Novikov (USSR)
1979 Yasuhiro Yamashita (Jap)
1980* Angelo Parisi (Fra)

95 kg (Middleweight)
1979 Timur Khubul (USSR)
1980* Robert van de Walle (Bel)

93 kg (Light heavyweight)
1967 Nobuyaki Sato (Jap)
1969 Fumio Sasahara (Jap)
1971 Fumio Sasahara (Jap)
1972* Shota Chochoshvily (USSR)
1973 Nobuyaki Sato (Jap)
1975 Jean-Luc Rouge (Fra)
1976* Kazuhiro Ninomiya (Jap)

86 kg (Middleweight)
1979 Detlef Ultsch (GDR)
1980* Juerg Roethlisberger (Swi)

80 kg (Middleweight)
1964* Isao Okano (Jap)
1965 Isao Okano (Jap)
1967 Eiji Maruki (Jap)
1969 Isamu Sonoda (Jap)
1971 Shozo Fujii (Jap)
1972* Shinobu Sekine (Jap)

1973 Shozo Fujii (Jap)
1975 Shozo Fujii (Jap)
1976* Isamu Sonoda (Jap)

78 kg (Light middleweight)
1979 Shozo Fujii (Jap)
1980* Shota Khabareli (USSR)

71 kg (Lightweight)
1979 Kyoto Katsuki (Jap)
1980* Ezio Gamba (Ita)

70 kg (Light middleweight or Welterweight)
1967 Hiroshi Minatoya (Jap)
1969 Hiroshi Minatoya (Jap)
1971 Hizashi Tsuzawa (Jap)
1972* Kazutoyo Nomura (Jap)
1973 Kazutoyo Nomura (Jap)
1975 Vladimir Nevzorov (USSR)
1976* Vladimir Nevzorov (USSR)

65 kg (Middle lightweight)
1979 Nikolai Solodukhin (USSR)
1980* Nikolai Solodukhin (USSR)

63 kg (Lightweight)
1964* Takehide Nakatani (Jap)
1965 H. Matsuda (Jap)
1967 Takosumi Shigeoka (Jap)
1969 Yoshio Sonoda (Jap)
1971 Takao Kawaguchi (Jap)
1972* Takao Kawaguchi (Jap)
1973 Yoshiharu Minamo (Jap)
1975 Yoshiharu Minamo (Jap)
1976* Hector Rodriguez (Cub)

60 kg (Super lightweight)
1979 Thierry Ray (Fra)
1980* Thierry Ray (Fra)

WOMEN'S JUDO WORLD CHAMPIONSHIPS

First held in 1980 when the winners were:

Open
Inge Berghmans (Bel)

48 kg
Jane Bridge (GB)

52 kg
Edith Hrovat (Aut)

56 kg
Gerda Winklbauer (Aut)

61 kg
Anita Staps (Hol)

66 kg
Edith Simon (Aut)

72 kg
Jocelyne Triadou (Fra)

Over 72 kg
Margarita de Cal (Ita)

Karate

WORLD CHAMPIONSHIPS (KARATE-DO)

Team
First held in 1970. Winners:
1970 Japan

1972 France
1975 Great Britain
1977 Holland

Individual
1977 Otti Roethof (Hol)

Kendo

WORLD KENDO CHAMPIONSHIPS

First held in 1970 in Japan, and subsequently every three years.

Individual
1970 M. Kobayashi (Jap)
1973 T. Sakuragi (Jap)
1976 Eiji Yoko (Jap)
1979 Hironori Yamada (Jap)

Team
1970 Japan
1973 Japan
1976 Japan
1979 Japan

Lacrosse

WORLD CHAMPIONSHIPS

The first men's world championships for field lacrosse were held in 1967 in Toronto. Winners:

1967 USA
1974 USA
1978 Canada

The first women's world championships were held in 1969. Winners:

1969 Great Britain
1974 USA
1978 Canada

An early lacrosse contest between Canadian settlers and Iroquois Indians, from whose game of baggataway the modern game derived

Lawn Tennis

DAVIS CUP
The world's premier international team competition is contested on a best of five matches basis by men's teams. The Cup was first contested as a challenge match between USA and Great Britain in 1900. Winners since 1974:

1974	South Africa	1978	USA
1975	Sweden	1979	USA
1976	Italy	1980	Czechoslovakia
1977	Australia		

Most wins:
USA 26 (1900, 1902, 1913, 1920–26, 1937–38, 1946–49, 1954, 1958, 1963, 1968–72, 1978–79)
Australia/Australasia 24 (1907–9, 1911, 1914, 1919, 1939, 1950–53, 1955–57, 1959–62, 1964–67, 1973, 1977).
Great Britain/British Isles 9 (1903–6, 1912, 1933–36)
France 6 (1927–32)

WIGHTMAN CUP
Contested annually by women's teams from the USA and Great Britain on a best of seven matches basis. First held in 1923, the United States have won 43 times to 1980, Great Britain have won 10 times – 1924, 1925, 1928, 1930, 1958, 1960, 1968, 1974, 1975, 1978.

FEDERATION CUP
Contested by women's teams annually on a knock-out basis. First played in 1963.

1963	USA	1972	South Africa
1964	Australia	1973	Australia
1965	Australia	1974	Australia
1966	USA	1975	Czechoslovakia
1967	USA	1976	USA
1968	Australia	1977	USA
1969	USA	1978	USA
1970	Australia	1979	USA
1971	Australia	1980	USA

WIMBLEDON CHAMPIONSHIPS
The most celebrated of the world's major championships, the Wimbledon championships were first played in 1877. Winners:

MEN'S SINGLES
1877	Spencer W. Gore (GB)
1878	Frank Hadow (GB)
1879	Rev. John Hartley (GB)
1880	Rev. John Hartley (GB)
1881	William Renshaw (GB)
1882	William Renshaw (GB)
1883	William Renshaw (GB)
1884	William Renshaw (GB)
1885	William Renshaw (GB)
1886	William Renshaw (GB)
1887	Herbert Lawford (GB)
1888	Ernest Renshaw (GB)
1889	William Renshaw (GB)
1890	Willoughby Hamilton (GB)
1891	Wilfred Baddeley (GB)
1892	Wilfred Baddeley (GB)
1893	Joshua Pim (GB)
1894	Joshua Pim (GB)
1895	Wilfred Baddeley (GB)
1896	Harold Mahony (GB)
1897	Reginald Doherty (GB)
1898	Reginald Doherty (GB)
1899	Reginald Doherty (GB)
1900	Reginald Doherty (GB)
1901	Arthur W. Gore (GB)
1902	Laurence Doherty (GB)
1903	Laurence Doherty (GB)
1904	Laurence Doherty (GB)
1905	Laurence Doherty (GB)
1906	Laurence Doherty (GB)
1907	Norman Brookes (Aus)
1908	Arthur W. Gore (GB)
1909	Arthur W. Gore (GB)
1910	Tony Wilding (NZ)
1911	Tony Wilding (NZ)
1912	Tony Wilding (NZ)
1913	Tony Wilding (NZ)
1914	Norman Brookes (Aus)
1919	Gerald Patterson (Aus)
1920	Bill Tilden (USA)
1921	Bill Tilden (USA)
1922	Gerald Patterson (Aus)
1923	William Johnston (USA)
1924	Jean Borotra (Fra)
1925	René Lacoste (Fra)
1926	Jean Borotra (Fra)
1927	Henri Cochet (Fra)
1928	René Lacoste (Fra)
1929	Henri Cochet (Fra)
1930	Bill Tilden (USA)
1931	Sidney Wood (USA)
1932	Ellsworth Vines (USA)
1933	Jack Crawford (Aus)
1934	Fred Perry (GB)
1935	Fred Perry (GB)
1936	Fred Perry (GB)
1937	Donald Budge (USA)
1938	Donald Budge (USA)
1939	Bobby Riggs (USA)
1946	Yvon Petra (Fra)
1947	Jack Kramer (USA)
1948	Bob Falkenburg (USA)
1949	Ted Schroeder (USA)
1950	Budge Patty (USA)
1951	Dick Savitt (USA)
1952	Frank Sedgman (Aus)
1953	Vic Seixas (USA)
1954	Jaroslav Drobny (Cze)
1955	Tony Trabert (USA)
1956	Lew Hoad (Aus)
1957	Lew Hoad (Aus)
1958	Ashley Cooper (Aus)
1959	Alex Olmedo (USA)
1960	Neale Fraser (Aus)
1961	Rod Laver (Aus)
1962	Rod Laver (Aus)
1963	Chuck McKinley (USA)
1964	Roy Emerson (Aus)
1965	Roy Emerson (Aus)

1966 Manuel Santana (Spa)	1899 Blanche Hillyard (GB)
1967 John Newcombe (Aus)	1900 Blanche Hillyard (GB)
1968 Rod Laver (Aus)	1901 Charlotte Sterry (née Cooper) (GB)
1969 Rod Laver (Aus)	1902 Muriel Robb (GB)
1970 John Newcombe (Aus)	1903 Dorothea Douglass (GB)
1971 John Newcombe (Aus)	1904 Dorothea Douglass (GB)
1972 Stan Smith (USA)	1905 May Sutton (USA)
1973 Jan Kodes (Cze)	1906 Dorothea Douglass (GB)
1974 Jimmy Connors (USA)	1907 May Sutton (USA)
1975 Arthur Ashe (USA)	1908 Charlotte Sterry (GB)
1976 Bjorn Borg (Swe)	1909 Dora Boothby (GB)
1977 Bjorn Borg (Swe)	1910 Dorothea Lambert Chambers (née Douglass) (GB)
1978 Bjorn Borg (Swe)	1911 Dorothea Lambert Chambers (GB)
1979 Bjorn Borg (Swe)	1912 Ethel Larcombe (GB)
1980 Bjorn Borg (Swe)	1913 Dorothea Lambert Chambers (GB)
1981 John McEnroe (USA)	1914 Dorothea Lambert Chambers (GB)

WOMEN'S SINGLES

First played in 1884. Winners:

1884 Maud Watson (GB)	1919 Suzanne Lenglen (Fra)
1885 Maud Watson (GB)	1920 Suzanne Lenglen (Fra)
1886 Blanche Bingley (GB)	1921 Suzanne Lenglen (Fra)
1887 Lottie Dod (GB)	1922 Suzanne Lenglen (Fra)
1888 Lottie Dod (GB)	1923 Suzanne Lenglen (Fra)
1889 Blanche Hillyard (née Bingley) (GB)	1924 Kathleen McKane (GB)
1890 Helene Rice (GB-Ire)	1925 Suzanne Lenglen (Fra)
1891 Lottie Dod (GB)	1926 Kathleen Godfree (née McKane) (GB)
1892 Lottie Dod (GB)	1927 Helen Wills (USA)
1893 Lottie Dod (GB)	1928 Helen Wills (USA)
1894 Blanche Hillyard (GB)	
1895 Charlotte Cooper (GB)	
1896 Charlotte Cooper (GB)	
1897 Blanche Hillyard (GB)	
1898 Charlotte Cooper (GB)	

Evonne Cawley holds aloft the women's singles trophy after her success in 1980, nine years after she had first won under her maiden name of Evonne Goolagong (Sporting Pictures)

1929 Helen Wills (USA)
1930 Helen Wills Moody (USA)
1931 Cilly Aussem (Ger)
1932 Helen Wills Moody (USA)
1933 Helen Wills Moody (USA)
1934 Dorothy Round (GB)
1935 Helen Wills Moody (USA)
1936 Helen Jacobs (USA)
1937 Dorothy Round (GB)
1938 Helen Wills Moody (USA)
1939 Alice Marble (USA)
1946 Pauline Betz (USA)
1947 Margaret Osborne (USA)
1948 Louise Brough (USA)
1949 Louise Brough (USA)
1950 Louise Brough (USA)
1951 Doris Hart (USA)
1952 Maureen Connolly (USA)
1953 Maureen Connolly (USA)
1954 Maureen Connolly (USA)
1955 Louise Brough (USA)
1956 Shirley Fry (USA)
1957 Althea Gibson (USA)
1958 Althea Gibson (USA)
1959 Maria Bueno (Bra)
1960 Maria Bueno (Bra)
1961 Angela Mortimer (GB)
1962 Karen Susman (USA)
1963 Margaret Smith (Aus)
1964 Maria Bueno (Bra)
1965 Margaret Smith (Aus)
1966 Billie Jean King (USA)
1967 Billie Jean King (USA)
1968 Billie Jean King (USA)
1969 Ann Jones (GB)
1970 Margaret Court (née Smith) (Aus)
1971 Evonne Goolagong (Aus)
1972 Billie Jean King (USA)
1973 Billie Jean King (USA)
1974 Christine Evert (USA)
1975 Billie Jean King (USA)
1976 Christine Evert (USA)
1977 Virginia Wade (GB)
1978 Martina Navratilova (Cze)
1979 Martina Navratilova (Cze)
1980 Evonne Cawley
     (née Goolagong) (Aus)
1981 Christine Evert-Lloyd (USA)

MEN'S DOUBLES
First held 1884.
Winners since 1965:

1965 John Newcombe and Tony Roche (Aus)
1966 Ken Fletcher and John Newcombe (Aus)
1967 Bob Hewitt and Frew McMillan (SA)
1968 John Newcombe and Tony Roche (Aus)
1969 John Newcombe and Tony Roche (Aus)
1970 John Newcombe and Tony Roche (Aus)
1971 Roy Emerson and Rod Laver (Aus)
1972 Bob Hewitt and Frew McMillan (SA)
1973 Jimmy Connors (USA) and Ilie Nastase (Rom)
1974 John Newcombe and Tony Roche (Aus)
1975 Vitas Gerulaitis and Sandy Mayer (USA)
1976 Brian Gottfried (USA) and Raul Ramirez (Mex)
1977 Ross Case and Geoff Masters (Aus)
1978 Bob Hewitt and Frew McMillan (SA)

Bob Hewitt (left) *and Frew McMillan* (right), *specialists in men's doubles, and Wimbledon champions in 1967, 1972 and 1978* (Diana Burnett)

1979 Peter Fleming and John McEnroe (USA)
1980 Peter McNamara and Paul McNamee (Aus)
1981 Peter Fleming and John McEnroe (USA)

Most wins:
8 Laurence Doherty and Reginald Doherty (GB) 1897–1901, 1903–5

WOMEN'S DOUBLES
First held 1899, but not a championship event until 1913.
Winners since 1965:

1965 Maria Bueno (Bra) and Billie Jean Moffitt (USA)
1966 Maria Bueno (Bra) and Nancy Richey (USA)
1967 Rosemary Casals and Billie Jean King (née Moffitt) (USA)
1968 Rosemary Casals and Billie Jean King (USA)
1969 Margaret Court and Judy Tegart (Aus)
1970 Rosemary Casals and Billie Jean King (USA)
1971 Rosemary Casals and Billie Jean King (USA)
1972 Billie Jean King (USA) and Betty Stove (Hol)
1973 Rosemary Casals and Billie Jean King (USA)
1974 Evonne Goolagong (Aus) and Peggy Michel (USA)
1975 Ann Kiyomura (USA) and Kazuko Sawamatsu (Jap)
1976 Christine Evert (USA) and Martina Navratilova (Cze)
1977 Helen Cawley (Aus) and Joanne Russell (USA)
1978 Kerry Reid and Wendy Turnbull (Aus)
1979 Billie Jean King (USA) and Martina Navratilova (Cze)
1980 Kathy Jordan and Anne Smith (USA)
1981 Martina Navratilova (Cze) and Pam Shriver (USA)

Most wins:
12 Elizabeth Ryan (USA): 1 with Agatha Morton 1914, 6 with Suzanne Lenglen 1919–23, 1925; 1 with Mary Browne 1926, 2 with Helen Wills Moody 1927, 1930; 2 with Simone Mathieu 1933–34

MIXED DOUBLES
First held 1900, but not a championship event until 1913.

Winners since 1965:
1965 Ken Fletcher and Margaret Smith (Aus)
1966 Ken Fletcher and Margaret Smith (Aus)
1967 Owen Davidson (Aus) and Billie Jean King (USA)
1968 Ken Fletcher and Margaret Court (née Smith) (Aus)
1969 Fred Stolle (Aus) and Ann Jones (GB)
1970 Ilie Nastase (Rom) and Rosemary Casals (USA)
1971 Owen Davidson (Aus) and Billie Jean King (USA)
1972 Ilie Nastase (Rom) and Rosemary Casals (USA)
1973 Owen Davidson (Aus) and Billie Jean King (USA)
1974 Owen Davidson (Aus) and Billie Jean King (USA)
1975 Marty Reissen (USA) and Margaret Court (Aus)
1976 Tony Roche (Aus) and Françoise Durr (Fra)
1977 Bob Hewitt and Greer Stevens (SA)
1978 Frew McMillan (SA) and Betty Stove (Hol)
1979 Bob Hewitt and Greer Stevens (USA)
1980 John Austin and Tracy Austin (USA)
1981 Frew McMillan (SA) and Betty Stove (Hol)
Most wins:
7 Elizabeth Ryan (USA) 1919, 1921, 1923, 1927–8, 1930, 1932 with 5 different partners

UNITED STATES CHAMPIONSHIPS
The US Lawn Tennis Association (USLTA) championships were first held in 1881 and continued until 1969. The tournament was superseded in 1970 by the US Open Championships which had first been held in 1968. Now held at Flushing Meadow, New York.

US Open winners:
MEN'S SINGLES
1968 Arthur Ashe (USA)
1969 Rod Laver (Aus)
1970 Ken Rosewall (Aus)
1971 Stan Smith (USA)
1972 Ilie Nastase (Rom)
1973 John Newcombe (Aus)
1974 Jimmy Connors (USA)
1975 Manuel Orantes (Spa)
1976 Jimmy Connors (USA)
1977 Guillermo Vilas (Arg)
1978 Jimmy Connors (USA)
1979 John McEnroe (USA)
1980 John McEnroe (USA)

WOMEN'S SINGLES
1968 Virginia Wade (GB)
1969 Margaret Court (Aus)
1970 Margaret Court (Aus)
1971 Billie Jean King (USA)
1972 Billie Jean King (USA)
1973 Margaret Court (Aus)
1974 Billie Jean King (USA)
1975 Christine Evert (USA)
1976 Christine Evert (USA)

Tracy Austin in her Wimbledon debut at the age of 14 (Syndication International)

1977 Christine Evert (USA)
1978 Christine Evert (USA)
1979 Tracy Austin (USA)
1980 Christine Evert-Lloyd (USA)
Most wins in the USLTA championships:
Men's Singles
7 Richard D. Sears 1881–87; William T. Tilden 1920–25, 1929
Women's Singles
7 Helen Wills Moody 1923–25, 1927–29, 1931

FRENCH CHAMPIONSHIPS
First held in 1891. Held on hard courts at the Stade Roland Garros, near Paris. Singles winners since 1968:

MEN'S SINGLES
1968 Ken Rosewall (Aus)
1969 Rod Laver (Aus)
1970 Jan Kodes (Cze)
1971 Jan Kodes (Cze)
1972 Andres Gimeno (Spa)
1973 Ilie Nastase (Rom)

1974 Bjorn Borg (Swe)
1975 Bjorn Borg (Swe)
1976 Adriano Panatta (Ita)
1977 Guillermo Vilas (Arg)
1978 Bjorn Borg (Swe)
1979 Bjorn Borg (Swe)
1980 Bjorn Borg (Swe)
1981 Bjorn Borg (Swe)

WOMEN'S SINGLES
1968 Nancy Richey (USA)
1969 Margaret Court (Aus)
1970 Margaret Court (Aus)
1971 Evonne Goolagong (Aus)
1972 Billie Jean King (USA)
1973 Margaret Court (Aus)
1974 Christine Evert (USA)
1975 Christine Evert (USA)
1976 Susan Barker (GB)
1977 Mima Jausovec (Yug)
1978 Virginia Ruzici (Rom)
1979 Christine Evert-Lloyd (USA)
1980 Christine Evert-Lloyd (USA)
1981 Hana Mandlikova (Cze)

AUSTRALIAN CHAMPIONSHIPS
First held in 1905. Singles' winners since 1968
(year shown is second half of winter season):

MEN'S SINGLES
1968 William Bowrey (Aus)
1969 Rod Laver (Aus)
1970 Arthur Ashe (USA)
1971 Ken Rosewall (Aus)
1972 Ken Rosewall (Aus)

*John McEnroe in action at Wimbledon in 1980,
when he overcame the opposition of the crowds
to be acclaimed after losing a great final to
Bjorn Borg* (Sporting Pictures)

1973 John Newcombe (Aus)
1974 Jimmy Connors (USA)
1975 John Newcombe (Aus)
1976 Mark Edmondson (Aus)
1977 Roscoe Tanner (USA)
1978 Vitas Gerulaitis (USA)
1979 Guillermo Vilas (Arg)
1980 Guillermo Vilas (Arg)
1981 Brian Teacher (USA)

WOMEN'S SINGLES
1968 Billie Jean King (USA)
1969 Margaret Court (Aus)
1970 Margaret Court (Aus)
1971 Margaret Court (Aus)
1972 Virginia Wade (GB)
1973 Margaret Court (Aus)
1974 Evonne Goolagong (Aus)
1975 Evonne Goolagong (Aus)
1976 Evonne Cawley (née Goolagong) (Aus)
1977 Kerry Reid (Aus)
1978 Evonne Cawley (Aus)
1979 Christine O'Neill (Aus)
1980 Barbara Jordan (USA)
1981 Hana Mandlikova (Cze)

GRAND SLAM
Winners of the Grand Slam are those players
who have won the singles' events at the world's
four major tournaments in the same year.
Tournaments are Wimbledon, USA, French
and Australian championships. Grand Slams
have been achieved by:

MEN
Donald Budge (USA) 1938: Rod Laver (Aus) 1962,
1969

WOMEN
Maureen Connolly (USA) 1953: Margaret Court
(Aus) 1970

WCT CHAMPIONS
World Championship Tennis (WCT) has held
a series of championships since 1971.

1971 Ken Rosewall (Aus)
1972 Ken Rosewall (Aus)
1973 Stan Smith (USA)
1974 John Newcombe (Aus)
1975 Arthur Ashe (USA)
1976 Bjorn Borg (Swe)
1977 Jimmy Connors (USA)
1978 Vitas Gerulaitis (USA)
1979 John McEnroe (USA)
1980 Jimmy Connors (USA)
1981 John McEnroe (USA)

WCT DOUBLES
Winners of the WCT Doubles tournament (sponsored by Braniff Airways), first held in 1973.

1973 Bob Lutz and Stan Smith (USA)
1974 Bob Hewitt and Frew McMillan (SA)
1975 Brian Gottfried (USA) and Raul Ramirez
     (Mex)
1976 Wojtek Fibak (Pol) and Karl Meiler (Ger)
1977 Vijay Amritraj (Ind) and Dick Stockton
     (USA)

1978 Wojtek Fibak (Pol) and Tom Okker (Hol)
1979 Peter Fleming and John McEnroe (USA)
1980 Brian Gottfried (USA) and Raul Ramirez (Mex)
1981 Peter McNamara and Paul McNamee (Aus)

GRAND PRIX
Winners on points gained in major tournaments since 1970:

1970 Cliff Richey (USA)
1971 Stan Smith (USA)
1972 Ilie Nastase (Rom)
1973 Ilie Nastase (Rom)
1974 Guillermo Vilas (Arg)
1975 Guillermo Vilas (Arg)
1976 Raul Ramirez (Mex)
1977 Guillermo Vilas (Arg)
1978 Jimmy Connors (USA)
1979 John McEnroe (USA)
1980 John McEnroe (USA)

GRAND PRIX MASTERS TOURNAMENT
Contested annually since 1970 by the top points scorers in the Grand Prix. Now held in the January of the following year to that shown.

1970 Stan Smith (USA)
1971 Ilie Nastase (Rom)
1972 Ilie Nastase (Rom)
1973 Ilie Nastase (Rom)

1974 Guillermo Vilas (Arg)
1975 Ilie Nastase (Rom)
1976 Manuel Orantes (Spa)
1977 Jimmy Connors (USA)
1978 John McEnroe (USA)
1979 Bjorn Borg (Swe)
1980 Bjorn Borg (Swe)

MASTERS DOUBLES CHAMPIONS
(first held 1975)
1975 Manuel Orantes and Juan Gisbert (Spa)
1976 Fred McNair and Sherwood Stewart (USA)
1977 Bob Hewitt and Frew McMillan (SA) (Jan '78)
1978 John McEnroe and Peter Fleming (USA) (Jan '79)
1979 John McEnroe and Peter Fleming (USA) (Jan '80)
1980 John McEnroe and Peter Fleming (USA) (Jan '81)

WORLD CHAMPIONSHIPS
Officially designated by the International Tennis Federation for the first time in 1978.

MEN
1978 Bjorn Borg (Swe)
1979 Bjorn Borg (Swe)
1980 Bjorn Borg (Swe)

WOMEN
1978 Christine Evert-Lloyd (USA)
1979 Martina Navratilova (USA, ex Cze)
1980 Christine Evert-Lloyd (USA)

Literature

THE BOOKER McCONNELL PRIZE
Inaugurated in 1968, this most prestigious annual prize for fiction of £10 000 is sponsored by Booker McConnell Ltd, and administered by the National Book League. The prize is awarded to the best novel, in the opinion of the judges, published each year. The prize is open to novels written in English by citizens of the British Commonwealth, the Republic of Ireland and the Republic of South Africa, and published for the first time in the UK by a British publisher.

1969 *Something to Answer For*, P. H. Newby.
1970 *The Elected Member*, Bernice Rubens
1971 *In a Free State*, V. S. Naipaul.
1972 *G*, John Berger
1973 *The Siege of Krishnapur*, James Gordon Farrell
1974 *The Conservationist*, Nadine Gordimer
      Holiday, Stanley Middleton
1975 *Heat and Dust*, Ruth Prawer Jhabvala.
1976 *Saville*, David Storey
1977 *Staying On*, Paul Scott
1978 *The Sea, The Sea*, Iris Murdoch
1979 *Offshore*, Penelope Fitzgerald
1980 *Rites of Passage*, William Golding

William Golding, 1980 winner of the Booker McConnell prize

THE GUARDIAN AWARD FOR CHILDREN'S FICTION

This award which dates from 1967 is made for an outstanding contribution to imaginative literature for children. The winner is chosen by a panel of regular *Guardian* reviewers.

1967 *Devil in the Fog*, Leon Garfield
1968 *The Owl Service*, Alan Garner
1969 *The Whispering Mountain*, Joan Aiken
1970 *Flambards Trilogy*, K. M. Peyton
1971 *The Guardians*, John Christopher
1972 *A Likely Lad*, Gillian Avery
1973 *Watership Down*, Richard Adams
1974 *The Iron Lily*, Barbara Willard
1975 *Gran at Coalgate*, Winifred Cawley
1976 *The Peppermint Pig*, Nina Bawden
1977 *The Blue Hawk*, Peter Dickinson
1978 *Charmed Life*, Dianna Wynne Jones
1979 *Conrad's War*, Andrew Davies
1980 *The Vandal*, Ann Schlee
1981 *The Sentinels*, Peter Carter

THE GUARDIAN FICTION PRIZE

This award has been given since 1965 for the best new fiction book of the year. A cash prize of £500 was given in 1980.

1965 *Crumb Borne*, Clive Barry
1966 *The Dear Green Place*, Archie Hind
1967 *Winter Journey*, Eva Figes
1968 *A Song and Dance*, Patrick Joseph Kavanagh
1969 *Poor Lazarus*, Maurice Leitch
1970 *When Did You Last See your Father?* Margaret Blount
1971 *The Big Chapel*, Thomas Kilroy
1972 *G*, John Berger
1973 *In the Country of the Skin*, Peter Redgrove
1974 *The Bottle Factory Outing*, Beryl Bainbridge
1975 *Friends and Romans*, Sylvia Clayton
1976 *Falstaff*, Robert Nye
1977 *The Condition of Muzak*, Michael Moorcock
1978 *The Murderer*, Roy A. K. Heath
1979 *Night in Tunisia*, Neil Jordan
     The House of Hunger, Dambudzo Marechera
1980 *A Month in the Country*, J. L. Carr

THE HAWTHORNDEN PRIZE

The Hawthornden Prize, the oldest of the famous British literary prizes, was founded in 1919 by Miss Alice Warrender. It consists of £100 awarded annually to an English writer under 41 years of age for the best work of imaginative literature. It is especially designed to encourage young authors, and the word 'imaginative' is given a broad interpretation. Biographies are not necessarily excluded. Books do not have to be submitted for the prize. It is awarded without competition, and a panel of judges decides upon the winner. Winners since 1958 (prize not awarded, 1945–57)

1958 *A Beginning*, Dom Moraes
1959 No award
1960 *The Loneliness of the Long Distance Runner*, Alan Sillitoe
1961 *Lupercal*, Ted Hughes

1962 *The Sun Doctor*, Robert Shaw
1963 *The Price of Glory: Verdun 1916*, Alistair Horne
1964 *Mr Stone and the Knights Companions*, V. S. Naipaul
1965 *The Old Boys*, William Trevor
1966 No award
1967 *The Russian Interpreter*, Michael Frayn
1968 *Early Renaissance*, Michael Levey
1969 *King Log*, Geoffrey Hill
1970 *Monk Dawson*, Piers Paul Read
1971 No award
1972 No award
1973 No award
1974 *Awakenings*, Oliver Sacks
1975 *Changing Places*, David Lodge
1976 *Falstaff*, Robert Nye
1977 *In Patagonia*, Bruce Chatwin
1978 *Walter*, David Cook
1979 *Kindergarten*, P. S. Rushforth
1980 *Arcadia,* Christopher Reid

NOBEL PRIZE FOR LITERATURE

The Nobel Prize for Literature is one of the awards stipulated in the will of the late Alfred Nobel, the Swedish scientist who invented dynamite. The awarding authority is the Swedish Academy (for Literature). For further details see under main heading of Nobel Prizes.

1901 Sully Prudhomme (René Prudhomme) (Fra)
1902 C. M. T. Mommsen (Ger)
1903 Bjornstjerne Bjornson (Nor)
1904 Frederic Mistral (Fra)
     Jose Echegaray (Spa)
1905 Henryk Sienkiewicz (Pol)
1906 Giosue Carducci (Ita)
1907 Rudyard Kipling (GB)
1908 Rudolf C. Eucken (Ger)
1909 Selma Lagerlof (Swe)
1910 Paul J. L. Heyse (Ger)
1911 Count Maurice Maeterlinck (Bel)
1912 Gerhart Hauptmann (Ger)
1913 Rabindranath Tagore (Ind)
1914 No award
1915 Romain Rolland (Fra)
1916 Carl G. von Heidenstam (Swe)
1917 Karl A. Gjellerup (Den)
     Henrik Pontoppidan (Den)
1918 No award
1919 Carl F. G. Spitteler (Swi)
1920 Knut Hamsun (Nor)
1921 Anatole France (Fra)
1922 Jacinto Benavente (Spa)
1923 William Butler Yeats (Ire)
1924 Wladyslaw S. Reymont (Pol)
1925 George Bernard Shaw (GB) (Irish-born)
1926 Grazia Deledda (Ita)
1927 Henri Bergson (Fra)
1928 Sigrid Undset (Nor) (Danish-born)
1929 Thomas Mann (Ger)
1930 Sinclair Lewis (USA)
1931 Erik A. Karlfeldt (Swe)
1932 John Galsworthy (GB)
1933 Ivan A. Bunin (Fra) (Russian-born)
1934 Luigi Pirandello (Ita)

1935 No award
1936 Eugene O'Neill (USA)
1937 Roger Martin du Gard (Fra)
1938 Pearl S. Buck (USA)
1939 Frans E. Sillanpaa (Fin)
1940 No award
1941 No award
1942 No award
1943 No award
1944 Johannes V. Jensen (Den)
1945 Gabriela Mistral (Chi)
1946 Hermann Hesse (Swi) (German-born)
1947 André Gide (Fra)
1948 T. S. Eliot (GB) (USA-born)
1949 William Faulkner (USA)
1950 Bertrand Russell (GB)
1951 Par F. Lagerkvist (Swe)
1952 François Mauriac (Fra)
1953 Sir Winston Churchill (GB)
1954 Ernest Hemingway (USA)
1955 Halldor K. Laxness (Ice)
1956 Juan Ramon Jimenez (PR) (Spanish-born)
1957 Albert Camus (Fra)
1958 Boris L. Pasternak (USSR) Prize declined
1959 Salvatore Quasimodo (Ita)
1960 Saint-John Perse (Fra)
1961 Ivo Andric (Yug)
1962 John Steinbeck (USA)
1963 George Seferis (Gre)
1964 Jean-Paul Sartre (Fra) Prize declined
1965 Mikhail Sholokhov (USSR)
1966 Shmuel Yosef Agnon (Isr) (Austrian-born)
     Nelly Sachs (Swe) (German-born)
1967 Miguel Angel Asturias (Gua)
1968 Yasunari Kawabata (Jap)
1969 Samuel Beckett (Ire)
1970 Aleksandr. I. Solzhenitsyn (USSR)
1971 Pablo Neruda (Chi)
1972 Heinrich Boll (Ger)
1973 Patrick White (Aus)
1974 Eyvind Johnson (Swe)
     Harry Edmund Martinson (Swe)
1975 Eugenio Montale (Ita)
1976 Saul Bellow (USA)
1977 Vicente Aleixandre (Spa)
1978 Isaac Bashevis Singer (USA)
1979 Odysseus Elytis (Odysseus Alepoudelis) (Gre)
1980 Czeslaw Milosz (Pol)

PULITZER PRIZE FOR LITERATURE

For further details see under main heading of Pulitzer Prizes.

FICTION

1917 No award
1918 *His Family,* Ernest Poole
1919 *The Magnificent Ambersons*, Booth Tarking-
     ton
1920 No award
1921 *The Age of Innocence*, Edith Wharton
1922 *Alice Adams*, Booth Tarkington
1923 *One of Ours*, Willa Cather
1924 *The Able McLaughlins*, Margaret Wilson
1925 *So Big*, Edna Ferber
1926 *Arrowsmith*, Sinclair Lewis
1927 *Early Autumn*, Louis Bromfield
1928 *The Bridge of San Luis Rey*, Thornton Wilder
1929 *Scarlet Sister Mary*, Julia Peterkin

1930 *Laughing Boy*, Oliver LaFarge
1931 *Years of Grace*, Margaret Ayer Barnes
1932 *The Good Earth*, Pearl S. Buck
1933 *The Store*, T. S. Stribling
1934 *Lamb in His Bosom*, Caroline Miller
1935 *Now in November*, Josephine Winslow
     Johnson
1936 *Honey in the Horn*, Harold L. Davis
1937 *Gone with the Wind*, Margaret Mitchell
1938 *The Late George Apley*, John Phillips Mar-
     quand
1939 *The Yearling*, Marjorie Kinnan Rawlings
1940 *The Grapes of Wrath*, John Steinbeck
1941 No award
1942 *In This Our Life*, Ellen Glasgow
1943 *Dragon's Teeth*, Upton Sinclair
1944 *Journey in the Dark*, Martin Flavin
1945 *A Bell for Adano*, John Hersey
1946 No award
1947 *All the King's Men*, Robert Penn Warren
1948 *Tales of the South Pacific*, James Michener
1949 *Guard of Honor*, James Gould Cozzens
1950 *The Way West*, A. B. Guthrie Jr
1951 *The Town*, Conrad Richter
1952 *The Caine Mutiny*, Herman Wouk
1953 *The Old Man and the Sea*, Ernest Hemingway
1954 No award
1955 *A Fable*, William Faulkner
1956 *Andersonville*, MacKinlay Kantor
1957 No award
1958 *A Death in the Family*, James Agee
1959 *The Travels of Jaime McPheeters*, Robert
     Lewis Taylor
1960 *Advise and Consent*, Allen Drury
1961 *To Kill a Mockingbird*, Harper Lee
1962 *The Edge of Sadness*, Edwin O'Connor
1963 *The Reivers*, William Faulkner
1964 No award
1965 *The Keepers of the House*, Shirley Ann Grau
1966 *The Collected Stories of Katherine Anne
     Porter*, Katherine Anne Porter
1967 *The Fixer*, Bernard Malamud
1968 *The Confessions of Nat Turner*, William Styron
1969 *House Made of Dawn*, Navarre Scott
     Momaday
1970 *Collected Stories*, Jean Stafford
1971 No award
1972 *Angle of Repose*, Wallace Stegner
1973 *The Optimist's Daughter*, Eudora Welty
1974 No award
1975 *The Killer Angels*, Michael Shaara
1976 *Humboldt's Gift*, Saul Bellow
1977 No award
1978 *Elbow Room*, James Allan McPherson
1979 *The Stories of John Cheever*, John Cheever
1980 *The Executioner's Song*, Norman Mailer
1981 *A Confederacy of Dunces*, John Kennedy
     Toole

GENERAL NONFICTION

This prize was first awarded in 1962.

1962 *The Making of the President 1960*, Theodore
     H. White
1963 *The Guns of August*, Barbara Tuchman
1964 *Anti-intellectualism in American Life*, Richard
     Hofstadter
1965 *O Strange New World*, Howard Mumford
     Jones

1966	*Wandering Through Winter*, Edwin Way Teale
1967	*The Problem of Slavery in Western Culture*, David Brion Davis
1968	*Rousseau and Revolution*, Will and Ariel Durant
1969	*So Human an Animal: How We are Shaped by Surroundings and Events*, Rene Dubos
	The Armies of the Night, Norman Mailer
1970	*Gandhi's Truth*, Erik H. Erikson
1971	*The Rising Sun*, John Toland
1972	*Stilwell and the American Experience in China, 1911–1945*, Barbara W. Tuchman
1973	*Fire in the Lake*, Frances Fitzgerald
	Children of Crisis, Robert Coles
1974	*The Denial of Death*, Ernest Becker
1975	*Pilgrim at Tinker Creek*, Annie Dillard
1976	*Why Survive? Being Old in America*, Robert N. Butler
1977	*Beautiful Swimmers: Watermen, Crabs and the Chesapeake Bay*, William W. Warner
1978	*The Dragons of Eden*, Carl Sagan
1979	*On Human Nature*, Edward O. Wilson
1980	*Gödel, Escher, Bach: an Eternal Golden Braid*, Douglas R. Hofstadter
1981	*Fin-de-Siecle Vienna: Politics and Culture*, Carl E. Schorske

THE JAMES TAIT BLACK MEMORIAL PRIZES

One of the oldest literary awards, the James Tait Black Memorial prizes, founded in memory of the publisher, were instituted in 1918. The two prizes are for the best biography or work of that nature, and for the best novel. Winners since 1945:

	Novel	*Biography*
1945	*Travellers*, L. A. G. Strong	*Wilson Steer*, D. S. MacColl
1946	*Poor Man's Tapestry*, G. Oliver	*Wellington*, R. Aldington
1947	*Eustace and Hilda*, L. P. Hartley	*English Naturalists from Neckham to Ray*. Rev. C. C. E. Raven
1948	*The Heart of the Matter*, G. Greene	*The Great Dr. Burney*, P. A. Scholes
1949	*The Far Cry*, E. Smith	*W. E. Henley*, J. Connell
1950	*Along the Valley*, R. Henriquez	*Florence Nightingale*, Mrs. C. Woodham-Smith
1951	*Father Goose*, W. C. Chapman-Mortimer	*Leslie Stephen*, Noel G. Annah
1952	*Men at Arms*, Evelyn Waugh	*Stanley Baldwin*, G. M. Young
1953	*Troy Chimneys*, Margaret Kennedy	*Sir John Moore*, Carola Oman
1954	*The New Man* (and *The Masters*, in sequence), C. P. Snow	*Warren Hastings*, Keith Feiling
1955	*Mother and Son*, Ivy Compton-Burnett	*Thomas Gray*, R. W. Ketton-Cremer
1956	*The Towers of Trebizond*, Rose Macauley	*George Bernard Shaw*, St. John Ervine.
1957	*At Lady Molly's*, Anthony Powell	*Life of John Locke*, Maurice Cranston
1958	*The Middle Age of Mrs Eliot*, Angus Wilson	*The History of Fanny Burney*, Joyce Hernlow
1959	*The Devil's Advocate*, Morris West	*Edward Marsh*, Christopher Hassall
1960	*Imperial Caesar*, Rex Warner	*The Life of Dean Inge*, Canon Adam-Fox
1961	*The Ha-Ha*, Jennifer Dawson	*Joseph Ashby of Tysoe*, Miss M. K. Ashby
1962	*Act of Destruction,* Ronald Hardy	*John Henry Newman: The Pillar of the Cloud* and *John Henry Newman: Light in Winter*, Meriol Trevor
1963	*A Slanting Light*, Gerda Charles	*John Keble: A Study in Limitation*, Georgina Battiscombe
1964	*The Ice Saints*, Frank Tuohy	*Queen Victoria*, Lady Longford
1965	*The Mandelbaum Gate*, Muriel Spark	*William Wordsworth, the Later Years*, Mary Moorman
1966	*Such*, Christine Brooke-Rose	*The Life of William Harvey*, Geoffrey Keynes
	Langrishe, Go Down, Aidan Higgins (Joint Award)	
1967	*Jerusalem the Golden*, Margaret Drabble	*Charlotte Bronte, the Evolution of Genius*, Winifred Gerin
1968	*The Gasterapod*, Maggie Ross	*George Eliot*, Prof. Gordon S. Haight
1969	*Eva Trout*, Elizabeth Bowen	*Mary Queen of Scots*, Lady Antonia Fraser
1970	*The Bird of Paradise*, Lily Powell	*Lord Palmerston*, Jasper Ridley
1971	*A Guest of Honour*, Nadine Gordimer	*Lewis Namier*, Julia Namier
1972	*G*, John Berger	*Virginia Woolf*, Quentin Bell
1973	*The Black Prince*, Iris Murdoch	*Alexander the Great*, Robin Fox Lane
1974	*Monsieur, or The Prince of Darkness*, Lawrence Durrell	*Samuel Johnson*, John Wain
1975	*The Great Victorian Collection*, Brian Moore	*Cockburn's Millennium*, Karl Miller
1976	*Doctor Copernicus*, John Vanville	*A New Life of Anton Chekhov*, Ronald Hingley
1977	*The Honourable Schoolboy*, John Le Carré	*Chateaubriand: The Longed-for Tempests, 1768–93, Vol. 1*, George Painter
1978	*Plumb*, Maurice Gee	*The Older Hardy*, Robert Gittings
1979	*Darkness Visible*, William Golding	*Christopher Isherwood*, Brian Finney
1980	*Waiting for the Barbarians*, J. M. Coetzee	*Tennyson: The Unquiet Heart*, Robert B. Martin

THE ROYAL SOCIETY OF LITERATURE BENSON MEDAL

Established in 1916, the award is given from time to time by the Council of the Royal Society of Literature for meritorious work in poetry, fiction, history, biography, and belles-lettres.

1917 Gabrielle d'Annunzio
     Benito Peréz Galdós
     Maurice Parrès
1923 Lytton Strachey
1926 Percy Lubbock
     Robert Lynd
     Harold Nicolson
1928 Gordon Bottomley
     George Santayana
1929 Helen Waddell
     F. A. Simpson
1932 Stella Benson
1934 Dame Edith Sitwell
1938 E. M. Forster
     G. M. Young
1939 F. L. Lucas
     Andrew Young
1940 John Galsworthy
     Christopher Hassall
1941 Christopher La Farge
1952 Frederick S. Boas
1966 J. R. R. Tolkien
     Dame Rebecca West
1968 E. V. Rieu
1969 C. Woodham-Smith
1975 Philip Larkin
1981 Odysseus Elytis

THE ROYAL SOCIETY OF LITERATURE HEINEMANN AWARD

Established in 1944 through the will of the late William Heinemann. The award, organised by the Royal Society of Literature, is 'primarily to reward those classes of literature which are less remunerative, namely, poetry, criticism, biography, history, etc.' and 'to encourage the production of works of real merit'.

1945 *Five Rivers*, Norman Nicholson
1946 *In Search of Two Characters*, D. Colston-Baynes
     Prospect of Flowers, Andrew Young
1947 *History of Western Philosophy*, Bertrand Russell
     The Garden, V. Sackville-West
1948 *Down to Earth*, J. Stuart Collis
     Letters to Malaya, Martyn Skinner
1949 *Selected Poems*, John Betjeman
     Travelling Home, Frances Cornford
1950 *Broken Images*, John Guest
     John Ruskin, Peter Quennell
1951 *Travellers Tree*, Patrick Leigh-Fermor
     Glassblowers and Gormanghast, Mervyn Peake
1952 *The Cruel Sea*, Nicholas Monsarrat
     Mountains with a Difference, G. Winthrop Young
1953 *Collected Poems*, Edwin Muir
     Arnold Bennett, Reginald Pound

1954 *The Ermine*, Ruth Pitter
     The Go-Between, L. P. Hartley
1955 *John Keats: The Living Years*, Robert Gittings
     Song at the Years Turning, R. S. Thomas
1956 *Wise Man from the West*, Vincent Cronin
     Thomas Gray, R. W. Ketton-Cremer
1957 *The Bourbons of Naples*, Harold Acton
     Roman Mornings, James Lees-Milne
1958 *Sword of Pleasure*, Peter Green
     A Reed Shaken by the Wind, Gavin Maxwell
1959 *The Last Tudor King*, Hester Chapman
     The Chequer'd Shade, John Press
1960 *The Cocks of Hades*, Constantine A. Trypanis
     The Devil's Advocate, Morris West
1961 *Venice*, James Morris
     The Masks of Love, Vernon Scannell
1962 *Curtmantle*, Christopher Fry
     The Destruction of Lord Raglan, Christopher Hibbert
1963 *Mrs. Browning*, Alethea Hayter
1964 *Rosebery*, Robert Rhodes James
     Cooper's Creek, Alan Moorehead
1965 *Journey from Obscurity, II, Youth*, Harold Owen
     The Marsh Arabs, Wilfred Thesiger
1966 *Jonathan Swift*, Nigel Dennis
     The Castaway, Derek Walcott
1967 *Wide Sargasso Sea*, Jean Rhys
     Surroundings, Norman MacCaig
     Tolstoy and the Novel, John Bayley
1968 *Charlotte Brontë*, Winifred Gerin
     The Maze Maker, Michael Ayrton
1969 *George Eliot*, Gordon S. Haight
     Writing in the Dust, Jasmine Rose Innes
     A Cab at the Door, V. S. Pritchett
1970 *Akenfield: Portrait of an English Village*, Ronald Blythe
     Sir William Hamilton, Brian Fothergill
     Pharaoh's Chicken, Nicholas Wollaston
1971 *Britain and Her Army*, Corelli Barnett
     Medieval Humanism, Richard W. Southern
1972 *Granite Islands: Portrait of Corsica*, Dorothy Carrington
     Mercian Hymns, Geoffrey Hill
     The Big Chapel, Thomas Kilroy
1973 *That Greece Might Still Be Free*, William St. Clair
     The Chant of Jimmy Blacksmith, Thomas Keneally
1974 *Alexander the Great*, Robin Lane Fox
     From the Wilderness, Alasdair Maclean
     Mooncranker's Gift, Barry Unsworth
1975 *Samuel Johnson*, John Wain
     William Wilberforce, Robin Furneaux
1976 *Melbourne*, Philip Ziegler
     Shadow of the Winter Palace, Edward Crankshaw
1977 *Parnell*, F. S. L. Lyons
     The First Fabians, Norman and Jeanne Mackenzie
     Milton and the English Revolution, Christopher Hill
1978 *Live Bait*, Frank Tuohy
     The Older Hardy, Robert Gittings
1979 *Beckford of Fonthill*, Brian Fothergill
     Moortown, Ted Hughes
1980 *Tennyson: The Unquiet Heart*, Robert Martin
     Seeing the World, Dick Davis

Isabel Colegate, 1981 winner of the W. H. Smith annual literary award

THE W.H. SMITH ANNUAL LITERARY AWARD

The prize of £2500, awarded annually since 1959, goes to a Commonwealth author (including a citizen of the UK) whose book, written in English and published in the UK, within 12 months ending on December 31st preceding the date of the award, in the opinion of the judges makes the most outstanding contribution to literature. Previous winners include:

1959 *Voss*, Patrick White
1960 *Cider with Rosie*, Laurie Lee
1961 *Friday's Footprint*, Nadine Gordimer
1962 *We Think the World of You*, J. R. Ackerley
1963 *The Birthday King*, Gabriel Fielding
1964 *Meditations on a Hobby Horse*, Ernst H. Gombrich
1965 *Beginning Again*, Leonard Woolf
1966 *A Child Possessed*, Ray Coryton Hutchinson
1967 *Wide Sargasso Sea*, Jean Rhys
1968 *The Mimic Men*, V. S. Naipaul
1969 *John Keats*, Robert Gittings
1970 *The French Lieutenant's Woman*, John Fowles
1971 *New Lives, New Landscapes*, Nan Fairbrother
1972 *The Lost Country*, Kathleen Raine
1973 *Catholics*, Brian Moore
1974 *Temporary Kings*, Anthony Powell
1975 *Wilfred Owen: A Biography*, Jon Stallworthy
1976 *North*, Seamus Heaney
1977 *Slim: The Standardbearer*, Ronald Lewin
1978 *A Time of Gifts*, Patrick Leigh Fermor

1979 *Life in the English Country House*, Mark Girouard
1980 *Selected Poems 1950–1975*, Thom Gunn
1981 *The Shooting Party*, Isabel Colegate

THE WHITBREAD LITERARY AWARDS

Instituted in 1971, the awards of £1500 each in three categories, Novel, Biography/Autobiography and Children's Book, are selected from books by writers who have lived in Great Britain and Ireland for five or more years. A fourth prize was given in 1980, in celebration of the tenth year of the awards. This was for the Whitbread Book of the Year. The winner, chosen from the winners of the three categories, was David Lodge for *How Far Can You Go?*

1971
Fiction: *The Destiny Waltz*, Gerda Charles
Biography: *Henrik Ibsen*, Michael Meyer
Poetry: *Mercian Hymns*, Geoffrey Hill

1972
Fiction: *The Bird of Night*, Susan Hill
Biography: *Trollope*, James Pope-Hennessy
Children's book: *The Diddakoi*, Rumer Godden

1973
Fiction: *The Chip Chip Gatherers*, Shiva Naipaul
Biography: *CB – A Life of Sir Henry Campbell-Bannerman*, John Wilson
Children's book: *The Butterfly Ball and the Grasshopper's Feast*, Alan Aldridge and William Plomer

1974
Fiction: *The Sacred and Profane Love Machine*, Iris Murdoch
Biography: *Poor Dear Brendan*, Andrew Boyle
Joint children's books: *How Tom Beat Captain Najork and His Hired Sportsmen*, Russell Hoban and Quentin Blake
The Emperor's Winding Sheet, Jill Paton Walsh
First book: *The Life and Death of Mary Wollstonecraft*, Claire Tomalin

1975
Fiction: *Docherty*, William McIlvanney
Biography: *In Our Infancy (An Autobiography 1882–1912)*, Helen Corke
First book: *The Improbable Puritan (A Life of Bulstrode Whitelock 1605–1675)*, Ruth Spalding

1976
Fiction: *The Children of Dynmouth*, William Trevor
Biography: *Elizabeth Gaskell*, Winifred Gerin
Children's book: *A Stitch in Time*, Penelope Lively

1977
Fiction: *Injury Time*, Beryl Bainbridge
Biography: *Mary Curzon*, Nigel Nicolson
Children's book: *No End of Yesterday*, Shelagh Macdonald

1978
Fiction: *Picture Palace*, Paul Theroux
Biography: *Lloyd George: The People's Champion, 1902–1911*, John Grigg
Children's book: *The Battle of Bubble and Squeak*, Philippa Pearce

1979
Fiction: *Old Jest*, Jennifer Johnston
Autobiography: *About Time*, Penelope Mortimer
Children's book: *Tulku*, Peter Dickinson

1980
Fiction: *How Far Can You Go?*, David Lodge
Biography: *On the Edge of Paradise: A.C. Benson the Diarist*, David Newsome
Children's book: *John Diamond*, Leon Garfield

Livestock

THE ROYAL SMITHFIELD SHOW LIVESTOCK CHAMPIONS

The Royal Smithfield Club has held its annual show at Earls Court, London, since 1949, but the club dates from 1798 when the original Smithfield Cattle and Sheep Society was founded. The first Smithfield Show was organised in Wootton's Dolphin Yard, Smithfield, London in 1799.

The greatest number of wins, within each category, by one owner:

Champion Cattle		
Supreme Champion Beast of the Show	Scottish Malt Distillers Ltd, Pencaitland, E. Lothian	Shorthorn × Aberdeen Angus Steer (1949)
		Aberdeen Angus × Shorthorn Steer (1952)
		Aberdeen Angus Steer (1953)
		Aberdeen Angus × Shorthorn Steer (1954)
Best Beast in the Show bred by Exhibitor	David B. Sinclair, Inchture, Perthshire	Aberdeen Angus Heifer (1968)
		Aberdeen Angus Cross Steer (1971)
		Charolais × Aberdeen Angus Steer (1972)
Supreme Champion Beast of the Show	James Donald, Glenalmond, Perthshire	Charolais × Aberdeen Angus Steer – Named Super Star (1974)
Champion Sheep		
Champion Pen of Lambs in the Show	Late Sir Wm. Rootes, Nr. Hungerford, Berks	Hampshire Down (1950, 1954, 1955, 1956, 1957)
Best Pen of Lambs in the Show bred by Exhibitor	Late Sir Wm. Rootes, Nr. Hungerford, Berks	Hampshire Down (1950, 1954, 1955, 1956, 1957)

The Supreme Champion Cup being presented to Scott Watson of Lewis Watson & Son at the 1980 Smithfield Show

Champion Pigs

Champion Pen of Two Pigs in the Show	C. N. Flack & Co. Ltd. Culford, Bury St. Edmunds, Suffolk	Large White (1955, 1956, 1977) Landrace (1973)
	Croxton Park Ltd, Thetford, Norfolk	Welsh (1963, 1971, 1974, 1978)
Champion Single Pig in the Show	C. N. Flack & Co. Ltd, Culford, Bury St. Edmunds, Suffolk	Large White (1955, 1965, 1973) Landrace (1970)

Champion Carcase

Champion Beef Carcase	Hatch Gate Farms Ltd, Wargrave, Berks	Aberdeen Angus Steer (1960, 1965, 1968) Aberdeen Angus Heifer (1961)
Champion Beef Carcase Sold for Show Record Price. Fetched £5319 at Auction. (581 lbs at £9) World Record	J. H. Cridlan, Henley-on-Thames, Oxon	Aberdeen Angus Steer (1971)
Champion Lamb Carcase	J. M. Lenthall, Burton Bradstock, Dorset	Dorset Horn (1957, 1959) Polled Dorset Horn (1960) Suffolk × Dorset Horn (1963)
	A. W. Lang, Curry Rivel, Langport, Somerset	Dorset Down (1965, 1969, 1970, 1976)
Champion Pork Carcase	D. W. P. Gough & Co. Ltd, Lackford, Bury St. Edmunds, Suffolk	Landrace (1965, 1970, 1977)
Champion Bacon Carcase	Alan Tew, Bledlow Ridge, High Wycombe, Bucks	Welsh (1976, 1977, 1978)
Champion Veal Carcase	Mrs B. Wrixton, Toller Porcorum, Dorchester, Dorset	British Friesian (1970, 1971) British Friesian × Aberdeen Angus (1977)

Magic

THE MAGIC CIRCLE AWARDS

The first award is a direct competition open to those aged 12 to 18, who have to present a short magic act which is judged on standard of technique, ability, personality and presentation. The competition is held every two years and is open to entrants from all over the world. The eliminating rounds are held wherever necessary with the final at a London theatre.

YOUNG MAGICIAN OF THE YEAR
1961 Johnny Hart
1963 Airaksinen
1965 Keith Cooper
1967 Colin Rose
1969 David Lait
1971 Christopher Payne
1973 Colin Boardman
1975 *Joint:* David Owen, Martin Welford
1977 *Joint:* Stephen Hill, David Metcalf
1979 Phillip Theodore
1981 Andrew O'Connor

The other award made by the Magic Circle is the Maskelyne. This is given to the magician who has made an outstanding contribution either by performance, invention, writing or, in fact, in any way that will help to develop the art of magic. The award takes the shape of a bronze head of John Nevil Maskelyne who was a great magician 100 years ago and who did much to help the Magic Circle when it was founded in 1905.

THE MASKELYNE
1970 Robert Harbin
1971 David Nixon
1972 Ali Bongo
1973 John Nevil Maskelyne (posthumously)
1974 Peter Warlock
1975–7 No award
1978 Goodliffe
1979 No award
1980 No award
1981 No award

142

Medicine

NOBEL PRIZE FOR MEDICINE
For further details see under main heading of
Nobel Prizes.

1901 Emil A. von Behring (Ger)
1902 Sir Ronald Ross (GB)
1903 Niels R. Finsen (Den)
1904 Ivan P. Pavlov (Rus)
1905 Robert Koch (Ger)
1906 Camillo Golgi (Ita)
      Santiago Ramon y Cajal (Spa)
1907 Charles L. A. Laveran (Fra)
1908 Paul Ehrlich (Ger)
      Elie Metchnikoff (Fra) (Russian-born)
1909 Emil T. Kocher (Swi)
1910 Albrecht Kossel (Ger)
1911 Allvar Gullstrand (Swe)
1912 Alexis Carrel (USA)
1913 Charles R. Richet (Fra)
1914 Robert Bárány (Hun)
1915–18 No award
1919 Jules Bordet (Bel)
1920 Schack A. S. Krogh (Den)
1921 No award
1922 Archibald V. Hill (GB)
      Otto F. Meyerhof (Ger)
1923 Frederick G. Banting (Can)
      John J. R. Macleod (Can)
1924 Willem Einthoven (Hol)
1925 No award
1926 Johannes A. G. Fibiger (Den)
1927 Julius Wagner-Jauregg (Aut)
1928 Charles J. H. Nicolle (Fra)
1929 Christiaan Eijkman (Hol)
      Sir Frederick G. Hopkins (GB)
1930 Karl Landsteiner (USA) (Austrian-born)
1931 Otto H. Warburg (Ger)
1932 Edgar D. Adrian (GB)
      Sir Charles S. Sherrington (GB)
1933 Thomas H. Morgan (USA)
1934 George R. Minot (USA)
      William P. Murphy (USA)
      George H. Whipple (USA)
1935 Hans Spemann (Ger)
1936 Sir Henry H. Dale (GB)
      Otto Loewi (USA) (Austrian-born)
1937 Albert Szent-Györgyi von Nagyrapolt (USA)
      (Hungarian-born)
1938 Corneille J. F. Heymans (Bel)
1939 Gerhard Domagk (Ger)
1940–42 No award
1943 Henrik C. P. Dam (Den)
      Edward A. Doisy (USA)
1944 Joseph Erlanger (USA)
      Herbert S. Gasser (USA)
1945 Sir Alexander Fleming (GB)
      Ernst B. Chain (GB) (German-born)
      Sir Howard W. Florey (GB) (Australian-born)
1946 Hermann J. Muller (USA)
1947 Carl F. Cori (USA) (Czech-born)
      Gerty T. Cori (USA) (Czech-born)
      Bernardo A. Houssay (Arg)
1948 Paul H. Müller (Swi)
1949 Walter R. Hess (Swi)
      Antonio Moniz (Por)

1950 Philip S. Hench (USA)
      Edward C. Kendall (USA)
      Tadeus Reichstein (Swi) (Polish-born)
1951 Max Theiler (USA) (S. African-born)
1952 Selman A. Waksman (USA)
1953 Hans A. Krebs (GB) (German-born)
      Fritz A. Lipmann (USA) (German-born)
1954 John F. Enders (USA)
      Frederick C. Robbins (USA)
      Thomas H. Weller (USA)
1955 Alex H. T. Theorell (Swe)
1956 André F. Cournand (USA) (French-born)
      Werner Forssmann (Ger)
      Dickinson W. Richards Jr (USA)
1957 Daniel Bovet (Ita) (Swiss-born)
1958 George W. Beadle (USA)
      Edward L. Tatum (USA)
      Joshua Lederberg (USA)
1959 Arthur Kornberg (USA)
      Severo Ochoa (USA) (Spanish-born)
1960 Sir F. Macfarlane Burnet (Aus)
      Peter B. Medawar (GB) (Brazilian-born)
1961 Georg von Békèsy (USA) (Hungarian-born)
1962 Francis H. C. Crick (GB)
      James D. Watson (USA)
      Maurice H. F. Wilkins (GB)
1963 Sir John C. Eccles (Aus)
      Alan L. Hodgkin (GB)
      Andrew F. Huxley (GB)
1964 Konrad E. Bloch (USA)
      Feodor Lynen (Ger)
1965 François Jacob (Fra)
      André Lwoff (Fra)
      Jacques Monod (Fra)
1966 Charles B. Huggins (USA)
      Francis Peyton Rous (USA)
1967 Ragnar Granit (Swe) (Finnish-born)
      Haldan Keffer Hartline (USA)
      George Wald (USA)
1968 Robert W. Holley (USA)
      Har Gobind Khorana (USA) (Indian-born)
      Marshall W. Nirenberg (USA)
1969 Max Delbrück (USA) (German-born)
      Alfred D. Hershey (USA)
      Salvador D. Luria (USA) (Italian-born)
1970 Julius Axelrod (USA)
      Ulf von Euler (Swe)
      Bernard Katz (GB)
1971 Earl W. Sutherland Jr (USA)
1972 Gerald M. Edelman (USA)
      Rodney Porter (GB)
1973 Karl von Frisch (Aut)
      Konrad Lorenz (Aut)
      Nikolaas Tinbergen (GB) (Dutch-born)
1974 Albert Claude (USA) (Lux-born)
      Christian René de Duve (Bel)
      George Emil Palade (USA) (Romanian-born)
1975 David Baltimore (USA)
      Howard Martin Temin (USA)
      Renato Dulbecco (USA) (Italian-born)
1976 Baruch S. Blumberg (USA)
      D. Carleton Gajdusek (USA)
1977 Rosalyn S. Yalow (USA)
      Roger C. L. Guillemin (USA) (French-born)
      Andrew V. Schally (USA)

1978 Werner Arber (Swi)
     Daniel Nathans (USA)
     Hamilton Smith (USA)
1979 Dr Hounsfield (GB)

     Allan Cormack (USA)
1980 Baruy Benacerraf (Ven)
     Jean Dausset (Fra)
     George Snell (USA)

Milk

MILKMAN OF THE YEAR

The National Dairy Council's Personality Milkman is chosen from thousands of nominations by customers throughout England and Wales. A prize of £500 is awarded to both the Milkman of the Year and the customer who nominated him. Winners:

1979 William Jones, Blackwood, Gwent – nominated by Mrs Mary Charles of Blackwood. Her summing up: 'He is always very pleasant in all winds and weathers and very helpful'.

1980 Dennis Buckley, London – nominated by Mrs Bishop of London. Mr Buckley won the award for his punctuality, helpfulness and cheerful attitude.

1981 Alan Donnelly, Birmingham – nominated by Mrs. A. M. Jones of Sutton Coldfield. 'His obliging and friendly service is as reliable as he is'.

NATIONAL DAIRY COUNCIL'S DAIRY QUEEN

Inaugurated in 1956 by the National Dairy Council, the title is awarded for personality, good looks and knowledge of the dairy industry. The winner receives a car, a trip to North America, clothes, and a modelling and grooming course at the London Academy of

Dennis Buckley, 1980 Personality Milkman of the Year, receives congratulations from Lulu

Jane Alexander, 1980 National Dairy Queen

Modelling. The winners, since 1956, are as follows:

1956 Evelyn Clegg, Coulsdon, Surrey
1957 Mona Griffiths, Denbigh, Clwyd
1958 Eirlys Morgan, Llanelli, Dyfed
1959 Marjorie Watson, Howden, East Yorks
1960 Eirian Evans, Holt, nr Wrexham, Clwyd
1961 Jean Walling, Kendal, Cumbria
1962 Heather Bomford, Kidderminster, Worcestershire
1963 Rosemary Manister, Ipswich, Suffolk
1964 Christine Hewitt, Norwich, Norfolk
1965 Mary Lewellin, Dyfed
1966 Pamela Cox, Buxton, Derbyshire
1967 Christine Ginns, Bury, Lancashire
1968 Joan Harland, Thirsk, North Yorkshire
1969 Mary Vincent, Wymondham, Norfolk
1970 Julia Greenleaf, Colchester, Essex
1971 Josephine Ayre, South Molton, North Devon
1972 Karen Langstaff, RAF Coltishall, Norfolk
1973 Helen Richardson, Bedale, Yorkshire
1974 Rachael Reddaway, Crediton, Devon
1975 Janet Barnett, Wheatley Hill, Co. Durham
1976 Diana Tibbs, Stanton Drew, Bristol
1977 Angela Watkins, South Wales
1978 Sabrina Jones, Garthmyl, Powys
1979 Fiona Pooler, Dorridge, Solihull
1980 Jane Alexander, Eynsford, Kent

Modern Pentathlon

Modern pentathlon comprises the sports of cross-country riding, fencing, shooting, swimming and cross-country running. It was first included in the Olympic Games of 1912 and world championships were first held in 1949.

OLYMPIC CHAMPIONSHIPS
Since 1948

	Individual	Team
1948	William Grut (Swe)	–
1952	Lars Hall (Swe)	Hungary
1956	Lars Hall (Swe)	USSR
1960	Ferenc Németh (Hun)	Hungary
1964	Ferenc Török (Hun)	USSR
1968	Björn Ferm (Swe)	Hungary
1972	Andras Balczo (Hun)	USSR
1976	Janusz Pyciak-Peciak (Pol)	Great Britain
1980	Anatoliy Starostin (USSR)	USSR

MEN'S WORLD CHAMPIONSHIPS
Held annually except in Olympic years.

	Individual	Team
1949	Tage Bjurefelt (Swe)	Sweden
1950	Lars Hall (Swe)	Sweden
1951	Lars Hall (Swe)	Sweden
1953	Dabor Benedek (Hun)	Sweden
1954	Björn Thofelt (Swe)	Hungary
1955	Konstantin Salnikov (USSR)	Hungary
1957	Igor Novikov (USSR)	USSR
1958	Igor Novikov (USSR)	USSR
1959	Igor Novikov (USSR)	USSR
1961	Igor Novikov (USSR)	USSR
1962	Eduard Dobnikov (USSR)	USSR
1963	Andras Balczo (Hun)	Hungary
1965	Andras Balczo (Hun)	Hungary
1966	Andras Balczo (Hun)	Hungary
1967	Andras Balczo (Hun)	Hungary
1969	Andras Balczo (Hun)	USSR
1970	Paul Kelemen (Hun)	Hungary
1971	Boris Onischenko (USSR)	USSR
1973	Pavel Lednev (USSR)	USSR
1974	Pavel Lednev (USSR)	USSR
1975	Pavel Lednev (USSR)	Hungary
1977	Janusz Pyciak-Peciak (Pol)	Poland
1978	Pavel Lednev (USSR)	Poland
1979	Robert Neiman (USA)	USA

WOMEN'S WORLD CHAMPIONSHIPS
First contested 1977.

1977 Virginia Swift (USA)

WOMEN'S WORLD CUP

	Individual	Team
1978	Wendy Norman (GB)	Great Britain
1979	Kathy Taylor (GB)	Great Britain
1980	Wendy Norman (GB)	Great Britain

Moto Cross

European championships were first held at 500 cc in 1952 and world championships were first held at this category in 1957, at which time a 250 cc category was introduced as a European championship. The latter was upgraded to world championship status in 1962. Winners since 1957:

250 cc
European championships
1957 Fritz Betzelbacher (Ger)
1958 Jaromir Cizek (Cze)
1959 Rolf Tibblin (Swe)
1960 Dave Bickers (GB)
1961 Dave Bickers (GB)

World Championships
1962 Torsten Hallman (Swe)
1963 Torsten Hallman (Swe)
1964 Joël Robert (Bel)
1965 Victor Arbekov (USSR)
1966 Torsten Hallman (Swe)
1967 Torsten Hallman (Swe)
1968 Joël Robert (Bel)
1969 Joël Robert (Bel)
1970 Joël Robert (Bel)
1971 Joël Robert (Bel)
1972 Joël Robert (Bel)
1973 Hakan Andersson (Swe)
1974 Gennadiy Moisseyev (USSR)
1975 Harry Everts (Bel)
1976 Heikki Mikkola (Fin)
1977 Gennadiy Moisseyev (USSR)
1978 Gennadiy Moisseyev (USSR)
1979 Håkan Carlqvist (Swe)
1980 Georges Jobé (Bel)

500 cc
World Championships
1957 Bill Nilsson (Swe)
1958 René Baeten (Bel)
1959 Sten Lundin (Swe)
1960 Bill Nilsson (Swe)
1961 Sten Lundin (Swe)
1962 Rolf Tibblin (Swe)
1963 Rolf Tibblin (Swe)
1964 Jeff Smith (GB)
1965 Jeff Smith (GB)
1966 Paul Friedrichs (GDR)
1967 Paul Friedrichs (GDR)
1968 Paul Friedrichs (GDR)
1969 Bengt Aberg (Swe)
1970 Bengt Aberg (Swe)
1971 Roger de Coster (Bel)
1972 Roger de Coster (Bel)
1973 Roger de Coster (Bel)
1974 Heikki Mikkola (Fin)
1975 Roger de Coster (Bel)

Graham Noyce the 1979 world 500 cc moto-cross champion (Diana Burnett)

1976 Roger de Coster (Bel)
1977 Heikki Mikkola (Fin)
1978 Heikki Mikkola (Fin)
1979 Graham Noyce (GB)
1980 André Malherbe (Bel)

125 cc
World Championships
First held 1975
1975 Gaston Rahier (Bel)
1976 Gaston Rahier (Bel)
1977 Gaston Rahier (Bel)
1978 Akira Watanabe (Jap)
1979 Harry Everts (Bel)
1980 Harry Everts (Bel)

Moto-cross des nations
The international team championship for 500 cc has been contested annually since 1947. Winning nations: Great Britain: 1947, 1949–50, 1952–54, 1956–57, 1959–60, 1963–67
Belgium: 1948, 1951, 1969, 1972–73, 1976–77, 1979–80
Sweden: 1955, 1958, 1961–62, 1970–71, 1974
USSR: 1969, 1978
Czechoslovakia: 1975

Trophée des nations
The international team championship for 250 cc has been contested annually since 1961. Winning nations:
Great Britain: 1961–62, 1965
Sweden: 1963–64, 1966–68
Belgium: 1969–78, 1980
USSR: 1979

Trials
World Championships (first recognised 1975)
1975 Martin Lampkin (GB)
1976 Yrjo Vesterinen (Fin)
1977 Yrjo Vesterinen (Fin)
1978 Yrjo Vesterinen (Fin)
1979 Bernie Schreiber (USA)
1980 Ulf Karlsson (Swe)

Motorcycling

WORLD CHAMPIONSHIPS
The most important world championship category is undoubtedly the 500 cc. For this and the other categories riders gain points based on their performances in a series of Grand Prix events. The world championships were first held under the auspices of the FIM in 1949. Individual winners:

50 cc
1962 Ernst Degner (Ger)
1963 Hugh Anderson (NZ)
1964 Hugh Anderson (NZ)
1965 Ralph Bryans (Ire)
1966 Hans-Georg Anscheidt (Ger)
1967 Hans-Georg Anscheidt (Ger)
1968 Hans-Georg Anscheidt (Ger)
1969 Angel Nieto (Spa)
1970 Angel Nieto (Spa)
1971 Jan de Vries (Hol)

1972 Angel Nieto (Spa)
1973 Jan de Vries (Hol)
1974 Henk van Kessel (Hol)
1975 Angel Nieto (Spa)
1976 Angel Nieto (Spa)
1977 Angel Nieto (Spa)
1978 Rocardo Tormo (Spa)
1979 Eugenio Lazzarini (Ita)
1980 Eugenio Lazzarini (Ita)

125 cc
1949 Nello Pagani (Ita)
1950 Bruno Ruffo (Ita)
1951 Carlo Ubbiali (Ita)
1952 Cecil Sandford (GB)
1953 Werner Haas (Ger)
1954 Rupert Hollaus (Aut)
1955 Carlo Ubbiali (Ita)
1956 Carlo Ubbiali (Ita)
1957 Tarquinio Provini (Ita)

Barry Sheene on a Yamaha (Leo Vocelzang)

1958	Carlo Ubbiali (Ita)		1956	Carlo Ubbiali (Ita)
1959	Carlo Ubbiali (Ita)		1957	Cecil Sandford (GB)
1960	Carlo Ubbiali (Ita)		1958	Tarquinio Provini (Ita)
1961	Tom Phillis (Aus)		1959	Carlo Ubbiali (Ita)
1962	Luigi Taveri (Swi)		1960	Carlo Ubbiali (Ita)
1963	Hugh Anderson (NZ)		1961	Mike Hailwood (GB)
1964	Luigi Taveri (Swi)		1962	Jim Redman (Rho)
1965	Hugh Anderson (NZ)		1963	Jim Redman (Rho)
1966	Luigi Taveri (Swi)		1964	Phil Read (GB)
1967	Bill Ivy (GB)		1965	Phil Read (GB)
1968	Phil Read (GB)		1966	Mike Hailwood (GB)
1969	Dave Simmonds (GB)		1967	Mike Hailwood (GB)
1970	Dieter Braun (Ger)		1968	Phil Read (GB)
1971	Angel Nieto (Spa)		1969	Kel Caruthers (Aus)
1972	Angel Nieto (Spa)		1970	Rod Gould (GB)
1973	Kent Andersson (Swe)		1971	Phil Read (GB)
1974	Kent Andersson (Swe)		1972	Jarno Saarinen (Fin)
1975	Paolo Pileri (Ita)		1973	Dieter Braun (Ger)
1976	Pier-Paolo Bianchi (Ita)		1974	Walter Villa (Ita)
1977	Pier-Paolo Bianchi (Ita)		1975	Walter Villa (Ita)
1978	Eugenio Lazzarini (Ita)		1976	Walter Villa (Ita)
1979	Angel Nieto (Spa)		1977	Mario Lega (Ita)
1980	Pier-Paolo Bianchi (Ita)		1978	Kork Ballington (SA)
			1979	Kork Ballington (SA)
			1980	Anton Mang (Ger)

250 cc

1949	Bruno Ruffo (Ita)
1950	Dario Ambrosini (Ita)
1951	Bruno Ruffo (Ita)
1952	Enrico Lorenzetti (Ita)
1953	Werner Haas (Ger)
1954	Werner Haas (Ger)
1955	Herman Müller (Ger)

350 cc

1949	Freddie Frith (GB)
1950	Bob Foster (GB)
1951	Geoff Duke (GB)
1952	Geoff Duke (GB)
1953	Fergus Anderson (GB)

1954 Fergus Anderson (GB)
1955 Bill Lomas (GB)
1956 Bill Lomas (GB)
1957 Keith Campbell (Aus)
1958 John Surtees (GB)
1959 John Surtees (GB)
1960 John Surtees (GB)
1961 Gary Hocking (Rho)
1962 Jim Redman (Rho)
1963 Jim Redman (Rho)
1964 Jim Redman (Rho)
1965 Jim Redman (Rho)
1966 Mike Hailwood (GB)
1967 Mike Hailwood (GB)
1968 Giacomo Agostini (Ita)
1969 Giacomo Agostini (Ita)
1970 Giacomo Agostini (Ita)
1971 Giacomo Agostini (Ita)
1972 Giacomo Agostini (Ita)
1973 Giacomo Agostini (Ita)
1974 Giacomo Agostini (Ita)
1975 Johnnie Cecotto (Ven)
1976 Walter Villa (Ita)
1977 Takazumi Katayama (Jap)
1978 Kork Ballington (SA)
1979 Kork Ballington (SA)
1980 Jon Ekerold (SA)

500 cc
1949 Leslie Graham (GB)
1950 Umberto Masetti (Ita)
1951 Geoff Duke (GB)
1952 Umberto Masetti (Ita)
1953 Geoff Duke (GB)
1954 Geoff Duke (GB)
1955 Geoff Duke (GB)
1956 John Surtees (GB)
1957 Libero Liberati (Ita)
1958 John Surtees (GB)
1959 John Surtees (GB)
1960 John Surtees (GB)
1961 Gary Hocking (Rho)
1962 Mike Hailwood (GB)
1963 Mike Hailwood (GB)
1964 Mike Hailwood (GB)
1965 Mike Hailwood (GB)
1966 Giacomo Agostini (Ita)
1967 Giacomo Agostini (Ita)
1968 Giacomo Agostini (Ita)
1969 Giacomo Agostini (Ita)
1970 Giacomo Agostini (Ita)
1971 Giacomo Agostini (Ita)
1972 Giacomo Agostini (Ita)
1973 Phil Read (GB)
1974 Phil Read (GB)
1975 Giacomo Agostini (Ita)
1976 Barry Sheene (GB)
1977 Barry Sheene (GB)
1978 Kenny Roberts (USA)
1979 Kenny Roberts (USA)
1980 Kenny Roberts (USA)

Side-cars
1949 Eric Oliver (GB)
1950 Eric Oliver(GB)
1951 Eric Oliver (GB)
1952 Cyril Smith (GB)

1953 Eric Oliver (GB)
1954 Wilhelm Noll (Ger)
1955 Wilhelm Faust (Ger)
1956 Wilhelm Noll (Ger)
1957 Fritz Hillebrand (Ger)
1958 Walter Schneider (Ger)
1959 Walter Schneider (Ger)
1960 Helmut Fath (Ger)
1961 Max Deubel (Ger)
1962 Max Deubel (Ger)
1963 Max Deubel (Ger)
1964 Max Deubel (Ger)
1965 Fritz Scheidegger (Swi)
1966 Fritz Scheidegger (Swi)
1967 Klaus Enders (Ger)
1968 Helmut Fath (Ger)
1969 Klaus Enders (Ger)
1970 Klaus Enders (Ger)
1971 Horst Owesle (Ger)
1972 Klaus Enders (Ger)
1973 Klaus Enders (Ger)
1974 Klaus Enders (Ger)
1975 Rolf Steinhausen (Ger)
1976 Rolf Steinhausen (Ger)
1977 George O'Dell (GB)
1978 Rolf Biland (Swi)
1979 Rolf Biland (Swi)
1980 Jock Taylor (GB)

Formula 750
1977 Steve Baker (USA)
1978 Johnnie Cecotto (Ven)
1979 Patrick Pons (Fra)
1980 Lost world championship status

Endurance
1980 Marc Fontan and Herve Moinean (Fra)

MOTOR CYCLE NEWS 'MAN OF THE YEAR' COMPETITION
This prestigious annual poll is for the man voted by readers of *Motor Cycle News* as their most popular motorcycle racer. Inaugurated in 1958. Winners (GB except where shown):

1958 John Surtees
1959 John Surtees
1960 Dave Bickers
1961 Mike Hailwood
1962 Derek Minter
1963 Mike Hailwood
1964 Jeff Smith
1965 Bill Ivy
1966 Giacomo Agostini (Ita)
1967 Mike Hailwood
1968 Helmut Fath (Ger)
1969 Rod Gould
1970 John Cooper
1971 John Cooper
1972 Ray Pickrell
1973 Barry Sheene
1974 Phil Read
1975 Barry Sheene
1976 Barry Sheene
1977 Barry Sheene
1978 Mike Hailwood
1979 Barry Sheene
1980 Jock Taylor

Motoring

AUTOMOBILE ASSOCIATION NATIONAL MOTORING AWARDS

These awards are given to mark notable inventions and developments which help the motoring public. The gold medal awards made are as follows.

1965 The Rover Company Ltd (for the Rover 2000 car)
1967 The Corporation of London (for the Blackfriars Underpass)
1968 Dover Harbour Board (for their efforts to facilitate the outward and inward passage of record numbers of motor vehicles)
1969 Britax (London) Ltd (for their Centre-Lok car seat belt)
1971 Sir William Lyons (in recognition of his long and distinguished service to motoring in Great Britain and to mark his recent retirement)
1972 National Motor Museum, Beaulieu
1973 Dunlop Ltd (for its Denovo Total Mobility Tyre)
1974 The Forestry Commission (for the advancement of conservation and leisure facilities in Scotland)
1976 Leyland Cars (for the new Rover 3500)
     Triplex Safety Glass Company Ltd (for the development of the Ten Twenty laminated windscreen)
1978 Quinton Hazell Automotive (for the Underider safety device designed to minimise the effects of collisions between cars and lorries)
1979 Anton Blankert (for his outstanding contribution to motoring and tourism throughout his 18 years as Director General of ANWB, the Dutch motoring and touring club)
1980 No award

ROYAL AUTOMOBILE CLUB AWARDS

DIAMOND JUBILEE TROPHY
This is the major award of the RAC. The trophy has been awarded to the following:

1958
Sir Vivian Fuchs, David Pratt and members of the Trans-Antarctic Expedition, who used advanced Snowcats in their explorations.

1962
Christopher Cockerell, inventor of the Hovercraft.

1969
The United States National Aeronautics and Space Administration for their giant rocket transporter.

1976
The British Aircraft Corporation and Aerospatiale (France) for the design and construction of Concorde.

1977
Cosworth Engineering Ltd, coupled with the names of Keith Duckworth and the Ford Motor Company, for their achievement in designing and building the engines which have won 100 Grand Prix races.

THE DEWAR TROPHY
This trophy is awarded irregularly and recognises properly authenticated British achievement in research, development, design, manufacture, utilisation or performance, or in any combination of these. Winners since 1960:

1963
Coventry-Climax Engines Ltd., for design, development and production of engines which brought British racing cars to forefront of Grand Prix racing.

1967
Motor Industry Research Association in recognition of the valuable work done to prevent road accidents caused by lorries jack-knifing.

1969
Keith Duckworth, for the design of the Ford Formula One engine which has retained the supremacy of British engineering in Grand Prix racing.

1971
British Leyland Motor Corporation coupled with the name of Peter Wilks, for advanced development in automobile design displayed in the corporation's Range Rover.

1972
The British Leyland Motor Corporation (Truck and Bus Division) for the design, development and construction of the Leyland National Bus which represents a radical new approach to the development of a public service vehicle incorporating maximum payload and security at minimal cost and maintenance.

1973
Dunlop Company Limited for the development of the Denovo fail-safe tyre and wheel system as an outstanding contribution to road safety.

1977
Triplex Safety Glass Company for the development, manufacture and application to production models of the Ten Twenty safety glass as an outstanding contribution to the safety of automobile occupants.

1981
British Leyland Cars Ltd for efficiency in automobile design in respect of the utilisation of interior space, and predicted low cost of ownership of the Austin Metro car.

Motor Racing

WORLD DRIVERS' CHAMPIONSHIP
Inaugurated in 1950, the World Drivers' Championship is made up of specified Formula One Grand Prix races each season. Winners:

Jim Clark, here driving a Lotus Ford, during his second World Drivers Championship in 1965

1950 Giuseppe Farina (Ita)	1979 Jody Scheckter (SA)
1951 Juan Manuel Fangio (Arg)	1980 Alan Jones (Aus)
1952 Alberto Ascari (Ita)	
1953 Alberto Ascari (Ita)	

MANUFACTURER'S WORLD CHAMPIONSHIP (FORMULA ONE)

1954 Juan Manuel Fangio (Arg)	1958 Vanwall
1955 Juan Manuel Fangio (Arg)	1959 Cooper-Climax
1956 Juan Manuel Fangio (Arg)	1960 Cooper-Climax
1957 Juan Manuel Fangio (Arg)	1961 Ferrari
1958 Mike Hawthorn (GB)	1962 BRM
1959 Jack Brabham (Aus)	1963 Lotus-Climax
1960 Jack Brabham (Aus)	1964 Ferrari
1961 Phil Hill (USA)	1965 Lotus-Climax
1962 Graham Hill (GB)	1966 Repco-Brabham
1963 Jim Clark (GB)	1967 Repco-Brabham
1964 John Surtees (GB)	1968 Lotus-Ford
1965 Jim Clark (GB)	1969 Matra-Ford
1966 Jack Brabham (Aus)	1970 Lotus-Ford
1967 Denny Hulme (NZ)	1971 Tyrell-Ford
1968 Graham Hill (GB)	1972 J.P.S. Lotus
1969 Jackie Stewart (GB)	1973 J.P.S. Lotus
1970 Jochen Rindt (Ger)	1974 McLaren
1971 Jackie Stewart (GB)	1975 Ferrari
1972 Emerson Fittipaldi (Bra)	1976 Ferrari
1973 Jackie Stewart (GB)	1977 Ferrari
1974 Emerson Fittipaldi (Bra)	1978 J.P.S. Lotus
1975 Niki Lauda (Aut)	1979 Ferrari
1976 James Hunt (GB)	1980 Williams-Ford
1977 Niki Lauda (Aut)	
1978 Mario Andretti (USA)	

BRITISH GRAND PRIX

First run as the RAC Grand Prix at Brooklands in 1926, and later as the Donington Grand Prix in 1937 and 1938. The name British Grand Prix was first used in 1949. Full list of winners, circuits distance and speed:

	Driver	Car	Circuit	Distance (miles)	Speed (mph)
1926	Robert Sénéchal/Louis Wagner (Fra)	Delage	Brooklands	287	71·61
1927	Robert Benoist (Fra)	Delage	Brooklands	325	85·59
1935	Richard Shuttleworth (GB)	Alfa Romeo	Donington	306	63·97
1936	Hans Ruesch (Ger) Richard Seaman (GB)	Alfa Romeo	Donington	306	69·23
1937	Bernd Rosemeyer (Ger)	Auto-Union	Donington	250	82·85
1938	Tazio Nuvolari (Ita)	Auto-Union	Donington	250	80·49
1948	Luigi Villoresi (Ita)	Maserati	Silverstone	250	72·28
1949	Baron Emmanuel de Graffenried (Swi)	Maserati	Silverstone	300	77·31
1950	Giuseppe Farina (Ita)	Alfa Romeo	Silverstone	202	90·95
1951	Froilan Gonzalez (Arg)	Ferrari	Silverstone	253	96·11

1952 Alberto Ascari (Ita)	Ferrari	Silverstone	249	90·92
1953 Alberto Ascari (Ita)	Ferrari	Silverstone	263	92·97
1954 José Froilan Gonzalez (Arg)	Ferrari	Silverstone	270	89·69
1955 Stirling Moss (GB)	Mercedes-Benz	Aintree	270	86·47
1956 Juan Manuel Fangio (Arg)	Ferrari	Silverstone	300	98·65
1957 Tony Brooks/Stirling Moss (GB)	Vanwall	Aintree	270	86·80
1958 Peter Collins (GB)	Ferrari	Silverstone	225	102·05
1959 Jack Brabham (Aus)	Cooper-Climax	Aintree	225	89·88
1960 Jack Brabham (Aus)	Cooper-Climax	Silverstone	231	108·69
1961 Wolfgang von Trips (Ger)	Ferrari	Aintree	225	83·91
1962 Jim Clark (GB)	Lotus-Climax	Aintree	225	92·25
1963 Jim Clark (GB)	Lotus-Climax	Silverstone	246	107·75
1964 Jim Clark (GB)	Lotus-Climax	Brands Hatch	212	94·14
1965 Jim Clark (GB)	Lotus-Climax	Silverstone	240	112·02
1966 Jack Brabham (Aus)	Repco Brabham	Brands Hatch	212	95·48
1967 Jim Clark (GB)	Lotus-Ford	Silverstone	240	117·64
1968 Joseph Siffert (Swi)	Lotus-Ford	Brands Hatch	212	104·83
1969 Jackie Stewart (GB)	Matra-Ford	Silverstone	246	127·25
1970 Jochen Rindt (Ger)	Lotus-Ford	Brands Hatch	212	108·69
1971 Jackie Stewart (GB)	Tyrell-Ford	Silverstone	199	130·48
1972 Emerson Fittipaldi (Bra)	J.P.S.-Ford	Brands Hatch	201	112·06
1973 Peter Revson (US)	McLaren-Ford	Silverstone	196	131·75
1974 Jody Scheckter (SA)	Tyrell-Ford	Brands Hatch	199	115·73
1975 Emerson Fittipaldi (Bra)	McLaren-Ford	Silverstone	164	120·01
1976 Niki Lauda (Aut)	Ferrari	Brands Hatch	198	114·24
1977 James Hunt (GB)	McLaren-Ford	Silverstone	199	130·36
1978 Carlos Reutemann (Arg)	Ferrari	Brands Hatch	199	116·61
1979 'Clay' Regazzoni (Swi)	Williams-Ford	Silverstone	199	138·80
1980 Alan Jones (Aus)	Williams-Ford	Brands Hatch	198	125·69

THE RAC'S HAWTHORN MEMORIAL TROPHY

To the highest placed British or Commonwealth driver in the world championship. Winners since foundation in 1960:

1960 Jack Brabham
1961 Stirling Moss
1962 Graham Hill
1963 Jim Clark
1964 John Surtees
1965 Jim Clark
1966 Jack Brabham
1967 Denis Hulme
1968 Graham Hill
1969 Jackie Stewart
1970 Denis Hulme
1971 Jackie Stewart
1972 Jackie Stewart
1973 Jackie Stewart
1974 Denis Hulme
1975 James Hunt
1976 James Hunt
1977 James Hunt
1978 John Watson
1979 John Watson
1980 John Watson

INDIANAPOLIS 500

America's most famous motor race was first held in 1911. Anthony (A. J.) Foyt is the only man to have won on four occasions. Winners since 1946 (USA except where stated):

	Driver	*Car*	*Speed* (mph)
1946	George Robson	Thorne Engineering	114·820
1947	Mauri Rose	Blue Crown Special	116·338
1948	Mauri Rose	Blue Crown Special	119·814
1949	Bill Holland	Blue Crown Special	121·327
1950	Johnny Parsons	Wynn Kurtis Kraft	124·002
1951	Lee Wallard	Belanger	126·224
1952	Troy Ruttman	Agajanian	128·922

1953	Bill Vukovich	Fuel Injection	128·740
1954	Bill Vukovich	Fuel Injection	130·840
1955	Bob Sweikert	John Zink Special	128·209
1956	Pat Flaherty	John Zink Special	128·490
1957	Sam Hanks	Belond Exhaust	135·601
1958	Jimmy Bryan	Belond A. P.	133·791
1959	Rodger Ward	Leader Card Special	135·857
1960	Jim Rathmann	Ken-Paul Special	138·767
1961	A. J. Foyt	Bowes Seal Fast	139·130
1962	Rodger Ward	Leader Card Special	140·293
1963	Parnelli Jones	Agajanian Special	143·137
1964	A. J. Foyt	Sheraton-Thompson Special	147·350
1965	Jim Clark (GB)	Lotus-Ford	150·686
1966	Graham Hill (GB)	American Red Ball	144·317
1967	A. J. Foyt	Sheraton-Thompson Special	151·207
1968	Bobby Unser	Rislone Special	152·882
1969	Mario Andretti	STP Oil Treatment Special	156·867
1970	Al Unser	Johnny Lightning Special	155·749
1971	Al Unser	Johnny Lightning Special	157·735
1972	Mark Donohue	Sunoco McLaren	162·962
1973	Gordon Johncock	STP Double Oil Filter	159·036
1974	Johnny Rutherford	McLaren	158·589
1975	Bobby Unser	Jorgensen Eagle	149·213
1976	Johnny Rutherford	Hygain McLaren	148·725
1977	A. J. Foyt	Gilmore Coyote-Foyt	161·331
1978	Al Unser	Lola-Chapparal Cosworth	161·363
1979	Rick Mears	Penske-Cosworth	158·899
1980	Johnny Rutherford	Chapparal Cosworth	142·862
1981	Mario Andretti	Wildcat-Cosworth	139·084

LE MANS 24-HOUR RACE

The world's most important race for sports cars was first held in 1923. The most wins by one man is four by Olivier Gendebien (Bel) and Jackie Ickx (Bel). Winners since 1949 when the race was revived after the Second World War:

Driver	Car	Average Speed (mph)
1949 Luigi Chinetti/Lord Peter Selsdon	Ferrari	82·27
1950 Louis Rosier/Jean-Louis Rosier	Talbot	89·73
1951 Peter Walker/Peter Whitehead	Jaguar	93·50
1952 Hermann Lang/Fritz Riess	Mercedes	96·67
1953 Anthony Rolt/Duncan Hamilton	Jaguar	105·85
1954 Froilan Gonzalez/Maurice Trintignant	Ferrari	105·15
1955 Mike Hawthorn/Ivor Bueb	Jaguar	107·07
1956 Ron Flockhart/Ninian Sanderson	Jaguar	104·46
1957 Ron Flockhart/Ivor Bueb	Jaguar	113·85
1958 Phil Hill/Olivier Gendebien	Ferrari	106·20
1959 Roy Salvadori/Carroll Shelby	Aston Martin	112·57
1960 Paul Frère/Olivier Gendebien	Ferrari	109·19
1961 Phil Hill/Olivier Gendebien	Ferrari	115·90
1962 Phil Hill/Olivier Gendebien	Ferrari	115·24
1963 Ludovico Scarfiotti/Lorenzo Bandini	Ferrari	118·10
1964 Jean Guichet/Nino Vaccarella	Ferrari	121·55
1965 Masten Gregory/Jochen Rindt	Ferrari	121·09
1966 Bruce McLaren/Chris Amon	Ford	126·01

1967 Anthony Joseph Foyt/Dan Gurney	Ford	132·49
1968 Pedro Rodriguez/Lucien Bianchi	Ford	115·29
1969 Jackie Ickx/Jackie Oliver	Ford	125·44
1970 Hans Herrmann/Richard Attwood	Porsche	119·29
1971 Helmut Marko/Gijs van Lennep	Porsche	138·14
1972 Graham Hill/Henri Pescarolo	Matra-Simca	121·47
1973 Henri Pescarolo/Gerard Larrousse	Matra-Simca	125·68
1974 Henri Pescarolo/Gerard Larrousse	Matra-Simca	119·27
1975 Jackie Ickx/Derek Bell	Gulf Ford	118·99
1976 Jackie Ickx/Gijs van Lennep	Porsche	123·50
1977 Jackie Ickx/Jurgen Barth/Hurley Haywood	Porsche	120·95
1978 Didier Peroni/Jean-Pierre Jaussaud	Renault Alpine	130·60
1979 Klaus Ludwig/Bill and Don Whittington	Porsche	108·06
1980 Jean-Pierre Jaussaud/Jean Rondeau	Rondeau	119·17
1981 Jackie Ickx/Derek Bell	Porsche	124·87

Museums

THE MUSEUM OF THE YEAR AWARD

This is an annual award sponsored by the *Illustrated London News* in conjunction with National Heritage, a voluntary organisation set up to protect the interests of museums and galleries throughout the country. The *Illustrated London News* donates the first prize (of not less than £2000), and the ILN Award, a Henry Moore porcelain sculpture called 'Moon Head'. The award began in 1973 to induce industry to promote the arts. The museums are judged for their enterprise, general improvements and improved facilities.

1973 Abbot Hall Museum of Lakeland Life and Industry, Kendal
1974 National Motor Museum, Beaulieu, Hants
1975 Weald and Downland Open Air Museum, Chichester
1976 Gladstone Pottery Museum, Stoke on Trent
1977 Ironbridge Gorge Museum, Telford, Salop
1978 *Joint winners:* Museum of London, and Erddig, a country house near Wrexham in Clwyd
1979 Museum and Art Gallery of St Peter Port, Guernsey

One of the Natural History Museum's exhibitions on dinosaurs

1980 British Museum (Natural History), South Kensington, London
1981 The National Tractor and Farm Museum, Stocksfield

Music

AUDIO AWARDS

An annual presentation, organised by *Hi-Fi News & Record Review*, to musicians and others for their services to music via the gramophone record. This dates back to 1967, and is supported by the Composers' Guild of Great Britain, the Mechanical Copyright Protection Society, the National Federation of Gramophone Societies, the National Music Council, the Songwriters' Guild of GB and the Performing Rights Society. Those who have received this since 1970 have been:

1970–71 Neville Marriner
1971–72 Sir Adrian Boult
1973 Raymond Leppard
1974 Peter Pears
     Kinloch Anderson
1975 Colin Davis

John Williams and Julian Bream receiving the 1977 Audio Award

1976 Dame Janet Baker
1977 John Williams
     Julian Bream
1978 André Previn
1979 Arthur Haddy
     Tony Griffith
1980 Norma del Mar
     Richard Itter
1981 Sir Charles Groves
     Kenneth Wilkinson

BLUES & SOUL MAGAZINE READERS' POLL

Readers of *Blues & Soul* magazine vote for their favourites in this annual poll. Recent winners:

BEST MALE VOCALIST
1977 Teddy Pendergrass
1978 Teddy Pendergrass
1979 Michael Jackson
1980 Stevie Wonder

BEST FEMALE VOCALIST
1977 Deniece Williams
1978 Chaka Khan
1979 Donna Summer
1980 Randy Crawford

BEST GROUP
1977 Commodores
1978 Earth Wind and Fire
1979 Earth Wind and Fire
1980 Earth Wind and Fire

BEST INSTRUMENTALIST
1977 George Benson
1978 Grover Washington Jnr
1979 George Benson
1980 Grover Washington Jnr

BEST LIVE ACT
1977 Commodores
1978 Commodores
1979 Earth Wind and Fire
1980 Stevie Wonder

MOST PROMISING NEWCOMER
1977 Pockets
1978 Hi-Tension
1979 Randy Crawford
1980 Linx

BEST SONGWRITER
1977 Stevie Wonder
1978 Lionel Ritchie
1979 Ashford and Simpson
1980 Rod Temperton

BEST PRODUCER
1977 Maurice White
1978 Maurice White
1979 Maurice White
1980 Quincy Jones

BEST SOUL SINGLE
1977 The Best of My Love, The Emotions
1978 Three Times a Lady, Commodores
1979 Street Life, Crusaders
1980 One Day I'll Fly Away, Randy Crawford

BEST DISCO SINGLE
1977 Do What You Wanna Do, T-Connection
1978 You Make Me Feel (Mighty Real), Sylvester
1979 Ain't No Stoppin' Us Now, McFadden and Whitehead
Discontinued

BEST SOUL ALBUM
1977 Teddy Pendergrass, Teddy Pendergrass
1978 All 'n' All, Earth Wind and Fire
1979 I Am, Earth Wind and Fire
1980 Hotter than July, Stevie Wonder

BEST DISCO ALBUM
1977 In Full Bloom, Rose Royce
1978 Step 11, Sylvester
1979 Off the Wall, Michael Jackson
1980 Discontinued

MOST ANNOYING SINGLE
1979 Ring My Bell, Anita Ward
1980 Ottowan, Disco

BEST RADIO DJ
1980 Robbie Vincent

BEST CLUB DJ
1980 Chris Hill

BRITISH ROCK AND POP AWARDS

These have been organised since 1978 jointly by the *Daily Mirror*, BBC Nationwide and BBC Radio 1. Winners:

BEST MALE SINGER
1978 Leo Sayer
1979 Gary Numan
1980 David Bowie

BEST FEMALE SINGER
1978 Kate Bush
1979 Kate Bush
1980 Sheena Easton

The Police, 'Best Band' in the British Rock and Pop Awards for 1979 and 1980, shown here during their recent tour in Japan

BEST BAND OR GROUP
1978 Bee Gees
1979 The Police
1980 The Police

BEST SINGLE
1978 Baker Street, Gerry Rafferty
1979 I Don't Like Mondays, The Boomtown Rats
1980 Going Underground, The Jam

BEST ALBUM
1978 Out of the Blue, ELO
1979 Regatta de Blanc, The Police
1980 Zenyatta Mondatta, The Police

DAILY MIRROR AWARD FOR THE OUTSTANDING MUSIC PERSONALITY
1978 Ian Dury
1979 Paul McCartney
1980 Cliff Richard

THE NATIONWIDE GOLDEN AWARD FOR THE ARTIST WITH MOST ALL-ROUND FAMILY APPEAL
1978 Barron Knights
1979 Cliff Richard
1980 The Nolans

BBC RADIO 1 DISC JOCKEY AWARD FOR OUTSTANDING CONTRIBUTION TO BRITISH MUSIC
1978 Nick Lowe
1979 Jerry Dammers (The Specials)
1980 John Lennon

Capital Radio award winners. Left to right: *Ian Dury, Reginald Bosanquet, Nigel Harrison of Blondie, Sheena Easton*

CAPITAL RADIO MUSIC AWARDS
Capital broadcasts in the Greater London area and has a listening audience of over 5 million each week. Listeners are asked to make nominations for the music awards and to vote for the winners.

BEST SINGLE
1976 Don't Go Breaking My Heart, Elton John and Kiki Dee
1977 Mull of Kintyre, Paul McCartney and Wings
1978 Night Fever, Bee Gees
1979 Message in a Bottle, The Police
1980 Don't Stand So Close To Me, The Police

BEST ALBUM
1976 How Dare You, 10 CC
1977 Out of the Blue, ELO
1978 A Single Man, Elton John
1979 Regatta De Blanc, The Police
1980 Zenyatta Mondatta, The Police

BEST MALE SINGER
1976 Elton John
1977 Elton John
1978 Elton John
1979 Gary Numan
1980 David Bowie

BEST FEMALE SINGER
1976 Kiki Dee
1977 Julie Covington
1978 Kate Bush
1979 Kate Bush
1980 Kate Bush

BEST LONDON BAND/ARTIST
1976 Dr Feelgood
1977 Tom Robinson Band
1978 Ian Dury
1979 Ian Dury
1980 Ian Dury

MOST PROMISING NEWCOMER
1976 Climax Blues Band
1977 Tom Robinson Band
1978 Kate Bush
1979 The Police
1980 Sheena Easton

MOST REQUESTED RECORD ON THE CAPITAL HITLINE
1976 I'm Mandy Fly Me, 10 CC
1977 We Are The Champions, Queen
1978 Night Fever, Bee Gees
1979 Heart of Glass, Blondie
1980 Don't Stand So Close To Me, The Police

BEST SONGWRITER OF THE YEAR
1978 The Gibb Brothers (Bee Gees)
1979 Elvis Costello
1980 No award

BEST INTERNATIONAL ARTIST
1978 Earth Wind and Fire
1979 Michael Jackson
1980 Blondie

BEST BRITISH GROUP
1978 The Bee Gees
1979 The Police
1980 The Police

PRESENTER'S CHOICE
1980 Don't Stand So Close To Me, The Police

BESTSELLING SINGLE
1980 Don't Stand So Close To Me, The Police

DAVE CASH'S COUNTRY TOP 10
1980 I Believe in You, Don Williams

WORLD'S WORST RECORD
1980 Dance With Me, Reginald Bosanquet

GRAMMY AWARDS
The Grammy Award is sponsored by the National Academy of Recording Arts and Sciences of America, founded in 1957 by recording artists, composers and craftsmen to advance the arts and sciences of recording.

Recordings are nominated and voted on by members of the National Academy of Recording Arts and Sciences. These members are the individuals directly and creatively involved in the making of phonograph records.

Awards are announced annually on the Academy's Grammy Awards telecast over the CBS network in early spring.

A selection from the ninety or so categories for which awards have been made since 1958.

RECORD OF THE YEAR
1958 Nel Blu Dipinto di Blu (Volare) Domenico Modugno
1959 Mack the Knife, Bobby Darin
1960 Theme from 'A Summer Place', Percy Faith
1961 Moon River, Henry Mancini
1962 I Left My Heart in San Francisco, Tony Bennett
1963 The Days of Wine and Roses, Henry Mancini
1964 The Girl from Ipanema, Stan Getz and Astrud Gilberto
1965 A Taste of Honey, Herb Alpert and the Tijuana Brass
1966 Strangers in the Night, Frank Sinatra
1967 Up, Up and Away, 5th Dimension
1968 Mrs. Robinson, Simon and Garfunkel
1969 Aquarius, Let the Sunshine In, 5th Dimension
1970 Bridge Over Troubled Water, Simon and Garfunkel
1971 It's Too Late, Carole King
1972 The First Time Ever I Saw Your Face, Roberta Flack
1973 Killing Me Softly With His Song, Roberta Flack
1974 I Honestly Love You, Olivia Newton-John
1975 Love Will Keep Us Together, Captain and Tenille
1976 This Masquerade, George Benson
1977 Hotel California, The Eagles
1978 Just the Way You Are, Billy Joel
1979 What A Fool Believes, The Doobie Brothers
1980 Sailing, Christopher Cross

ALBUM OF THE YEAR
1958 The Music from Peter Gunn, Henry Mancini
1959 Come Dance With Me, Frank Sinatra
1960 Button Down Mind, Bob Newhart
1961 Judy at Carnegie Hall, Judy Garland
1962 The First Family, Vaughn Meader
1963 The Barbra Streisand Album, Barbra Streisand
1964 Getz/Gilberto, Stan Getz and Joao Gilberto
1965 September of My Years, Frank Sinatra
1966 Sinatra: A Man and His Music, Frank Sinatra
1967 Sgt. Pepper's Lonely Hearts Club Band, The Beatles
1968 By the Time I Get to Phoenix, Glen Campbell
1969 Blood, Sweat and Tears, Blood Sweat and Tears
1970 Bridge Over Troubled Water, Simon and Garfunkel
1971 Tapestry, Carole King

1980 Grammy award winners Christopher Cross, who won five Grammys, and producer Michael Omartian, perform their winning song 'Sailing'

© NARAS

1972 The Concert for Bangla Desh, George Harrison, Ravi Shankar, Bob Dylan, Leon Russell, Ringo Starr, Billy Preston, Eric Clapton and Klaus Voormann
1973 Innervisions, Stevie Wonder
1974 Fulfillingness' First Finale, Stevie Wonder
1975 Still Crazy After All These Years, Paul Simon
1976 Songs in the Key of Life, Stevie Wonder
1977 Rumors, Fleetwood Mac
1978 Saturday Night Fever, Bee Gees
1979 52nd Street, Billy Joel
1980 Christopher Cross, Christopher Cross

SONG OF THE YEAR (Award to Songwriter)
1958 Domenico Modugno, for Nel Blu Dipinto di Blu
1959 Jimmy Driftwood, for The Battle of New Orleans
1960 Ernest Gold, for Theme from Exodus
1961 Henry Mancini and Johnny Mercer, for Moon River

1962 Leslie Bricusse and Anthony Newley, for What Kind of Fool Am I.
1963 Henry Mancini and Johnny Mercer, for The Days of Wine and Roses
1964 Jerry Herman, for Hello Dolly!
1965 Paul Francis Webster and Johnny Mandel, for The Shadow of Your Smile
1966 John Lennon and Paul McCartney, for Michelle
1967 Jim Webb, for Up, Up and Away
1978 Bobby Russell, for Little Green Apples
1969 Joe South, for Games People Play
1970 Paul Simon, for Bridge Over Troubled Water
1971 Carole King, for You've Got a Friend
1972 Ewan MacColl, for The First Time Ever I Saw Your Face
1973 Norman Gimbel and Charles Fox, for Killing Me Softly With His Song
1974 Marilyn and Alan Bergman and Marvin Hamlisch, for The Way We Were
1975 Stephen Sondheim, for Send in the Clowns

157

1976 Bruce Johnson, for I Write the Songs
1977 Barbra Streisand and Paul Williams, for Evergreen
     Joe Brooks, for You Light Up My Life
1978 Billy Joel, for Just the Way You Are
1979 Kenny Loggins, Michael McDonald, for What a Fool Believes
1980 Christopher Cross, for Sailing

BEST NEW ARTIST OF THE YEAR
1959 Bobby Darin
1960 Bob Newhart
1961 Peter Nero
1962 Robert Goulet
1963 Swingle Singers
1964 The Beatles
1965 Tom Jones
1966 Category not voted on
1967 Bobbie Gentry
1968 Jose Feliciano
1969 Crosby, Stills and Nash
1970 The Carpenters
1971 Carly Simon
1972 America
1973 Bette Midler
1974 Marvin Hamlisch
1975 Natalie Cole
1976 Starland Vocal Band
1977 Debby Boone
1978 A Taste of Honey
1979 Rickie Lee Jones
1980 Christopher Cross

BEST FEMALE VOCAL PERFORMANCE
1958 Ella Fitzgerald, Ella Fitzgerald Sings the Irving Berlin Song Book
1959 Ella Fitzgerald, But Not for Me
1960 Ella Fitzgerald, Mack the Knife (single)
     Ella Fitzgerald, Mack the Knife – Ella in Berlin (album)
1961 Judy Garland, Judy at Carnegie Hall (album)
1962 Ella Fitzgerald, Ella Swings Brightly With Nelson Riddle (album)
1963 Barbra Streisand, The Barbra Streisand Album (album)
1964 Barbra Streisand, People (single)
1965 Barbra Streisand, My Name Is Barbra (album)
1966 Eydie Gormé, If He Walked into My Life (single)
1967 Bobbie Gentry, Ode to Billy Joe (single)
1968 Dionne Warwick, Do You Know the Way to San Jose? (single)
1969 Peggy Lee, Is That All There Is (single)
1970 Dionne Warwick, I'll Never Fall in Love Again (album)
1971 Carole King, Tapestry (album)
1972 Helen Reddy, I Am Woman (single)
1973 Roberta Flack, Killing Me Softly With His Song (single)
1974 Olivia Newton-John, I Honestly Love You (single)
1975 Janis Ian, At Seventeen (single)
1976 Linda Ronstadt, Hasten Down the Wind (album)
1977 Barbra Streisand, Evergreen (single)
1978 Anne Murray, You Needed Me
1979 Dionne Warwick, I'll Never Love This Way Again (single)
1980 Bette Midler, The Rose

BEST MALE VOCAL PERFORMANCE
1958 Perry Como, Catch a Falling Star
1959 Frank Sinatra, Come Dance With Me
1960 Ray Charles, Georgia On My Mind (single)
     Ray Charles, Genius of Ray Charles (album)
1961 Jack Jones, Lollipops and Roses (single)
1962 Tony Bennett, I Left My Heart in San Francisco (album)
1963 Jack Jones, Wives and Lovers (single)
1964 Louis Armstrong, Hello, Dolly! (single)
1965 Frank Sinatra, It Was a Very Good Year (single)
1966 Frank Sinatra, Strangers in the Night (single)
1967 Glen Campbell, By the Time I Get to Phoenix (single)
1968 Jose Feliciano, Light My Fire (single)
1969 Harry Nilsson, Everybody's Talkin
1970 Ray Stevens, Everything is Beautiful (single)
1971 James Taylor, You've Got a Friend (single)
1972 Harry Nilsson, Without You (single)
1973 Stevie Wonder, You Are the Sunshine of My Life (single)
1974 Stevie Wonder, Fulfillingness' First Finale (album)
1975 Paul Simon, Still Crazy After All These Years (album)
1976 Stevie Wonder, Songs in the Key of Life (album)
1977 James Taylor, Handy Man (single)
1978 Barry Manilow, Copacabana (at the Copa) (single)
1979 Billy Joel, 52nd Street (album)
1980 Kenny Loggins, This is it (track)

BEST PERFORMANCE BY A VOCAL GROUP
1960 Steve Lawrence and Eydie Gormé, We Got Us
1961 Lambert, Hendricks and Ross, High Flying
1962 Peter, Paul and Mary, If I Had A Hammer
1963 Peter, Paul and Mary, Blowin' in the Wind
1964 The Beatles, A Hard Day's Night
1965 Anita Kerr Singers, We Dig Mancini
1966 Anita Kerr Singers, A Man and a Woman
1967 5th Dimension, Up, Up and Away
1968 Simon and Garfunkel, Mrs. Robinson
1969 5th Dimension, Aquarius/Let the Sunshine In
1970 Carpenters, Close to You
1971 Carpenters, Carpenters
1972 Roberta Flack and Donny Hathaway, Where Is the Love?
1973 Gladys Knight and The Pips, Neither One of Us (Wants to Be the First to Say Goodbye)
1974 Paul McCartney and Wings, Band on the Run
1975 Eagles, Lyin' Eyes
1976 Chicago, If You Leave Me Now
1977 Bee Gees, How Deep is Your Love?
1978 Bee Gees, Saturday Night Fever
1979 Doobie Brothers, Minute by Minute (album)
1980 Barbra Streisand and Barry Gibb, Guilty (track)

BEST FEMALE COUNTRY (AND WESTERN) VOCAL PERFORMANCE
1964 Dottie West, Here Comes My Baby
1965 Jody Miller, Queen of the House
1966 Jeannie Seely, Don't Touch Me
1967 Tammy Wynette, I Don't Wanna Play House
1968 Jeannie C. Riley, Harper Valley P.T.A.

Kenny Loggins, 1980 Grammy award winner for 'Best Pop Vocal Performance'

The Bee Gees after winning five Grammys in 1979

1969 Tammy Wynette, Stand By Your Man
1970 Lynn Anderson, Rose Garden
1971 Sammi Smith, Help Me Make It Through the Night
1972 Donna Fargo, Happiest Girl in the Whole USA
1973 Olivia Newton-John, Let Me Be There
1974 Anne Murray, Love Song
1975 Linda Ronstadt, I Can't Help It (If I'm Still in Love with You)
1976 Emmylou Harris, Elite Hotel
1977 Crystal Gayle, Don't It Make My Brown Eyes Blue
1978 Dolly Parton, Here You Come Again
1979 Emmylou Harris, Blue Kentucky Girl
1980 Anne Murray, Could I Have This Dance?

BEST MALE COUNTRY (AND WESTERN) VOCAL PERFORMANCE
1964 Roger Miller, Dang Me
1965 Roger Miller, King of the Road
1966 David Houston, Almost Persuaded
1967 Glen Campbell, Gentle on My Mind
1968 Johnny Cash, Folsom Prison Blues
1969 Johnny Cash, A Boy Named Sue
1970 Ray Price, For the Good Times
1971 Jerry Reed, When You're Hot, You're Hot
1972 Charley Pride, Charley Pride Sings Heart Songs
1973 Charlie Rich, Behind Closed Doors
1974 Ronnie Milsap, Please Don't Tell Me How the Story Ends
1975 Willie Nelson, Blue Eyes Cryin' in the Rain
1976 Ronnie Milsap, (I'm a) Stand By My Woman Man
1977 Kenny Rogers, Lucille
1978 Willie Nelson, Georgia on my Mind
1979 Kenny Rogers, The Gambler
1980 George Jones, He Stopped Loving Her Today

BEST FEMALE RHYTHM AND BLUES VOCAL PERFORMANCE
1967 Aretha Franklin, Respect
1968 Aretha Franklin, Chain of Fools
1969 Aretha Franklin, Share Your Love With Me
1970 Aretha Franklin, Don't Play That Song
1971 Aretha Franklin, Bridge Over Troubled Water
1972 Aretha Franklin, Young, Gifted and Black

1973 Aretha Franklin, Master of Eyes
1974 Aretha Franklin, Ain't Nothing Like the Real Thing
1975 Natalie Cole, This Will Be
1976 Natalie Cole, Sophisticated Lady (She's a Different Lady)
1977 Thelma Houston, Don't Leave Me This Way
1978 Donna Summer, Last Dance
1979 Dionne Warwick, Deja Vu
1980 Stephanie Mills, Never Knew Love Like This Before

BEST MALE RHYTHM AND BLUES VOCAL PERFORMANCE
1967 Lou Rawls, Dead End Street
1968 Otis Redding, (Sittin' on) The Dock of the Bay
1969 Joe Simon, The Chokin' Kind
1970 B.B. King, The Thrill Is Gone
1971 Lou Rawls, A Natural Man
1972 Billy Paul, Me and Mrs. Jones
1973 Stevie Wonder, Superstition
1974 Stevie Wonder, Boogie on Reggae Woman
1975 Ray Charles, Living for the City
1976 Stevie Wonder, I Wish
1977 Lou Rawls, Unmistakably Lou
1978 George Benson, On Broadway
1979 Michael Jackson, Don't Stop Till You Get Enough
1980 George Benson, Give me the Night

BEST RHYTHM AND BLUES VOCAL GROUP
1969 Isley Brothers, It's Your Thing
1970 The Delfonics, Didn't I (Blow Your Mind This Time)?
1971 Ike and Tina Turner, Proud Mary
1972 The Temptations, Papa Was A Rolling Stone
1973 Gladys Knight and The Pips, Midnight Train to Georgia
1974 Rufus, Tell Me Something Good
1975 Earth, Wind and Fire, Shining Star
1976 Marilyn McCoo and Billy Davis, Jr., You Don't Have to be a Star (to Be in My Show)
1977 Emotions, Best of My Love
1978 Earth, Wind and Fire, All 'n All
1979 Earth, Wind and Fire, After the Love Has Gone
1980 Manhattans, Shining Star

159

BEST ALBUM FOR FILM SCORE OR TELEVISION (Award to Composer)

1959 Duke Ellington, Anatomy of a Murder
1960 Ernest Gold, Exodus
1961 Henry Mancini, Breakfast at Tiffany's
1962 Category not voted on
1963 John Addison, Tom Jones
1964 Richard M. and Roger B. Sherman, Mary Poppins
1965 Johnny Mandel, The Sandpiper
1966 Maurice Jarre, Dr. Zhivago
1967 Lalo Shifrin, Mission Impossible
1968 Paul Simon (additional music by David Grusin), The Graduate
1969 Burt Bacharach, Butch Cassidy and the Sundance Kid
1970 John Lennon, Paul McCartney, George Harrison and Ringo Starr, Let It Be
1971 Isaac Hayes, Shaft
1972 Nino Rota, The Godfather
1973 Neil Diamond, Jonathan Livingston Seagull
1974 Marvin Hamlisch, Alan and Marilyn Bergman, The Way We Were
1975 John Williams, Jaws
1976 Norman Whitfield, Car Wash
1977 John Williams, Star Wars
1978 John Williams, Close Encounters of the Third Kind
1979 John Williams, Superman
1980 John Williams, The Empire Strikes Back

CLASSICAL ALBUM OF THE YEAR

1961 Igor Stravinsky conducting the Columbia Symphony, Stravinsky Conducts, 1960: Le Sacre du Printemps; Petrouchka
1962 Vladimir Horowitz, Columbia Records Presents Vladimir Horowitz
1963 Benjamin Britten conducting the London Symphony Orchestra and Chorus, Britten: War Requiem
1964 Leonard Bernstein conducting the New York Philharmonic, Bernstein Symphony No. 3 (Kaddish)
1965 Vladimir Horowitz (prod. by Thomas Frost), Horowitz at Carnegie Hall (An Historic Return)
1966 Morton Gould conducting the Chicago Symphony (prod. by Howard Scott), Ives: Symphony No. 1 in D Minor
1967 Pierre Boulez and the Paris National Opera (prod. by Thomas Z. Shepard), Berg, Wozzeck
Leonard Bernstein and the London Symphony Orchestra (prod. by John McClure), Mahler: Symphony No. 8 in E Flat Major (Symphony of a Thousand)
1968 Category not voted on
1969 Walter Carlos (prod. by Rachel Elkind), Switched-on Bach
1970 Colin Davis and the Royal Opera House Orchestra (prod. by Erik Smith), Berlioz: Les Troyens
1971 Vladimir Horowitz (prod. by Richard Killough and Thomas Frost), Horowitz Plays Rachmaninoff
1972 Georg Solti conducting the Chicago Symphony Orchestra, Vienna Boys' Choir, Vienna State Opera Chorus and Vienna Sangerverein chorus and soloists (prod. by David Harvey), Mahler: Symphony No. 8
1973 Pierre Boulez conducting the New York Philharmonic (prod. by Thomas Z. Shepard), Bartok: Concerto for Orchestra
1974 Georg Solti conducting the Chicago Symphony Orchestra (prod. by David Harvey), Berlioz: Symphonie Fantastique
1975 Sir Georg Solti conducting the Chicago Symphony Orchestra (prod. by Ray Minshull), Beethoven: Symphonies (9) Complete
1976 Artur Rubinstein and Daniel Barenboim conducting the London Philharmonic (prod. by Ray Minsheill), Beethoven: The Five Piano Concertos
1977 Leonard Bernstein, Vladimir Horowitz, Isaac Stern, Mstislav Rostropovich, Dietrich Fischer-Dieskau, Yehudi Menuhin and Lyndon Woodside (prod. by Thomas Fronts), Concert of the Century
1978 Carlo Guilini, conductor, and Itzhak Perlman, soloist, and the Chicago Orchestra, Brahms: Concerto for Violin in D Major
1979 Sir Georg Solti, conductor, and the Chicago Symphony Orchestra, Brahms: Symphonies Complete
1980 Pierre Boulez, conductor, and the Orchestre de l'Opera de Paris, Berg: Lulu (complete version)

New Awards 1979:

BEST FEMALE ROCK VOCAL PERFORMANCE

1979 Donna Summer, Hot Stuff
1980 Pat Benatar, Crimes of Panic

BEST MALE ROCK VOCAL PERFORMANCE

1979 Bob Dylan, Gotta Serve Somebody
1980 Billy Joel, Glass Houses

BEST ROCK GROUP'S VOCAL PERFORMANCE

1979 Eagles, Heartache Tonight
1980 Bob Seger and The Silver Bullet Band, Against the Wind

LEEDS INTERNATIONAL PIANOFORTE COMPETITION

The Princess Mary Gold Medal goes to the winner, together with prize money of £2000. The competition is triennial.

1963 Michael Roll (GB)
1966 Rafael Orozco (Spa)
1969 Radu Lupu (Rom)
1972 Murray Perahia (USA)
1975 Dmitri Alexeev (USSR)
1978 Michel-Jean-Jacques Dalberto (Fra)

THE *MELODY MAKER* JAZZ AWARDS

This poll by readers of the magazine was introduced in 1946, and separate British (B) and world (W) national sections were operated from 1955 until 1974 when the poll was discon-

Archery

Darrell Pace, the computer expert who won an Olympic archery gold medal at the age of 19 (All Sport/Don Morley) (see p. 9)

Athletics

Sebastian Coe beats Jürgen Straub and Steve Ovett to win the 1980 Olympic 1500 metres gold medal and gain revenge for his defeat by Ovett at 800 metres (Provincial Sports Photography) (see p. 17)

"I wouldn't dream of paying £4 for a suntan oil."

"I can see that!"

When you stretch out in the sun you can do one of three things.

You can use no sun tan oil. You can use an ordinary sun tan oil. Or you can use Bergasol.

If you don't use any sun tan oil at all when you're in sun that is stronger than you're used to, you will burn surprisingly quickly.

If you use an ordinary sun tan oil you will protect your skin to a lesser or greater degree. How much

depends on the 'protection-factor number' on the bottle.

Some of these oils block out so many of the sun's rays you can stay in the sun all day without burning—but you won't go very brown, either.

Bergasol will protect your skin like an ordinary sun tan oil. But Bergasol oil also has a tan accelerator which comes from the oil of the Bergamot fruit.

It speeds up the rate at which the sun activates the skin cells that produce melanin.

And it is melanin which gives the skin its brown colour.

So when you use Bergasol sun tan oil you go brown faster, and as the days pass the difference will become more and more obvious.

Unfortunately this special formulation isn't cheap to prepare. So Bergasol is rather more expensive than ordinary sun tan oil.

However the price looks more attractive as you do.

bergasol

It makes you go brown faster.

Advertising

Wight Collins Rutherford Scott Ltd won a 1981 Campaign *Gold Award for this advertisement for Chefaro Proprietaries Ltd entitled 'Sitting' (see p. 5)*

Cartoons

'Wicked Wanda' created by Ron Embleton won a 1979 award from The Society of Strip Illustration (see p. 48)

tinued. A special poll for jazz critics on newspapers and magazines was also held, and in 1977 *Melody Maker* organised a poll of international jazz critics to find the world's best jazz musicians and artists.

The following are just a selection of some of the winners of the *Melody Maker* readers' poll jazz awards:

BIG BANDS/BANDLEADER OF THE YEAR
1946 Geraldo
1947 Ted Heath
1952 Geraldo
1953–54 Ted Heath
1955 Ted Heath (B) and Stan Kenton (W)
1957 Johnny Dankworth (B) and Count Basie (W)
1961–63 Johnny Dankworth (B) and Count Basie (W)
1964–65 Johnny Dankworth (B) and Duke Ellington (W)
1967 Harry South (B) and Duke Ellington (W)
1969–70 Mike Westbrook (B) and Duke Ellington (W)
1971 Mike Westbrook (B) and Sun Ra (W)
1972 Centipede (B) and Duke Ellington (W)
1973–74 Mike Gibbs (B) and Duke Ellington (W)

MUSICIAN OF THE YEAR
1949–52 Johnny Dankworth
1953 Jack Parnell
1954 Johnny Dankworth
1955 Eric Delaney (B) and Gerry Mulligan (W)
1957 Johnny Dankworth (B) and Count Basie (W)
1961 Johnny Dankworth (B) and Miles Davis (W)
1962–69 Tubby Hayes (B) and Duke Ellington (W)
1970–72 John Surman (B) and Miles Davis (W)
1973 John McLaughlin and Mike Gibbs (B) and Miles Davis (W)
1974 Mike Gibbs (B) and Duke Ellington (W)

OTHER TOP BANDS AND SMALL GROUPS
1946–47 Ted Heath (swing), Jack Parnell (combo) and Geraldo (sweet)
1949 Ted Heath (swing), Ray Ellington (combo), Geraldo (sweet), and Edmundo Ross (Latin American)
1950–51 Ted Heath (swing), Johnny Dankworth (combo), Geraldo (sweet) and Edmundo Ross (Latin American)
1952–53 Ted Heath (swing), Johnny Dankworth (modern), Edmundo Ross (Latin), Humphrey Lyttelton (trad)
1954 Ronnie Scott (modern) and Humphrey Lyttelton (trad)
1955 Ronnie Scott (modern) (B), Humphrey Lyttelton (trad) (B) and Gerry Mulligan (modern) (W), Louis Armstrong (trad) (W)
1957 Tony Kinsey (B) and Modern Jazz Quartet (W)
1961 Tubby Hayes (B) and Modern Jazz Quartet (W)
1962–63 Chris Barber (trad), Tubby Hayes (B) and Dave Brubeck (W)
1964 Tubby Hayes (B) and Modern Jazz Quartet (W)
1965 Tubby Hayes, Georgie Fame (R & B) (B) and Modern Jazz Quartet, Rolling Stones (R & B) (W)

1966 Freddy Randall (B) and Modern Jazz Quartet (W)
1967 Don Rendell/Ian Carr (B) and Modern Jazz Quartet (W)
1969 Georgie Fame (B) and Miles Davis (W)
1970 Alex Welsh (B) and Miles Davis (W)
1971–72 Nucleus (B) and Miles Davis (W)
1973 Nucleus (B) and Mahavishau Orchestra (W)
1974 Soft Machine (B) and Mahavishau Orchestra (W)

MALE VOCALIST OF THE YEAR
('British', from 1955)
1946–47 Benny Lee
1949–52 Alan Dean
1953–55 Dickie Valentine
1957 Denis Lotis
1959–63 George Melly (trad)
1962–65 Matt Monro
1966–71 Georgie Fame
1972 Jack Bruce
1973–74 George Melly

FEMALE VOCALIST OF THE YEAR
('British', from 1955)
1946–57 Anne Shelton
1949 Terry Devon
1950–51 Pearl Carr
1952–55 Lita Roza
1957 Cleo Laine
1961 Cleo Laine
1962–63 Ottilie Patterson (trad) and Cleo Laine
1964–70 Cleo Laine
1971–73 Norma Winstone
1974 Cleo Laine

WORLD'S TOP MALE SINGER
1955–68 Frank Sinatra
1969–70 Jon Hendricks
1971–74 Leon Thomas

WORLD'S TOP FEMALE SINGER
1955 Sarah Vaughan
1957 Ella Fitzgerald

Matt Monro, Male Vocalist of the Year 1962–65

1961–70 Ella Fitzgerald
1971 Norma Winstone
1972 Ella Fitzgerald
1973 Norma Winstone
1974 Ella Fitzgerald

VOCAL GROUP OF THE YEAR
('British', from 1955)
1950–51 Keynotes
1952–57 Stargazers
1961–65 The Polka Dots
1966–67 Morgan James Duo
Discontinued

WORLD'S TOP VOCAL GROUP
1955 Four Aces
1957 Hi-lo's
1961–62 Four Freshmen
1963 Lambert, Hendricks and Ross
1964 Four Freshmen
1965–67 Swingle Singers
Discontinued

World's Top Musicians include:
GUITAR
1955 Barney Kessel
1965 Wes Montgomery

CLARINET
1955 Buddy de Franco
1965 Pee Wee Russell
1972 Benny Goodman

SAXOPHONE
1953 Ronnie Scott
1955 Gerry Mulligan, Lee Konitz, Stan Getz
1965 Tubby Hayes, Johnny Hodges, John Coltrane
and Gerry Mulligan

TOP BLUES ARTISTS
1965 Jimmy Witherspoon
1966 Georgie Fame (B) and Jimmy Witherspoon
1969 John Mayall (B) and Muddy Waters
1970 John Mayall (B) and Jimmy Witherspoon
1971 John Mayall (B) and Muddy Waters
1972–74 John Mayall (B) and B B King

There were no *Melody Maker* readers' polls
after 1974

CRITICS' SECTION
1961
Critics' awards

Musician of the Year	Miles Davis
Small Combo	Miles Davis
New Star	Ray Bryant
Big Band	Duke Ellington
Male Singer	Jimmy Rushing
Female Singer	Ella Fitzgerald
Vocal Group	Lambert, Hendricks and Ross

1963
Critics' section

Musician of the Year	Duke Ellington
Big Band	Duke Ellington
Combo	Miles Davis
Male Singer	Louis Armstrong
Female Singer	Sarah Vaughan

1964
Critics' section

Musician of the Year	Duke Ellington
Big Band	Duke Ellington
Combo	Charlie Mingus
Arranger/Composer	Duke Ellington
Male Singer	Louis Armstrong
Female Singer	Sarah Vaughan
Blues/Gospel	Marion Williams
New Star	Anthony Williams

1966
Critics' poll

Musician of the Year	Ornette Coleman
Big Band	Duke Ellington
Small Group	Clark Terry/Bob Brookmeyer

1969
Critics' section

Top Musician	John Surman
Big Band	Duke Ellington
Small Group	Miles Davis
Male Singer	Louis Armstrong
Female Singer	Sarah Vaughan

1977
International Jazz critics' Awards

Big Band	Thad Jones/Mel Lewis
Ensemble	McCoy Tyner
Composer	Keith Jarrett
Arranger	Gil Evans
Trumpet	Dizzy Gillespie
Soprano Sax	Steve Lacy
Alto Sax	Anthony Braxton
Tenor Sax	Sonny Rollins
Baritone Sax	Gerry Mulligan
Clarinet	Anthony Braxton
Flute	Hubert Laws
Trombone	Albert Mangelsdorff
Piano	Cecil Taylor
Organ	Jimmy Smith
Synthesiser	Joe Zawinul
Guitar	Jim Hall
Violin	Jean-Luc Ponty
Acoustic Bass	Niels-Henning Orsted-Pedersen
Electric Bass	Stanley Clarke
Vibes	Gary Burton
Drums	Elvin Jones
Percussion	Airto Moreira
Misc. Instruments	Roland Kirk
Male Vocal	Joe Williams
Female Vocal	Sarah Vaughan

MELODY MAKER READERS' POP POLL AND ANNUAL AWARDS
This annual poll by readers of the magazine
was inaugurated in 1960. The separate British
(B) and world (W) Sections, introduced in
1963, were abandoned in 1978.

TOP MALE SINGER OF THE YEAR
1960–62 Cliff Richard
1963–65 Cliff Richard (B) and Elvis Presley (W)

1966 Tom Jones (B) and Elvis Presley (W)
1967 Cliff Richard (B) and Otis Redding (W)
1968 Scott Walker (B) and Bob Dylan (W)
1969 Tom Jones (B) and Bob Dylan (W)
1970 Robert Plant (B) and Bob Dylan (W)
1971–72 Rod Stewart (B) and Neil Young (W)
1973 David Bowie (B) and Robert Plant (W)
1974 Paul Rodgers (B) and David Bowie (W)
1975 Robert Plant (B and W)
1976 Jon Anderson (B) and Robert Plant (W)
1977 Jon Anderson (B and W)
1978 Jon Anderson
1979 Robert Plant
1980 Peter Gabriel

FEMALE SINGER OF THE YEAR
1960–62 Shirley Bassey
1962 Helen Shapiro
1963 Susan Maughan (B) and Brenda Lee (W)
1964 Cilla Black (B) and Mary Wells (W)
1965 Sandie Shaw (B) and Brenda Lee (W)
1966–67 Dusty Springfield (B and W)
1968 Julie Driscoll (B) and Aretha Franklin (W)
1969 Christine Perfect (B) and Janis Joplin (W)
1970–71 Sandy Denny (B) and Joni Mitchell (W)
1972 Maggie Bell (B) and Joni Mitchell (W)
1973 Maggie Bell (B) and Carly Simon (W)
1974–75 Maggie Bell (B) and Joni Mitchell (W)
1976–77 Kiki Dee (B) and Joni Mitchell (W)
1978–80 Kate Bush

Melody Maker *award
winners*. Above:
*Kate Bush at the 1980
presentation
ceremony with
Rowan Atkinson;
below: Rod Stewart
receiving his award in
1972*

BRIGHTEST HOPE OF THE YEAR
1960 Emile Ford
1961 The Allisons
1962 Helen Shapiro
1963 Billy J. Kramer (B) and Lesley Gore (W)
1964 Lulu and the Lovers (B) and P. J. Proby (W)
1965 Donovan (B) and Walker Bros (W)
1966 The Troggs (B) and Mama's and Papa's (W)
1967 Procol Harum (B and W)
1968 Julie Driscoll and Brian Auger Trinity (B and W)
1969 Blind Faith (B and W)
1970 Mungo Jerry (B) and Emerson, Lake and Palmer (W)
1971 Wishbone Ash (B) and Mountain (W)
1972 Roxy Music (B) and Focus (W)
1973 Nazareth (B) and Beck, Bogert and Appice (W)
1974 Bad Company (B) and Sparks (W)
1975 Camel (B and W)
1976 Thin Lizzy (B) and Peter Frampton (W)
1977 Stranglers (B) and Television (W)
1978 Kate Bush
1979 Gary Numan
1980 Saxon

INSTRUMENTALIST OF THE YEAR
1960 Russ Conway
1961 Bert Weedon
1962 Acker Bilk
1963 Jet Harris (B) and Duane Eddy (W)
Discontinued

MALE TV ARTIST OF THE YEAR
1960 Bruce Forsyth
1961 Anthony Newley
1962 Bruce Forsyth
1963 Norman Vaughan
1964–65 Cliff Richard
1966 Barry Fantoni
1967–68 Simon Dee
1969 Tom Jones
Discontinued

Billy Connolly with John Peel, receiving his award, at the 1975 awards ceremony

FEMALE TV ARTIST OF THE YEAR
1960–61 Alma Cogan
1962 Helen Shapiro
1963 Millicent Martin
1964 Kathy Kirby
1965–66 Cathy McGowan
1967–69 Lulu
Discontinued

RADIO SHOW OF THE YEAR
1960–62 Saturday Club
1963 Pick of the Pops
1964–66 Saturday Club
1967 Radio London Fab 40
1968–70 Top Gear, John Peel
1971 John Peel's In Concert Sunday Show
1972–73 Sounds of the Seventies
1974–78 Alan Freeman's Saturday Show
1979–80 Friday Rock Show

TV SHOW OF THE YEAR
1960 Boy Meets Girl (ITV)
1961 Juke Box Jury (BBC)
1962 Thank Your Lucky Stars (ITV)
1963 Lucky Stars – Summer Spin (ITV)
1964–65 Ready Steady Go (ITV)
1966–68 Top of the Pops (BBC)
1969 Colour Me Pop
1970–71 Disco 2
1972–77 Old Grey Whistle Test (BBC 2)
1978 Revolver
1979–80 Old Grey Whistle Test (BBC 2)

VOCAL DISC OF THE YEAR
(British section)
1960 Living Doll, Cliff Richard
1961 Portrait of my Love, Matt Monro
1962 The Young Ones, Cliff Richard
1963 From Me to You, Beatles
1964 Not Fade Away, Rolling Stones
1965 Ticket to Ride, Beatles
1966 Paperback Writer, Beatles
Discontinued

INSTRUMENTAL DISC OF THE YEAR
(British section)
1960 Petite Fleur, Chris Barber
1961 Apache, The Shadows
1962 Stranger on the Shore, Acker Bilk
1963 Diamonds, Jet Harris and Tony Meeham
1964 Rise and Fall of Flingel Bunt, Shadows
1965 Cast Your Fate to the Winds, Sounds Orchestral
1966 The War Lord, Shadows
Discontinued

VOCAL GROUP OF THE YEAR
1960 Polka Dots
1961 King Brothers
1962 Springfields
1963 Beatles (B) and Four Seasons (W)
1964 Rolling Stones (B) and Beatles (W)
1965–69 Beatles (B and W)
1970 Led Zeppelin (B and W)
1971 Emerson, Lake and Palmer (B) and Crosby, Stills, Nash and Young (W)
1972–73 Emerson, Lake and Palmer (B and W)
Discontinued

1966 awards: left to right, *Paul McCartney, Dusty Springfield, Tom Jones and Ringo Starr*

DISC JOCKEY OF THE YEAR
1960–63 David Jacobs
1964–67 Jimmy Savile
1968–79 John Peel
1980 Tommy Vance

MUSICIAN OF THE YEAR
(British section)
1964–66 Hank Marvin
1967–69 Eric Clapton
Discontinued

TOP MUSICIAN
(World section)
1964 Chuck Berry
1965 Burt Bacharach
1966 Herb Alpert
1967 Jimi Hendrix
1968–69 Eric Clapton
Discontinued

TOP GUITARIST
1970–71 Eric Clapton
1972 Rory Gallagher
1973 Jan Akkerman
1974 Eric Clapton
1975 Jimmy Page
1976 Steve Howe

1977 Jimmy Page
1978 Steve Howe
1979 Jimmy Page
1980 Ritchie Blackmore

TOP KEYBOARDS
1970–72 Keith Emerson
1973–76 Rick Wakeman
1977 Keith Emerson
1978–79 Rick Wakeman
1980 Tony Banks

VOCAL DISC OF THE YEAR
(World section)
1963 Can't Get Used to Losing You, Andy Williams
1964 It's Over, Roy Orbison
1965 Crying in the Chapel, Elvis Presley
1966 Paperback Writer, Beatles
Discontinued

INSTRUMENTAL DISC OF THE YEAR
(World section)
1963 Pipeline, Chantays
1964 Rise and Fall of Flingel Bunt, Shadows
1965 Cast Your Fate to the Winds, Sounds Orchestral
1966 Spanish Flea, Herb Alpert
Discontinued

SINGLE DISC OF THE YEAR
(British section)
1967 Whiter Shade of Pale, Procol Harum
1968 Jumpin' Jack Flash, Rolling Stones

1978 awards: Peter Cook and Rick Wakeman receiving his award

1969 Get Back, Beatles
1970 All Right Now, Free
1971 My Sweet Lord, George Harrison
1972 Lady Eleanor, Lindisfarne
1973 Jean Genie, David Bowie
1974 Can't Get Enough, Bad Company
1975 I'm Not in Love, 10cc
1976 Bohemian Rhapsody, Queen
1977 Fanfare for the Common Man, Emerson, Lake and Palmer
Discontinued

LP/ALBUM OF THE YEAR
(British section)
1967 Sgt Pepper's Lonely Hearts Club Band, Beatles
1968 Scott 2, Scott Walker
1969 Goodbye, Cream
1970 Led Zeppelin II
1971 Tarkus, Emerson, Lake and Palmer
1972 Argus, Wishbone Ash
1973 Dark Side of the Moon, Pink Floyd
1974 Tubular Bells, Mike Oldfield
1975 Physical Graffiti, Led Zeppelin
1976 A Trick of the Tail, Genesis
1977 Works, Emerson, Lake and Palmer
Discontinued

BEST LIVE ACT OF THE YEAR
(British section)
1973 Emerson, Lake and Palmer
1974–77 Genesis
Discontinued

SINGLE DISC OF THE YEAR
(World section)
1967 Whiter Shade of Pale, Procol Harum
1968 US Male, Elvis Presley
1969 The Boxer, Simon and Garfunkel
1970 Bridge Over Troubled Water, Simon and Garfunkel
1971 My Sweet Lord, George Harrison
1972 American Pie, Don McLean
1973 Walk on the Wild Side, Lou Reed
1974 This Town Ain't Big Enough for Both of Us, Sparks
1975 I'm Not in Love, 10cc
1976 Bohemian Rhapsody, Queen
1977 Fanfare for the Common Man, Emerson, Lake and Palmer
1978 Baker Street, Gerry Rafferty
1979 I Don't Like Mondays, Boomtown Rats
1980 Another Brick in the Wall (Part 2), Pink Floyd

LP/ALBUM OF THE YEAR
(World section)
1967 Sgt Pepper's Lonely Hearts Club Band, Beatles
1968 John Wesley Harding, Bob Dylan
1969 Nashville Skyline, Bob Dylan
1970 Hot Rats, Frank Zappa
1971 After the Gold Rush, Neil Young
1972 Harvest, Neil Young
1973 Dark Side of the Moon, Pink Floyd
1974 Tubular Bells, Mike Oldfield
1975 Physical Graffiti, Led Zeppelin
1976 A Trick of the Tail, Genesis
1977 Works, Emerson, Lake and Palmer
1978 Live and Dangerous, Thin Lizzy
1979 In Through the Out Door, Led Zeppelin
1980 The Wall, Pink Floyd

TOP BAND OF THE YEAR
(British section)
1973–76 Yes
1977 Genesis
Discontinued

TOP RECORD PRODUCER
1970 Frank Zappa
1971 Bob Johnson
1972 Greg Lake
1973 David Bowie
1974–75 Eddie Offord
1976–77 Jimmy Page
1978 David Hentschel
1979 Jimmy Page
1980 David Hentschel

TOP COMPOSER
1971 Neil Young
1972 Keith Emerson/Greg Lake
1973 David Bowie
1974 John Anderson /Steve Howe
1975–76 John Anderson
1977 Jimmy Page/Robert Plant

Above: *Keith Emerson, Greg Lake and Carl Palmer in 1972*

Right: *Phil Collins receiving the Genesis awards in 1977*

1978 Genesis
1979 Led Zeppelin
1980 Pink Floyd

TOP ARRANGER
1971 Paul Buckmaster
1972–73 Emerson, Lake and Palmer
1974 David Bowie
1975–76 Yes
1977–78 Genesis
1979 Yes
1980 No award

TOP BAND
1973–74 Yes
1975 Led Zeppelin
1976–77 Yes
1978 Genesis
1979 Led Zeppelin
1980 Genesis

TOP LIVE ACT
1973 Alice Cooper
1974 Emerson, Lake and Palmer
1975 Led Zeppelin
1976–78 Genesis
1979 Led Zeppelin
1980 Genesis

BEST DISCO RECORD
1978 Night Fever, Bee Gees
1979 Heart of Glass, Blondie
1980 Upside Down, Diana Ross

BEST JAZZ ACT
1978–80 Brand X

BEST REGGAE ACT
1978–80 Bob Marley and the Wailers

MUSICIAN OF THE YEAR AWARD
This award is given by the Incorporated Society of Musicians for the most outstanding contribution to music. Each winner is chosen by a committee of musicians, from a list of nominations. Winners since foundation:

1976 Sir Alexander Gibson
1977 Sir William Walton
1978 Sir Peter Pears
1979 Sir Adrian Boult
     James Galway
1980 Jacqueline du Pré

PULITZER PRIZE FOR MUSIC
For further details see under main heading of Pulitzer Prizes.

1943 *Secular Cantata No. 2*, William Schuman
1944 *Symphony No. 4, opus 34*, Howard Hanson
1945 *Appalachian Spring*, Aaron Copland
1946 *The Canticle of the Sun*, Leo Sowerby
1947 *Symphony No. 3*, Charles Ives
1948 *Symphony No. 3*, Walter Piston
1949 *Louisiana Story*, Virgil Thomson
1950 *The Consul*, Gian-Carlo Menotti
1951 *Giants in the Earth*, Douglas S. Moore
1952 *Symphony Concertante*, Gail Kubik
1953 No award
1954 *Concerto for Two Pianos and Orchestra*, Quincy Porter
1955 *The Saint of Bleecker Street*, Gian-Carlo Menotti
1956 *Symphony No. 3*, Ernst Toch

Jacqueline du Pré (with Daniel Barenboim, her husband) 1980 'Musician of the Year'

1957 *Meditations on Ecclesiastes*, Norman Dello Joio
1958 *The Score of Vanessa*, Samuel Barber
1959 *Concerto for Piano and Orchestra*, John la Montaine

1960 *Second String Quartet*, Elliott C. Carter Jr.
1961 *Symphony No. 7,* Walter Piston
1962 *The Crucible*, Robert Ward
1963 *Piano Concerto No. 1,* Samuel Barber
1964–65 No award
1966 *Variations for Orchestra*, Leslie Bassett
1967 *Quartet No. 3,* Leon Kirchner
1968 *Echoes of Time and the River,* George Crumb
1969 *String Quartet No. 3,* Karel Husa
1970 *Time's Economium,* Charles W. Wuorinen
1971 *Synchronisms No. 6,* Mario Davidovsky
1972 *Windows*, Jacob Druckman
1973 *String Quartet No. 3,* Elliott Carter
1974 *Notturno*, Donald Martino; special citation to Roger Sessions
1975 *From the Diary of Virginia Woolf*, Dominick Argento
1976 *Air Music, 10 études for orchestra,* Ned Rorem
1977 *Visions of Terror and Wonder,* Richard Wernick
1978 *Déjà Vu for Percussion Quartet and Orchestra*, Michael Colgrass
1979 *Aftertones of Infinity*, Joseph Schwantner
1980 *In Memory of a Summer Day*, David Del Tredici
1981 No award

YOUNG MUSICIAN OF THE YEAR
A contest organised by BBC to select the most talented and outstanding young musician. It is held every two years.The winners:

1978
Michael Hext, bassoon

1980
Nicholas Daniel, oboe

Netball

WORLD CHAMPIONSHIPS
World championships for women's netball teams were first held in 1963. Winners:

1963 Australia
1967 New Zealand

1971 Australia
1975 Australia
1979 Australia, New Zealand, Trinidad & Tobago (shared)

Nobel Prizes

Nobel Prizes are awarded each year to persons who have made important contributions for the good of humanity.

The awards were established in the will of Alfred Bernhard Nobel (1833–96), a Swedish chemist who became wealthy from his invention of dynamite in 1867. He regretted that dynamite had been used as an instrument of war, and left a fund of about $9 million to establish the Nobel Prizes to encourage peace and progress.

Six prizes are awarded each year in chemistry, economics, literature, peace, physics and physiology or medicine. The first prizes were awarded in 1901. The economics prize was added in 1969. Recent prizes carry a monetary award of about $150 000, divided when there is more than one recipient.

The Royal Academy of Science in Sweden picks the prizewinners in physics, chemistry, and economics. The medical faculty of Stockholm's Caroline Institute chooses the winner in the field of physiology or medicine. The Swedish Academy of Literature names the winner in the field of literature. The Norwegian parliament elects a committee of five persons to select the winner of the prize for peace.

(*See* under Chemistry, Economics, Literature, Medicine, Peace and Physics for details of winners.)

Alfred Bernhard Nobel

Nursing

THE DETTOL NATIONAL NURSING AWARDS

These have been organised annually since 1973 by the Royal College of Nursing and sponsored by Reckitt & Colman Pharmaceutical Division. Nurses are nominated by a nursing or medical colleague, or a member of the general public. Each entrant initially answers a questionnaire, and the finalists are judged by a panel of individuals from the nursing and medical profession. The winner in 1980 received a Mini, a cheque for £1000 and the Dettol Sword Trophy. The nominator also received a Mini. Winners:

1974 Alison Cumming, Western Infirmary, Glasgow
1975 Mary Fearon, Musgrave Park Hospital, Belfast
1976 Margaret Height, Royal Victoria Hospital, Edinburgh
1977 Betty Earnshaw, Royal Ordnance Factory, Crewe
1978 No award

Philip Darbyshire with nursing staff from the Gogarburn Hospital receiving the Dettol National Nursing Award

1979 Renee Hartley, Cheshire County Council
1980 Philip Darbyshire, Gogarburn Hospital, Edinburgh

NURSE OF THE YEAR
This competition is organised each year by the *Daily Express* and featured on television. Readers vote to give their favourite nurse a chance to win the title of 'The Nurse of the Year', together with a luxury holiday and' pocket money presented by Cunard.

Anyone can nominate a nurse for the title – patients, colleagues, relatives and friends. Academic achievement and experience are not the main criteria – kindness, efficiency, manner, general disposition and aspirations are more likely to influence the independent panel of judges.

The winners to date are:

1970 Madeline Ambrose
1971 Dilys Owen
1972 Patricia Henry
1973 Barbara Murray
1974 Jenny Denham
1975 Joy Dyer
1976 Tessa Dodds
1977 Nancy Farley
1978 Cecilia Holden
1979 Susan Hemming
1980 Barbara Lockett

Olympic Games

The first Olympic Games of the modern era were held in Athens, Greece in 1896. Since then, with the exception of the war years (1916, 1940 and 1944), Games have been held every four years, and additionally in Athens in 1906. Separate Winter Olympics were first held in 1924. The dates and venues have been allocated as follows:

I	Athens	6–15 Apr 1896
II	Paris	20 May–28 Oct 1900
III	St. Louis	1 Jul–23 Nov 1904
†	Athens	22 Apr–2 May 1906
IV	London	27 Apr–31 Oct 1908
V	Stockholm	5 May–22 Jul 1912
VI	*Berlin	1916
VII	Antwerp	20 Apr–12 Sep 1920
VIII	Paris	4 May–27 Jul 1924
IX	Amsterdam	17 May–12 Aug 1928
X	Los Angeles	30 Jul–14 Aug 1932
XI	Berlin	1–16 Aug 1936
XII	*Tokyo, then Helsinki 1940	

The Olympic Stadium in Rome for the 1960 Games

XIII	*London	1944
XIV	London	29 Jul–14 Aug 1948
XV	Helsinki	19 Jul–3 Aug 1952
XVI	‡Melbourne	22 Nov–8 Dec 1956
XVII	Rome	25 Aug–11 Sep 1960
XVIII	Tokyo	10–24 Oct 1964
XIX	Mexico City	12–27 Oct 1968
XX	Munich	26 Aug–10 Sep 1972
XXI	Montreal	17 Jul–1 Aug 1976
XXII	Moscow	19 Jul–3 Aug 1980
XXIII	Los Angeles	28 Jul–12 Aug 1984

The Winter Olympics were inaugurated in 1924 and have been allocated as follows:

I	Chamonix, France	25 Jan–4 Feb 1924
II	St. Moritz, Switzerland	11–19 Feb 1928
III	Lake Placid, USA	4–15 Feb 1932
IV	Garmisch-Partenkirchen, Germany	6–16 Feb 1936
V	St. Moritz, Switzerland	30 Jan–8 Feb 1948
VI	Oslo, Norway	14–25 Feb 1952
VII	Cortina d'Ampezzo, Italy	26 Jan–5 Feb 1956
VIII	Squaw Valley, California	18–28 Feb 1960
IX	Innsbruck, Austria	29 Jan–9 Feb 1964
X	Grenoble, France	6–18 Feb 1968
XI	Sapporo, Japan	3–13 Feb 1972
XII	Innsbruck, Austria	4–15 Feb 1976
XIII	Lake Placid, USA	14–23 Feb 1980
XIV	Sarajevo, Yugoslavia	8–19 Feb 1984

*Cancelled due to World Wars
†Intercalated celebration not numbered but officially organised by the IOC (International Olympic Committee)
‡Equestrian events held in Stockholm, Sweden 10–17 Jun 1956

See the following sports for additional details: Archery, Association Football, Athletics, Basketball, Bobsleigh and Tobogganing, Boxing, Canoeing, Cycling, Equestrian Events, Fencing, Gymnastics, Handball,

Hockey, Ice Hockey, Ice Skating, (Speed skating), Judo, Modern Pentathlon, Rowing, Shooting, Skiing (and Biathlon), Swimming, Volleyball, Water Polo, Weightlifting, Wrestling, Yachting

Most individual gold medals:

MEN
10 Ray Ewry (USA): track and field athletics 1900–08

WOMEN
7 Vera   Caslavska   (Cze):   gymnastics 1964–68

Opera

THE NEW STANDARD OPERA AWARD
Instituted in 1973 by the London *Evening Standard* (*The New Standard* from 1980), this award for the 'Most Outstanding Achievement in Opera' aims to promote the arts in London. The winner is chosen by a panel of judges composed of critics from London newspapers. Winners:

1973 Reginald Goodall
1974 Glyndebourne Festival Opera
1975 Scottish Opera
1976 Colin Davis
1977 Charles Mackerras
1978 Jon Vickers
1979 English National Opera
1980 Carlos Kleiber

Orienteering

WORLD CHAMPIONSHIPS
World championships were first held in 1966.

Men's Individual
1966 Aage Hadler (Nor)
1968 Karl Johansson (Swe)
1970 Stig Berge (Nor)
1972 Aage Hadler (Nor)
1974 Bernt Frilen (Swe)
1976 Egil Johansen (Nor)
1978 Egil Johansen (Nor)
1979 Ogvin Thon (Nor)

Women's Individual
1966 Ulla Lindqvist (Swe)
1968 Ulla Lindqvist (Swe)
1970 Ingrid Hadler (Nor)
1972 Sarolta Monspart (Fin)
1974 Mona Norgaard (Den)
1976 Liisa Veijalainen (Fin)
1978 Anne Berit Eid (Nor)
1979 Outi Bergonstrom (Fin)

Men's Relay
1966 Sweden
1968 Sweden
1970 Norway
1972 Sweden
1974 Sweden
1976 Sweden
1978 Norway
1979 Sweden

Women's Relay
1966 Sweden   1974 Sweden
1968 Norway   1976 Sweden
1970 Sweden   1978 Finland
1972 Finland   1979 Finland

Ulla Lindqvist won the first two women's world orienteering championships (Arild Jakobsen)

Peace

ALBERT EINSTEIN PEACE PRIZE
Founded in 1980 in New York and awarded for contributions to world peace, the first winner was:

Alva Reiner Myrdal (78) of Sweden for her work towards arms control.

The prize is worth around £25 000.

NOBEL PRIZE FOR PEACE
For further details see under main heading of Nobel Prizes.

1901 Jean H. Dunant (Swi)
     Frederic Passy (Fra)
1902 Elie Ducommun (Swi)
     Charles A. Gobat (Swi)
1903 Sir William R. Cremer (GB)
1904 Institute of International Law
1905 Baroness Bertha von Suttner (Aut)
1906 Theodore Roosevelt (USA)
1907 Ernesto T. Moneta (Ita)
     Louis Renault (Fra)
1908 Klas P. Arnoldson (Swe)
     Fredrik Bajer (Den)
1909 Auguste M. F. Beernaert (Bel)
     Paul H. B. B. d'Estournelles de Constant (Fra)
1910 Permanent International Peace Bureau
1911 Tobias M. C. Asser (Hol)
     Alfred H. Fried (Aut)
1912 Alihu Root (USA)
1913 Henri Lafontaine (Bel)
1914–16 No award
1917 International Committee of the Red Cross
1918 No award
1919 Woodrow Wilson (USA)
1920 Léon V. A. Bourgeois (Fra)
1921 Karl H. Branting (Swe)
     Christian L. Lange (Nor)
1922 Fridtjof Nansen (Nor)
1923–24 No award
1925 Sir J. Austen Chamberlain (GB)
     Charles G. Dawes (USA)
1926 Aristide Briand (Fra)
     Gustav Stresemann (Ger)
1927 Ferdinand Buisson (Fra)
     Ludwig Quidde (Ger)
1928 No award
1929 Frank B. Kellogg (USA)
1930 Lårs O. N. Söderblom (Swe)
1931 Jane Addams (USA)
     Nicholas Murray Butler (USA)

1932 No award
1933 Sir Norman Angell (GB)
1934 Arthur Henderson (GB)
1935 Carl von Ossietzky (Ger)
1936 Carlos Saavedra Lamas (Arg)
1937 Viscount Cecil of Chelwood (GB)
1938 International Office for Refugees
1939–43 No award
1944 International Committee of the Red Cross
1945 Cordell Hull (USA)
1946 Emily G. Balch (USA)
     John R. Mott (USA)
1947 Friends Service Council (GB)
     American Friends Service Committee
1948 No award
1949 Lord John Boyd Orr of Brechin (GB)
1950 Ralph J. Bunche (USA)
1951 Léon Jouhaux (Fra)
1952 Albert Schweitzer (Fra) (German-born)
1953 George C. Marshall (USA)
1954 Office of UN High Commissioner for Refugees
1955–56 No award
1957 Lester B. Pearson (Can)
1958 Georges Pire (Bel)
1959 Philip J. Noel-Baker (GB)
1960 Albert J. Luthuli (SA)
1961 Dag Hammarskjöld (Swe) posthumous
1962 Linus C. Pauling (USA)
1963 International Committee of the Red Cross
     Red Cross Societies League
1964 Martin Luther King Jr (USA)
1965 United Nations Children's Fund (UNICEF)
1966–67 No award
1968 René Cassin (Fra)
1969 International Labour Organisation (ILO)
1970 Norman E. Borlaug (USA)
1971 Willy Brandt (Ger)
1972 No award
1973 Henry A. Kissinger (USA) (German-born)
     Le Duc Tho (N. Viet)
1974 Eisaku Sato (Jap)
     Sean MacBride (Ire)
1975 Andrei D. Sakharov (USSR)
1976 Betty Williams and Mairead Corrigan (GB)
1977 Amnesty International
1978 Anwar el Sadat (Egy)
     Menachem Begin (Isr)
1979 Mother Theresa of Calcutta (Alb)
1980 Adolfo Pérez Esquivel (Arg)

Pets

PET OF THE YEAR
The Pet of the Year award was first presented in 1978. Organised by the Junglies Club – an off-shoot of the World Wildlife Fund's Wildlife Youth Service – the competition is open to any child who has a pet of any description.

Entrants are invited to send a photograph of their pet together with, in no more than 100 words, their reasons why they think their animal should be the Pet of the Year. The winner's owner is presented with a cash prize and various other Junglies products, together with a brass plaque commemorating the Pet of Year award.

1978 Alsatian called Sherry, owned by two sisters, Julie and Gina Wilding from Bolton, Lancs

1979 Shelty dog called Bengie, owned by Carol Ann Iles from Haywards Heath, Sussex.

1980 A mongrel dog called Bella, owned by Alison Jayes from London

Photography

BRITISH PHOTOGRAPHY COMPETITION

The competition, held annually since 1975, is organised by the *Telegraph Sunday Magazine* in association with Kodak Limited, British Airways, the National Trust and the National Trust for Scotland. It is open to all photographers resident in the UK. The overwall winner is named British Photographer of the Year and wins a cash prize of £1500 and a British Airways holiday

1975
Theme: The British Weekend
Winner: Rosemary Drayson

1976
Theme: The British on Holiday
Winners: Professional Category G. P. Eisen, LRPS
Amateur Category Andrew Polakowski

1977
Theme: Britain '77
Winners:
Section 1 – On The Move
John Eyett (Two Hurdlers)

Section 2 – National Trust and British Heritage (open to amateur and professional photographers)
P. Lacey (West Clandon)

Section 3 – A Sense of Community (open to amateur photographers only)
Clive B. Harrison

Overall Winner: John Eyett

1978
Theme: A Sense of Beauty
Winners:
People Barney Edwards (Man and Dog in Mist)
Places K. Taylor (St. Kilda)
Things J. G. Corbett (Sun Clocks)
National Trust Patricio Goycolea (Glastonbury Tor)
Overall winner: Barney Edwards

1979
Theme: A Time to Remember
Winners:
People Ian Torrance

Lawrence Englesberg's winning photograph in the 1979 British Photography Competition

Places Lawrence Englesberg
Things Mary Fane-Gladwin
National Trust R. Snell
Overall Winner: Lawrence Englesberg

1980
Theme: Assignment 1980
Winners:
People Peter Whitaker
Places Niall Sinclair Cotton
Things Robert Ashby
National Trust Ernest Cooke
Overall winner: Niall Sinclair Cotton

BRITISH PRESS PHOTOGRAPHER OF THE YEAR

This has been an annual award since 1969, sponsored by the Midland Bank Limited from 1974 to 1979

1969 Kent Gavin, *Daily Mirror*
1970 Michael Brennan, *The Sun*
1971 David Cairns, *Daily Express*
1972 William Lovelace, *Daily Express*
1973 David Cairns, *Daily Express*
1974 Jim McLagan, *The Argus* (Cape Town)
1975 Ronald G. Bell, The Press Association
1976 Monty Fresco, *Daily Mail*
1977 Frank Barrett, Keystone Press Agency
1978 Monty Fresco, *Daily Mail*
1979 Ian Torrance, *Scottish Daily Record*
1980 No award

KODAK UNDER FIVES PORTRAIT AWARDS

In this annual competition, which dates from 1976, parents are invited to have their young children (five years or under) photographed in colour by a professional photographer. Two cash prizes are awarded each month for the photographs of the girl and boy judged to look 'the most lovable and appealing'. There is an annual cash prize each for the two overall winners.

1976 Helen Ann Clark, Dalton in Furness
1977 Twins Wendy and Amanda Henoq, South Croydon, Kent
1978 Robb Halley, Edinburgh and Rhiannon James, Dawlish, Devon
1979 Samantha Martin, Ilford, Essex and Luke Fresle, Hampton Dene, Hereford
1980 Lisa Coppin, Chatham, Kent and Sam Parkes, Hemel Hempstead, Herts

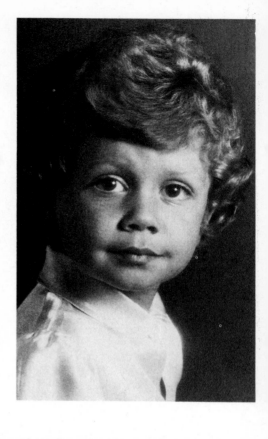

Sam Parkes (top) *and Lisa Coppin* (right) *winners of the 1980 Kodak Under Fives Portrait Awards*

174

Physics

NOBEL PRIZE FOR PHYSICS
For further details see under main heading of
Nobel Prizes

1901 Wilhelm C. Roentgen (Ger)
1902 Hendrik A. Lorentz (Hol)
     Pieter Zeeman (Hol)
1903 Antoine Henri Becquerel (Fra)
     Marie Curie (Fra) (Polish-born)
     Pierre Curie (Fra)
1904 Lord Rayleigh (John W. Strutt) (GB)
1905 Philipp E. A. von Lenard (Ger) (Hungarian-
     born)
1906 Sir Joseph John Thomson (GB)
1907 Albert A. Michelson (USA) (German-born)
1908 Gabriel Lippmann (Fra) (Lux-born)
1909 Guglielmo Marconi (Ita)
     Carl F. Braun (Ger)
1910 Johannes D. van der Waals (Hol)
1911 Wilhelm Wien (Ger)
1912 Nils G. Dalén (Swe)
1913 Heike Kamerlingh-Onnes (Hol)
1914 Max von Laue (Ger)
1915 Sir William H. Bragg (GB)
1916 No award
1917 Charles G. Barkla (GB)
1918 Max K. E. L. Planck (Ger)
1919 Johannes Stark (Ger)
1920 Charles E. Guillaume (Fra) (Swiss-born)
1921 Albert Einstein (USA) (German-born)
1922 Niels Bohr (Den)
1923 Robert A. Millikan (USA)
1924 Karl M. G. Siegbahn (Swe)
1925 James Franck (Ger)
     Gustav Hertz (Ger)
1926 Jean B. Perrin (Fra)
1927 Arthur H. Compton (USA)
     Charles T. R. Wilson (GB)
1928 Owen W. Richardson (GB)
1929 Prince Louis-Victor de Broglie (Fra)
1930 Sir Chandrasekhara V. Raman (Ind)
1931 No award
1932 Werner Heisenberg (Ger)
1933 Paul A. M. Dirac (GB)
     Erwin Schrödinger (Aut)
1934 No award
1935 Sir James Chadwick (GB)
1936 Carl D. Anderson (USA)
     Victor F. Hess (Aut)
1937 Clinton J. Davisson (USA)
     George P. Thomson (GB)
1938 Enrico Fermi (USA) (Italian-born)
1939 Ernst O. Lawrence (USA)
1940 No award
1941 No award
1942 No award
1943 Otto Stern (USA) (German-born)
1944 Isidor Isaac Rabi (USA)
1945 Wolfgang Pauli (USA)
1946 Percy Williams Bridgman (USA)
1947 Sir Edward V. Appleton (GB)
1948 Patrick M. S. Blackett (GB)
1949 Hideki Yukawa (Jap)
1950 Cecil F. Powell (GB)

1951 Sir John D. Cockroft (GB)
     Ernest T. S. Walton (Ire)
1952 Felix Bloch (USA) (Swiss-born)
     Edward M. Purcell (USA)
1953 Fritz Zernike (Hol)
1954 Max Born (GB) (German-born)
     Walther Bothe (Ger)
1955 Polykarp Kusch (UDS) (German-born)
     Willis E. Lamb (USA)
1956 John Bardeen (USA)
     Walter H. Brattain (USA)
     William Shockley (USA)
1957 Tsung-Dao Lee (USA) (Chinese-born)
     Chen Ning Yang (USA) (Chinese-born)
1958 Paval A. Cherenkov (USSR)
     Ilya M. Frank (USSR)
     Igor J. Tamm (USSR)
1959 Owen Chamberlain (USA)
     Emilio G. Segrè (USA) (Italian-born)
1960 Donald A. Glaser (USA)
1961 Robert Hofstadter (USA)
     Rudolf L. Mössbauer (Ger)
1962 Lev D. Landau (USSR)
1963 Maria Goeppert-Mayer (USA)
     J. Hans D. Jensen (Ger)
     Eugene P. Wigner (USA)
1964 Nikolai G. Basov (USSR)
     Aleksandr M. Prokhorov (USSR)
     Charles H. Townes (USA)
1965 Richard P. Feynman (USA)
     Julian S. Schwinger (USA)
     Sin-itiro Tomonaga (Jap)
1966 Alfred Kastler (Fra)
1967 Hans A. Bethe (USA) (German-born)
1968 Luis W. Alvarez (USA)
1969 Murray Gell-Man (USA)
1970 Hannes O. G. Alfven (Swe)
     Louis E. F. Néel (Fra)
1971 Dennis Gabor (GB) (Hungarian-born)
1972 John Bardeen (USA)
     Leon N. Cooper (USA)
     John R. Schrieffer (USA)
1973 Ivar Giaever (USA) (Norwegian-born)
     Leo Esaki (Jap)
     Brian D. Josephson (GB)
1974 Antony Hewish (GB)
     Sir Martin Ryle (GB)
1975 L. James Rainwater (USA)
     Aage Bohr (Den)
     Ben Roy Mottelson (Den) (USA-born)
1976 Burton Richter (USA)
     Samuel C. C. Ting (USA)
1977 John H. Van Vleck (USA)
     Philip W. Anderson (USA)
     Sir Nevill F. Mott (GB)
1978 Piotr Leontevich Kapitsa (USSR)
     Arno A. Penzias (USA) (German-born)
     Robert W. Wilson (USA)
1979 Abdus Salam (GB)
     Sheldon Glashow (USA)
     Steven Weinberg (USA)
1980 James Cronin (USA)
     Val Fitch (USA)

Ploughing

BRITISH NATIONAL PLOUGHING CHAMPIONSHIPS

The following list of British competitors in the World Ploughing Contest was supplied by the Society of Ploughmen, which was formed in 1951. From 1968, Britain's international representatives were also the winners and runners up of the British National Ploughing Championship. The winners from 1951, and location of contest:

1951 ⎱
1952 ⎰ Class Winners Only
1953 (Canada) Leslie Dixon and R. A. Hogg
1954 (Ireland) R. L. Roberts and Leslie Dixon
1955 (Sweden) E. J. Walker and T. C. Watkins
1956 (England) E. J. Walker and J. D. Lomas
1957 (USA) John Mason and R. J. Miller
1958 (Germany) T. L. Goodwin and John Dixon
1959 (N. Ireland) J. H. Nott and E. S. Davies
1960 (Italy) J. A. Gwilliam and H. R. Jones
1961 (France) W. T. Phillips and G. W. Hoskins
1962 (Holland) H. R. Jones and J. W. Sandford
1963 (Canada) L. J. Williams and D. W. J. Bonning

1964 (Austria) J. W. Cole and J. Mason
1965 (Norway) J. L. Nixon and D. W. J. Bonning
1966 (England) Robert Anderson and Raymond Goodwin
1967 (New Zealand) Raymond Goodwin and Philip Skyrme
1968 (Rhodesia) Robert Anderson and Ken Chappell
1969 (Yugoslavia) Gerald I. Smith and Geo. F. Allwood
1970 (Denmark) Raymond H. Robson and David Dick
1971 (England) J. J. Metcalfe and F. H. Millington
1972 (USA) J. B. Smith and Philip Skyrme
1973 (Ireland) J. Milnes and D. W. J. Bonning
1974 (Finland) L. F. Waudby and L. Iredale
1975 (Canada) Robert Anderson and V. E. Samuel
1976 (Sweden) J. T. Smith and Raymond Goodwin
1977 (Netherlands) J. T. Smith and David Chappell
1978 (West Germany) V. E. Samuel and C. T. W. Potter
1979 (N. Ireland) V. E. Samuel and F. H. Millington
1980 (New Zealand) T. R. Goodwin and V. E. Samuel

Poetry

POETS LAUREATE

The office of poet laureate is one of great honour, conferred on a poet of distinction. In 1616, James I granted a pension to the poet Ben Jonson, but it was not until 1668 that the laureateship was created as a royal office. When the position of poet laureate falls vacant, the prime minister is responsible for putting forth names for a new laureate, to be chosen by the sovereign. The sovereign then commands the Lord Chamberlain to appoint the poet laureate, and he does so by issuing a warrant to the laureate-elect. The Chamberlain also arranges for the appointment – for life – to be announced in the *London Gazette*.

John Dryden (1631–1700; laureate 1668–88)
Thomas Shadwell (1642?–92; laureate 1688–92)
Nahum Tate (1652–1715; laureate 1692–1715)
Nicholas Rowe (1674–1718; laureate 1715–18)
Laurence Eusden (1688–1730; laureate 1718–30)
Colley Cibber (1671–1757; laureate 1730–57)
William Whitehead (1715–85; laureate 1757–85)
　(Appointed after Thomas Gray declined the offer)
Thomas Warton (1728–90; laureate 1785–90)
Henry James Pye (1745–1813; laureate 1790–1813)
Robert Southey (1774–1843; laureate 1813–43)
William Wordsworth (1770–1850; laureate 1843–50)
Alfred, Lord Tennyson (1809–92; laureate 1850–92)
　(Appointed after Samuel Russell declined the offer)
Alfred Austin (1835–1913; laureate 1896–1913)

Robert Bridges (1844–1930; laureate 1913–30)
John Masefield (1878–1967; laureate 1930–67)
Cecil Day-Lewis (1904–72; laureate 1968–72)
Sir John Betjeman (1906–; laureate 1972–)

PULITZER PRIZE FOR POETRY

For further details see under main heading of Pulitzer Prizes.

1918 *Love Songs*, Sara Teasdale
1919 *Corn Huskers*, Carl Sandburg
　　 Old Road to Paradise, Margaret Widdemer
1920 No award
1921 No award
1922 *Collected Poems*, Edwin Arlington Robinson
1923 *The Ballad of the Harp-Weaver; A Few Figs from Thistles*; eight sonnets in *American Poetry, 1922, A Miscellany*, Edna St. Vincent Millay
1924 *New Hampshire: A Poem with Notes and Grace Notes*, Robert Frost
1925 *The Man Who Died Twice*, Edwin Arlington Robinson
1926 *What's O'Clock*, Amy Lowell
1927 *Fiddler's Farewell*, Leonora Speyer
1928 *Tristram*, Edwin Arlington Robinson
1929 *John Brown's Body*, Stephen Vincent Benet
1930 *Selected Poems*, Conrad Aiken
1931 *Collected Poems*, Robert Frost
1932 *The Flowering Stone*, George Dillon
1933 *Conquistador*, Archibald MacLeish

1934 *Collected Verse*, Robert Hillyer
1935 *Bright Ambush*, Audrey Wurdemann
1936 *Strange Holiness*, R. P. Tristram Coffin
1937 *A Further Range*, Robert Frost
1938 *Cold Morning Sky*, Marya Zaturenska
1939 *Selected Poems*, John Gould Fletcher
1940 *Collected Poems*, Mark Van Doren
1941 *Sunderland Capture*, Leonard Bacon
1942 *The Dust Which is God*, William Benet
1943 *A Witness Tree*, Robert Frost
1944 *Western Star,* Stephen Vincent Benet
1945 *V-Letter and Other Poems*, Karl Shapiro
1946 No award
1947 *Lord Weary's Castle*, Robert Lowell
1948 *The Age of Anxiety*, W. H. Auden
1949 *Terror and Decorum*, Peter Viereck
1950 *Annie Allen*, Gwendolyn Brooks
1951 *Complete Poems*, Carl Sandburg
1952 *Collected Poems*, Marianne Moore
1953 *Collected Poems 1917–1952,* Archibald MacLeish
1954 *The Waking*, Theodore Roethke
1955 *Collected Poems*, Wallace Stevens
1956 *Poems – North & South*, Elizabeth Bishop
1957 *Things of This World*, Richard Wilbur
1958 *Promises: Poems 1954–56,* Robert Penn Warren
1959 *Selected Poems 1928–1958*, Stanley Kunitz
1960 *Heart's Needle*, W. D. Snodgrass
1961 *Times Three: Selected Verse from Three Decades*, Phyllis McGinley
1962 *Poems*, Alan Dugan
1963 *Pictures from Breughel,* William Carlos Williams
1964 *At the End of the Open Road*, Louis Simpson
1965 *77 Dream Songs*, John Berryman
1966 *Selected Poems*, Richard Eberhart
1967 *Live or Die*, Anne Sexton
1968 *The Hard Hours*, Anthony Hecht
1969 *Of Being Numerous*, George Oppen
1970 *Untitled Subjects*, Richard Howard
1971 *The Carrier of Ladders*, W. S. Merwin
1972 *Collected Poems,* James Wright
1973 *Up Country,* Maxine Winokur Kumin
1974 *The Dolphin*, Robert Lowell
1975 *Turtle Island,* Gary Snyder
1976 *Self-Portrait in a Convex Mirror,* John Ashbery
1977 *Divine Comedies*, James Merrill

Robert Graves being presented with the Queen's Gold Medal for Poetry in 1968 (BBC copyright)

1978 *Collected Poems*, Howard Nemerov
1979 *Now and Then*, Robert Penn Warren
1980 *Selected Poems*, Donald Justice
1981 *The Morning of the Poem*, James Schuyler

QUEEN'S GOLD MEDAL FOR POETRY

This award, which was instituted in 1933 by King George V, at the suggestion of the Poet Laureate, John Masefield, is given from time to time for a book of verse.

1934 Laurence Whistler	1963 William Plomer
1936 W. H. Auden	1964 R. S. Thomas
1940 Michael Thwaites	1965 Philip Larkin
1952 Andrew Young	1967 Charles Causley
1953 Arthur Whaley	1968 Robert Graves
1954 Ralph Hodgson	1969 Stevie Smith
1955 Ruth Pitter	1970 Roy Fuller
1956 Edmund Blunden	1971 Stephen Spender
1957 Siegfried Sassoon	1973 John Heath-Stubbs
1959 Frances Cornford	1974 Ted Hughes
1960 John Betjeman	1977 Norman Nicholson
1962 Christopher Fry	

Popularity

Each year at the Madame Tussaud's wax museums in London and Amsterdam a questionnaire is handed out to visitors to discover their favourite heroes and heroines. Full lists are available from Madame Tussaud's, and recent London results appear below.

POLITICS

1978
1 Jimmy Carter
2 Margaret Thatcher
3 Sadat
  Churchill
5 Edward Heath

1979
1 Margaret Thatcher
2 Jimmy Carter
3 David Steel
4 Cyril Smith
5 J. F. Kennedy

1980
1 Margaret Thatcher

Left: *Margaret Thatcher with her wax portrait. She was voted second in the 'Most Hated and Feared' category in the 1980 Madame Tussaud's poll*

Below: *Wax portrait of Bjorn Borg, 'Sporting Favourite'*

2 Churchill
3 Michael Foot
Sir Harold Wilson
5 J. F. Kennedy

SPORTING FAVOURITES

1978
1 Muhammad Ali
2 Pele
3 Kevin Keegan
4 Bjorn Borg
5 Ilie Nastase

1979
1 Bjorn Borg
2 Muhammad Ali
3 Kevin Keegan
4 Pele
5 Sebastian Coe

1980
1 Bjorn Borg
2 Kevin Keegan

3 Muhammad Ali
4 Johan Cruyff
5 Geoffrey Boycott

ENTERTAINMENT

1978
1 Bruce Forsyth
2 Elton John
3 Charlie Chaplin
Liza Minnelli
5 Frank Sinatra

1979
1 Freddie Starr
2 Ronnie Barker
Kojak
Frank Sinatra
5 Elvis Presley

1980
1 Bruce Forsyth
2 Cliff Richard
3 Liza Minnelli
The Beatles
5 Elvis Presley

ARTS

1978
1 Picasso
2 Margot Fonteyn
3 Salvador Dali
Rembrandt
5 Nureyev

1979
1 Picasso
2 Margot Fonteyn
3 Salvador Dali
4 Constable
Van Gogh

1980
1 Picasso
2 Beethoven
Rembrandt
Shakespeare
5 Van Gogh

BEAUTY

1978
1 Sophia Loren

Marilyn Monroe
Elizabeth Taylor
4 Liza Minnelli
5 Raquel Welch

1979
1 Sophia Loren
2 Debbie Harry
3 Brigitte Bardot
4 Marilyn Monroe
5 Raquel Welch

1980
1 Sophia Loren
2 Marilyn Monroe
3 Debbie Harry
4 Brigitte Bardot
Bo Derek

HATE AND FEAR

1978
1 Hitler
2 General Amin
3 Margaret Thatcher
4 Dracula
5 Jack the Ripper

1979
1 Ayatollah Khomeini
2 General Amin
3 Hitler
4 Dracula
5 Yorkshire Ripper

1980
1 Hitler
2 Margaret Thatcher
3 General Amin
4 Ayatollah Khomeini
5 Yorkshire Ripper

HERO OR HEROINE IN MADAME TUSSAUD'S

1978
1 Agatha Christie
2 Kojak
3 Elton John
4 Elvis Presley
5 The Queen

1979
1 Kojak
  Elvis Presley
3 Bjorn Borg
4 Pope John Paul II
5 The Queen

1980
1 Tom Baker
2 Lord Carrington
  Liza Minnelli
4 Elvis Presley
5 Larry Hagman

HERO OR HEROINE OF ALL TIME

1978
1 Churchill
  Superman
3 Muhammad Ali
4 Nelson
  J. F. Kennedy

1979
1 Churchill
2 Joan of Arc
3 Lord Mountbatten
4 Nelson
5 Bjorn Borg

1980
1 Superman
2 Churchill
  Martin Luther King
4 Lord Mountbatten
5 John Lennon

Wax portrait of HM The Queen, 'Heroine in Madame Tussauds'

Powerboat Racing

DAILY EXPRESS INTERNATIONAL COWES–TORQUAY OFFSHORE POWERBOAT RACE
From 1968 held from Cowes to Torquay and back (199·1 miles/320·4 km)

	Boat	Pilot	Average speed	
			mph	km/h
1961	Thunderbolt	Tommy Sopwith (GB)	25	40
1962	Tramontana	Jeffrey Quill (GB)	37	60
1963	A'Speranzella	Renato Levi (Ita)	41	66
1964	Surfrider	Charles Gardner (GB)	49	79
1965	Brave Moppie	Dick Bertram (USA)	39	63
1966	Ghost Rider	Jim Wynne (USA)	41	66
1967	Surfury	Charles Gardner (GB)	53	85
1968	Telstar	Tommy Sopwith (GB)	38	61
1969	The Cigarette	Don Aronow (USA)	66·7	107·3
1970	Miss Enfield 2	Tommy Sopwith (GB)	58·5	94·1
1971	Lady Nara	Ronny Bonelli (Ita)	39	63
1972	Aeromarine IX	Carlo Bonomi (Ita)	55	88
1973	Unowot	Don Shead (GB)	62	100
1974	Dry Martini	Carlo Bonomi (Ita)	66·9	107·7
1975	Uno Embassy	Don Shead (GB)	72·86	117·26
1976	I Like It Too	Charles Gill (GB)	69·9	112·5
1977	Yellowdrama III	Ken Cassir (GB)	75·13	120·91
1978	Kaama	Betty Cook (USA)	77·42	124·59
1979	Dry Martini 2	Guido Nicolai (Ita)	63·71	102·54
1980	Satisfaction	Bill Elswick (USA)	79·8	128·42

Miss Enfield II, *driven by Tommy Sopwith – the winner of the 1970* Daily Express *Power Boat Race*

BRITISH INTERNATIONAL (OR HARMSWORTH) TROPHY FOR MOTORBOATS

	Nationality	Boat	Venue	Speed mph	km/h
1903	England	*Napier I*	Queenstown, Ireland	19·53	31·43
1904	France	*Trefle-A-Quatre*	Solent, England	26·63	42·86
1905	England	Napier II	Arachon, France	26·03	41·89
1906	England	*Yarrow-Napier*	Solent, England	15·48	24·91
1907	USA	*Dixie I*	Solent, England	31·78	51·14
1908	USA	*Dixie II*	Huntington Bay, NY	31·35	50·45
1910	USA	*Dixie III*	Huntington Bay, NY	36·04	58·00
1911	USA	*Dixie IV*	Huntington Bay, NY	40·28	64·82
1912	England	*Maple Leaf IV*	Huntington Bay, NY	43·18	69·49
1913	England	*Maple Leaf IV*	Osborne Bay, England	57·45	92·46
1920	USA	*Miss America I*	Osborne Bay, England	61·51	98·99
1921	USA	*Miss America II*	Detroit River	59·75	96·16
1926	USA	*Miss America V*	Detroit River	61·118	98·359
1928	USA	*Miss America VII*	Detroit River	59·325	95·474
1929	USA	*Miss America VIII*	Detroit River	75·287	121·163
1930	USA	*Miss America IX*	Detroit River	77·233	124·294
1931	USA	*Miss America VIII*	Detroit River	85·861	138·180
1932	USA	*Miss America X*	Lake St Clair	78·489	126·315
1933	USA	*Miss America X*	St Clair River	86·939	139·915
1949	USA	*Skip-A-Long*	Detroit River	94·285	151·737
1950	USA	*Slo-Mo-Shun IV*	Detroit River	100·680	162·029
1956	USA	*Shanty I*	Detroit River	89·750	144·439
1959	Canada	*Miss Supertest III*	Detroit River	99·789	160·595
1960	Canada	*Miss Supertest III*	Lake Ontario, Canada	115·483	185·852
1961	Canada	*Miss Supertest III*	Lake Ontario, Canada	98·218	158·066

After a lapse of some 15 years, the rules of this Trophy were re-written and it became known as

THE HARMSWORTH BRITISH & COMMONWEALTH TROPHY FOR MOTORBOATS

1977	England	*Limit-Up*	Michael Doxford and Tim Powell
1978	England	*Limit-Up*	Michael Doxford and Tim Powell
1979	England	*Uno-Mint-Jewellery*	Derek Pobjoy
1980	USA	*Satisfaction*	Bill Elswick

The most wins: 8 Commodore Garfield A. Wood 1920–21, 1926, 1928, 1929, 1930, 1932 and 1933. The only boat to win three times: *Miss Supertest III* (1959–61) owned by James G. Thompson (Can).

AMERICAN POWER BOAT ASSOCIATION GOLD CHALLENGE CUP
Instituted in 1903 and contested annually. Winners since 1970:

	Boat	Pilot	Average speed of fastest heat mph	km/h
1970	Miss Budweiser	Dean Chenoweth	101·848	163·908
1971	Miss Madison	Jim McCormick	101·522	163·384
1972	Atlas Van Lines	Bill Muncey	103·547	166·643
1973	Miss Budweiser	Dean Chenoweth	104·046	167·446
1974	Pay'N Pak	George Henley	112·056	180·337
1975	Pay'N Pak	George Henley	113·350	182·419
1976	Miss US	Tom d'Eath	108·021	173·843
1977	Atlas Van Lines	Bill Muncey	114·849	184·832
1978	Atlas Van Lines	Bill Muncey	104·448	167·330
1979	Atlas Van Lines	Bill Muncey	107·892	173·631
1980	Miss Budweiser	Dean Chenoweth	117·391	188·922

Most wins: 8 Bill Muncey (1956–7, 1961–2, 1972, 1977–79)
5 Garfield Wood (1917–21)

Publishing

PUBLISHER OF THE YEAR
The Booksellers' Association instituted this annual award in 1979. The winner is chosen through a poll of the Association's members, who are asked to nominate candidates for the award on the basis of four criteria: editorial quality, terms and conditions, distribution (including accuracy of invoicing, returns policy, etc.), and promotion and publicity.

1979 Thames & Hudson
1980 Chatto, Bodley Head and Cape Services
1981 Chatto, Bodley Head and Cape Services

THE ODDEST TITLE
Founded in 1978 the Diagram Group Prize is awarded to the oddest title spotted at the Frankfurt Book Fair. The prize is awarded to the person who submits the entry which, in the opinion of the editor of The Bookseller, 'most outrageously exceeds all bounds of credibility'.

1978 Proceedings of the Second International Workshop on Nude Mice, University of Tokyo Press
1979 The Madam as Entrepreneur: Career Management in House Prostitution, Transaction Press
1980 The Joy of Chickens, Prentice-Hall

Pubs

THE NEW STANDARD PUB OF THE YEAR
The London Evening Standard, now The New Standard, has organised this annual competition since 1967 to find the best pub in London. The judges are sent to inspect all the pubs nominated by readers, and the winning landlord, his wife and the nominator all get a free holiday.

1967 The Red Lion, Brentford (Fullers)
     The White Hart, Newenden (Courage)
1968 The Jolly Millers, Bexleyheath (Charrington)
     The Swan, West Peckham (Courage)
1969 The White Lion, Selling (Shepherd Neame)
1970 The Rose and Crown, Wimbledon (Youngs)
1971 Duke of Cumberland, Parsons Green (Youngs)
1972 The Victoria, Bermondsey (Trumans)

1973 Pied Bull, Streatham (Youngs)
1974 Flask, Highgate (Ind Coope)
1975 Greyhound, Kensington Square (Watneys)
1976 Orange Tree, Richmond (Youngs)
1977 The Angel, Bermondsey (Courage)
     (River Pub of the Year – Jubilee Year)
1978 The Old Ship, Hammersmith (Watneys)
1979 Royal Oak, New Malden (Ind Coope)
1980 The Rose of York, Richmond (Sam Smith)

EGON RONAY PUB OF THE YEAR
This annual award in Britain for the best pub is given by the gourmet and critic, Egon Ronay. The award is made to the pub which combines a high standard of food and good accommodation with a warm, welcoming atmosphere. The winner receives and keeps for a year an

engraved Pewter Plate. Winners since inception:

1980 The Fox, Ansty, Dorset, Wendy and Peter Amey
1981 The Greyhound Inn, Staple Fitzpaine, Somerset, Miriam and Christopher Goss

The Greyhound Inn, 1981 Egon Ronay Pub of the Year

Pulitzer Prizes

The Pulitzer prizes are the most prestigious awards made each year in the United States for journalism, literature, and music. The prizes are established under the terms of the will of Joseph Pulitzer (1847–1911), a Hungarian immigrant who in 1878 founded one of America's great newspapers, the *St. Louis Post-Dispatch*, and then in 1883 purchased New York City's *The World*, making it into a crusading newspaper with the largest circulation in the United States.

Upon his death in 1911, Pulitzer left $2 million to found a graduate school of journalism at Columbia University in New York City with the provision that after the school had op-

erated for at least three years prizes should be awarded annually for the advancement of journalism, literature, music, and public service. The Columbia University School of Journalism was founded in 1912. The first Pulitzer Prizes began to be awarded in 1917.

Each prize carries an award of $1000 except for the gold medal award to a newspaper for meritorious public service.

Prizes in journalism are awarded in 11 categories. Prizes in literature, drama, and music are awarded in seven areas. In addition, special awards are made from time to time. (For further details see entries under Drama, Journalism, Literature, Music and Poetry.)

Quiz

BRAIN OF BRITAIN
BBC Radio organises this annual nationwide general knowledge quiz. The winners have been:

1953–54 Martin Dakin
1955 Arthur Maddocks
1956 Anthony Carr
1957 Rosemary Watson
1958 David Keys
1959 Dr Reginald Webster
1960 Patrick Bowles
1961 Irene Thomas
1962 Henry Button
1963 Ian Barton
1964 Ian Gillies
1965 Robert Crampsey
1966 Richard Best
1967 Lieut.-Commander Julian Loring
1968 Ralph Raby
1969 T. D. Thomson
1970 Iain Matheson
1971 Fred Morgan
1972 Aubrey Lawrence
1973 Dr Glyn Court

1974 Dr Roger Pritchard
1975 Winifred Lawson
1976 Thomas Dyer
1977 Martin Costelow
1978 James Nesbitt
1979 Arthur Gerard
1980 Tim Paxton

BRAIN OF BRAINS
This is competed for every three years.

1956 Anthony Carr
1959 Dr Reginald Webster
1962 Irene Thomas
1965 Ian Gillies
1968 Ralph Raby
1971 Iain Matheson
1974 Dr Roger Pritchard
1977 Thomas Dyer
1980 James Nesbitt

THE NEW STANDARD BRAIN OF LONDON
This was introduced in the *Evening News* (*The*

New Standard from 1980) in 1973. Readers are asked to solve problems which call for common sense, imagination and a little determination, rather than a vast store of knowledge. The questions, published daily for a week – some simple, some a little harder – are devised by MENSA, the high-IQ organisation. The 50 readers who give the best performance in answering the questions are invited to the final and the winner receives a cheque for £500. The winners have been:

1973 Colin Williams, telecommunications engineer
1974 Janet Langmaid, librarian
1975 Michael Davies, student
1976 Alan Deas, insurance inspector
1977 Paul Light, trainee accountant
1978 Richard Saunders, computer programmer
1979 Michael Jarrard, teacher
1980 Richard Ellis, systems analyst

BRAIN OF SPORT

'Brain of Sport' is transmitted on BBC Radio 2, and the first competition in the series was held in 1975.

The competition is open to anyone in the UK over the age of 16. All applicants are required to take part in an eliminating test and the 24 contestants with the highest marks take part in the quiz.

The 'Brain of Sport' since the start of the programmes has been as follows:

1975 Patricia Arthur
1976 Paul Hewett
1977 David Ball
1978 Julian Pincher
1979 Tony Shaw
1980 Arthur Palfreyman

MASTERMIND

This competition has been organised each year since 1972 by BBC Television. The entrants answer detailed questions on a special subject of their own choice, and then face further questions on general knowledge. If unsure of an answer the competitor may 'pass', rather than lose time whilst the compère Magnus Magnusson corrects a mistake. The top scorers in each round go forward to the semi-finals and finals, and the eventual winner is awarded the Mastermind trophy. Winners, with their special subjects in the final:

1972 Nancy Wilkinson, History of Music, 1550–1900
1973 Patricia Owen, Byzantine Art
1974 Elizabeth Horrocks, The Detective Stories of Dorothy L. Sayers
1975 John Hart, Athens in 5th Century BC
1976 Roger Pritchard, Life of the Duke of Wellington
1977 Sir David Hunt, The Roman Revolution, 60 BC – AD 14

Winifred Lawson, 1975 winner of the Brain of Britain contest (BBC copyright)

Fred Housego, taxi driver, winner of the 1980 Mastermind series (BBC copyright)

1978 Rosemary James, Mythology of the Greeks and Romans
1979 Philip Jenkins, History of Wales, 400–1100
1980 Fred Housego, The Tower of London

MASTERMIND INTERNATIONAL

Copies of the British competition have spread to many countries, and all the winners take part in an international championship which is held in the Old Library, Guildhall, London.

1979

Winner: John Mulcahy (Ire), Irish History, 1916–22
Other contestants: John Bond (Aus), Barbara Eddy (Can), Mark Allan (NZ), Godwin Anaba (Nig), Rosemary James (UK), Sir David Hunt (UK)

1980

Winner: Rachel Stewart (Aus), Life and Times of Julius Caesar
Other contestants: Gina Barreca (USA), Ehud Fuchs (Isr), Gerrit Jan Korteling (Net), Lewis Clohessy (Ire), Paul Bowden (NZ), Philip Jenkins (UK)

TOP OF THE FORM

One of BBC Radio's long-established and popular annual competitions for teams of children representing secondary schools throughout the country. The teams, each made up of four members with ages ranging from 11 to 18, are tested on general knowledge. The winners have been:

1948 Royal High School, Edinburgh
1949 Elgin Academy, Scotland
1950 Robert Gordon's College, Aberdeen
1951 Morgan Academy, Dundee
1952 Bangor Grammar School, North Wales
1953 Nicholson Institute, Stornoway
1954 Grove Park School, Wrexham
1955 Newtown Girls' County Grammar School, Wales
1956 Sutton Coldfield High School
1957 Wycombe High School for Girls, High Wycombe
1958 Gordon Schools, Huntly, Aberdeenshire
1959 Mackie Academy, Stonehaven, Kincardine
1960 Grove Park Grammar School for Girls, Wrexham
1961 Archbishop Holgate's Grammar School, York

1962 Hull Grammar School
1963 Cambridge High School for Boys, Cambridge
1964 The Academy, Montrose
1965 The High School, Falkirk
1966 St Martin-in-the-Fields High School, London
1967 Greenock Academy
1968 Grove Park School, Wrexham
1969 Queen Elizabeth Grammar School for Girls, Carmarthen
1970 Wyggeston Boys' School, Leicester
1971 Cheadle Hulme School, Cheadle, Cheshire
1972 The County Girls' Grammar School, Newbury
1973 Kirkcudbright Academy, Kirkcudbright
1974 The Grammar School, Cheltenham
1975 King William's College, Isle of Man
1976 County High School for Girls, Macclesfield
1977 Wellington School, Somerset
1978 Brinkburn School, Hartlepool
1979 Chislehurst and Sidcup Grammar School, Kent
1980 Wycombe High School for Girls, High Wycombe

UNIVERSITY CHALLENGE

Granada Television has organised since 1964 this competition between teams from British universities, which calls for a very detailed and wide general knowledge and speed in answering the questions put by compère, Bamber Gascoigne. Each year there is a final knock-out competition between all the teams who have won three games. The winners are:

1964 Leicester University
1965 New College, Oxford
1966 Oriel College, Oxford
1967 University of Sussex
1968 Keble College, Oxford
1969 University of Sussex
1970 Churchill College Cambridge
1971 Sidney Sussex College, Cambridge
1972 University College, Oxford
1973 Fitzwilliam College, Cambridge
1974 Trinity College, Cambridge
1975 Keble College, Oxford
1976 University College, Oxford
1977 University of Durham
1978 Sidney Sussex College, Cambridge
1979 Bradford University
1980 Merton College, Oxford

Merton College, Oxford – 1980 University Challenge winning team (BBC copyright)

Rackets

WORLD CHAMPIONSHIPS
The first recognised world champion was Robert Mackay in 1820, since when champions have been:

1820 Robert Mackay (GB)
1825–34 Thomas Pittman (GB)
1834–38 John Pittman (GB)
1838–46 John Lamb (GB)
1846–60 L. C. Mitchell (GB)
1860 Francis Erwood (GB)
1860–63 Sir William Hart-Dyke (GB)
1863–66 Henry Gray (GB)

1866–75 William Gray (GB)
1876–77 H. B. Fairs (GB)
1878–87 Joseph Gray (GB)
1887–1902 Peter Latham (GB)
1903–11 J. Jamsetji (Ind)
1911–14 Charles Williams (GB)
1914–28 Jock Souter (USA)
1928–35 Charles Williams (GB)
1937–47 David Milford (GB)
1947–52 James Dear (GB)
1952–71 Geoffrey Atkins (GB)
1972– William Surtees (USA)

Radio

THE SOCIETY OF AUTHORS' PYE RADIO AWARDS
Founded in 1975 by Imperial Tobacco in conjunction with the Association of Radio Writers of the Society of Authors, these awards are given annually. They are open to anyone working in radio. As from 1979 the sponsorship and name were changed to the Society of Authors' Pye Radio Awards. A selection of these awards is as follows:

BEST ACTOR OF THE YEAR
1975–76 Nigel Anthony, Oscar
1977 Colin Blakely, Judgement, BBC Radio 3
1978 Dennis Quilley, Peer Gynt, BBC Radio 3
1979 David Suchet, The Kreutzer Sonata, BBC World Service
1980 Norman Rodway and Warren Mitchell, Faith Healer, BBC Radio 3

BEST ACTRESS OF THE YEAR
1975–76 Beatrix Lehmann, Hecuba
1977 Rosemary Leach, Moonshine, BBC Radio 4
1978 Sarah Badel, A Moon for the Misbegotten, BBC Radio 3
1979 Maureen O'Brien, By Grand Central Station I Sat Down and Wept, BBC Radio 3
1980 Yvonne Bryceland, Boesman and Lena, BBC Radio 3

DOCUMENTARY FEATURE OF THE YEAR
1975–76 Peter Everett, The Cookham Resurrection
1977 Desmond Briscoe, A Wall Walks Slowly, BBC Radio 3
1978 Chris Bryer and John Smithson, If the Bombs Dropped Now, Piccadilly Radio
1979 John Theocharis, Spring of Memory, BBC Radio 3
1980 Kevin d'Arcy, Right to Work, Radio Orwell

TALKS OF THE YEAR
1975–76 Madeau Stewart, Interval Talk Introducing Movements in Sound
1977 Ray Gosling, Battle for the Slums, BBC Radio 3

1978 John Barrett and Dilys Breese, Elephants Can Tell Jokes, BBC Radio 4
1979 Arthur Good and Arthur Berry, Lament for the Lost Pubs of Burslem, Radio Stoke
1980 Michael Elkins, A Jew at Christmas, BBC Radio 4

LOCAL RADIO OF THE YEAR
1977 Robin Hall, The Singing Streets, Radio Clyde
1978 Hazel Fowlie and Andrew Monaghan, The Lanthorn, Radio Forth
1979 No award
1980 Tony Cartledge and Jackie France, Go Freight, Metro Radio

OUTSTANDING RADIO PRODUCTION OR DIRECTION OF THE YEAR
1975–76 Richard Wortley, The Cookham Resurrection, and One Day in Summer in a Garden
1977 Desmond Briscoe, A Wall Walks Slowly, BBC Radio 3
1978 No award
1979 David Spenser, Strands, BBC Radio 3
1980 David Spenser, Equus, BBC Radio 4

DRAMATISED FEATURE OF THE YEAR
1977 Inez Heron, When Trees Were Green, BBC Radio 4
1978 Gerald Frow, Beau Brummell, Prince of Dandies, BBC Radio 4
1979 Angela Cater, Come Unto These Yellow Sands, BBC Radio 3
1980 Alan Haydock, Dunkirk 1940, BBC Radio 4

BEST RADIO COMEDY SCRIPT
1979 John Howard and Derek Graham, That Was the West That Was, Radio Bristol
1980 Week Ending, BBC Radio 4

DRAMA ADAPTATION OF THE YEAR
1975–76 Desmond Hawkins, The Return of the Native
1977 Malcolm Clarke, August 2026, BBC Radio 4
1978 Desmond Hawkins, The Woodlanders, BBC Radio 4
1979 Tom McGrath, The Hardman, Radio Scotland

185

1980 Denys Hawthorne, How Many Miles to Babylon?, BBC Radio 4

DRAMA ORIGINAL OF THE YEAR
1975–76 Don Howarth, On a Day in Summer in a Garden
1977 Philip Martin, Dead Soldiers, BBC Radio 3
1978 Peter Redgrove, The God of Glass, BBC Radio 3
1979 Shirley Gee, Typhoid Mary, BBC Radio 4
1980 Catherine Lucy Czerkawska, O Flower of Scotland, Radio Scotland

SPORTS PERSONALITY OF THE YEAR
1979 Freddie Trueman, Test Match Specials, BBC
1980 John Arlott, Cricket Commentary Team, BBC Radio 3

RADIO PERSONALITY OF THE YEAR
1979 Roger Cook, Checkpoint, BBC Radio 4
1980 Terry Wogan

MOST OUTSTANDING CONTRIBUTION TO RADIO
1979 Henry Reed, poet, playwright and critic
1980 Alfred Bradley

PROGRAMME OR SERIES OF PROGRAMMES FOR YOUNG LISTENERS
1980 Douglas Adams, Hitchhiker's Guide to the Galaxy, BBC Radio 4

TELEVISION AND RADIO INDUSTRIES CLUB AWARDS
These awards are decided by the membership of the club which is composed of representatives of firms involved in the television and audio equipment industry. Recent prizewinners include:

RADIO PERSONALITY OF THE YEAR
1972 John Dunn
1973 Pete Murray
1974 Robert Robinson
1975 Terry Wogan
1976 Pete Murray
1977 Terry Wogan
1978 Terry Wogan
1979 Terry Wogan
1980 Kenny Everett

RADIO PROGRAMME OF THE YEAR
1972 Today, BBC Radio 4
1973 Today, BBC Radio 4
1974 Today, BBC Radio 4
1975 Today, BBC Radio 4
1976 The World At One, BBC Radio 4
1977 Today, BBC Radio 4
1978 Noel Edmonds' Breakfast Show, BBC Radio 1
1979 The World At One, BBC Radio 4
1980 Desert Island Discs, BBC Radio 4

Terry Wogan (below left) *and Noel Edmonds* (below right) *recipients of Television and Radio Industries Club Awards*

Railways

LONDON TRANSPORT'S TOP STATIONS AND UNDERGROUND PROFICIENCY AWARDS

London Transport Underground stations are given awards annually for their proficiency and general high standards.

In addition to marks for the standard of service to the public, account is taken of commendations to staff from passengers, economy in the use of stores, and the condition of equipment. Marks are deducted for public complaints and for delays caused by the actions of station staff.

All station staff at winning stations receive a small cash payment, and a framed certificate is displayed in the station booking hall for a year. The award-winning stations since 1977 are:

1977
Acton Town
Becontree
Belsize Park
Eastcote
Golders Green
Hanger Lane
Holland Park
Leyton
Northwood Hills
Osterley
Paddington (Metropolitan Line)
Royal Oak
Upney
Victoria
Walthamstow Central

1978
Burnt Oak
Chancery Lane
East Acton
Edgware
Finsbury Park
Heathrow Central
Moor Park
Russell Square
St John's Wood
St Paul's
Stepney Green
Trafalgar Square
Walthamstow Central
Willesden Green
Wood Green

1979
Aldgate
Angel
Bond Street
Brent Cross
Finsbury Park
Goodge Street
Harrow-on-the Hill
Hounslow Central
North Harrow
Oxford Circus
Park Royal
Roding Valley
St John's Wood
St Paul's
Wood Green

1980
Bond Street
Cannon Street
Eastcote
High Barnet
Hyde Park Corner
Latimer Road
North Weald
Roding Valley
Ruislip
Totteridge
Victoria
Warren Street
Westbourne Park
West Kensington
Wood Green

BEST UNDERGROUND STATION GARDEN
1977 Devdatt Sethi, Rayners Lane Station
1978 Fred Pearce, Totteridge
1979 Colin Whitehead and Donald Mapp, Hainault (West Bound Platform Garden)
1980 George Hillier, Ratilal Shah and Dennis Cleveland, Sudbury Town

RAILWAY PRESERVATION SOCIETY'S ANNUAL AWARD
This is made to a member Group making an outstanding contribution to voluntary railway preservation during the year of the Award.

The awards have been made to:

1975 Great Western Society Ltd.
1976 Princess Elizabeth Locomotive Society
1977 Peterborough Railway Society Ltd. (Nene Valley Railway)
1978 Ffestiniog Railway Society
1979 Severn Valley Railway Co. Ltd.
1980 Scottish Railway Preservation Society

Colin Whitehead and Donald Mapp took the Best Underground Station award in 1979 for Hainault station

STEAM PRESERVATION
Best Preserved Station in Britain

This competition is sponsored by Travel Britain Company and Ian Allen Ltd and the first award was presented by Sir Peter Parker in January 1979 to a 'beautifully restored and maintained genuine Midland Railway Station – complete in every detail, including gas lamps, fire bucket notices etc.'

1979 Oakworth, Keighley and Worth Valley Railway
1980 Staverton Bridge, Dart Valley Railway

Oakworth station on the Keighley and Worth Valley Railway, 1979 Best Preserved Station in Britain

Rallying

MONTE CARLO RALLY

The world's most famous car rally event is held annually, the drivers converging on Monte Carlo from all over Europe. Winners:

MONTE CARLO RALLY

1911 Henri Rougier, Turcat-Mery 25hp
1912 J. Beutler, Berliet 16hp
1924 Jean Ledure, Bignan 2 litre
1925 Francois Repusseau, Renault 40 CV
1926 Hon Victor Bruce, AC Bristol
1927 M. Lefebvre, Amilcar 1100cc
1928 Jacques Bignan, Fiat 990cc
1929 Dr Sprenger Van Eijk, Graham-Paige 4·7 litre
1930 Hector Petit, Licorne 904cc
1931 Donald Healey, Invicta 4·5 litre
1932 M. Vasselle, Hotchkiss 2·5 litre

World champion Bjorn Waldegard and co-driver Hans Thorzelius in their Ford Escort in the 1977 Lombard RAC rally

1933 M. Vasselle, Hotchkiss 3·5 litre
1934 M. Gas, Hotchkiss 3·5 litre
1935 Christian Lahaye, Renault Nervasport 5·6 litre
1936 I. Zamfirescu, Ford 3·6 litre
1937 René le Begue, Delahaye 3·6 litre
1938 Bakker Schut, Ford 3·6 litre
1939 { Jean Trevoux, Hotchkiss 3·5 litre
      { M. Paul, Delahaye 3·6 litre
1949 Jean Trevoux, Hotchkiss 3·5 litre
1950 Marcel Becquart, Hotchkiss 3·5 litre
1951 Jean Trevoux, Delahaye 4·6 litre
1952 Sidney Allard, Allard P2 4·4 litre
1953 Maurice Gatsonides, Ford Zephyr 2·3 litre
1954 Louis Chiron, Lancia-Aurelia 2·5 litre
1955 Per Malling, Sunbeam-Talbot 2·3 litre
1956 Ronnie Adams, Jaguar Mk VII 3·4 litre
1957 Not held (Suez Crisis)
1958 Guy Monraisse, Renault Dauphine 845cc
1959 Paul Coltelloni, Citroen ID 19 1·9 litre
1960 Walter Schock, Mercedes 220 SE
1961 Maurice Martin, Panhard PL17 848cc
1962 Erik Carlsson/Gunnar Haggbom, Saab 96 848cc
1963 Erik Carlsson/Gunnar Palm, Saab 96 848cc
1964 Paddy Hopkirk/Henry Liddon, Mini-Cooper 'S' 1071cc
1965 Timo Makinen/Paul Easter, Mini-Cooper 'S' 1275cc
1966 Pauli Toivonen/Ensio Mikander, Citroen DS21
1967 Rauno Aaltonen/Henry Liddon, Mini-Cooper 'S' 1275cc
1968 Vic Elford/David Stone, Porsche 911T
1969 Bjorn Waldegaard/Lars Helmer, Porsche 911
1970 Bjorn Waldegaard/Lars Helmer, Porsche 911 S
1971 Ove Andersson/David Stone, Alpine Renault A110

1972 Sandro Munari/Mario Manucci, Lancia Fulvia 1.6
1973 Jean-Claude Andruet/'Biche', Alpine Renault A110
1974 Not held (fuel crisis)
1975 Sandro Munari/Mario Manucci, Lancia Stratos
1976 Sandro Munari/Silvio Maiga, Lancia Stratos
1977 Sandro Munari/Mario Manucci, Lancia Stratos
1978 Jean-Pierre Nicolas/Vincent Laverne, Porsche Carrera
1979 Bernard Darniche/Alain Mahe, Lancia Stratos
1980 Walter Rohrl/Christian Geistdorfer, Fiat 131 Abarth
1981 Jean Ragnotti/Jean-Marc Andrié, Renault 5 Turbo

(Co-drivers names included after 1962 when special stages and pace notes used for first time)

WORLD RALLYING CHAMPIONSHIPS

For makes of car. Winners since inception:

1968 Ford GB
1969 Ford Europe
1970 Porsche
1971 Renault Alpine
1972 Lancia
1973 Renault Alpine
1974 Lancia
1975 Lancia
1976 Lancia
1977 Fiat
1978 Fiat
1979 Ford
1980 Fiat

THE SAFARI RALLY

The first event was held in 1953 as the Coronation Safari in Kenya, Tanzania and Uganda, when it was won by Alan Dix in a Volkswagen. It has since been held annually. The name was changed in 1960 to the East African Safari Rally, but since 1974 has been confined within Kenya. In 1970 the event was included for the first time in the International (now World) Rallying Championship. Winners since 1970 (leading driver only named):

1970 Edgar Herrmann (Ger), Datsun 1600 SSS
1971 Edgar Herrmann (Ger), Datsun 2402
1972 Hannu Mikkola (Fin), Ford Escort
1973 Shekhar Mehta (Uga), Datsun 250Z
1974 Joginder Singh (Ken), Colt Galant 1600
1975 Ove Andersson (Swe), Peugeot 504
1976 Joginder Singh (Ken), Mitsubishi Lancer
1977 Bjorn Waldegaard (Swe), Ford Escort
1978 Jean-Pierre Nicolas (Fra), Peugeot 504
1979 Shekhar Mehta (Uga), Datsun 160J
1980 Shekhar Mehta (Uga), Datsun 160J

Most wins: 3 Joginder Singh (Ken) 1965, 1974, 1976; 3 Shekhar Mehta (Uga) 1973, 1979, 1980

RAC INTERNATIONAL RALLY OF GREAT BRITAIN

The first RAC rally was held in 1932, and in 1951 this event was recognised by the Fédér-

Hannu Mikkola with his co-driver Arne Hertz, winners of the 1979 Lombard RAC rally

ation International de l'Automobile as of international status. Since then the winning drivers and cars have been:

1951 Ian Appleyard (GB), Jaguar XK
1952 Goff Imhof (GB), Cadillac-Allard
1953 Ian Appleyard (GB), Jaguar XK
1954 Johnny Wallwork (GB), Triumph
1955 Jimmy Ray (GB), Standard
1956 Lyndon Sims (GB), Aston-Martin
1957 Not held (petrol rationing)
1958 Peter Harper (GB), Sunbeam Rapier
1959 Gerry Burgess (GB), Ford Zephyr
1960 Erik Carlsson (Swe), Saab 96
1961 Erik Carlsson (Swe), Saab 96
1962 Erik Carlsson (Swe), Saab 96
1963 Tom Trana (Swe), Volvo PV 544
1964 Tom Trana (Swe), Volvo 122 S
1965 Rauno Aaltonen (Fin), Mini Cooper S 1275
1966 Bengt Soderstrom (Swe), Ford Cortina Lotus
1967 Not held (foot and mouth epidemic)
1968 Simo Lampinen (Fin), Saab 96 V4
1969 Harry Kallström (Fin), Lancia Fulvia
1970 Harry Kallström (Fin), Lancia Fulvia
1971 Stig Blomqvist (Swe), Saab 96 V4
1972 Roger Clark (GB), Ford Escort
1973 Timo Mäkinen (Fin), Ford Escort
1974 Timo Mäkinen (Fin), Ford Escort
1975 Timo Mäkinen (Fin), Ford Escort
1976 Roger Clark (GB), Ford Escort
1977 Bjorn Waldegaard (Swe), Ford Escort
1978 Hannu Mikkola (Fin), Ford Escort
1979 Hannu Mikkola (Fin), Ford Escort
1980 Henri Toivonen (Fin), Talbot Sunbeam Lotus

Real Tennis

WORLD CHAMPIONSHIPS
The list of world champions at real tennis extends further back than just about any sport – it begins with Clergé of France in 1740. Since then:

The Basque Pierre Etchebaster, world tennis champion from 1928 to 1952

1765–85 Raymond Masson (Fra)
1785–1816 Joseph Barcellon (Fra)
1816–19 Marchesio (Ita)
1819–29 Philip Cox (GB)
1829–62 Edmond Barre (Fra)
1862–71 Edmund Tomkins (GB)
1871–85 George Lambert (GB)
1885–90 Tom Pettitt (USA)
1890–95 Charles Saunders (GB)
1895–1905 Peter Latham (GB)
1905–07 Cecil Fairs (GB)
1907–08 Peter Latham (GB)
1908–12 Cecil Fairs (GB)
1912–14 George Covey (GB)
1914–16 Jay Gould (USA)
1916–28 George Covey (GB)
1928–55 Pierre Etchebaster (Fra)
1955–57 James Dear (GB)
1957–59 Albert Johnson (GB)
1959–69 Northrup Knox (USA)
1969–72 George 'Pete' Bostwick (USA)
1972–75 Jimmy Bostwick (USA)
1976–80 Howard Angus (GB)
1981– Christopher Ronaldson (GB)

Restaurants

EGON RONAY RESTAURANT OF THE YEAR
This annual award in Britain for the best restaurant is given by the gourmet and critic, Egon Ronay. The award is made to the restaurant whose consistent excellence or enterprise is found to be outstanding. The winner receives, and keeps for a year, an engraved Gold Plate. Winners since inception:

1969 Thornbury Castle, Thornbury (Avon)
1970 Le Poulbot, London EC2
1971 Box Tree Cottage, Ilkley (West Yorkshire)
1972 Le Gavroche, London SW1
1973 Kildwick Hall, Kildwick (West Yorkshire)
1974 Shezan, London SW7
1975 Wilton's, London SW1
1976 Horn of Plenty, Gulworthy (Devon)
1977 Carrier's, London N1
1978 McCoy's, Staddle Bridge (North Yorkshire)
1979 Les Quat' Saisons, Oxford
1980 Sharrow Bay Country House Hotel Restaurant, Ullswater (Cumbria)

Roller Skating

WORLD CHAMPIONSHIPS
World championships were first held in 1947. Just as in ice skating both speed skating and figure skating events are held. Winners since 1972:

FIGURE SKATING
MEN
1972 Michael Obrecht (Ger)
1973 Randy Dayney (USA)
1974 Michael Obrecht (Ger)
1975 Leonardo Lienhard (Swi)
1976 Thomas Nieder (Ger)
1977 Thomas Nieder (Ger)
1978 Thomas Nieder (Ger)
1979 Michael Butzke (GDR)
1980 Michael Butzke (GDR)

Most wins: 5 Karl-Heinz Losch (Ger) 1958, 1959, 1961, 1962, 1966

WOMEN
1972 Petra Hausler (Ger)
1973 Sigrid Mullenbach (Ger)
1974 Sigrid Mullenbach (Ger)
1975 Sigrid Mullenbach (Ger)
1976 Natalie Dunn (USA)
1977 Natalie Dunn (USA)
1978 Natalie Dunn (USA)
1979 Petra Schneider (GDR)
1980 Petra Ernert (née Schneider) (GDR)

Most wins: 4 Astrid Bader (Ger) 1965–68

Pairs
1972 Ronald Robovitsky and Gail Robovitsky (USA)
1973 Louis Stovel and Vicki Handyside (USA)
1974 Ron Sabo and Susan McDonald (USA)
1975 Ron Sabo and Darlene Waters(USA)
1976 Ron Sabo and Darlene Waters (USA)
1977 Ray Chapatta and Karen Mejia (USA)
1978 Pat Jones and Rooie Coleman (USA)
1979 Ray Chapatta and Karen Mejia (USA)
1980 Paul Price and Tina Kneisley (USA)

Most wins: 3 Dieter Fingerle and Ute Keller (Ger) 1965–67 (Fingerle also won in 1959 with S. Schneider)

Dance
1972 Tom Straker and Bonnie Lambert (USA)
1973 James Stephens and Jane Puracchio (USA)
1974 Udo Donsdorf and Christine Henke (Ger)
1975 Kerry Cavazzi and Jane Puracchio (USA)
1976 Kerry Cavazzi and Jane Puracchio (USA)
1977 Dan Littel and Fleurette Arsenault (USA)
1978 Dan Littel and Fleurette Arsenault (USA)
1979 Dan Littel and Fleurette Arsenault (USA)

The world roller skating pairs ceremony of 1978 (Keystone)

1980 Torsten Carels and Gabriele Achenbach (GDR)

Rowing

WORLD CHAMPIONSHIPS
World championships were first held in 1962 at Lucerne and have subsequently been held in 1966, 1970, 1974, 1975, 1977, 1978 and 1979. Women's world championships were first held in 1974.

Winners (in all coxed events, the name of the cox is shown last):

MEN

Single Sculls
1962 Vyacheslav Ivanov (USSR)
1966 Don Spero (USA)
1970 Alberto Demiddi (Arg)
1974 Wolfgang Honig (GDR)
1975 Peter-Michael Kolbe (Ger)
1977 Joachim Dreifke (GDR)
1978 Peter-Michael Kolbe (Ger)
1979 Pertti Karppinen (Fin)

Double Sculls
1962 France (René Duhamel and Bernard Monnereau)
1966 Switzerland (Melchior Buergin and Martin Studach)
1970 Denmark (J. Engelbrecht and N. Secher)
1974 GDR (Hans-Ulrich Schmied and Christof Kreuziger)
1975 Norway (Frank Hansen and Alf Hansen)
1977 GB (Chris Baillieu and Michael Hart)
1978 Norway (Frank Hansen and Alf Hansen)
1979 Norway (Frank Hansen and Alf Hansen)

Coxless Pairs
1962 W. Germany (Bander, Z. Keller)
1966 GDR (P. Kremitz, A. Göhler)
1970 W. Germany (W. Klatt, P. Gorniv)
1974 GDR (B. Landvoigt, J. Landvoigt)
1975 GDR (B. Landvoigt, J. Landvoigt)
1977 USSR (V. Elisev, A. Kulagine)
1978 GDR (B. Landvoigt, J. Landvoigt)
1979 GDR (B. Landvoigt, J. Landvoigt)

Coxed Pairs
1962 W. Germany (Jordan, Neuss)
1966 Holland (H. van Nes, J. van de Graaf)
1970 Romania (S. Tudor, P. Ceapura)
1974 USSR (V. Ivanov, V. Eshinov)
1975 GDR (J. Lucke, W. Gunkel, B. Fritsch)
1977 Bulgaria (T. Mrankov, S. Yanakiev, S. Stoykov)
1978 GDR (J. Pfeiffer, G. Vebeler, O. Beyer)
1979 GDR (J. Pfeiffer, G. Vebeler, G. Spohr)

The champion Australian sculler Stewart Mackenzie (Central Press)

Coxless Fours
1962 W. Germany
1966 GDR
1970 GDR
1974 GDR
1975 GDR (S. Brietzke, A. Decker, S. Semmler, W. Mager)
1977 GDR (S. Brietzke, A. Decker, S. Semmler, W. Mager)
1978 USSR (V. Preobrazenski, N. Kuznyetsov, V. Dolinin, A. Nemtiriov)
1979 GDR (S. Brietzke, A. Decker, S. Semmler, W. Mager)

Coxed Fours
1962 W. Germany
1966 GDR
1970 W. Germany
1974 GDR
1975 USSR (V. Eshinov, N. Ivanov, A. Sema, A. Klepikov, A. Lukianov)
1977 GDR (U. Diessner, G. Döhn, W. Diessner, D. Wendisch, A. Gregor)
1978 GDR (U. Diessner, G. Döhn, W. Diessner, D. Wendisch, A. Gregor)
1979 GDR (W. Schlufter, W. Diessner, J. Doberschutz, U. Diessner, W. Lutz)

Quadruple Sculls
First held 1974
1974 GDR
1975 GDR (S. Weisse, W. Guldenpfennig, W. Hönig, C. Kreuziger)
1977 GDR (W. Guldenpfennig, K.-H. Bussert, M. Winter, F. Dundr)
1978 GDR (J. Dreifke, K.-H. Bussert, M. Winter, F. Dundr)
1979 GDR (P. Kersten, K. Kröppelin, K.-H. Bussert, J. Dreifke)

Eights

1962 W. Germany	1975 GDR
1966 W. Germany	1977 GDR
1970 GDR	1978 GDR
1974 USA	1979 GDR

WOMEN

Single Sculls
1974 Christine Scheiblich (GDR)
1975 Christine Scheiblich (GDR)
1977 Christine Scheiblich (GDR)
1978 Christine Hann (née Scheiblich) (GDR)
1979 Sanda Toma (Rom)

Double Sculls
1974 USSR (G. Yermoleyeva, E. Antonova)
1975 USSR (G. Yermoleyeva, E. Antonova)
1977 GDR (R. Zobelt, A. Borchmann)
1978 Bulgaria (S. Olzetova, Z. Yordanova)
1979 GDR (H. Westphal, C. Linse)

Coxless Pairs
1974 Romania (C. Neascu, M. Ghita)
1975 GDR (A. Noack, S. Dähne)
1977 GDR (A. Noack, S. Dähne)
1978 GDR (C. Bugel, U. Steindorf)
1979 GDR (C. Bugel, U. Steindorf)

Quadruple Sculls	1977 GDR
1974 GDR	1978 GDR
1975 GDR	1979 USSR
1977 GDR	
1978 Bulgaria	**Eights**
1979 GDR	1974 GDR
	1975 GDR
Coxed Fours	1977 GDR
1974 GDR	1978 USSR
1975 GDR	1979 USSR

OLYMPIC CHAMPIONSHIPS
Rowing has been included in each Olympic Games since 1900. Winners at each event since 1964 have been:

MEN

Single Sculls
1964 Vyacheslav Ivanov (USSR)
1968 Henri Wienese (Hol)
1972 Yuriy Malishev (USSR)
1976 Pertti Karppinen (Fin)
1980 Pertti Karppinen (Fin)

Double Sculls
1964 USSR (Oleg Tyurin and Boris Dubrovsky)
1968 USSR (Anatoliy Sass and Aleksandr Timoshinin)
1972 USSR (Aleksandr Timoshinin and Gennadiy Korshikov)
1976 Norway (Frank Hansen and Alf Hansen)
1980 GDR (Joachim Dreifke and Klaus Kroppelien)

Coxless Pairs
1964 Canada (G. Hungerford, R. Jackson)
1968 GDR (J. Lucke, H.–J. Bothe)
1972 GDR (S. Brietzke, W. Mager)
1976 GDR (J. Landvoigt, B. Landvoigt)
1980 GDR (J. Landvoigt, B. Landvoigt)

Coxed Pairs
1964 USA (E. Ferry, C. Findlay, K. Mitchell)
1968 Italy (P. Baron, R. Sambo, B. Cipolla)
1972 GDR (W. Gunkel, J. Lucke, K.–D. Neubert)
1976 GDR (H. Jahrling, F.–W. Ulrich, G. Spohr)
1980 GDR (H. Jahrling, F.–W. Ulrich, G. Spohr)

Swimming

Vladimir Salnikov, world and Olympic champion and the first man to swim 1500 metres freestyle in less than a quarter of an hour (Allsport/Mark Moylan) (see p. 218)

Billiards and Snooker

Steve Davis Embassy world champion after displaying devastating form during the 1981 season (Dave Muscroft) (see p. 33)

Hotels

A Royal Crescent Hotel bedroom suite, Egon Ronay Hotel of the Year 1980 (see p. 117)

Restaurants

1980 Egon Ronay Restaurant of the Year – the Sharrow Bay Hotel (Keith Scott Morton) (see p. 190)

Coxless Fours
1964 Denmark (J. O. Hansen, B. Haslöv, E. Petersen, K. Helmudt)
1968 GDR (F. Forberger, D. Grahn, F. Rühle, D. Schubert)
1972 GDR (F. Forberger, F. Rühle, D. Grahn, D. Schubert)
1976 GDR (S. Brietzke, A. Decker, S. Semmler, W. Mager)
1980 GDR (J. Thiele, A. Decker, S. Semmler, S. Brietzke)

Coxed Fours
1964 W. Gemany (P. Neusel, B. Britting, J. Werner, E. Hirschfelder, J. Oelke)
1968 New Zealand (R. Joyce, D. Storey, W. Cole, R. Collinge, S. Dickie)
1972 W. Germany (P. Berger, H.-J. Faerber, G. Auer, A. Bierl, U. Benter)
1976 USSR (V. Eshinov, N. Ivanov, M. Kuznyetsov, A. Klepikov, A. Lukianov)
1980 GDR (D. Wendisch, U. Diessner, W. Diessner, G. Dohn, A. Gregor)

Quadruple Sculls
First held 1976.
1976 GDR (W. Guldenpfennig, R. Reiche, K.-H. Bussert, M. Wolfgramm)
1980 GDR (F. Dundr, K. Bunk, U. Heppner, M. Winter)

Eights
1964 USA
1968 W. Germany
1972 New Zealand
1976 GDR
1980 GDR

WOMEN
First included in 1976.

Single Sculls
1976 Christine Scheiblich (GDR)
1980 Sanda Toma (Rom)

Double Sculls
1976 Bulgaria (Svetla Otzetova, Zdravka Yordanova)
1980 USSR (Yelena Khloptseva, Larisa Popova)

Coxless Pairs
1976 Bulgaria (Siika Kelbetcheva, S. Grouitcheva)
1980 GDR (Ute Steindorf, Cornelia Klier)

Coxed Fours
1976 GDR (K. Metze, B. Schwede, G. Lohs, A. Kurth, S. Hess)
1980 GDR (R. Kapheim, S. Frohlich, A. Noack R. Saalfeld, K. Wenzel)

Coxed Quadruple Sculls
1976 GDR (A. Borchmann, J. Lau, V. Poley, R. Zobelt, L. Weigelt)
1980 GDR (S. Reinhardt, J. Ploch, J. Lau, R. Zobelt, L. Buhr)

Eights
1976 GDR
1980 GDR

HENLEY ROYAL REGATTA
The annual regatta on the Thames at Henley was first held in 1839. Many events are held, but perhaps the two most famous are the Grand Challenge Cup for Eights, first held 1839 and the Diamond Challenge Sculls, first held 1844. Winners of these events since 1965 have been:

GRAND CHALLENGE CUP
1965 Ratzeburg (Ger)
1966 TSC Berlin (GDR)
1967 SCW Leipzig (GDR)
1968 Univ. of London (GB)
1969 SC Einheit, Dresden (GDR)
1970 ASK Rostock (GDR)
1971 Tideway Scullers (GB)
1972 WMF Moscow (USSR)
1973 Trud Kolomna (USSR)
1974 Trud Kolomna (USSR)
1975 Leander/Thames Tradesmen (GB)
1976 Thames Tradesmen (GB)
1977 Univ. of Washington (USA)
1978 Trakia Club (Bul)
1979 Thames Tradesmen (GB)
1980 Charles River RA (USA)

The 1980 Grand Challenge Cup final. Charles River RA of the USA beating Wairu Rowing Club of New Zealand (Gerry Paknadel)

DIAMOND CHALLENGE SCULLS

1965 Don Spero (USA)
1966 Achim Hill (Ger)
1967 Martin Studach (Swi)
1968 Hugh Wardell-Yerburgh (GB)
1969 Hans-Joachim Böhmer (GDR)
1970 Jochen Meissner (Ger)
1971 Alberto Demiddi (Arg)
1972 Aleksandr Timoshinin (USSR)
1973 Sean Drea (Ire)
1974 Sean Drea (Ire)
1975 Sean Drea (Ire)
1976 Edward Hale (Aus)
1977 Tim Crooks (GB)
1978 Tim Crooks (GB)
1979 Hugh Matheson (GB)
1980 Riccardo Ibarra (Arg)

Most wins: 6 Stuart Mackenzie (Aus) 1957–62

UNIVERSITY BOAT RACE
The boat race between the Universities of Oxford and Cambridge is rowed annually on the Thames from Putney to Mortlake over a distance of 4 miles 374 yards. It was first contested in 1829 at Henley. Winners have been:

OXFORD
1829, 1842, 1849, 1852, 1854, 1857, 1859, 1861–69, 1875, 1878, 1880–83, 1885, 1890–98, 1901, 1905, 1909–13, 1923, 1937–38, 1946, 1952, 1954, 1959–60, 1963, 1965–67, 1974, 1976–81 — Total 58

CAMBRIDGE
1836, 1839–41, 1845–46, 1849, 1856, 1858, 1860, 1870–74, 1876, 1879, 1884, 1886–89, 1899–1900, 1902–04, 1906–08, 1914, 1920–22, 1924–36, 1939, 1947–51, 1953, 1955–58, 1961–62, 1964, 1968–73, 1975 — Total 68

There was a dead heat in 1877.

Rugby Fives

AMATEUR SINGLES CHAMPIONSHIP
Contested annually for the Jesters Cup. First held in 1932. Winners since 1970:

1970 John Watkinson
1971–72 Andrew Cowie
1973–78 Wayne Enstone
1979 David Hebden
1980 Wayne Enstone

Most wins: 6 Wayne Enstone 1973–78
4 John Pretlove 1953, 1955–56, 1958;
Eric Marsh 1960–63

AMATEUR DOUBLES CHAMPIONSHIP
Contested annually for the Cyriax Cup. First held in 1934, but preceded by a club doubles championship. Winners since 1970:

1970–72 David Gardner and Stuart Reid
1973 John East and Andrew Cowie
1974 David Gardner and Stuart Reid
1975–79 Wayne Enstone and John East
1980 Ian Fuller and David Hebden

Most wins: 7 John Pretlove 1952, 1954, 1956–59, 1961; David Gardner 1960, 1965–66, 1970–72, 1974
Most wins by one pair: 5 Wayne Enstone and John East 1975–79

Rugby League

WORLD CUP
First held in 1954. Winners:

1954 England
1957 Australia
1960 England
1968 Australia
1970 Australia
1972 Great Britain

INTERNATIONAL CHAMPIONSHIP
Replaced the World Cup in 1975:

1975 Australia
1977 Australia

CHALLENGE CUP
First held in 1897; since 1929, with the exception of 1932, all finals have been at Wembley (except for the war-time finals, 1941–45). Winners:

1897 Batley
1898 Batley
1899 Oldham
1900 Swinton
1901 Batley
1902 Broughton R.
1903 Halifax
1904 Halifax
1905 Warrington
1906 Bradford
1907 Warrington
1908 Hunslet
1909 Wakefield Trinity
1910 Leeds
1911 Broughton R.
1912 Dewsbury

1913 Huddersfield
1914 Hull
1915 Huddersfield
1920 Huddersfield
1921 Leigh
1922 Rochdale R.
1923 Leeds
1924 Wigan
1925 Oldham
1926 Swinton
1927 Oldham
1928 Swinton
1929 Wigan
1930 Widnes
1931 Halifax
1932 Leeds
1933 Huddersfield
1934 Hunslet
1935 Castleford
1936 Leeds
1937 Widnes
1938 Salford
1939 Halifax
1940 Not held
1941 Leeds
1942 Leeds
1943 Dewsbury
1944 Bradford Northern
1945 Huddersfield
1946 Wakefield Trinity
1947 Bradford Northern
1948 Wigan
1949 Bradford Northern
1950 Warrington
1951 Wigan
1952 Workington Town
1953 Huddersfield
1954 Warrington
1955 Barrow
1956 St Helens
1957 Leeds
1958 Wigan
1959 Wigan
1960 Wakefield Trinity
1961 St Helens
1962 Wakefield Trinity
1963 Wakefield Trinity
1964 Widnes
1965 Wigan
1966 St Helens
1967 Featherstone R.
1968 Leeds
1969 Castleford
1970 Castleford
1971 Leigh
1972 St Helens
1973 Featherstone R.
1974 Warrington
1975 Widnes
1976 St Helens
1977 Leeds
1978 Leeds
1979 Widnes
1980 Hull K. R.
1981 Widnes

LANCE TODD TROPHY

Awarded to the man of the match in the Challenge Cup final. Presented annually since 1946 in memory of Lance Todd, the New Zealand and Wigan player and Salford manager, who was killed in a car accident in 1942. Winners and team:

1946 Billy Stott, Wakefield Trinity
1947 Willie Davies, Bradford Northern
1948 Frank Whitcombe, Bradford Northern
1949 Ernest Ward, Bradford Northern
1950 Gerry Helme, Warrington
1951 Ces Mountford, Wigan
1952 Billy Iveson, Workington Town
1953 Peter Ramsden, Huddersfield
1954 Gerry Helme, Warrington
1955 Jack Grundy, Barrow
1956 Alan Prescott, St. Helens
1957 Jeff Stevenson, Leeds
1958 Rees Thomas, Wigan
1959 Brian McTigue, Wigan
1960 Tommy Harris, Hull
1961 Dick Huddart, St. Helens
1962 Neil Fox, Wakefield Trinity
1963 Harold Poynton, Wakefield Trinity
1964 Frank Collier, Widnes
1965 Ray Ashby, Wigan
     Brian Gabbitas, Hunslet
1966 Len Killeen, St. Helens
1967 Carl Dooler, Featherstone Rovers
1968 Don Fox, Wakefield Trinity
1969 Malcolm Reilly, Castleford
1970 Bill Kirkbride, Castleford
1971 Alex Murphy, Leigh
1972 Kel Coslett, St. Helens
1973 Steve Nash, Featherstone Rovers
1974 Derek Whitehead, Warrington
1975 Ray Dutton, Widnes
1976 Geoff Pimblett, St. Helens
1977 Steve Pitchford, Leeds
1978 George Nicholls, St. Helens
1979 David Topliss, Wakefield Trinity
1980 Brian Lockwood, Hull K.R.
1981 Mick Burke, Widnes

LEAGUE CHAMPIONS

From 1907 the first four teams in the Northern League played off for the title of league champions. For two seasons, 1962–63 and 1963–64 there were two divisions and no play-off. From 1964 to 1973 the top clubs again played off for the title and from 1973–74 there were again two divisions.

1906–07 Halifax
1907–08 Hunslet
1908–09 Wigan
1909–10 Oldham
1910–11 Oldham
1911–12 Huddersfield
1912–13 Huddersfield
1913–14 Salford
1914–15 Huddersfield
1919–20 Hull
1920–21 Hull
1921–22 Wigan
1922–23 Hull K.R.
1923–24 Batley
1924–25 Hull K.R.
1925–26 Wigan
1926–27 Swinton

Celebrations after the 1980 John Player Trophy final between Bradford Northern and Warrington

1927–28 Swinton
1928–29 Huddersfield
1929–30 Huddersfield
1930–31 Swinton
1931–32 St Helens
1932–33 Salford
1933–34 Wigan
1934–35 Swinton
1935–36 Hull
1936–37 Salford
1937–38 Hunslet
1938–39 Salford
1945–46 Wigan
1946–47 Wigan
1947–48 Warrington
1948–49 Huddersfield
1949–50 Wigan
1950–51 Workington Town
1951–52 Wigan
1952–53 St Helens
1953–54 Warrington
1954–55 Warrington
1955–56 Hull
1956–57 Oldham
1957–58 Hull
1958–59 St Helens
1959–60 Wigan

1960–61 Leeds
1961–62 Huddersfield
1962–63 Swinton (Div. 1)
1963–64 Swinton (Div. 1)
1964–65 Halifax
1965–66 St Helens
1966–67 Wakefield Trinity
1967–68 Wakefield Trinity
1968–69 Leeds
1969–70 St Helens
1970–71 St Helens
1971–72 Leeds
1972–73 Dewsbury
1973–74 Salford (Div. 1)
1974–75 St Helens (Div. 1)
1975–76 Salford (Div. 1)
1976–77 Featherstone Rovers (Div. 1)
1977–78 Widnes (Div. 1)
1978–79 Hull K.R. (Div. 1)
1979–80 Bradford Northern (Div. 1)
1980–81 Bradford Northern (Div. 1)

PREMIERSHIP TROPHY
First held in the 1974–75 season, and contested by the leading teams in the League. Winners (year shown is that of second half of each season):

1975 Leeds
1976 St Helens
1977 St Helens
1978 Bradford Northern

1979 Leeds
1980 Widnes
1981 Hull K.R.

LANCASHIRE CUP

First held in 1905 and now sponsored by Forshaws.

1905 Wigan	1946 Wigan
1906 Broughton R.	1947 Wigan
1907 Oldham	1948 Wigan
1908 Wigan	1949 Wigan
1909 Wigan	1950 Wigan
1910 Oldham	1951 Wigan
1911 Rochdale H.	1952 Leigh
1912 Wigan	1953 St Helens
1913 Oldham	1954 Barrow
1914 Rochdale H.	1955 Leigh
1915–17 Not held	1956 Oldham
1918 Rochdale H.	1957 Oldham
1919 Oldham	1958 Oldham
1920 Broughton R.	1959 Warrington
1921 Warrington	1960 St Helens
1922 Wigan	1961 St Helens
1923 St Helens	1962 St Helens
1924 Oldham	1963 St Helens
1925 Swinton	1964 St Helens
1926 St Helens	1965 Warrington
1927 Swinton	1966 Wigan
1928 Wigan	1967 St Helens
1929 Warrington	1968 St Helens
1930 St Helens	1969 Swinton
1931 Salford	1970 Leigh
1932 Warrington	1971 Wigan
1933 Oldham	1972 Salford
1934 Salford	1973 Wigan
1935 Salford	1974 Wigan
1936 Salford	1975 Widnes
1937 Warrington	1976 Widnes
1938 Wigan	1977 Widnes
1939 Swinton	1978 Workington Town
1940–44 Not held	1979 Widnes
1945 Widnes	1980 Warrington

YORKSHIRE CUP

First held in 1905 and now sponsored by Esso.

1905 Hunslet	1908 Halifax
1906 Bradford	1909 Huddersfield
1907 Hunslet	1910 Wakefield T.

1911 Huddersfield	1948 Bradford N.
1912 Batley	1949 Bradford N.
1913 Huddersfield	1950 Huddersfield
1914 Huddersfield	1951 Wakefield T.
1919 (May) Huddersfield	1952 Huddersfield
1919 (Nov) Huddersfield	1953 Bradford N.
1920 Hull K.R.	1954 Halifax
1921 Leeds	1955 Halifax
1922 York	1956 Wakefield T.
1923 Hull	1957 Huddersfield
1924 Wakefield T.	1958 Leeds
1925 Dewsbury	1959 Featherstone R.
1926 Huddersfield	1960 Wakefield T.
1927 Dewsbury	1961 Wakefield T.
1928 Leeds	1962 Hunslet
1929 Hull K.R.	1963 Halifax
1930 Leeds	1964 Wakefield T.
1931 Huddersfield	1965 Bradford N.
1932 Leeds	1966 Hull K.R.
1933 York	1967 Hull K.R.
1934 Leeds	1968 Leeds
1935 Leeds	1969 Hull
1936 York	1970 Leeds
1937 Leeds	1971 Hull K.R.
1938 Huddersfield	1972 Leeds
1939 Featherstone R.	1973 Leeds
1940 Bradford N.	1974 Leeds
1941 Bradford N.	1975 Hull K.R.
1942 Dewsbury	1976 Leeds
1943 Bradford N.	1977 Leeds
1944 Halifax	1978 Castleford
1945 Bradford N.	1979 Leeds
1946 Wakefield T.	1980 Leeds
1947 Wakefield T.	

JOHN PLAYER TROPHY

First contested in the 1971–72 season. Winners (year shown is that of second half of each season):

1972 Halifax	1977 Castleford
1973 Leeds	1978 Warrington
1974 Warrington	1979 Widnes
1975 Bradford Northern	1980 Bradford N.
1976 Widnes	1981 Warrington

Rugby Union

THE INTERNATIONAL CHAMPIONSHIP

Contested annually by England, France, Ireland, Scotland and Wales. First decided in 1884, France entered for the first time in 1910. In 1885, 1888, 1889, 1897, 1898, and 1972 not all matches were completed, but winners in the other years have been:

1884 England	1890 England, Scotland
1886 England, Scotland	1891 Scotland
1887 Scotland	1892 England

1893 Wales	1905 Wales
1894 Ireland	1906 Ireland, Wales
1895 Scotland	1907 Scotland
1896 Ireland	1908 Wales
1899 Ireland	1909 Wales
1900 Wales	1910 England
1901 Scotland	1911 Wales
1902 Wales	1912 England, Ireland
1903 Scotland	1913 England
1904 Scotland	1914 England

1920 England, Scotland, Wales
1921 England
1922 Wales
1923 England
1924 England
1925 Scotland
1926 Scotland, Ireland
1927 Scotland, Ireland
1928 England
1929 Scotland
1930 England
1931 Wales
1932 England, Wales, Ireland
1933 Scotland
1934 England
1935 Ireland
1936 Wales
1937 England
1938 Scotland
1939 England, Wales, Ireland
1947 Wales, England
1948 Ireland
1949 Ireland
1950 Wales
1951 Ireland
1952 Wales
1953 England
1954 England, France, Wales
1955 France, Wales
1956 Wales
1957 England
1958 England
1959 France
1960 France, England
1961 France
1962 France
1963 England
1964 Scotland, Wales
1965 Wales
1966 Wales
1967 France
1968 France
1969 Wales
1970 France, Wales
1971 Wales
1973 Quintuple tie
1974 Ireland
1975 Wales
1976 Wales
1977 France
1978 Wales
1979 Wales
1980 England
1981 France

TRIPLE CROWN
Won when one of the four British countries beats the other three in the same season. Winners have been:

England
1884, 1892, 1913, 1914, 1921, 1923, 1924, 1928, 1934, 1937, 1954, 1957, 1960
Wales
1893, 1900, 1902, 1905, 1908, 1909, 1911, 1950, 1952, 1965, 1969, 1971, 1976, 1977, 1978, 1979
Scotland
1891, 1895, 1901, 1903, 1907, 1925, 1933, 1938

Ireland
1894, 1899, 1948, 1949

CALCUTTA CUP
The annual contest between England and Scotland. To the end of the 1981 season, England have won 47 times, Scotland 34 and 15 have been drawn.

ENGLISH COUNTY CHAMPIONSHIP
First held in 1889, the county championship is contested annually, firstly on a regional league basis and then by knock-out. Winners since 1965 have been:

1965 Warwickshire
1966 Middlesex
1967 Durham and Surrey
1968 Middlesex
1969 Lancashire
1970 Staffordshire
1971 Surrey
1972 Gloucestershire
1973 Lancashire
1974 Gloucestershire
1975 Gloucestershire
1976 Gloucestershire
1977 Lancashire
1978 East Midlands
1979 Middlesex (played 31 Dec 1978)
1980 Lancashire
1981 Northumberland

Most wins: 13 Gloucestershire 1910, 1913, 1920–22, 1930–32, 1937, 1972, 1974–76

RUGBY FOOTBALL UNION KNOCK-OUT CUP
First held in the 1971–72 season. Contested by English clubs. Winners (year shown is that of second half of each season):

1972 Gloucester
1973 Coventry
1974 Coventry
1975 Bedford
1976 Gosforth
1977 Gosforth
1978 Gloucester
1979 Leicester
1980 Leicester
1981 Leicester

WELSH RUGBY UNION CHALLENGE CUP
First held in the 1971–72 season. Contested by Welsh clubs. Winners (year shown is that of second half of each season):

1972 Neath
1973 Llanelli
1974 Llanelli
1975 Llanelli
1976 Llanelli

1977 Newport
1978 Swansea
1979 Bridgend
1980 Bridgend

BRITISH LIONS

The four home countries – England, Ireland, Scotland and Wales – come together to provide players for the British Isles touring teams (The Lions). Summarised results of Internationals are:

Australia: British Isles 6, Australia 1, Drawn 0
New Zealand: British Isles 5, New Zealand 17, Drawn 2
South Africa: British Isles 8, South Africa 18, Drawn 4

SCOTTISH CLUB CHAMPIONSHIP

Scottish League Division One was won by Hawick for the competition's first five seasons, from 1973–74 to 1977–78.

1978–79 Heriot's F.P.   1980–81 Gala
1979–80 Gala

RUGBY WORLD PLAYER OF THE YEAR

Voted annually by readers of *Rugby World* magazine, since 1970.

1970 Ken Goodall
1971 Barry John
1972 Barry John
1973 David Duckham
1974 Mike Gibson
1975 Mervyn Davies
1976 Gareth Edwards
1977 Phil Bennett
1978 Gareth Edwards
1979 Tony Ward
1980 Billy Beaumont
1981 Huw Davies

The Thorn County Championship final between Northumberland and Gloucestershire in 1981 (Colorsport)

Science

YOUNG SCIENTISTS OF THE YEAR

This is the annual competition organised by BBC Television

1966 Bexley Erith Technical High School
Subject: Measuring water in moulding sand
Team: Michael Breton, Barry Lewis
1967 Heywood Grammar School
Subject: Peat
Team: Nicholas Pickvance, David Lord, Marilyn Hadfield, Neil Brocklehurst, Susan Blackburn, Jose England
1968 Erdington Girls Grammar School
Subject: Crease Resistance in the Family Wash
Team: Linda Hodgets, Janice Checketts, Marilyn Cook, Christine Scoins, June Carrington, Camilla Wickins, June Harvey, Jennifer Dowsett, Pauline Jones
1969 Golspie High School
Subject: Trout in Scottish Lochs
Team: Sarah Mackay, Katie McLellan, Walter Sutherland
1970 Gateway School, Leicester
Subject: Fingerprints
Team: David May, Peter Hall, Peter Kitson, Mervyn Hall
1971 Sittingbourne Girls Grammar School
Subject: Difference in Eye Colour
Team: Judith Greaves, Rosemary Underdown, Susan Whitesman, Susan Jury
1972 Lincoln School
Subject: Sowing Wild Oats
Team: Christopher O'Brien, David Smith, Christopher Dennison
1973 Neath Grammar School, Glamorgan
Subject: Runner Beans and Fungicide
Team: Keith Jones, Hugh Jones

1974 Ifield School, Crawley, Sussex
Subject: Magnetism Affecting Plant Growth
Team: Kings Dobson, Malcolm MacGarvin, David Law
1975 Codsall Comprehensive School, Codsall, Staffs.
Subject: Kinks caused by reaction between Magnesium and Hydrochloric acid
Team: Wendy Heath, Jane Darling
1976 Pocklington School, Pocklington, Yorks
Subject: Oscillating Aerofoil
Team: Nick Ramsden, Nick Pollard, Andrew Blacker, David Quarton
1977 Yeovil College, Yeovil
Subject: Wool De-crimping
Team: Ben Holt, Jonathan Stagg, Alyson Wreford, Anthony Brown
1978 Royal Grammar School, Newcastle upon Tyne
Subject: Hovercraft Crop Sprayer
Team: Paul Brown, Alistair Wolf
1979 Madras College, St Andrews
Subject: Psychology of Blushing
Team: Nicola Pyke, Angela McLean, Matthew Allen, Patrick Seymour, Andrew Cormack
1980 Royal Grammar School, Newcastle upon Tyne
Subject: Microprocessor system for controlling theatre lights
Team: Anthony McKay, Graeme Harker
1981 Yeovil College, Somerset
Subject: New types of solvent for regenerating cellulose as a film for kidney machines
Team: Mandy Curtis, Elizabeth Ponter, Bridget Stinson

1977 Young Scientists of the Year: Yeovil College (BBC copyright)

Scrabble

BRITISH NATIONAL CHAMPIONSHIPS

These were inaugurated in 1971. Anyone of any age can enter. The contestants play qualifying games and regional finals, the top 100 players going through to the grand finals. Here the contestants play three games against different opponents, very strict word rules apply and only two minutes are allowed for each move. The player with the highest aggregate score becomes the champion. Winners and scores:

1971 Stephen Haskell, 1345
1972 Olive Behan, 1215
1973 Anne Bradford, 1266
1974 Richard Sharp, 1288
1975 Olive Behan, 1363
1976 Alan Richter, 1359
1977 Michael Goldman, 1478
1978 Philip Nelkon, 1521
1979 Christine Jones, 1453
1980 Joyce Cansfield, 1540
1981 Philip Nelkon, 1551

Secretaries

THE TOP SECRETARY AWARD

This has been given each year since 1956 to the candidate who obtains the highest marks in the Private Secretary's Diploma Examination offered by the Commercial Education Scheme of the London Chamber of Commerce and Industry as a professional secretarial qualification. It is generally regarded as the highest award of its kind and is designed for the secretary at top management level. The winners have been:

1956 Miss E. J. Phillips, British Transport Commission
1957 Miss S. A. Mitcher, Private tuition
1958 Mrs E. I. Phillips, Liverpool College of Commerce
1959 Miss R. M. Anderson, Municipal College of Commerce, Newcastle
1960 Miss D. M. Moore, Ealing Technical College
1961 Mrs A. M. Billingsley, Secretary to the Borough Treasurer, Solihull
1962 M. J. Newton, Westminster College
1963 Mrs C. F. McClaren, Holborn College of Law, Languages and Commerce
1964 Susan Darwin, College of Technology, Sheffield
1965 Nancy Hall, West London College of Commerce
1966 Jennifer Tattersall, Ealing Technical College
1967 Gwen Weightman, Municipal College of Commerce, Newcastle
1968 Jacqueline Barlow, College of Technology, Slough
    Judith Fairhurst, College of Commerce, Liverpool
1969 Jeanne Priddle, Private tuition
1970 Thelma Jenkins, Private tuition
1971 Ruth A. Jarman, James Neill (Sheffield) Ltd
    Diana P. Tidd, Croydon Technical College
1972 Judith Wilkinson, Calder Water Board
1973 Jane Morrison, Birmingham Polytechnic
1974 Patricia Gibson, Croydon Technical College

Julia Sherring, Top Secretary for 1980

1975 Christina Eveleigh, Highbury College, Portsmouth
1976 Heather Paterson, South East London College
1977 Jean Anderson, Westminster College
1978 Andrea Mullaney, South East Derbyshire College, Ilkeston
1979 Jane Gillet, Filton Technical College, Bristol
1980 Julie Sherring, Eastleigh College, Hants

Sheepdogs

The skills of the shepherd and his dog are tested each year at various competitive 'trials'.

THE 'JAMES A. REID' CHAMPIONSHIP SHIELD
Founded in 1922. The winners since 1970:

1970 Kilmartin, D. McTier, Peebles, with 'Wiston Bill'
1971 Cardiff, J. Murray, Sanquhar, with 'Glen'
1972 Newcastle, J. J. Templeton, Kilmarnock, with 'Cap'
1973 Bala, H. G. Jones, Bodfari, with 'Gel'
1974 Kilmartin, G. Jones, Penmachno, with 'Bill'
1975 York, R. C. MacPherson, Brampton, with 'Zac'
1976 Lockerbie G. Jones, Penmachno, with 'Shep'
1977 Libanus, J. R. Thomas, Llandovery, with 'Craig'
1978 Chatsworth, R. J. Shennan, Girvan, with 'Mirk'
1979 Stranraer, R. C. MacPherson, Brampton, with 'Zac'
1980 Bula, T. Watson, Lauder, with 'Jen'

Tom Watson with Bula after winning the 1980 James A. Reid championship shield

A scene from 'One Man and His Dog', the sheepdog championships (BBC copyright)

ONE MAN AND HIS DOG
This BBC Television programme organises its own championship, of which the winners are:

1976
Singles: David Shennan with 'Maid'
Doubles: Glyn Jones with 'Gel' and 'Bracken'

1977
Singles: Martin O'Neill with 'Risp'
Doubles: Tot Longton with 'Jed' and 'Kerry'

1978
Singles: Alan Jones with 'Spot'
Doubles: Alan Jones with 'Spot' and 'Craig'

1979
Singles: Bob Shennan with 'Mirk'
Doubles: Glyn Jones with 'Gel' and 'Bracken'

1980
Singles: Martin O'Neill with 'Risp'
Doubles: George Hutton with 'Nip' and 'Roy'

Shepherds

SHEPHERD OF THE YEAR
This award was founded in 1973 by *Livestock Farming* magazine and Rumenco Ltd. It aims to highlight and identify the contribution the full-time shepherd makes to agriculture and the community as a whole. On this basis, a Shepherd of the Year is selected from entrants: Winners:

1973 Dorothy Bell, Cumbria. Responsible for 1800 Swaledale ewes and 500 ewe hoggs.

1974 Richard Lund, Dorset. Responsible for 2000 ewe flock.
1975 Bill Graham, Berwick-on-Tweed. Responsible for 1000 ewe flock.
1976 Ray Dent, Co. Durham. Responsible for 1218 Swaledale ewes.
1977 Tom Williams, N. Wales. Responsible for 1250 Welsh Mountain sheep.
1978 Jack Thomas, Cornwall. Responsible for 700 pedigree polled Dorset sheep.
1979 Harry Hutchinson, Lancs. Responsible for 1200 ewe flock.
1980 John Read, Hants. Responsible for 3000 ewe flock.

Harry Hutchinson, 1979 Shepherd of the Year, tending his flock

Shooting

OLYMPIC CHAMPIONSHIPS
Seven men have won five gold medals at the Olympic Games at shooting, including Carl Townsend Osburn (USA), who also won four silver and two bronze medals for a record total of 11 medals.

The events in the Olympics have varied considerably since shooting was first included in 1908, and all events are now for individuals. The most individual gold medals won is three by Gulbrandsen Skatteboe (Nor) in 1906, 1908, 1912. Winners in 1976 and 1980 were:

Free pistol (50 m)
1976 Uwe Potteck (GDR) 573/600
1980 Aleksandr Melemtev (USSR) 581
Small-bore rifle prone (50 m)
1976 Karl Heinz Smieszek (Ger) 599/600
1980 Karoly Varga (Hun) 599
Small-bore rifle 3 positions (50 m)
1976 Lanny Bassham (USA) 1162/1200
1980 Viktor Vlasov (USSR) 1173
Rapid-fire pistol (25 m)
1976 Norbert Klaar (GDR) 597/600
1980 Corneliu Ion (Rom) 596
Trap shooting
1976 Donald Haldeman (USA) 190/200
1980 Luciano Giovanetti (Ita) 198
Skeet shooting
1976 Josef Panacek (Cze) 198/200

1980 Hans-Kjeld Rasmussen (Den) 196
Running game target (50 m)
1976 Aleksandr Gazov (USSR) 579/600
1980 Igor Sokolov (USSR) 589

WORLD CHAMPIONSHIPS
World champions at the 1978 championships held in Seoul, South Korea, were:

MEN
Free pistol (50 m): Moritz Minder (Swi) 577/600
Small-bore rifle prone (50 m): Alister Allan (GB) 599/600
Small-bore rifle 3 positions (50 m): Lanny Bassham (USA) 1165/1200
Rapid fire pistol (25 m): Ove Gunnarsson (Swe) 595/600
Trap shooting: Eladio Vallduvi (Spa) 198/200
Skeet shooting: Luciano Brunetti (Ita) 197/200
Running game target: Guha Rannikko (Fin) 572/600

WOMEN
Small-bore rifle prone (50 m): Sue-Ann Sandusky (USA) 596/600
Small-bore rifle 3 positions (50 m): Wanda Oliver (USA) 580/600
Trap shooting: Susan Nattrass (Can) 195/200
Skeet shooting: Bianca Hansberg (Ita) 189/200
(*Note*: in all cases the total possible score is shown last)

Show Business

VARIETY CLUB OF GREAT BRITAIN SHOW BUSINESS AWARDS

Britain's entertainment industry honours its leading members with these annual awards. The presentations were first made in 1952. A selection of these follow:

BEST STAGE ACTOR
1954 Jack Hawkins
1955 No award
1956 Paul Scofield
1957 Sir Laurence Olivier
1958 Michael Redgrave
1959 Peter O'Toole

1960 Nigel Patrick
1961 Albert Finney
1962 Paul Scofield
1963 Sir Michael Redgrave
1964 Sir Laurence Olivier
1965 Robert Stephens
1966 David Warner
1967 Donald Pleasance
1968 Sir John Gielgud
1969 Leonard Rossiter
1970 Alec McCowen
1971 Alan Badel
1972 Tom Courtenay
1973 Alastair Sim
1974 Tom Courtenay
1975 Alan Bates
1976 Donald Sinden
1977 Sir Alec Guinness
1978 Tom Conti
1979 Paul Scofield
1980 Alan Howard

BEST STAGE ACTRESS
1953 Dorothy Tutin
1954 No award
1955 No award
1956 Mary Ure
1957 Yvonne Mitchell
1958 No award
1959 Elizabeth Seal
1960 Billie Whitelaw
1961 Vanessa Redgrave
1962 Sheila Hancock
1963 Maggie Smith
1964 Dame Peggy Ashcroft
1965 Dorothy Tutin
1966 Vanessa Redgrave
1967 Irene Worth
1968 Jill Bennett
1969 Margaret Leighton
1970 Eileen Atkins
1971 Moira Lister
1972 Maggie Smith
1973 Wendy Hiller
1974 Claire Bloom
1975 Helen Mirren
1976 Joan Plowright
1977 Glynis Johns
1978 Felicity Kendal
1979 Jane Lapotaire
1980 Judi Dench

BEST FILM ACTOR
1957 Alec Guinness
1958 Richard Attenborough
1959 Laurence Harvey
1960 Peter Sellers
1961 No award
1962 Peter O'Toole
1963 Dirk Bogarde
1964 Richard Attenborough
1965 Sean Connery
1966 Michael Caine
1967 Paul Scofield
1968 Ron Moody
1969 Nicol Williamson
1970 Albert Finney
1971 Peter Finch

1972 Simon Ward
1973 Malcolm McDowell
1974 Albert Finney
1975 Robert Shaw
1976 Sir Laurence Olivier
1977 Norman Beaton
1978 Peter Ustinov
1979 John Hurt
1980 John Hurt

BEST FILM ACTRESS
1958 Sylvia Sims
1959 Audrey Hepburn
1960 Hayley Mills
1961 Deborah Kerr
1962 Leslie Caron
1963 Margaret Rutherford
1964 Rita Tushingham and
     Millicent Martin
1965 Julie Christie
1966 Virginia McKenna
1967 Edith Evans
1968 Maggie Smith
1969 Glenda Jackson
1970 Sarah Miles
1971 Nanette Newman
1972 Dorothy Tutin
1973 Glenda Jackson
1974 Susannah York
1975 Glenda Jackson
1976 Gemma Craven
1977 Billie Whitelaw
1978 Glenda Jackson
1979 Karen Dotrice
1980 Hazel O'Connor

SHOW BUSINESS PERSONALITY
1955 Diana Dors
1956 Tommy Trinder
1957 Frankie Vaughan
1958 Max Bygraves
1959 Harry Secombe
1960 Lionel Bart
1961 Cliff Richard
1962 Billy Cotton
1963 The Beatles
1964 Morecambe and Wise
1965 Ken Dodd
1966 Frankie Howerd
1967 Englebert Humperdinck
1968 Tom Jones
1969 Danny La Rue
1970 Derek Nimmo
1971 Frankie Howerd
1972 Jimmy Savile
1973 Max Bygraves
1974 Michael Crawford
1975 Bruce Forsyth
1976 Penelope Keith
1977 John Dankworth and
     Cleo Laine
1978 David Essex and
     Elaine Page
1979 Tommy Steele
1980 Ronnie Corbett and Ronnie Barker

BBC TV PERSONALITY
1959 Richard Dimbleby

1980 Variety Club of Great Britain Show Business Awards. Top left: *Jon Pertwee, ITV Personality;* Top right: *John Hurt, Best Film Actor;* Below: *Ronnie Corbett* (left) *and Ronnie Barker, Show Business Personalities*

1960 David Jacobs
1961 Cliff Michelmore
1962 Harry Worth
1963 Wilfred Brambell and
     Harry H. Corbett
1964 Eric Sykes
1965 Benny Hill
1966 Val Doonican
1967 Warren Mitchell
1968 Marty Feldman and
     Rolf Harris
1969 Wendy Craig
1970 Arthur Lowe, John Le Mesurier, Clive Dunn,
     John Laurie, Arnold Ridley, James Beck and
     Ian Lavender
1971 Stratford Johns
1972 Dick Emery
1973 Mike Yarwood
1974 Ronnie Barker
1975 John Cleese and
     Esther Rantzen
1976 John Inman and
     Derek Jacobi
1977 Terry Scott and
     June Whitfield
1978 Christopher Timothy, Robert Hardy, Carol
     Drinkwater and Peter Davidson
1979 Penelope Keith
1980 Rowan Atkinson

ITV PERSONALITY
1959 Bruce Forsyth
1960 Alfie Bass and
     Bill Fraser
1961 Arthur Haynes
1962 Violet Carson
1963 Honor Blackman and
     Patrick Macnee
1964 Bernard Braden
1965 Patrick McGoohan
1966 David Frost
1967 Dave Allen
1968 Ronnie Corbett and
     Tommy Cooper
1969 Ronnie Barker
1970 Reg Varney, Doris Hare, Michael Robbins,
     Bob Grant, Stephen Lewis and Anna Karen
1971 Benny Hill
1972 Jack Smethurst, Rudolph Walker, Nina
     Baden-Semper, and Kate Williams
1973 Wendy Craig
1974 Jean Marsh
1975 Gordon Jackson
1976 Dennis Waterman, John Thaw, Yootha Joyce
     and Brian Murphy
1977 Jim Henson and Frank Oz
1978 Francesca Annis
1979 Benny Hill
1980 Jon Pertwee

BBC SOUND RADIO PERSONALITY
1960 Freddie Grisewood
1961 Franklin Engelman
1962 Eamonn Andrews
1963 Jean Metcalfe
1964 Jack De Manio
1965 Peter Haigh
1966 Nicholas Parsons
1967 Kenneth Horne

1968 Jimmy Young
1969 Eric Robinson
1970 Sam Costa
1971 Tony Blackburn
1972 Pete Murray
1973 Terry Wogan
1974 Ed Stewart
1975 David Jacobs
1976 Roy Hudd
1977 Frank Muir and Denis Norden
1978 Charlie Chester
1979 Roy Plomley
1980 Robert Robinson

INDEPENDENT RADIO PERSONALITY
1977 Kenny Everett
1978 Maggie Norden
1979 Bob Holness and Douglas Cameron
1980 Bryan Hayes

MOST PROMISING ARTISTE
1956 Elizabeth Seal
1957 Heather Sears
1958 Bernard Bresslaw
1959 Anthony Newley
1960 Albert Finney
1961 Helen Shapiro and Rita Tushingham
1962 Tom Courtenay and
     Sarah Miles
1963 Julie Christie and James Fox
1964 Jimmy Tarbuck
1965 Michael Crawford
1966 Barbara Ferris
1967 Carol White
1968 Alan Bennett
1969 Polly James
1970 Jenny Agutter
1971 Murray Head
1972 Jon Finch
1973 David Essex
1974 Felicity Kendal
1975 Lisa Harrow
1976 Andrew Sachs
1977 Susan Littler
1978 Muriel Odunton
1979 Liz Robertson and Trevor Eve
1980 Julie Walters

SPECIAL AWARDS
1963 Sean Connery
1964 No award
1965 Michael Miles and Hughie Green
1966 Anna Neagle
1967 Stanley Baker and
     Dame Gladys Cooper
1968 Dame Sybil Thorndike
1969 Bernard Delfont
1970 Fred Emney
1971 Keith Michell, Cicely Courtneidge and Jack
     Hulbert
1972 Jack Warner
1973 Lord Willis and Evelyn Laye
1974 John Woolf
1975 Max Wall
1976 Richard Goolden
1977 Stanley Holloway
1978 Arthur Askey
1979 Dame Margot Fonteyn
1980 Chesney Allen

Skiing

WORLD AND OLYMPIC CHAMPIONSHIPS — ALPINE SKIING

Alpine skiing has been included in the winter Olympic Games since 1948, and world championships were first held in 1932. Winners at world and Olympic (*) events since 1948 have been:

MEN

Alpine Combination
1948 Henri Oreiller (Fra)
1950 Not held
1952 Not held
1954 Stein Eriksen (Nor)
1956 Toni Sailer (Aut)
1958 Toni Sailer (Aut)
1960 Guy Perillat (Fra)
1962 Karl Schranz (Aut)
1964 Ludwig Leitner (Ger)
1966 Jean-Claude Killy (Fra)
1968 Jean-Claude Killy (Fra)
1970 William Kidd (USA)
1972 Gustavo Thoeni (Ita)
1974 Franz Klammer (Aut)
1976 Gustavo Thoeni (Ita)
1978 Andreas Wenzel (Lie)

Downhill
1948*Henri Oreiller (Fra)
1950 Zeno Colo (Ita)
1952* Zeno Colo (Ita)
1954 Christian Pravda (Aut)
1956* Toni Sailer (Aut)
1958 Toni Sailer (Aut)
1960* Jean Vuarnet (Fra)
1962 Karl Schranz (Aut)
1964* Egon Zimmermann (Aut)
1966 Jean-Claude Killy (Fra)
1968* Jean-Claude Killy (Fra)
1970 Bernhard Russi (Swi)
1972* Bernhard Russi (Swi)
1974 David Zwilling (Aut)
1976* Franz Klammer (Aut)
1978 Joseph Walcher (Aut)
1980* Leonhard Stock (Aut)

Slalom
1948* Edi Reinalter (Swi)
1950 Georges Schneider (Swi)
1952* Othmar Schneider (Aut)
1954 Stein Eriksen (Nor)
1956* Toni Sailer (Aut)
1958 Josl Reider (Aut)
1960* Ernst Hinterseer (Aut)
1962 Charles Bozon (Fra)
1964* Josef Stiegler (Aut)
1966 Carlo Senoner (Ita)
1968* Jean-Claude Killy (Fra)
1970 Jean-Noel Augert (Fra)
1972* Francesco Ochoa (Spa)
1974 Gustavo Thoeni (Ita)
1976* Piero Gros (Ita)
1978 Ingemar Stenmark (Swe)
1980* Ingemar Stenmark (Swe)

Giant Slalom
1948* Not held
1950 Zeno Colo (Ita)
1952* Stein Eriksen (Nor)
1954 Stein Eriksen (Nor)
1956* Toni Sailer (Aut)
1958 Toni Sailer (Aut)
1960* Roger Staub (Swi)
1962 Egon Zimmermann (Aut)
1964* Francois Bonlieu (Fra)
1966 Guy Perillat (Fra)
1968* Jean-Claude Killy (Fra)
1970 Karl Schranz (Aut)
1972* Gustavo Thoeni (Ita)
1974 Gustavo Thoeni (Ita)
1976* Heini Hemmi (Swi)
1978 Ingemar Stenmark (Swe)
1980* Ingemar Stenmark (Swe)

WOMEN

Alpine Combination
1948 Trude Jochum Beiser (Aut)
1950 Not held
1952 Not held
1954 Ida Schöpfer (Swi)
1956 Madeleine Berthod (Swi)
1958 Frieda Danzer (Swi)
1960 Anne Heggtveit (Can)
1962 Marielle Goitschel (Fra)
1964 Marielle Goitschel (Fra)
1966 Marielle Goitschel (Fra)
1968 Nancy Greene (Can)
1970 Michele Jacot (Fra)
1972 Annemarie Pröll (Aut)
1974 Fabienne Serrat (Fra)
1976 Rosi Mittermaier (Ger)
1978 Annemarie Moser (née Pröll) (Aut)

Jean-Claude Killy, the idol of France

Downhill
1948* Hedy Schlunegger (Swi)
1950 Trude Jochum Beiser (Aut)
1952* Trude Jochum Beiser (Aut)
1954 Ida Schöpfer (Aut)
1956* Madeleine Berthod (Swi)
1958 Lucille Wheeler (Can)
1960* Heidi Biebl (Ger)
1962 Christl Haas (Aut)
1964* Christl Haas (Aut)
1966 Erika Schinegger (Aut)
1968* Olga Pall (Aut)
1970 Anneroesli Zyrd (Swi)
1972* Marie-Thérèse Nadig (Swi)
1974 Annemarie Pröll (Aut)
1976* Rosi Mittermaier (Ger)
1978 Annemarie Moser (née Pröll) (Aut)
1980* Annemarie Moser (Aut)

Slalom
1948* Gretchen Fraser (USA)
1950 Dagmar Rom (Aut)
1952* Andrea Mead Lawrence (USA)
1954 Trude Klecker (Aut)
1956* Renée Colliard (Swi)
1958 Inger Björnbakken (Nor)
1960* Anne Heggtveit (Can)
1962 Marianne Jahn (Aut)
1964* Christine Goitschel (Fra)
1966 Annie Famose (Fra)
1968* Marielle Goitschel (Fra)
1970 Ingrid Lafforgue (Fra)
1972* Barbara Cochran (USA)
1974 Hanni Wenzel (Lie)
1976* Rosi Mittermaier (Ger)
1978 Lea Sölkner (Aut)
1980* Hanni Wenzel (Lie)

Giant Slalom
1948* Not held
1950 Dagmar Rom (Aut)
1952* Andrea Mead Lawrence (USA)
1954 Lucienne Schmith (Fra)
1956* Ossi Reichert (Ger)
1958 Lucille Wheeler (Can)
1960* Yvonne Rüegg (Swi)
1962 Marianne Jahn (Aut)
1964* Marielle Goitschel (Fra)
1966 Marielle Goitschel (Fra)
1968* Nancy Greene (Can)
1970 Betsy Clifford (Can)
1972* Marie-Thérèse Nadig (Swi)
1974 Fabienne Serrat (Fra)
1976* Kathy Kreiner (Can)
1978 Maria Epple (Ger)
1980* Hanni Wenzel (Lie)

ALPINE WORLD CUP
The Alpine World Cup, a points competition involving the season's major events, was introduced in 1967.

MEN
1967 Jean-Claude Killy (Fra)
1968 Jean-Claude Killy (Fra)
1969 Karl Schranz (Aut)
1970 Karl Schranz (Aut)
1971 Gustavo Thoeni (Ita)
1972 Gustavo Thoeni (Ita)

1973 Gustavo Thoeni (Ita)
1974 Piero Gros (Ita)
1975 Gustavo Thoeni (Ita)
1976 Ingemar Stenmark (Swe)
1977 Ingemar Stenmark (Swe)
1978 Ingemar Stenmark (Swe)
1979 Peter Luescher (Swi)
1980 Andreas Wenzel (Lie)
1981 Phil Mahre (USA)

WOMEN
1967 Nancy Greene (Can)
1968 Nancy Greene (Can)
1969 Gertrud Gabl (Aut)
1970 Michele Jacot (Fra)
1971 Annemarie Pröll (Aut)
1972 Annemarie Pröll (Aut)
1973 Annemarie Pröll (Aut)
1974 Annemarie Pröll (Aut)
1975 Annemarie Moser (née Pröll) (Aut)
1976 Rosi Mittermaier (Ger)
1977 Lise-Marie Morerod (Swi)
1978 Hanni Wenzel (Lie)
1979 Annemarie Moser (Aut)
1980 Hanni Wenzel (Lie)
1981 Marie-Thérèse Nadig (Swi)

WORLD AND OLYMPIC CHAMPIONSHIPS – NORDIC SKIING
Nordic skiing – jumping and cross-country – was first included in the Olympic Games in 1924 and separate world championships were first held in 1929. The Nordic combination is for 15 kilometres cross-country and jumping. Winners since 1948 (*=Olympics):

MEN
1948* Heikki Hasu (Fin)
1950 Heikki Hasu (Fin)
1952* Simon Slättvik (Nor)
1954 Sverre Stenersen (Nor)
1956* Sverre Stenersen (Nor)
1958 Paavo Korhonen (Fin)
1960* Georg Thoma (Ger)
1962 Arne Larsen (Nor)
1964* Tormod Knutsen (Nor)
1966 Georg Thoma (Ger)
1968* Franz Keller (Ger)
1970 Ladislav Rygl (Cze)
1972* Ulrich Wehling (GDR)
1974 Ulrich Wehling (GDR)
1976* Ulrich Wehling (GDR)
1978 Konrad Winkler (GDR)
1980* Ulrich Wehling (GDR)

CROSS-COUNTRY

MEN
The current Olympic cross-country events are 15, 30 and 50 kilometres for individuals as well as a 4 × 10 kilometres relay.
Winner of the **most titles** is Sixten Jernberg (Swe) with 8 (5 individual and 3 relay) between 1956 and 1964. **Most individual titles** have been won by Johan Grøttumsbraaten (Nor) with 6 between 1926 and 1932.

WOMEN
Women's Olympic events are at 5 and 10 kilometres for individuals and 4 × 5 kilometres relay.

Winner of the **most World and Olympic titles** is Galina Koulakova (USSR) with 9 between 1968 and 1978.

SKI-JUMPING
Since 1964 men have competed at the Olympic Games at ski-jumping on a 70-metre hill and on a 90-metre hill. Champions have been:

70 metres hill
1964 Veikko Kankkonen (Fin) 229·90
1968 Jiri Raska (Cze) 216·5
1972 Yukio Kasaya (Jap) 244·2
1976 Hans-Georg Aschenbach (GDR) 252·0
1980 Toni Innauer (Aut) 178·0

90 metres hill
1964 Toralf Engen (Nor) 230·70
1968 Vladimir Beloussov (USSR) 231·3
1972 Wojciech Fortuna (Pol) 219·9
1976 Karl Schnabl (Aut) 234·8
1980 Jouko Törmänen (Fin) 231·5

World Champions
World ski-jumping championships were first held in 1929. Winners since 1966:

1966 Björn Wirkola (Nor) (70m and 90m)
1970 Gurij Napalkov (USSR) (70m and 90m)
1974 Hans-Georg Aschenbach (GDR) (70m and 90m)
1978 Mathias Buse (GDR) (70m)
     Tapio Räisänen (Fin) (90m)

WORLD AND OLYMPIC CHAMPIONSHIPS – BIATHLON
The biathlon is a combination of skiing and shooting. World championships were first held in 1958 and Olympic championships in 1960. Champions (* = Olympics):

1958 Adolf Wiklund (Swe)
1959 Vladimir Melanin (USSR)
1960* Klas Lestander (Swe)
1961 Kalevi Huuskonen (Fin)
1962 Vladimir Melanin (USSR)
1963 Vladimir Melanin (USSR)
1964* Vladimir Melanin (USSR)
1965 Olav Jordet (Nor)
1966 Jon Istad (Nor)
1967 Viktor Mamatov (USSR)
1968* Magnar Solberg (Nor)
1969 Aleksandr Tikhonov (USSR)
1970 Aleksandr Tikhonov (USSR)
1971 Heinz Dieter Speer (GDR)
1972* Magnar Solberg (Nor)
1973 Aleksandr Tikhonov (USSR)
1974 Juhani Suutarinen (Fin) (10km and 20km)
1975 Aleksandr Elisarov (USSR) (10km)
     Heikki Ikola (Fin) (20km)
1976* Nikolay Kruglov (USSR) (20km)
     Juhani Suutarinen (Fin) (10km)
1977 Heikki Ikola (Fin) (20km)
     Aleksandr Tikhonov (USSR) (10km)
1978 Odd Lirhus (Nor) (20km)
     Frank Ullrich (GDR) (10km)
1979 Klaus Siebert (GDR) (20km)
     Frank Ullrich (GDR) (10km)
1980* Frank Ullrich (GDR) (10km)
     Anatoliy Alyabyev (USSR) (20km)
1981 Frank Ullrich (GDR) (10km)
     Heikki Ikola (Fin) (20km)

Biathlon Team (Relay (4 ✕ 7·5km) competition)
1958 Sweden
1959 USSR
1960 Not held
1961 Finland
1962 USSR
1963 USSR
1964 Not held
1965 Norway
1966 Norway
1967 Norway
1968* USSR
1969 USSR
1970 Norway
1971 USSR
1972* USSR
1973 USSR
1974 USSR
1975 Finland
1976* USSR
1977 USSR
1978 GDR
1979 GDR
1980* USSR
1981 GDR

Slimming

SLIMMER OF THE YEAR
Slimmer Magazine's 'Slimmer of the Year' contest was established in 1971. The contest winner is announced each year at a press reception held in September.

The winner is selected on the basis of physical weight-loss achieved to reach target weight, and in the view of the judges, a story which will be an inspiration to others. Details of past winners, with total weight-loss, are as follows:

1971 Jeannette Chappell, Stoke-on-Trent (6½ stone)
1972 Halina Smith, South Lancing (11 stone)
1973 Jeanette Edgar, Driffield, Yorks (10 stone)
1974 Brenda Smith, Rainham, Essex (5 stone)
1975 Marlene Johnson, Beverley (7 stone)
1976 Gail Ingham, Chester (6 stone)
1977 Helen Currie, Alloa, Clackmannanshire (7 stone)
1978 John and Linda Jenkins, Birmingham (11 stone)

Before and after: Hilary Hardman 1980 Slimmer of the Year

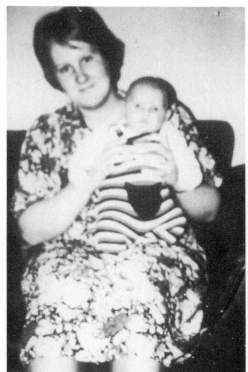

Smoking

PIPEMAN OF THE YEAR

The competition was first established in 1964 by the Briar Pipe Trade Association – which in 1978 changed its name to the Pipesmokers' Council – in association with *Tobacco Magazine*. Readers of *Tobacco Magazine* are presented with the names of several pipesmokers and invited to nominate one of these as 'Pipeman of the Year'.

The winner is invited to the Pipeman of the Year luncheon and is presented with the trophy, a pipe (not smoking) on a stand, on which his, and his predecessors' names are inscribed, which he keeps for one year. In addition he receives a replica of the trophy and a quantity of his favourite tobacco! Previous winning Pipemen:

1964 Rupert Davies
1965 Rt. Hon. Harold Wilson
1966 Andrew Cruickshank

James Galway, 1981 Pipeman of the Year

1967	Warren Mitchell	1975	Campbell Adamson
1968	Peter Cushing	1976	The Rt. Hon. Harold Wilson (Pipeman of the Decade)
1969	Jack Hargreaves		
1970	Eric Morecambe	1977	Brian Barnes
1971	The Right Hon. The Lord Shinwell	1978	Magnus Magnusson
1972	Not held	1979	J. B. Priestley
1973	Frank Muir	1980	Edward Fox
1974	Fred Trueman	1981	James Galway

Softball

WORLD CHAMPIONSHIPS

MEN
First held in 1966.
1966 USA
1968 USA
1972 Canada
1976 Canada, USA and New Zealand
1980 USA

WOMEN
First held in 1965.
1965 Australia
1970 Japan
1974 Japan
1978 USA

Songs

BRITAIN'S SONG FOR EUROPE
An annual competition in which BBC Television viewers vote for Britain's entry in the Eurovision Song Contest.

1956 No entry
1957 All, Patricia Bredin
1958 No entry
1959 Sing Little Birdie, Teddy Johnson and Pearl Carr
1960 Looking High, High, High, Bryan Johnson
1961 Are you Sure? The Allison Brothers
1962 Ring-a-Ding Girl, Ronnie Carroll
1963 Say Wonderful Things, Ronnie Carroll
1964 I Love the Little Things, Matt Monro
1965 I Belong, Kathy Kirby
1966 A Man Without Love, Kenneth McKellar
1967 Puppet on a String, Sandie Shaw
1968 Congratulations, Cliff Richard
1969 Boom Bang-a-Bang, Lulu
1970 Knock, Knock, Who's There?, Mary Hopkin
1971 Jack in the Box, Clodagh Rodgers
1972 Beg, Steal or Borrow, The New Seekers
1973 Power to All Our Friends, Cliff Richard
1974 Long Live Love, Olivia Newton-John
1975 Let Me Be The One, The Shadows
1976 Save Your Kisses For Me, Brotherhood of Man
1977 Rock Bottom, Lynsey de Paul and Mike Moran
1978 The Bad Old Days, Co-Co
1979 Mary Ann, Black Lace
1980 Love Enough for Two, Prima Donna
1981 Making Your Mind Up, Bucks Fizz

Bucks Fizz who won both 'Song for Europe' and the 'Eurovision Song Contest' with Making Your Mind Up *in 1981*

EUROVISION SONG CONTEST

An annual top award, the contest involves artists from over a dozen European countries, and attracts a huge television audience.

	Singer	Country	Song
1956	Lys Assia	Switzerland	Refrains
1957	Corry Brokken	Netherlands	Net Als Town
1958	André Claveau	France	Dors, Mon Amour
1959	Teddy Scholten	Netherlands	Een Beetje
1960	Jacqueline Boyer	France	Tom Pillibi
1961	Jean Claude Pascal	Luxembourg	Nous, Les Amoureux
1962	Isabelle Aubret	France	Un Premier Amour
1963	Grethe and Jørgen Ingmann	Denmark	Dansevise
1964	Gigliola Cinquetti	Italy	No Ho L'Eta per Amarti
1965	France Gall	Luxembourg	Poupee de Cire, Poupee de Son
1966	Udo Jurgens	Austria	Merci Cherie
1967	Sandie Shaw	United Kingdom	Puppet on a String
1968	Massiel	Spain	La, La, La
1969	(Four countries won – each with 18 points)		
	Salome	Spain	Vivo Cantando
	Lulu	United Kingdom	Boom Bang-a-Bang
	Lennie Kuhr	Holland	De Troubadour
	Frida Boccara	France	Un Jour, Un Enfant
1970	Dana	Ireland	All Kinds of Everything
1971	Severine	Monaco	Un Banc, Un Arbre, Une Rue
1972	Vicky Leandros	Luxembourg	Après Toi
1973	Anne Marie David	Luxembourg	Tu Te Reconnaitras
1974	Abba	Sweden	Waterloo
1975	Teach-In	Holland	Ding Ding A Dong
1976	Brotherhood of Man	United Kingdom	Save Your Kisses For Me
1977	Marie Myriam	France	L'Oiseau et l'Enfant
1978	Izhar Cohen and the Alphabeta	Israel	A-Ba-Ni-Bi
1979	Milk and Honey	Israel	Hallelujah
1980	Johnny Logan	Ireland	What's Another Year
1981	Bucks Fizz	United Kingdom	Making Your Mind Up

Abba, 1974 Eurovision Song Contest winners (BBC copyright)

YAMAHA MUSIC FOUNDATION GRAND PRIX

This is the main prize at the world popular music festival in Japan. It consists of $5000 and a gold medallion is given annually for the best original unpublished song.

1970
I Dream of Naomi, by David Krivoshei, performed by Hedva and David (Isr)

1971
The Song of Departure, by Hitoshi Komuro, performed by Kamijo and Rokumonsen (Jap)
Un Jour L'Amour, by Andre Popp, performed by Martine Clemenceau (Fra)

1972

Feeling, by Peter Yellowstone and Jane Schwarz, performed by Capricorn (GB)
Life Is Just for Livin', by Ernie Smith, performed by Ernie Smith (Jam)

1973

I Wish You Were Here With Me, by Akiko Kosaka, performed by Akiko Kosaka (Jap)
All the Kings and Castles, by Shawn Phillips, performed by Shawn Phillips (USA)
Head Over Heels, by Zack Laurence, performed by Keeley Ford (GB)
How Strange Paris is Sometimes, by Gino Mescoli and Alfred Ferrari, performed by Gilda Giuliani (Ita)

1974

Someday, by Yoshimi Hamada, performed by Yoshimi Hamada (Jap)
You Made Me Feel I Could Fly, by Kristian Lindeman, performed by Ellen Nikolaysen (Nor)

1975

Time Goes Around, by Miyuki Nakajima, performed by Miyuki Nakajima (Jap)
Lucky Man, by Jorge Garcia-Castil, performed by Mister Loco (Mex)

1976

Goodbye Morning, by Kaoru Nakajima, performed by Sandy (Jap)
My Love, by Gino Mescoli, performed by Franco and Regina (Ita)

1977

A Ballad For You, by Masanori Sera, performed by Masanori Sera and Twist (Jap)
Can't Hide My Love, by Richard Gillinson and David Hayes, performed by Rags (GB)

1978

Fly on all the Way, by Hiroshi Madoka, performed by Hiroshi Madoka (Jap)
Love Rocks, by Biddu, performed by Tina Charles (GB)

1979

In the City of Strangers, by Michio Yamashita, performed by The Crystal King (Jap)
Sitting on the Edge of the Ocean, by Ronnie Scott and Steve Wolfe, performed by Bonnie Tyler (GB)

1980

Oh My Good-Bye Town, by Tetsuya Itami, performed by Side by Side (Jap)

Mary Macgregor, 1980 winner of the Yamaha Music Foundation Grand Prix

What's The Use, by Mary Macgregor, Marty Rodgers and David Bluefield, performed by Mary Macgregor (USA)

Speedway

WORLD CHAMPIONSHIPS
First held in 1936 at Wembley

1936 Lionel Van Praag (Aus)	1954 Ronnie Moore (NZ)
1937 Jack Milne (USA)	1955 Peter Craven (Eng)
1938 Bluey Wilkinson (Aus)	1956 Ove Fundin (Swe)
1949 Tommy Price (Eng)	1957 Barry Briggs (NZ)
1950 Freddie Williams (Wal)	1958 Barry Briggs (NZ)
1951 Jack Young (Aus)	1959 Ronnie Moore (NZ)
1952 Jack Young (Aus)	1960 Ove Fundin (Swe)
1953 Freddie Williams (Wal)	1961 Ove Fundin (Swe)
	1962 Peter Craven (Eng)
	1963 Ove Fundin (Swe)
	1964 Barry Briggs (NZ)

Ronnie Moore, twice world speedway champion (Sport and General)

1965 Björn Knutsson (Swe)	1973 Jerzy Szczakiel (Pol)
1966 Barry Briggs (NZ)	1974 Anders Michanek (Swe)
1967 Ove Fundin (Swe)	1975 Ole Olsen (Den)
1968 Ivan Mauger (NZ)	1976 Peter Collins (Eng)
1969 Ivan Mauger (NZ)	1977 Ivan Mauger (NZ)
1970 Ivan Mauger (NZ)	1978 Ole Olsen (Den)
1971 Ole Olsen (Den)	1979 Ivan Mauger (NZ)
1972 Ivan Mauger (NZ)	1980 Mike Lee (Eng)

WORLD TEAM CUP
First contested in 1960.

1960 Sweden	1971 Great Britain
1961 Poland	1972 Great Britain
1962 Sweden	1973 Great Britain
1963 Sweden	1974 Great Britain
1964 Sweden	1975 Great Britain
1965 Poland	1976 Australia
1966 Poland	1977 Great Britain
1967 Sweden	1978 Denmark
1968 Great Britain	1979 New Zealand
1969 Poland	1980 England
1970 Sweden	

NATIONAL LEAGUE – BRITISH LEAGUE
Introduced in 1932 the National League varied between all the English divisions. In 1960 the Provincial League was founded, and the British League was formed in 1965 as a merger of these two leagues.

NATIONAL LEAGUE
1932 Wembley
1933 Belle Vue
1934 Belle Vue
1935 Belle Vue
1936 Belle Vue
1937 West Ham
1938 New Cross
1939 Belle Vue
1946 Wembley
1947 Wembley
1948 New Cross
1949 Wembley
1950 Wembley
1951 Wembley
1952 Wembley
1953 Wembley
1954 Wimbledon
1955 Southampton
1956 Wimbledon
1957 Swindon
1958 Wimbledon
1959 Wimbledon
1960 Wimbledon
1961 Wimbledon
1962 Southampton
1963 Belle Vue
1964 Oxford

BRITISH LEAGUE
1965 West Ham
1966 Halifax
1967 Swansea
1968 Coventry
1969 Poole
1970 Belle Vue
1971 Belle Vue
1972 Belle Vue
1973 Reading
1974 Exeter
1975 Ipswich
1976 Ipswich
1977 White City
1978 Coventry
1979 Coventry,
1980 Hackney

WORLD PAIRS CUP
First contested 1968.

1966 Sweden (Ove Fundin, Törbjorn Harrysson)
1969 New Zealand (Ivan Mauger, Bob Andrews)
1970 New Zealand (Ronnie Moore, Ivan Mauger)
1971 Poland (Jerzy Szczakiel, Andrzej Wyglenda)
1972 England (Ray Wilson, Terry Betts)
1973 Sweden (Anders Michanek, Tommy Jansson)
1974 Sweden (Anders Michanek, Soren Sjösten)
1975 Sweden (Anders Michanek, Tommy Jansson)
1976 England (John Louis, Malcolm Simmons)
1977 England (Peter Collins, Malcolm Simmons)
1978 England (Malcolm Simmons, Gordon Kennett)
1979 Denmark (Ole Olsen, Hans Nielsen)
1980 England (Dave Jessup, Peter Collins)
1981 USA (Bruce Penhall, Bobby Schwarz)

Spiritualism

SPIRITUALIST OF THE YEAR

This award was instituted by *Psychic News* in 1966, and a gift commemorating it is presented at an annual dinner.

1966 Geraldine Cummins, automatic writing medium
1967 Ena Twigg, medium for TV appearances
1968 Jessie Nason, medium for TV appearances
1969 Rosemary Brown, musical medium
1970 Gordon Higginson, president of the Spiritualists' National Union
1971 Ivy Northage, for her School for Mediums
1972 Harry Edwards, the healer
1973 Rev. David Kennedy, for his public exposition
1974 Grace Cook, veteran medium
1975 George Chapman, healer
1976 Leslie Flint, direct voice medium
1977 Coral Polge, psychic artist
1978 Doris Collins, medium
Doris Stokes, medium
1979 Joe Benjamin, medium
1980 David Walton, medium and spirit healer

Geraldine Cummins, with her automatic scripts, Spiritualist of the Year in 1966

Sport

THE BBC SPORTS PERSONALITY OF THE YEAR

Each year viewers of Grandstand and BBC Television sports programmes cast their votes to find the year's outstanding sports personality. Winners since the competition began:

1954 Christopher Chataway (athletics)
1955 Gordon Pirie (athletics)
1956 Jim Laker (cricket)
1957 Dai Rees (golf)
1958 Ian Black (swimming)
1959 John Surtees (motorcycling)
1960 David Broome (show jumping)
1961 Stirling Moss (motor racing)
1962 Anita Lonsborough (swimming)
1963 Dorothy Hyman (athletics)
1964 Mary Rand (athletics)
1965 Tommy Simpson (cycling)
1966 Bobby Moore (football)
1967 Henry Cooper (boxing)
1968 David Hemery (athletics)
1969 Ann Jones (tennis)
1970 Henry Cooper (boxing)
1971 Princess Anne (show jumping)
1972 Mary Peters (athletics)
1973 Jackie Stewart (motor racing)
1974 Brendan Foster (athletics)
1975 David Steele (cricket)
1976 John Curry (ice-skating)
1977 Virginia Wade (lawn tennis)
1978 Steve Ovett (athletics)
1979 Sebastian Coe (athletics)
1980 Robin Cousins (ice skating)

THE *DAILY EXPRESS* SPORTSMAN OF THE YEAR

1946 Bruce Woodcock (boxing)
1947 Denis Compton (cricket)
1948 Denis Compton (cricket)
1949 Reg Harris (cycling)
1950 Reg Harris (cycling)
1951 Geoffrey Duke (motorcycling)
1952 Len Hutton (cricket)
1953 Gordon Pirie (athletics)
1954 Roger Bannister (athletics)
1955 Gordon Pirie (athletics)
1956 Chris Brasher (athletics)
1957 Derek Ibbotson (athletics)
1958 Ian Black (swimming)
1959 John Surtees (motorcycling)
1960 Don Thompson (walking)
1961 Johnny Haynes (soccer)
1962 Brian Phelps (diving)
1963 Jim Clark (motor racing)
1964 Robbie Brightwell (athletics)
1965 Tommy Simpson (cycling)
1966 Bobby Moore (soccer)
1967 Harvey Smith (show jumping)
1968 Lester Piggott (horse racing)
1969 Tony Jacklin (golf)
1970 Henry Cooper (boxing)
1971 Jackie Stewart (motor racing)
1972 Gordon Banks (soccer)
1973 Jackie Stewart (motor racing)
1974 Willie John McBride (rugby union)
1975 David Steele (cricket)
1976 James Hunt (motor racing)
1977 Geoff Boycott (cricket)

Brian Jacks, Olympic middleweight judo bronze medallist in 1972, who went on to Superstardom

1978 Steve Ovett (athletics)	1962 Anita Lonsborough (swimming)
1979 Sebastian Coe (athletics)	1963 Dorothy Hyman (athletics)
1980 Sebastian Coe (athletics)	1964 Mary Rand (née Bignal) (athletics)
	1965 Marion Coakes (show jumping)
	1966 Ann Jones (lawn tennis)
SPORTSWOMAN OF THE YEAR	1967 Beryl Burton (cycling)
1952 Jeanette Altwegg (ice skating)	1968 Marion Coakes (show jumping)
1953 Pat Smythe (show jumping)	1969 Ann Jones (lawn tennis)
1954 Pat Smythe (show jumping)	1970 Lillian Board (athletics)
1955 Pat Smythe (show jumping)	1971 Princess Anne (equestrian three-day event)
1956 Judy Grinham (swimming)	1972 Mary Peters (athletics)
1957 Diana Wilkinson (swimming)	1973 Ann Moore (show jumping)
1958 Judy Grinham (swimming)	1974 Virginia Wade (lawn tennis)
1959 Mary Bignal (athletics)	1975 Virginia Wade (lawn tennis)
1960 Anita Lonsborough (swimming)	1976 Debbie Johnsey (equestrian three-day event)
1961 Angela Mortimer (lawn tennis)	1977 Virginia Wade (lawn tennis)

1978 Sharron Davies (swimming)
1979 Caroline Bradley (show jumping)
1980 Linsey Macdonald (athletics)

SUPERSTARS
The first Superstars, a multi-sport contest between invited top competitors in different sports, was held in the USA in 1973 and won by the pole vaulter, Bob Seagren.

UK NATIONAL CHAMPIONSHIPS
1973 David Hemery (athletics – hurdler)
1974 John Conteh (boxing)
1975 UK title not contested, but David Hemery leading UK competitor in European Final
1976 David Hemery (athletics – hurdler)
1977 Tim Crooks (rowing)
1978 Brian Jacks (judo)

1979 Brian Jacks (judo)
1980 Keith Fielding (rugby league)

EUROPEAN CHAMPIONSHIPS
1975 Kjell Isaksson (Sweden, athletics – pole vault)
1976 Kjell Isaksson (Sweden, athletics – pole vault)
1977 Ties Kruize (Netherlands, hockey)
1978 Brian Jacks (GB, judo) and Ties Kruize (Netherlands, hockey)
1979 Brian Jacks (GB, judo)
1980 Andy Ripley (GB, rugby union)

WORLD CHAMPIONSHIPS
1977 Bob Seagren (USA, athletics – pole vault)
1978 Brian Budd (Canada, association football)
1979 Brian Budd (Canada, association football)
1980 Brian Budd (Canada, association football)
1981 Jody Scheckter (South Africa, motor racing)

Squash Rackets

WORLD OPEN CHAMPIONSHIPS
First held in 1976 at Wembley.

MEN
1976 Geoff Hunt (Aus)
1977 Geoff Hunt (Aus)
1978 Postponed
1979 Geoff Hunt (Aus)

First held in 1976 in Australia.

WOMEN

Individual	Team
1976 Heather McKay (Aus)	Australia
1979 Heather McKay (Aus)	Great Britain

WORLD AMATEUR CHAMPIONSHIPS
First held in 1967, it is contested every two years. Individual and team winners:

Individual	Team
1967 Geoff Hunt (Aus)	Australia
1969 Geoff Hunt (Aus)	Australia
1971 Geoff Hunt (Aus)	Australia
1973 Cameron Nancarrow (Aus)	Australia
1975 Kevin Shawcross (Aus)	Great Britain
1977 Maqsood Ahmed (Pak)	Pakistan
1979 Jehangir Khan (Pak)	Great Britain

BRITISH OPEN CHAMPIONSHIP
First played in 1930, the British Open Championship in which both amateurs and professionals may compete was for years regarded as the unofficial world championship. Until 1947 the event was held on a challenge system with

Heather McKay in 1979 after a 20-year squash career in which she lost only two matches (Abbeydale Sports Centre)

217

two-leg matches between the holder and his challenger. Held annually.

1930–31 Don Butcher (GB)
1932–37 Abdel Fattah Amr Bey (Egy)
1938 James Dear (GB)
1946–49 Mahmoud el Karim (Egy)
1950–55 Hashim Khan (Pak)
1956 Roshan Khan (Pak)
1957 Hashim Khan (Pak)
1958–61 Azam Khan (Pak)
1962 Mohibullah Khan (Pak)
1963–66 Abou Taleb (Egy)
1967–68 Jonah Barrington (GB)
1969 Geoff Hunt (Aus)
1970–73 Jonah Barrington (GB)
1974 Geoff Hunt (Aus)
1975 Qamar Zaman (Pak)
1976–81 Geoff Hunt (Aus)

BRITISH WOMEN'S OPEN CHAMPIONSHIP
First held in 1922.

1922 Joyce Cave (GB)
1922 Sylvia Huntsman (GB)
1923 Nancy Cave (GB)
1924 Joyce Cave (GB)
1925–26 Cecily Fenwick (GB) (2)
1928 Joyce Cave (GB)
1929–30 Nancy Cave (GB)
1931 Cecily Fenwick (GB)
1932–34 Susan Noel (GB)

1934–39 Margot Lumb (GB)
1947–49 Joan Curry (GB)
1950–58 Janet Morgan/Shardlow (GB)
1960 Sheila Macintosh (GB)
1961 Fran Marshall (GB)
1962–77 Heather McKay (Aus)
1978 Susan Newman/King (Aus)
1979 Barbara Wall (Aus)
1980–81 Vicki Hoffman (Aus)

Note that there have occasionally been two championships in the same year, and that in other cases a year is missed. This is due to the championship being held in December or January.

BRITISH AMATEUR CHAMPIONSHIP
First held in 1922 and contested annually. Winners since 1963:

1963–66 Aftab Jawaid (Pak) (4)
1967–69 Jonah Barrington (GB) (3)
1970 Geoff Hunt (Aus)
1971 Gogi Alauddin (Pak)
1972 Cameron Nancarrow (Aus)
1973–74 Mohibullah Khan (Pak) (2)
1975–76 Kevin Shawcross (Aus).
1976–77 Bruce Brownlee (NZ)
1977–78 Gamal Awad (Egy)
1978–79 Gamal Awad (Egy)
1979–80 Jonathan Leslie (GB)
Discontinued
Most wins: 6 Abdel Fattah Amr Bey (Egy) 1931–33, 1935–57

Swimming

OLYMPIC CHAMPIONSHIPS
Swimming events have been held at each Olympic Games since 1896, when three men's events were included – 100, 500 and 1200 metres freestyle. Women's events were first included in 1912. Winners since 1948 have been:

MEN

100 metres freestyle
1948 Walter Ris (USA) 57·3
1952 Clarke Scholes (USA) 57·4
1956 Jon Henricks (Aus) 55·4
1960 John Devitt (Aus) 55·2
1964 Donald Schollander (USA) 53·4
1968 Michael Wenden (Aus) 52·2
1972 Mark Spitz (USA) 51·22
1976 Jim Montgomery (USA) 49·99
1980 Jorg Weithe (GDR) 50·40

200 metres freestyle
1968 Michael Wenden (Aus) 1:55·2
1972 Mark Spitz (USA) 1:52·78
1976 Bruce Furniss (USA) 1:50·29
1980 Sergei Kopliakov (USSR) 1·49·81

400 metres freestyle
1948 William Smith (USA) 4:41·0
1952 Jean Boiteaux (Fra) 4:30·7
1956 Murray Rose (Aus) 4:27·3
1960 Murray Rose (Aus) 4:18·3

1964 Donald Schollander (USA) 4:12·2
1968 Michael Burton (USA) 4:09·0
1972 Bradford Cooper (Aus) 4:00·27
1976 Brian Goodell (USA) 3:51·93
1980 Vladimir Salnikov (USSR) 3:51·31

1500 metres freestyle
1948 James McLane (USA) 19:18·5
1952 Ford Konno (USA) 18:30·0
1956 Murray Rose (Aus) 17:58·9
1960 Jon Konrads (Aus) 17:19·6
1964 Robert Windle (Aus) 17:01·7
1968 Michael Burton (USA) 16:38·9
1972 Michael Burton (USA 15:52·58
1976 Brian Goodell (USA) 15:02·40
1980 Vladimir Salnikov (USSR) 14:58·27

100 metres backstroke
1948 Allen Stack (USA) 1:06·4
1952 Yoshinobu Oyakawa (USA) 1:05·4
1956 David Thiele (Aus) 1:02·2
1960 David Thiele (Aus) 1:01·9
1964 Not held
1968 Roland Matthes (GDR) 58·7
1972 Roland Matthes (GDR) 56·58
1976 John Naber (USA) 55·49
1980 Bengt Baron (Swe) 56·53

200 metres backstroke
1964 Jed Graef (USA) 2:10·3
1968 Roland Matthes (GDR) 2:09·6

1972 Roland Matthes (GDR) 2:02·82
1976 John Naber (USA) 1:59·19
1980 Sandor Wladar (Hun) 2:01·93

100 metres butterfly
1968 Douglas Russell (USA) 55·9
1972 Mark Spitz (USA) 54·27
1976 Matt Vogel (USA) 54·35
1980 Par Arvidsson (Swe) 54·92

200 metres butterfly
1956 William Yorzyk (USA) 2:19·3
1960 Michael Troy (USA) 2:12·8
1964 Kevin Berry (Aus) 2:06·6
1968 Carl Robie (USA) 2:08·7
1972 Mark Spitz (USA) 2:00·70
1976 Michael Bruner (USA) 1:59·23
1980 Sergei Fesenko (USSR) 1:59·76

100 metres breaststroke
1968 Donald McKenzie (USA) 1:07·7
1972 Nobutaka Taguchi (Jap) 1:04·94
1976 John Hencken (USA) 1:03·11
1980 Duncan Goodhew (GB) 1:03·34

200 metres breaststroke
1948 Joseph Verdeur (USA) 2:39·3
1952 John Davies (Aus) 2:34·4
1956 Masura Furukawa (Jap) 2:34·7
1960 William Mulliken (USA) 2:37·4
1964 Ian O'Brien (Aus) 2:27·8
1968 Felipe Munoz (Mex) 2:28·7
1972 John Hencken (USA) 2:21·55
1976 David Wilkie (GB) 2:15·11
1980 Robertas Zulpa (USSR) 2:15·85

200 metres individual medley
1968 Charles Hickcox (USA) 2:12·0
1972 Gunnar Larsson (Swe) 2:07·17

400 metres individual medley
1964 Richard Roth (USA) 4:45·4
1968 Charles Hickcox (USA) 4:48·4
1972 Gunnar Larsson (Swe) 4:31·98
1976 Rod Strachan (USA) 4:23·68
1980 Aleksandr Sidorenko (USSR) 4:22·89

4 × 100 metres freestyle relay
1964 USA 3:33·2
1968 USA 3:31·7
1972 USA 3:26·42

4 × 200 metres freestyle relay
1948 USA 8:46·0
1952 USA 8:31·1
1956 Australia 8:23·6
1960 USA 8:10·2
1964 USA 7:52·1
1968 USA 7:52·3
1972 USA 7:35·78
1976 USA 7:23·22
1980 USSR 7:23·50

4 × 100 metres medley relay
1960 USA 4:05·4
1964 USA 3:58·4
1968 USA 3:54·9
1972 USA 3:48·16
1976 USA 3:42·22
1980 Australia 3:45·70

Vladimir Salnikov, double Olympic gold medallist in 1980 and the first man to swim 1 500 metres in less than 15 minutes (All-Sport)

Springboard diving
1948 Bruce Harlan (USA) 163·64
1952 David Browning (USA) 205·29
1956 Robert Clotworthy (USA) 159·56
1960 Gary Tobian (USA) 170·00
1964 Kenneth Sitzberger (USA) 159·90
1968 Bernard Wrightson (USA) 170·15
1972 Vladimir Vasin (USSR) 594·09
1976 Philip Boggs (USA) 619·05
1980 Aleksandr Portnov (USSR) 905·025

Platform diving (highboard)
1948 Samuel Lee (USA) 130·05
1952 Samuel Lee (USA) 156·28
1956 Joaquin Capilla (Mex) 152·44
1960 Robert Webster (USA) 165·56
1964 Robert Webster (USA) 148·58
1968 Klaus Dibiasi (Ita) 164·18
1972 Klaus Dibiasi (Ita) 504·12
1976 Klaus Dibiasi (Ita) 600·51
1980 Falk Hoffman (GDR) 835·650

WOMEN

100 metres freestyle
1948 Greta Andersen (Den) 1:06·3
1952 Katalin Szöke (Hun) 1:06·8
1956 Dawn Fraser (Aus) 1:02·0
1960 Dawn Fraser (Aus) 1:01·2
1964 Dawn Fraser (Aus) 59·5
1968 Jan Henne (USA) 1:00·0
1972 Sandra Neilson (USA) 58·59
1976 Kornelia Ender (GDR) 55·65
1980 Barbara Krause (GDR) 54·79

200 metres freestyle
1968 Debbie Meyer (USA) 2:10·5
1972 Shane Gould (Aus) 2:03·56
1976 Kornelia Ender (GDR) 1:59·26
1980 Barbara Krause (GDR) 1:58·33

400 metres freestyle
1948 Ann Curtis (USA) 5:17·8
1952 Valeria Gyenge (Hun) 5:12·1
1956 Lorraine Crapp (Aus) 4:54·6
1960 Christine von Saltza (USA) 4:50·6
1964 Virginia Duenkel (USA) 4:43·3

1968 Debbie Meyer (USA) 4:31·8
1972 Shane Gould (Aus) 4:19·04
1976 Petra Thuemer (GDR) 4:09·89
1980 Ines Diers (GDR) 4:08·76

800 metres freestyle
1968 Debbie Meyer (USA) 9:24·0
1972 Keena Rothhammer (USA) 8:53·68
1976 Petra Thuemer (GDR) 8:37·14
1980 Michelle Ford (Aus) 8:28·90

100 metres backstroke
1948 Karen Harup (Den) 1:14·4
1952 Joan Harrison (SA) 1:14·3
1956 Judy Grinham (GB) 1:12·9
1960 Lynn Burke (USA) 1:09·3
1964 Cathy Ferguson (USA) 1:07·7
1968 Kaye Hall (USA) 1:06·2
1972 Melissa Belote (USA) 1:05·78
1976 Ulrike Richter (GDR) 1:01·83
1980 Rica Reinisch (GDR) 1:00·86

200 metres backstroke
1968 Lillian Watson (USA) 2:24·8
1972 Melissa Belote (USA) 2:19·19
1976 Ulrike Richter (GDR) 2:13·43
1980 Rica Reinisch (GDR) 2:11·77

100 metres butterfly
1956 Shelley Mann (USA) 1:11·0
1960 Carolyn Schuler (USA) 1:09·5
1964 Sharon Stouder (USA) 1:04·7
1968 Lynette McClements (USA) 1:05·5
1972 Mayumi Aoki (Jap) 1:03·34
1976 Kornelia Ender (GDR) 1:00·13
1980 Caren Metschuck (GDR) 1:00·42

200 metres butterfly
1968 Ada Kok (Hol) 2:24·7
1972 Karen Moe (USA) 2:15·57
1976 Andrea Pollack (GDR) 2:11·41
1980 Ines Geissler (GDR) 2:10·44

100 metres breaststroke
1968 Djurdica Bjedov (Yug) 1:15·8
1972 Catherine Carr (USA) 1:13·58
1976 Hannelore Anke (GDR) 1:11·16
1980 Ute Geweniger (GDR) 1:10·22

200 metres breaststroke
1948 Petronella van Vliet (Hol) 2:57·2
1952 Eva Székely (Hun) 2:51·7
1956 Ursula Happe (Ger) 2:53·1
1960 Anita Lonsborough (GB) 2:49·5
1964 Galina Prozumenshchikova (USSR) 2:46·4
1968 Sharon Wichman (USA) 2:44·4
1972 Beverley Whitfield (Aus) 2:41·71
1976 Marina Koshevaia (USSR) 2:33·35
1980 Lina Kachushite (USSR) 2:29·54

200 metres individual medley
1968 Claudia Kolb (USA) 2:24·7
1972 Shane Gould (Aus) 2:23·07

400 metres individual medley
1964 Donna de Varona (USA) 5:18·7
1968 Claudia Kolb (USA) 5:08·5
1972 Gail Neall (Aus) 5:02·97
1976 Ulrike Tauber (GDR) 4:42·77
1980 Petra Schneider (GDR) 4:36·29

4 × 100 metres freestyle relay
1948 USA 4:29·2

1952 Hungary 4:24·4
1956 Australia 4:17·1
1960 USA 4:08·9
1964 USA 4:03·8
1968 USA 4:02·5
1972 USA 3:55·19
1976 USA 3:44·82
1980 GDR 3:42·71

4 × 100 metres medley relay
1960 USA 4:41·1
1964 USA 4:33·9
1968 USA 4:28·3
1972 USA 4:20·75
1976 GDR 4:07·95
1980 GDR 4:06·67

Springboard diving
1948 Victoria Draves (USA) 108·74
1952 Patricia McCormick (USA) 147·30
1956 Patricia McCormick (USA) 142·36
1960 Ingrid Krämer (Ger) 155·81
1964 Ingrid Engel (née Krämer) (Ger) 145·00
1968 Sue Gossick (USA) 150·77
1972 Micki King (USA) 450·03
1976 Jennifer Chandler (USA) 506·19
1980 Irina Kalinina (USSR) 725·910

Platform diving (highboard)
1948 Victoria Draves (USA) 68·87
1952 Patricia McCormick (USA) 79·37
1956 Patricia McCormick (USA) 84·85
1960 Ingrid Krämer (Ger) 91·28
1964 Lesley Bush (USA) 99·80
1968 Milena Duchková (Cze) 109·59
1972 Ulrika Knape (Swe) 390·00
1976 Elena Vaytsekhovskaya (USSR) 406·59
1980 Martina Jaschke (GDR) 596·250

Pat McCormick won four Olympic gold medals for diving

WORLD CHAMPIONSHIPS
First held in Belgrade in 1973.

MEN

100 metres freestyle
1973 Jim Montgomery (USA) 51·70
1975 Andrew Coan (USA) 51·25
1978 David McCagg (USA) 50·24

200 metres freestyle
1973 Jim Montgomery (USA) 1:53·02
1975 Tim Shaw (USA) 1:51·04
1978 William Forrester (USA) 1:51·02

400 metres freestyle
1973 Rick DeMont (USA) 3:58·18
1975 Tim Shaw (USA) 3:54·88
1978 Vladimir Salnikov (USSR) 3:51·94

1500 metres freestyle
1973 Steve Holland (Aus) 15:31·85
1975 Tim Shaw (USA) 15:28·92
1978 Vladimir Salnikov (USSR) 15:03·99

100 metres backstroke
1973 Roland Matthes (GDR) 57·47
1974 Roland Matthes (GDR) 58·15
1978 Robert Jackson (USA) 56·36

200 metres backstroke
1973 Roland Matthes (GDR) 2:01·87
1975 Zoltan Verraszto (Hun) 2:05·05
1978 Jesse Vassallo (USA) 2:02·16

100 metres butterfly
1973 Bruce Robertson (Can) 55·69
1975 Greg Jagenburg (USA) 55·63
1978 Joseph Bottom (USA) 54·30

200 metres butterfly
1973 Robin Backhaus (USA) 2:03·32
1975 William Forrester (USA) 2:01·95
1978 Michael Bruner (USA) 1:59·38

100 metres breaststroke
1973 John Hencken (USA) 1:04·02
1975 David Wilkie (GB) 1:04·26
1978 Walter Kusch (GDR) 1:03·56

200 metres breaststroke
1973 David Wilkie (GB) 2:19·28
1975 David Wilkie (GB) 2:18·23
1978 Nick Nevid (USA) 2:18·37

200 metres individual medley
1973 Gunnar Larsson (Swe) 2:08·36
1975 András Hargitay (Hun) 2:07·72
1978 Graham Smith (Can) 2:03·65

400 metres individual medley
1973 András Hargitay (Hun) 4:31·11
1975 András Hargitay (Hun) 4:32·57
1978 Jesse Vassallo (USA) 4:20·05

4 × 100 metres freestyle relay
1973 USA 3:27·18
1975 USA 3:24·85
1978 USA 3:19·74

4 × 200 metres freestyle relay
1973 USA 7:33·22
1975 West Germany 7:39·44
1978 USA 7:20·82

4 × 100 metres medley relay
1973 USA 3:49·49

1975 USA 3:49·00
1978 USA 3:44·63

Springboard diving
1973 Phil Boggs (USA) 618·57
1975 Phil Boggs (USA) 597·12
1978 Phil Boggs (USA) 913·95

Platform diving (highboard)
1973 Klaus Dibiasi (Ita) 559·53
1975 Klaus Dibiasi (Ita) 547·98
1978 Greg Louganis (USA) 844·11

WOMEN

100 metres freestyle
1973 Kornelia Ender (GDR) 57·54
1975 Kornelia Ender (GDR) 56·50
1978 Barbara Krause (GDR) 55·68

200 metres freestyle
1973 Keena Rothhammer (USA) 2:04·99
1975 Shirley Babashoff (USA) 2:02·50
1978 Cynthia Woodhead (USA) 1:58·53

400 metres freestyle
1973 Heather Greenwood (USA) 4:20·28
1975 Shirley Babashoff (USA) 4:16·87
1978 Tracey Wickham (Aus) 4:06·28

800 metres freestyle
1973 Novella Calligaris (Ita) 8:52·97
1975 Jenny Turrall (Aus) 8:44·75
1978 Tracey Wickham (Aus) 8:24·94

100 metres backstroke
1973 Ulrike Richter (GDR) 1:05·42
1975 Ulrike Richter (GDR) 1:03·30
1978 Linda Jezek (USA) 1:02·55

200 metres backstroke
1973 Melissa Belote (USA) 2:20·52
1975 Birgit Treiber (GDR) 2:15·46
1978 Linda Jezek (USA) 2:11·93

100 metres butterfly
1973 Kornelia Ender (GDR) 1:02·53
1975 Kornelia Ender (GDR) 1:01·24
1978 Mary-Joan Pennington (USA) 1:00·20

200 metres butterfly
1973 Rosemaria Kother (GDR) 2:13·76
1975 Rosemarie Kother (GDR) 2:13·82
1978 Tracy Caulkins (USA) 2:09·87

100 metres breaststroke
1973 Renate Vogel (GDR) 1:13·74
1975 Hannelore Anke (GDR) 1:12·72
1978 Julia Bogdanova (USSR) 1:10·31

200 metres breaststroke
1973 Renate Vogel (GDR) 2:40·01
1975 Hannelore Anke (GDR) 2:37·25
1978 Lina Kachushite (USSR) 2:31·42

200 metres individual medley
1973 Angela Hubner (GDR) 2:20·51
1975 Kathy Heddy (USA) 2:19·80
1978 Tracy Caulkins (USA) 2:14·07

400 metres individual medley
1973 Gudrun Wegner (GDR) 4:57·31
1975 Ulrike Tauber (GDR) 4:52·76
1978 Tracy Caulkins (USA) 4:40·83

4 × 100 metres freestyle relay
1973 GDR 3:52·45

1975 GDR 3:49·37
1978 USA 3:43·43

4 × 100 metres medley relay
1973 GDR 4:16·84
1975 GDR 4:14·74
1978 USA 4:08·21

Springboard diving
1973 Christine Kohler (GDR) 442·17
1975 Irina Kalinina (USSR) 489·81
1978 Irina Kalinina (USSR) 691·43

Platform diving (highboard)
1973 Ulrike Knape (Swe) 406·77
1975 Janet Ely (USA) 403·89
1978 Irina Kalinina (USSR) 412·71

Synchronised swimming

	Solo	Duet	Team
1973	Teresa Andersen 120·460 (USA)	USA	USA
1975	Gail Buzonas (USA) 133·083	USA	USA
1978	Helen Vanderburg 186·249	Canada	USA

EUROPEAN CUP
Competitions for European nations' teams fo
both men and women were first held in 1969
In December 1980 the events were held in a 25
metre pool, as compared to the usual 50-metr
pools used in the summer months.

MEN	WOMEN
1969 GDR	1969 GDR
1971 USSR	1971 GDR
1973 GDR	1973 GDR
1975 USSR	1975 GDR
1976 USSR	1976 USSR
1979 USSR	1979 GDR
1980 USSR	1980 GDR

WORLD CUP
Team competition first held in 1979, whe
both men's and women's events were won b
the USA.

*Tracy Caulkins, star of the 1978 world
swimming championships*
(All-Sport)

Table Tennis

SWAYTHLING CUP

The men's team world championship for the Swaythling Cup was first held in 1927, and from then until 1957, with the exception of the war years, it was contested annually; since then it has been held biennially.

1927–31 Hungary (5)
1932 Czechoslovakia
1933–35 Hungary (3)
1936 Austria
1937 USA
1938 Hungary
1939 Czechoslovakia
1947–48 Czechoslovakia (2)
1949 Hungary
1950–51 Czechoslovakia (2)
1952 Hungary
1953 England
1954–57 Japan (4)
1959 Japan
1961 China
1963 China
1965 China
1967 Japan
1969 Japan
1971 China
1973 Sweden
1975 China
1977 China
1979 Hungary
1981 China

CORBILLON CUP

The women's team world championship for the Marcel Corbillon Cup was first held in the 1933–34 season, and like the Swaythling Cup was contested annually until 1957 and biennially since then.

1934 Germany
1935–36 Czechoslovakia (2)
1937 USA
1938 Czechoslovakia
1939 Germany
1947–48 England (2)
1949 USA
1950–51 Romania (2)
1952 Japan
1953 Romania
1954 Japan
1955–56 Romania (2)
1957 Japan
1959 Japan
1961 Japan
1963 Japan
1965 China
1967 Japan
1969 USSR
1971 Japan
1973 South Korea
1975 China
1977 China
1979 China
1981 China

Fred Perry playing table tennis in 1932, three years after he had been world champion at that sport and two years before he won his first Wimbledon title at lawn tennis (RTHPL)

WORLD CHAMPIONSHIPS

First held in 1927. Winners:

MEN'S SINGLES

1927 Roland Jacobi (Hun)
1928 Zoltan Mechlovits (Hun)
1929 Fred Perry (GB)
1930 Viktor Barna (Hun)
1931 Miklos Szabados (Hun)
1932 Viktor Barna (Hun)
1933 Viktor Barna (Hun)
1934 Viktor Barna (Hun)
1935 Viktor Barna (Hun)
1936 Standa Kolar (Cze)
1937 Richard Bergmann (Aut)
1938 Bohumil Vana (Cze)
1939 Richard Bergmann (Aut)
1947 Bohumil Vana (Cze)
1948 Richard Bergmann (Eng)
1949 Johnny Leach (Eng)
1950 Richard Bergmann (Eng)
1951 Johnny Leach (Eng)
1952 Hiroji Satoh (Jap)
1953 Ferenc Sido (Hun)
1954 Ichiro Ogimura (Jap)
1955 Toshiaki Tanaka (Jap)
1956 Ichiro Ogimura (Jap)
1957 Toshiaki Tanaka (Jap)
1959 Jung Kuo-tuan (Chi)
1961 Chuang Tse-tung (Chi)
1963 Chuang Tse-tung (Chi)
1965 Chuang Tse-tung (Chi)
1967 Nobuhiko Hasegawa (Jap)
1969 Shigeo Ito (Jap)
1971 Stellan Bengtsson (Swe)
1973 Hsi En-ting (Chi)
1975 Istvan Jonyer (Hun)
1977 Mitsuru Kohno (Jap)
1979 Seiji Ono (Jap)
1981 Guo Yue-hua (Chi)

WOMEN'S SINGLES
1927–31 Maria Mednyanszky (Hun)
1932–33 Anna Sipos (Hun)
1934–35 Marie Kettnerova (Cze)
1936 Ruth Aarons (USA)
1937 Vacant (Ruth Aarons (USA) and Trude Pritzi (Aut) finalists)
1938 Trude Pritzi (Aut)
1939 Vlasha Depetrisova (Cze)
1947–49 Gizi Farkas (Hun)
1950–55 Angelica Rozeanu (Rom)
1956 Timo Okawa (Jap)
1957 Fujie Eguchi (Jap)
1959 Kimiyo Matsuzaki (Jap)
1961 Chiu Chung-hui (Chi)
1963 Kimiyo Matsuzaki (Jap)
1965 Naoko Fukazu (Jap)
1967 Sachiko Morisawa (Jap)
1969 Toshiko Kowada (Jap)
1971 Lin Hui-ching (Chi)
1973 Hu Yu-lan (Chi)
1975 Pak Yung Sun (N.Kor)
1977 Pak Yung Sun (N.Kor)
1979 Ke Hsin-ai (Chi)
1981 Tong Ling (Chi)

MEN'S DOUBLES
Winners since 1965:

1965 Chung Tse-tung and Hsu Yin-sheng (Chi)
1967 Hans Alser and Kjell Johansson (Swe)
1969 Hans Alser and Kjell Johansson (Swe)
1971 Istvan Jonyer and Tibor Klampar (Hun)
1973 Stellan Bengtsson and Kjell Johansson (Swe)
1975 Gabor Gergely and Istvan Jonyer (Hun)
1977 Chen-shih Li and Liang Ke-liang (Chi)
1979 Dragutin Surbek and Anton Stipancic (Yug)
1981 Cai Zhen-hua and Li Zhen-shi

Most wins: 8 Viktor Barna (Hun): 6 with Miklos Szabados 1929–32, 1934–35, with Sandor Glancz in 1933 and with Richard Bergmann 1939

WOMEN'S DOUBLES
Winners since 1965:

1965 Cheng Min-chih and Lin Hui-ching (Chi)
1967 Saeko Hirota and Sachiko Morisawa (Jap)
1969 Svyetlana Grinberg and Zoya Rudnova (USSR)
1971 Cheng Min-chih and Lin Hui-ching (Chi)
1973 Maria Alexandru (Rom) and Miho Hamada (Jap)
1975 Maria Alexandru (Rom) and Shoko Takashima (Jap)
1977 Yong Ok Pak (N.Kor) and Ying Yang (Chi)
1979 Zhang Li and Zhang Deijing (Chi)
1981 Cao Yan-hua and Zhang Deijing (Chi)

Most wins: Maria Mednyanszky (Hun): 6 with Anna Sipos 1930–35, 1 with Erika Flamm 1928

MIXED DOUBLES
Winners since 1965:

1965 Koji Kimura and Masako Seki (Jap)
1967 Nobuhiko Hasegawa and Noriko Yamanaka (Jap)
1969 Nobuhiko Hasegawa and Yasuka Konno (Jap)
1971 Chang Shih-lin and Lin Hui-ching (Chi)
1973 Liang Ko-liang and Li Li (Chi)
1975 Stanislav Gomozkov and Anna Ferdman (USSR)
1977 Jacques Secretin and Claude Bergeret (Fra)
1979 Liang Ke-liang and Ke Hsin-ai (Chi)
1981 Xie Saike and Huang Junquin (Chi)

Most wins: 6 Maria Mednyanszky (Hun): 3 with Miklos Szabados 1930–31, 1934, 2 with Zoltan Mechlovits 1927–28, 1 with Istvan Kelen 1933
4 Ferenc Sido (Hun) 2 with Gizi Farkas 1949–50, 2 with Angelica Rozeanu 1952–53

Tae Kwon-Do

The second world Tae Kwon-Do championships were held in 1980. Winners:

Pattern
Individual Men Puerto Rico
Individual Women Canada
Team Colombia

Sparring
MEN
Lightweight James Hong (USA)
Middleweight Don Jones (Can)
Heavyweight Jaine Morales (Dominica)

WOMEN
Lightweight Annette Sullivan (GB)
Middleweight Canada

TEAM
Canada

Power Test
MEN
Individual Cees Keukens (Can)
Team Paraguay

Teachers

TEACHER OF THE YEAR AWARD
Founded in 1974 this award is given by the *Daily Express*, the winner being chosen on the basis of letters written by pupils, parents and teachers. The prize is £500 and a set of New Caxton Encyclopaedias. Winners:

1974 Jean Miller (London), Algernon Road Junior School, London
1975 No competition
1976 No competition
1977 Nora Morris (London), Houndsfield School, London
1978 Yvonne Traves (Hants), Cams Hill Comprehensive, Fareham, Hants
1979 Hazel B. Roberts (Clwyd), Tirionfa School, Clwyd, N. Wales
1980 Sandra Gale (Berks), Mary Hare Grammar, Newbury, Berks

Nora Morris of Houndsfield School, London, 1977 Teacher of the Year

Television

BRITISH ACADEMY OF FILM AND TELEVISION ARTS AWARDS

Formerly the Society of Film and TV Arts and the Guild of Television Producers and Directors, the Academy gives Britain's most prestigious show business awards.

THE DESMOND DAVIS AWARD
1960 Richard Dimbleby
1961 Michael Barry
1962 Cecil McGivern
1963 Joan Kemp-Welch
1965 Humphrey Burton
1966 Alan Chivers
1967 Sydney Newman
1968 Ken Russell
1969 Richard Cawston
1970 David Attenborough
1971 Jeremy Isaacs
1972 Nigel Ryan
1973 James MacTaggart
1974 Denis Mitchell
1975 Jack Gold
1976 Bill Ward
1977 Norman Swallow
1978 Christopher Ralling
1979 Herbert Wise
1980 Roger Mills

BEST DRAMA PRODUCTION
1954 Christian Simpson
1955 Gill Calder
1956 Joy Harrington
1957 *Play:* Rudolph Cartier
1958 *Play:* Silvio Narizzano
1959 *Play:* William Kotcheff
1960 *Play:* Peter Dews
1961 *Play:* Andrew Osborn
1962 *Play:* David Rose and Charles Jarrott
1963 *Play:* John Jacobs
     Series: Philip Mackie
1964 *Play:* Philip Saville
     Series. Rex Firkin

Cheryl Campbell as Vera Brittain and Peter Woodward as Roland Leighton in 'Testament of Youth', 1979 BAFTA 'Best Drama Production' (BBC copyright)

Top: *Ronnie Corbett* (left) *and Ronnie Barker in their 1975 BAFTA award winning series for* 'Best Light Entertainment Production'.
Above: *A scene from 'Ripping Yarns' which won the 1979 BAFTA 'Best Light Entertainment Production'.* (BBC copyright)

1965 *Play:* Cyril Coke and Peter Hammond
       Series: Philip Mackie and Silvio Narizzano
1966 *Play:* Kenneth Loach
       Series: Peter Graham Scott
1967 *Play:* Kenneth Loach

1968 Anthony Page, Parachute
1969 *Play:* Christopher Morahan, The Letter;
       Nora You've Made Your Bed Now Lie on It
       Series: Verity Lambert, Somerset Maugham
       series
1970 Alan Bridges
1971 *Play:* Ted Kotcheff, Edna, The Inebriate
       Woman
       Series: John Hawkesworth, Upstairs Down-
       stairs
1972 *Single Play:* Jack Gold
       Series: Derek Granger
1973 *Single Play:* Michael Apted
       Series: John Hawkesworth, Upstairs Down-
       stairs
1974 *Single Play:* Jon Scoffield, Antony and Cleo-
       patra
       Series: James Ormerod, South Riding
1975 *Single Play:* Alan Parker, The Evacuees
       Series: Cecil Clarke and John Gorrie, Edward
       the VII
1976 *Single Play:* Michael Tuchner, Bar Mitzvah
       Boy
       Series: Andrew Brown, Rock Follies
1977 *Single Play:* John Goldschmidt, Spend Spend
       Spend
       Series: Peter Goodchild and John Glenister,
       Marie Curie
1978 *Single Play:* David Hare, Licking Hitler
       Series: Andrew Brown and Waris Hussein,
       Edward and Mrs Simpson
1979 *Single Play:* Brian Gibson, Blue Remembered
       Hills,
       Series: Jonathan Powell and Moira Arm-
       strong, Testament of Youth
1980 *Single Play:* Peter Duffell, Caught on a Train
       Series: Peter Goodchild and Barry Davis,
       Oppenheimer

BEST FACTUAL PRODUCTION
1957 Donald Baverstock and the Production Team
       of 'Tonight'
1958 The Production Team of 'Tonight'
1959 Denis Mitchell
1960 Michael Redington
       Current Affairs: 'Sportsview' Unit
1961 Tim Hewat
       Current Affairs: Bill Allenby
1962 Richard Cawston
1963 Peter Morley and Cyril Bennett
       Documentary: Anthony de Lotbiniere
1964 The Production Team of 'The World in
       Action'
       Documentary: Jack Gold
1965 Jeremy Isaacs and the Production Team of
       'This Week'
       Documentary: Charles Squires
1966 The Production Team of '24 Hours'
       Documentary: Kevin Billington
1967 Desmond Wilcox and Bill Morton
       Documentary: Kevin Billington
1968 *Documentary:* Michael Darlow and Mike
       Wooller
       *Current Affairs:*Phillip Whitehead and Produc-
       tion Team
1969 *Documentary:* Paul Watson, A Year in the
       Life
       Current Affairs: ITN Production Team

1970 Adrian Cowell
1971 Jeremy Wallington and Production Team, World in Action
1972 *Single Programme:* Mick Rhodes
Series: Peter Goodchild and Production Team
1973 *Single Programme:* Eric Davidson, Last Night Another Soldier . . .
Series: Gus MacDonald
1974 *Single Programme:* Frank Cvitanovich, Beauty, Bonny, Daisy, Violet, Grace, and Geoffrey Morton
Series: Peter Goodchild/Bruce Norman, Horizon
1975 *Single Programme:* John Willis, Johnny Go Home
Series: Brian Moser, Disappearing World
1976 *Single Programme:* John Purdie, The Rescue
Series: John Purdie/Roger Mills, Sailor
1977 *Documentary:* Tim King, Casualty
Series: Antony Thomas, The South African Experience
1978 *Documentary:* Adrian Cavell, The Opium Warlords
Series: Christopher Ralling, The Voyage of Charles Darwin
1979 *Documentary:* Fred Dibnah, Steeplejack, Don Haworth
Series: Mark Anderson, Circuit 11, Miami
1980 *Documentary:* Rex Bloomstein, Christmas (Strangeways)
Series: Rex Bloomstein, Strangeways

BEST LIGHT ENTERTAINMENT PRODUCTION
1957 Brian Tesler
1958 Joan Kemp-Welch
1959 Bill Ward
1960 James Gilbert
1961 George Inns
1962 Duncan Wood
1963 Colin Clews
1964 Francis Essex
Situation Comedy: Joe McGrath
1965 Joe McGrath
Situation Comedy: Michael Mills
1966 Ned Sherrin
Situation Comedy: Dick Clement
1967 James Gilbert
Situation Comedy: Michael Mills
1968 Dennis Main Wilson
1969 *Musical:* Yvonne Littlewood, Just Pet
Situation Comedy: Mark Stuart
1970 David Croft and Team
1971 John Robins and David Bell, The Benny Hill Show
1972 *Programme:* Ian McNaughton and Production Team
Situation Comedy: Graeme Muir
1973 *Programme:* David Bell
Situation Comedy: James Gilbert, Whatever Happened to the Likely Lads?
1974 *Programme:* David Bell
Situation Comedy: Sydney Lotterby
1975 *Programme:* Terry Hughes, Two Ronnies
Situation Comedy: John Howard Davies, Fawlty Towers
1976 *Programme:* The Muppet Show Production Team
Situation Comedy: Sydney Lotterby, Porridge

1977 *Programme:* Ernest Maxin, Morecambe and Wise Christmas Show
Situation Comedy: Ronnie Baxter, Rising Damp
1978 *Programme:* David Mallet, The Kenny Everett Video Show
Situation Comedy: Sydney Lotterby, Going Straight
1979 *Programme:* Alan Bell and Jim Franklin, Ripping Yarns
Situation Comedy: Douglas Argent and Bob Spiers, Fawlty Towers
1980 *Programme:* John Lloyd, Sean Hardie and Bill Wilson, Not the Nine O'Clock News
Situation Comedy: Sydney Lotterby, Yes Minister

BEST SPECIALISED PRODUCTION
1963 Margaret Dale
1964 Ned Sherrin
1965 Peter Watkins
1966 Ken Russell
1967 Basil Coleman
1968 Jack Gold
1969 Biddy Baxter, Edward Barnes and Rosemary Gill: Fred Burnley
1970 Christopher Burstall
1971 Norman Swallow
1972 *Programme:* Mai Zetterling and Team
Series: Michael Dibb
1973 *Programme:* Colin Nears
Series: Patrick Dowling
1974 *Programme:* Brian Gibson
Series: Humphrey Burton
1975 *Programme:* David Cobham
Series: Michael Latham
1976 *Programme:* David Hargreaves
Outside Broadcast Programme: F.A. Cup Final Production Team
Discontinued

OTHER AWARD
1979 Melvyn Bragg, The South Bank Show (LWT)
1980 Leslie Megahey, Omnibus

SPECIAL AWARDS
1964 The Great War
1965 Joy Whitby
1966 BBC-ITV World Cup Consortium
1967 Donald Wilson and Team for the Forsyte Saga
David Nicholas and John Phillips for Home is the Sailor
1968 ITN's News at Ten
Bryan Cowgill, David Coleman and the Olympics Production Team
1969 Monty Python's Flying Circus
Michael Gill and Peter Montagnon
1970 Ronald Travers and Mark Shivas
1971 Jenny Barraclough
Discontinued

MOST ORIGINAL PROGRAMME
1978 Pennies from Heaven, produced by Kenith Trodd (BBC)
Discontinued

BEST ACTUALITY COVERAGE
1977 Antony Craxton
1978 The Open Golf Championship, produced by A. P. Wilkinson (BBC)

BAFTA award winners. Top: *'The Forsyte Saga' – 1967 Special Award.* Centre: *Alex Guinness and Sian Phillips in a scene from 'Tinker, Tailor, Soldier, Spy' – 1979 Best Actor award to Alec Guinness.* Below: *'I Claudius' – Derek Jacobi (centre) 1976 Best Actor award.* (BBC copyright)

1979 Ian Engelmann, Last Night of the Proms (BBC)
1980 David Goldsmith and Production Team, Iranian Embassy Siege (ITN)

BEST ACTOR
1954 Paul Rogers
1955 Peter Cushing
1956 Michael Gough
1957 Michael Hordern
1958 Donald Pleasence
1959 Patrick McGoohan
1960 Lee Montague
1961 Rupert Davies
1962 Harry H. Corbett
1963 Alan Badel
1964 Patrick Wymark
1965 Alan Badel
1966 Warren Mitchell
1967 Eric Porter
1968 Roy Dotrice, Brief Lives
1969 Edward Woodward, Callan; A Dream Divided (Omnibus series); A Bit of a Holiday
1970 Keith Michell, The Six Wives of Henry VIII; An Ideal Husband
1971 John Le Mesurier, Traitor
1972 Anthony Hopkins, War and Peace
1973 Frank Finlay, Adventures of Don Quixote; The Death of Adolph Hitler; and Candide
1974 Peter Barkworth, Crown Matrimonial
1975 John Hurt, Naked Civil Servant
1976 Derek Jacobi, I Claudius
1977 Peter Barkworth, Professional Foul, The Country Party
1978 Edward Fox, Edward and Mrs Simpson
1979 Alec Guinness, Tinker, Tailor, Soldier, Spy
1980 Denholm Elliott, Gentle Folk; In Hiding; Blade on the Feather; The Stinker

BEST ACTRESS
1954 Googie Withers
1955 Virginia McKenna
1956 Rosalie Crutchley
1957 Heather Sears
1958 Gwen Watford
1959 Catherine Lacey
1960 Billie Whitelaw
1961 Ruth Dunning
1962 Brenda Bruce
1963 Vivien Merchant
1964 Katherine Blake
1965 Gwen Watford
1966 Vanessa Redgrave
1967 Judi Dench
1968 Wendy Craig, Not in Front of the Children
1969 Margaret Tyzack, The First Churchills
1970 Annette Crosbie, Catherine of Aragon (from The Six Wives of Henry VIII)
1971 Patricia Hayes, Edna, the Inebriate Woman
1972 Billie Whitelaw, The Sextet (series of 8 plays)
1973 Celia Johnson, Mrs Palfrey at the Claremont
1974 Lee Remick, Jennie
1975 Annette Crosbie, Edward the Seventh
1976 Sian Phillips, I Claudius; How Green Was My Valley
1977 Penelope Keith, Norman Conquests; Saving it from Albie
1978 Francesca Annis, Lillie
1979 Cheryl Campbell, Testament of Youth

1980 Dame Peggy Ashcroft, Cream in my Coffee;
     Caught on a Train

BEST LIGHT ENTERTAINMENT PERFORMANCE
1957 Tony Hancock
1958 Alan Melville
1959 Tony Hancock
1960 Stanley Baxter
1961 Eric Sykes
1962 Michael Bentine
1963 Morecambe and Wise
1964 Millicent Martin
1965 Peter Cook and Dudley Moore
1966 John Bird
1967 Alan Bennett
1968 Marty Feldman
1969 Eric Morecambe and Ernie Wise
1970 Eric Morecambe and Ernie Wise
1971 Ronnie Corbett and Ronnie Barker
1972 Eric Morecambe and Ernie Wise
1973 Eric Morecambe and Ernie Wise
1974 Stanley Baxter
1975 Ronnie Barker, Porridge
1976 Penelope Keith, The Good Life
1977 Ronnie Barker, Porridge
1978 Ronnie Barker, Going Straight and The Two Ronnies
1979 John Cleese, Fawlty Towers
1980 Rowan Atkinson, Not the Nine O'Clock News

THE RICHARD DIMBLEBY AWARD
(Most important contribution on screen in factual TV)
1963 Bernard Braden
1964 Alan Whicker
1965 Malcolm Muggeridge
1966 Alastair Burnet
1967 David Frost
1968 Julian Pettifer
1969 Kenneth Clark
1970 Alastair Burnet
1971 Desmond Wilcox
1972 Alistair Cooke
1973 Jonathan Dimbleby
1974 Robin Day
1975 Robert Kee
1976 Frank Bough
1977 Alan Whicker
1978 David Bellamy
1979 Alastair Burnet
1980 Barry Norman

BEST SCRIPT
1954 Iaian McCormack
1955 Colin Morris
1956 Spike Milligan
1957 Colin Morris
1958 Colin Morris
     Ken Hughes
1959 Alan Simpson and Ray Galton
1960 Alun Owen
1961 Giles Cooper
1962 Troy Kennedy Martin
1963 Harold Pinter
1964 Ken Taylor
1965 Michael Mills and Richard Waring
1966 Dennis Potter
1967 John Hopkins

A scene from 'Fawlty Towers' which won John Cleese (left) the 1979 BAFTA 'Best Light Entertainment Performance' award (BBC copyright)

1968 Marty Feldman and Barry Took
1969 John Terraine
1970 Colin Welland
1971 Benny Hill
1975 Dick Clement, Ian La Frenais
1976 Jack Rosenthal
1977 Tom Stoppard, Professional Foul
1978 Dennis Potter, Pennies From Heaven
1979 John Mortimer, Rumpole of the Bailey
1980 No award

BEST DESIGN
1954 Michael Yates
1955 Bruce Angrave
1956 Reece Pemberton
1957 Stephen Taylor
1958 Stephen Bundy
1959 Clifford Hatts
1960 Frederick Pusey
1961 Voytek
1962 Eileen Diss
1963 Richard Henry
1964 Richard Wilmot
1965 Eileen Diss
1966 Tony Abbott
1967 Julia Trevelyan Oman
1968 Roy Oxley
1969 Tony Abbott
1970 Peter Seddon
1971 The Rivals of Sherlock Holmes – Design Team
1972 Don Homfray
1973 Eileen Diss
1974 Bill McPherson
1975 Henry Graveney, Anthony Waller
1976 Tim Harvey
1977 Roy Stonehouse
1978 Alan Cameron and Martyn Hebert, Edward and Mrs Simpson
1979 Sally Hulke, Testament of Youth
1980 Therese Raquin, David Myerscough-Jones

TECHNICAL CRAFT
1972 Alan Tyrer
1973 Alan Afrait
1974 Lynda Beighton
1975 Jim Atkinson
1976 Mike Billing and Pam Meager
1977–79 A new set of ten awards for technical craft was introduced

Noel Edmonds, Maggie Philbin and Keith Chegwin at the 1979 Multi-Coloured Swap Shop award ceremony (BBC copyright)

GENERAL
1968 Tom Moncrieff
1969 Terry Gilliam
1970 John Bloomfield
1971 News Teams, BBC and ITV in Ulster
Discontinued

BRITISH ACADEMY FELLOWSHIP AWARD
1979 David Attenborough
1980 No award

BBC MULTI-COLOURED SWAP SHOP AWARDS
These are the only television awards voted for exclusively by children. There are only two rules: voters must be under 16 years of age, and Swap Shop hosts and everyone who is in it every week are disqualified. Winners:

FUNNIEST/FAVOURITE MAN
1978 Ronnie Barker
1979 Michael Crawford
1980 Dick Emery
1981 John Cleese

FUNNIEST/FAVOURITE WOMAN
1978 Penelope Keith
1979 Marti Cane
1980 Penelope Keith
1981 Barbara Woodhouse

TOP POP SINGER
1978 David Soul
1979 Debbie Harry of Blondie
1980 Cliff Richard
1981 Adam Ant

TOP POP GROUP
1978 Abba
1979 Showaddywaddy
1980 Boomtown Rats
1981 The Police

TOP SPORTSMAN
1978 Barry Sheene
1979 Kevin Keegan
      Brian Jacks
1980 Robin Cousins
Discontinued

TOP SPORTSWOMAN
1978 Virginia Wade
1979 Sonia Lannaman
1980 Sharron Davies
Discontinued

TOP TV PERSONALITY
1978 John Noakes
1979 Tony Hart
1980 Tony Hart
Discontinued

TOP TV PROGRAMME
1978 Blue Peter
1979 Grange Hill
1980 Grange Hill
1981 Grange Hill

TOP TV EXPERT
1978 Magnus Pyke
1979 David Attenborough
1980 David Bellamy
1981 David Bellamy

FUNNIEST PROGRAMME
1981 Little and Large

TOP SPORTS STAR
1981 Sebastian Coe

BROADCASTING PRESS GUILD ANNUAL AWARDS

Awards are presented each year by journalist members of the Broadcasting Press Guild and the Association of Television Critics.

BEST DRAMA SERIES
1978 Pennies from Heaven, by Dennis Potter (BBC 1)
1979 Tinker, Tailor, Soldier, Spy (BBC 2)
1980 To Serve Them All My Days (BBC 1)

BEST PLAY
1978 The Spongers, by Jim Allen (BBC 1)
1979 Blue Remembered Hills, by Dennis Potter (BBC 1)
1980 Caught on a Train, by Stephen Poliakoff (BBC 2)

BEST DOCUMENTARY
1978 The Voyage of Charles Darwin (BBC 2)
1979 Year Zero – The Silent Death of Cambodia (ATV)
1980 Single: Creggan (Thames TV)
      Series: Strangeways (BBC 1)

BEST ACTOR
1978 Edward Fox, Edward and Mrs Simpson (ITV)
1979 Sir Alec Guinness, Tinker, Tailor, Soldier, Spy (BBC 2)
1980 Nigel Hawthorne, Yes Minister (BBC 2)

BEST ACTRESS
1978 Geraldine McEwan, The Prime of Miss Jean Brodie (ITV)
1979 Cheryl Campbell, Testament of Youth (BBC 2)
1980 Dame Peggy Ashcroft, Cream in my Coffee (ATV) and Caught on a Train (BBC 2)

BEST NON-ACTING ROLE
1978 Jonathan Miller, The Body in Question (BBC 2)
1979 David Attenborough, Life on Earth (BBC 2)
1980 Sir Robin Day, Question Time (BBC 2)

OUTSTANDING CONTRIBUTION TO RADIO
1978 Checkpoint (BBC Radio 4)
1979 Sue MacGregor, Woman's Hour (BBC Radio 4)
1980 John Peel (Radio 1)

MOST ORIGINAL CONTRIBUTION TO TV
1978 Pennies from Heaven
Discontinued

BEST LIGHT ENTERTAINMENT
1978 The Kenny Everett Video Show (Thames TV)
Discontinued

BEST COMEDY
1979 Not the Nine O'Clock News (BBC 2)
1980 Yes Minister (BBC 2)

BEST IMPORTED PROGRAMME
1980 Lou Grant (ITV)

BEST RADIO MAGAZINE PROGRAMME
1980 Kaleidoscope (Radio 4)

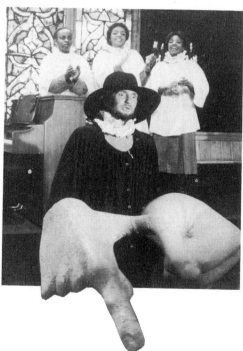

Broadcasting Press Guild Annual Awards: Bob Hoskins and Cheryl Campbell (top) *in 'Pennies From Heaven' which won the 1978 'Best Drama' award; Kenny Everett* (below) *won the 1978 'Best Light Entertainment' award for his show.* (BBC copyright)

EMMY AWARDS

The highest honours in American television, the awards were founded in 1948 and are given by the American Academy of Television Arts and Sciences. The categories change from year to year, and a selection of recent winners, familiar to television viewers on both sides of the Atlantic, is listed below.

BEST COMEDY SERIES
1973–74 M*A*S*H
1974–75 The Mary Tyler Moore Show
1975–76 The Mary Tyler Moore Show
1976–77 The Mary Tyler Moore Show
1977–78 All in the Family
1978–79 Taxi
1979–80 Taxi

BEST DRAMA SERIES
1973–74 Upstairs, Downstairs
1974–75 Upstairs, Downstairs
1975–76 Police Story
1976–77 Upstairs, Downstairs
1977–78 The Rockford Files
1978–79 Lou Grant
1979–80 Lou Grant

BEST COMEDY/VARIETY OR MUSIC PROGRAMME
1973–74 The Carol Burnett Show
1974–75 The Carol Burnett Show
1975–76 NBC's Saturday Night
1976–77 Dick Van Dyke and Company
1977–78 The Muppet Show
1978–79 Steve and Eydie Celebrate Irving Berlin
1979–80 Baryshnikov on Broadway

BEST LIMITED SERIES
1973–74 Columbo
1974–75 Benjamin Franklin
1975–76 Upstairs, Downstairs
         Eleanor and Franklin
1976–77 Roots
         Eleanor and Franklin

M.A.S.H. won an Emmy in 1973–74 for 'Best Comedy Series' (BBC copyright)

1977–78 Holocaust
1978–79 Roots: The Next Generations
1979–80 Edward and Mrs Simpson

BEST ACTOR AWARDS
1973–74 Alan Alda, M*A*S*H
         Telly Savalas, Kojak
1974–75 Tony Randall, The Odd Couple
         Robert Blake, Baretta
         Peter Falk, Columbo
         Lawrence Olivier, Love Among the Ruins
1975–76 Peter Falk, Columbo
         Jack Albertson, Chico and the Man
         Hal Holbrook, Sandburg's Lincoln
         Anthony Hopkins, The Lindbergh Kidnapping Case
         Edward Asner, Rich Man, Poor Man
1976–77 Louis Gossett, Roots
         Carroll O'Connor, All in the Family
         Christopher Plummer, The Money Changers
         James Garner, The Rockford Files
1977–78 Barnard Hughes, Lou Grant
         Carroll O'Connor, All in the Family
         Michael Moriarty, Holocaust
         Edward Asner, Lou Grant
1978–79 Carroll O'Connor, All in the Family
         Peter Strauss, The Jericho Mile
         Ron Liebman, Kaz
1979–80 Edward Asner, Lou Grant, Richard Mulligan, Soap
         Powers Boothe, Guyana Tragedy: The Story of Jim Jones

BEST ACTRESS
1970–71 Susan Hampshire, The First Churchills
         Jean Stapleton, All in the Family
1971–72 Glenda Jackson, Elizabeth R.
         Jean Stapleton, All in the Family
1972–73 Michael Learned, The Waltons
         Mary Tyler Moore, The Mary Tyler Moore Show
1973–74 Michael Learned, The Waltons
         Mary Tyler Moore, The Mary Tyler Moore Show
1974–75 Jean Marsh, Upstairs, Downstairs
         Valerie Harper, Rhoda
1975–76 Michael Learned, The Waltons
         Mary Tyler Moore, The Mary Tyler Moore Show
1976–77 Lindsay Wagner, The Bionic Woman
         Beatrice Arthur, Maude
         Patty Duke Astin, Captains and the Kings
         Beulah Bondi, The Waltons
1977–78 Sada Thompson, Family
         Jean Stapleton, All in the Family
         Meryl Streep, Holocaust
         Rita Moreno, Rockford Files
         Joanne Woodward, See How She Runs
1978–79 Mariette Hartley, The Incredible Hulk
         Ruth Gordon, Taxi
         Bette Davis, Strangers: The Story of a Mother and Daughter
1979–80 Barbara Bel Geddes, Dallas
         Catherine Damon, Soap
         Patty Duke Astin, The Miracle Worker

Television award winners:
Top: *'Not the Nine O'Clock News' – Silver Rose in the Montreux Festival in 1980.* Right: *Larry Hagman (J. R. Ewing from 'Dallas') – 1980* TV Times *'Most Compulsive Male TV Character'.* Below: *Michael Bentine in 'It's a Square World' – 1963 Press Prize in the Montreux Festival* (BBC copyright)

GOLDEN ROSE OF MONTREUX

This annual international contest for television light entertainment was first held in 1961. The event is organised by the Swiss Broadcasting Corporation in cooperation with the town of Montreux, under the patronage of the European Broadcasting Union. A Silver Rose is awarded to the best programme in each category and the best of these three winning entries is then awarded the Golden Rose. In addition a Special Prize is awarded, and a Press Prize is awarded by a jury of journalists. BBC and Independent Television winners:

GOLDEN ROSE
1961 The Black and White Minstrel Show (BBC)
1967 Frost Over England (BBC)
1972 Marty: The Best of the Comedy Machine (ATV)
1977 The Muppet Show (ATV)

SILVER ROSE
1969 Marty (BBC)
1971 Monty Python's Flying Circus (BBC)
1972 The Goodies (BBC)
1974 Barbra Streisand and other Musical Instruments (ATV)
1975 The Goodies (BBC)
1976 The Two Ronnies: The Picnic (BBC)
1978 Dave Allen at Large (BBC)
1980 It'll be Alright on the Night – 2 (LWT)
     Not the Nine O'Clock News (BBC)

PRESS PRIZE
1961 The Black and White Ministrel Show (BBC)
1963 It's a Square World (BBC)
1967 Frost Over England (BBC)
1980 The Plank (Thames)

SPECIAL PRIZE
First awarded in 1965
1968 The World of Charlie Drake (BBC)
1972 Marty: The Best of the Comedy Machine (ATV)

TV TIMES TOP TEN AWARDS

The magazine for Independent Television in Britain conducts an annual readers poll. Winners:

MOST COMPULSIVE MALE TV CHARACTER
1972 Callan (Callan), Edward Woodward
1973 Frank Marker (Public Eye), Alfred Burke
1974 Hadleigh (Hadleigh), Gerald Harper
1975 Hudson (Upstairs Downstairs), Gordon Jackson
1976 Detective Inspector Jack Regan (The Sweeney), John Thaw
1977 Detective Inspector Jack Regan (The Sweeney), John Thaw
1978 Hazell (Hazell), Nicholas Ball
1979 Simon Templar (Return of the Saint), Ian Ogilvy
1980 J. R. Ewing (Dallas), Larry Hagman
1981 Bodie and Doyle (The Professionals), Lewis Collins and Martin Shaw

MOST COMPULSIVE FEMALE CHARACTER
1972 Ena Sharples (Coronation Street), Violet Carson
1973 Kate (Kate), Phyllis Calvert
1974 Helen (Helen – A Woman of Today), Alison Fiske
1975 Meg Richardson (Crossroads), Noele Gordon
1976 Faye Boswell (Within These Walls), Googie Withers
1977 Purdey (The New Avengers), Joanna Lumley
1978 Amy Wide (The Wilde Alliance), Julia Foster
1979 Sarah (Thomas & Sarah), Pauline Collins
1980 Audrey fforbes-Hamilton (To the Manor Born), Penelope Keith
1981 Insp. Maggie Forbes (The Gentle Touch), Jill Gascoine

BEST TV ACTOR
1972 Edward Woodward
1973 Kenneth Haigh
1974 Gordon Jackson
1975 Kenneth More
1976 Timothy West
1977 Frank Finlay
1978 Robert Powell
1979 Edward Fox
1980 Robert Hardy
1981 John Duttine

BEST TV ACTRESS
1972 Margaret Lockwood
1973 Anne Stallybrass
1974 Alison Fiske
1975 Lee Remick
1976 Annette Crosbie
1977 Gemma Jones
1978 Geraldine McEwan
1979 Francesca Annis
1980 Diane Keen
1981 Vanessa Redgrave

FAVOURITE MALE TV PERSONALITY
1972 Des O'Connor
1973 Des O'Connor
1974 Des O'Connor
1975 John Alderton
1976 Bruce Forsyth
1977 Bruce Forsyth
1978 Bruce Forsyth
1979 Terry Wogan
1980 Terry Wogan
1981 Terry Wogan

FAVOURITE FEMALE TV PERSONALITY
1972 Noele Gordon
1973 Noele Gordon
1974 Noele Gordon
1975 Noele Gordon
1976 Noele Gordon
1977 Penelope Keith
1978 Penelope Keith
1979 Anna Ford
1980 Anna Ford
1981 Anna Ford

FUNNIEST MAN ON TV
1972 Benny Hill
1973 Larry Grayson

1974 Michael Crawford
1975 Sid James
1976 Leonard Rossiter
1977 John Inman
1978 Ronnie Barker
1979 John Cleese
1980 Jim Davidson
1981 John Cleese

FUNNIEST WOMAN ON TV
1972 Wendy Craig
1973 Wendy Craig
1974 Wendy Craig
1975 Pauline Collins
1976 Yootha Joyce
1977 Yootha Joyce
1978 Yootha Joyce
1979 Yootha Joyce
1980 Ruth Brown
1981 Janet Brown

MOST EXCITING MALE SINGER ON TV
1972 Sacha Distel
1973 Sacha Distel
1974 Gilbert O'Sullivan
1975 Val Doonican
1976 David Essex
1977 David Soul
1978 Paul McCartney
1979 Leo Sayer
1980 Cliff Richard
1981 Barry Manilow

MOST EXCITING FEMALE SINGER ON TV
1972 Shirley Bassey
1973 Shirley Bassey
1974 Shirley Bassey
1975 Petula Clark
1976 Dana
1977 Julie Covington
1978 Cleo Laine
1979 Kate Bush
1980 Marti Webb
1981 Sheena Easton

TV Times *Top Ten Awards:* Left: *Yootha Joyce 'Funniest Woman on TV' 1976–79;* Top: *Violet Carson as Ena Sharples from 'Coronation Street', 'Most Compulsive Female Character' 1972;* Above: *Noele Gordon 'Favourite Female TV Character' 1972–76*

Theatre

BRITISH THEATRE DRAMA AWARDS

Plays and Players published an annual list of award winning plays and artists chosen by London's theatre critics in 1978 and 1979. From 1980 *Drama*, published by the British Theatre Association, took on the awards. The winners:

BEST NEW PLAY
1978 Whose Life Is It Anyway?
1979 Amadeus
1980 The Dresser, Duet for One, and Make and Break

MOST PROMISING NEW PLAYWRIGHT
1978 Brian Clark, Whose Life Is It Anyway? and Nigel Williams, Class Enemy
1979 Victoria Wood, Talent
1980 Dusty Hughes, Commitments

BEST PERFORMANCE BY AN ACTRESS
1978 Diana Rigg, Night and Day
1979 Jane Lapotaire, Piaf
1980 Judi Dench, Juno and the Paycock and Frances de la Tour, Duet for One

BEST PERFORMANCE BY AN ACTOR
1978 Nicol Williamson, Inadmissible Evidence
1979 Warren Mitchell, Death of a Salesman
1980 Michael Gambon, Galileo and Tom Courtenay, The Dresser

BEST ACTRESS IN A SUPPORTING ROLE
1978 Dorothy Tutin, The Double Dealer
1979 Carmen du Sautoy, Once in a Lifetime
1980 Dearbhla Molloy, Juno and the Paycock and Yvonne Bryceland, Othello

BEST ACTOR IN A SUPPORTING ROLE
1978 Michael Bryant, The Double Dealer
1979 Richard Griffiths, Once in a Lifetime
1980 David Threlfall, Nicholas Nickleby, Edward Pethebridge, Nicholas Nickleby and David de Keyser, Duet for One

BEST NEW MUSICAL
1978 Annie
1979 Chicago
1980 Sweeney Todd

MOST PROMISING NEW PERFORMER
1978 David Threlfall, Royal Shakespeare Co.
1979 Actor: Alfred Molina, Accidental Death of an Anarchist
Actress: Lynsey Baxter, The Lady From the Sea
1980 Actor: Denis Lawson, Pal Joey
Actress: Julie Walters, Educating Rita and Carol Royle, Hamlet

BEST PRODUCTION
1978 Harold Prince, Evita
1979 William Dudley, Undiscovered Country
1980 Discontinued

BEST PRODUCTION (DESIGNER)
1978 Tanya Moiseiwitsch, The Double Dealer
1979 No award
1980 William Dudley, Hamlet

BEST NEW COMEDY
1979 Joking Apart, Alan Ayckbourn
A Day in Hollywood, A Night in the Ukraine, Dick Vosburgh
1980 Make and Break, Michael Frayn

BEST PRODUCTION (DIRECTOR)
1979 Trevor Nunn, Once in a Lifetime
1980 Trevor Nunn and John Caird, Nicholas Nickleby

BEST REVIVAL
1980 Juno and the Paycock, Sean O'Casey

THE NEW STANDARD DRAMA AWARDS

Instituted in 1955 by the London *Evening Standard*, (*The New Standard* from 1980) the awards aim to promote the arts in London. All major West End productions, writers, actors and actresses are eligible, and the winners are chosen by a panel of judges composed of critics from London newspapers.

BEST MUSICAL OF THE YEAR
1955 The Pajama Game
1956 Cranks ('Best Musical Entertainment')
1957 No award
1958 West Side Story
1959 Make Me an Offer
1960 Fings Ain't Wot They Used T'Be
1961 Beyond the Fringe
1962 No award
1963 Oh What A Lovely War
1964 Little Me
1965 No award
1966 Funny Girl
1967 Sweet Charity
1968 Cabaret
1969 Promises, Promises
1970 No award
1971 No award
1972 Applause
1973 Rocky Horror Show
1974 John, Paul, George, Ringo and Bert
1975 A Little Night Music
1976 Chorus Line
1977 Elvis
1978 Annie
1979 Songbook
1980 Sweeney Todd

BEST NEW PLAY OF THE YEAR
1955 Tiger at the Gates, J. Giraudoux
1956 Romanoff and Juliet, Peter Ustinov
1957 Summer of the Seventeenth Doll, Ray Lawler
1958 Cat on a Hot Tin Roof, Tennessee Williams

1959 The Long, the Short and the Tall, C. Shurr
1960 The Caretaker, Harold Pinter
1961 Becket, Jean Anouilh
1962 Caucasian Chalk Circle, B. Brecht
1963 Poor Bitos, Jean Anouilh
1964 Who's Afraid of Virginia Woolf, Edward Albee
1965 A Patriot for Me, John Osborne, and The Killing of Sister George, F. Marcus
1966 Loot, Joe Orton
1967 A Day in the Death of Joe Egg, Peter Nichols
1968 Hotel in Amsterdam, John Osborne
1969 National Health, Peter Nichols
1970 Home, David Storey
1971 Butley, Simon Gray
1972 Jumpers, Tom Stoppard
1973 Saturday, Sunday, Monday, Eduardo de Filippo
1974 Norman Conquests, Alan Ayckbourn
1975 Otherwise Engaged, Simon Gray
1976 Weapons of Happiness, Howard Brenton
1977 Just Between Ourselves, Alan Ayckbourn
1978 Night and Day, Tom Stoppard
1979 Amadeus, Peter Shaffer
1980 The Dresser, Ronald Harwood

BEST COMEDY OF THE YEAR (FROM 1970)
1970 The Philanthropist, Christopher Hampton
1971 Getting On, Alan Bennett
1972 Veterans, Charles Wood
1973 Absurd Person Singular, Alan Ayckbourn
1974 Travesties, Tom Stoppard
1975 Alphabetical Order, Michael Frayn
1976 Thoughts of Chairman Alf, Johnny Speight
1977 Privates on Parade, Peter Nicholls
1978 Gloo Joo, Michael Hastings
1979 A Day in Hollywood, A Night in the Ukraine, Dick Vosburgh
1980 Make and Break, Michael Frayn

MOST PROMISING PLAYWRIGHT ('BRITISH', 1956–59)
1956 John Osborne
1957 Roger Bolt
1958 Peter Shaffer
1959 John Arden; Arnold Walker
1960 J. P. Donleavy
1961 Gwyn Thomas; Henry Livings
1962 David Rudkin
1963 Charles Wood; James Saunders
1964 No award
1965 David Mercer
1966 David Halliwell
1967 Tom Stoppard; David Storey
1968 No award
1969 Peter Barnes
1970 David Hare; Heathcote Williams
1971 E. A. Whitehead
1972 Wilson John Haire
1973 David Williamson
1974 Mustapha Matura
1975 Stephen Poliakoff
1976 Stuart Parker
1977 Mary O'Malley; James Robson
1978 John Byrne; Brian Clark
1979 Victoria Wood; Richard Harris
1980 Paul Kember

BEST PERFORMANCE BY AN ACTOR IN THE YEAR
1955 Richard Burton
1956 Paul Scofield
1957 Laurence Olivier
1958 Sir Michael Redgrave
1959 Eric Porter
1960 Alec Guinness; Rex Harrison
1961 Christopher Plummer
1962 Paul Scofield
1963 Michael Redgrave
1964 Nicol Williamson
1965 Ian Holm
1966 Albert Finney
1967 Laurence Olivier
1968 Alec McCowen
1969 Nicol Williamson
1970 John Gielgud; Ralph Richardson
1971 Alan Bates
1972 Lord Olivier
1973 Alec McCowen
1974 John Wood
1975 John Gielgud
1976 Albert Finney
1977 Donald Sinden
1978 Alan Howard
1979 Warren Mitchell
1980 Tom Courtenay

BEST PERFORMANCE BY AN ACTRESS IN THE YEAR
1955 Sian McKenna
1956 Peggy Ashcroft
1957 Brenda De Banzie
1958 Gwen Ffrangcon-Davies
1959 Flora Robson
1960 Dorothy Tutin
1961 Vanessa Redgrave
1962 Maggie Smith
1963 Joan Plowright
1964 Peggy Ashcroft
1965 Eileen Atkins
1966 Irene Worth
1967 Lila Kedrova
1968 Jill Bennett
1969 Rosemary Harris
1970 Maggie Smith
1971 Peggy Ashcroft
1972 Rachel Roberts
1973 Janet Suzman
1974 Claire Bloom
1975 Dorothy Tutin
1976 Janet Suzman
1977 Alison Steadman
1978 Kate Nelligan
1979 Vanessa Redgrave
1980 Judi Dench; Francis de la Tour

SPECIAL AWARD
1979 Sir Peter Hall
1980 Sir Ralph Richardson

SYDNEY EDWARDS AWARD FOR BEST DIRECTOR
1979 Trevor Nunn, Once in a Lifetime
1980 Trevor Nunn and John Caird, Nicholas Nickleby

THE SCOTSMAN FRINGE FIRST AWARDS

These are presented at the Edinburgh Festival to outstanding productions of new plays, dance-works, or operas on the Edinburgh Festival Fringe. The awards have been made since 1973.

There are about 150 entries every year and the judges appointed by *The Scotsman* do not attempt to place them in any order of merit but select those which seem to be outstanding. The 1980 winners:

Company	Title	Author
Brighton Theatre	Vanity	Richard Crane and Faynia Williams
The Children's Music Theatre	The Roman Invasion of Ramsbottom	By The Company
The Cameri Theatre of Tel Aviv	Ya'acobi and Liedental	Hanoch Levine
The Lyric Studio, Hammersmith	The Ice Chimney	Barry Collins
The Cherub Company	For their new adaptation of 'The Trial'	Kafka
	Lyrics of the Hearthside	Joseph Mydell (US)
Californian State University, Fresno	Guys Like Me and Bogie	By The Company
	Chekhov on the Lawn	William Shust, (US)
The Children's Music Theatre	Captain Stirrick	By The Company
Cambridge Mummers	For an outstanding programme of new work	–
	Running Around the Stage Like a Lunatic	Walter Zerlin
	Newsrevue 1980	Strode Jackson
Borderline Theatre Company, Ayrshire	Play It Again, Tam!	By The Company
	Gru-Gru	Henri Gruvman
Wigan Young People's Theatre	Somewhere Resting	By The Company
Norman McDowell's Theatre Ballet of London	Summer Days	Jack Carter
Aella Theatre Company	I Die for None of Them	J. E. Cox

THE SOCIETY OF WEST END THEATRE AWARDS

From 1976 the Society has presented its own theatre awards, similar to the United States' Tony Awards, at a ceremony which takes place at the Café Royal on the first Sunday in December each year. The Society's presidents have included John Gale, Sir Emile Littler, Stephen Mitchell, Toby Rowland, Peter Saunders, David Conville and Ian B. Albery.

MUSICAL
1976 Chorus Line
1977 Comedy of Errors
1978 Evita
1979 Songbook
1980 Sweeney Todd

PLAY
1976 Dear Daddy
1977 The Fire That Consumes
1978 Whose Life is it Anyway?
1979 Betrayal (Harold Pinter)
1980 The Life and Adventures of Nicholas Nickleby

COMEDY
1976 Donkey's Years
1977 Privates on Parade
1978 Filumena
1979 Middle Age Spread
1980 Educating Rita

ACTOR (Revival)
1976 Alan Howard, Henry V/IV
1977 Ian McKellen, Pillars of the Community
1978 Alan Howard, Coriolanus
1979 Warren Mitchell, Death of a Salesman
1980 Jonathan Pryce, Hamlet

ACTOR (New Play)
1976 Paul Copley, King and Country
1977 Michael Bryant, State of Revolution
1978 Tom Conti, Whose Life is it Anyway?
1979 Ian McKellen, Bent
1980 Roger Rees, Nicholas Nickleby

BEST SUPPORTING ACTOR
1977 Nigel Hawthorne, Privates on Parade
1978 Rober Eddison, Twelfth Night
1979 Patrick Stewart, Antony and Cleopatra
1980 David Threlfall, Nicholas Nickleby

ACTRESS (Revival)
1976 Dorothy Tutin, A Month in the Country
1977 Judi Dench, Macbeth
1978 Dorothy Tutin, The Double Dealer
1979 Zoe Wanamaker, Once in a Lifetime
1980 Judi Dench, Juno and the Paycock

ACTRESS (New Play)
1976 Peggy Ashcroft, Old World
1977 Alison Fiske, Dusa Fish Stas and Vi
1978 Joan Plowright, Filumena

1979 Jane Lapotaire, Piaf
1980 Frances de la Tour, Duet For One

BEST SUPPORTING ACTRESS
1977 Mona Washbourne, Stevie
1978 Elizabeth Spriggs, Love Letters in Blue
1979 Doreen Mantle, Death of a Salesman
1980 Suzanne Bertish, Nicholas Nickleby

PERFORMER IN A MUSICAL
1977 Anna Sharkey, Maggie
1978 Elaine Paige, Evita
1979 Virginia McKenna, The King and I; Anton
     Rogers, Songbook
1980 Gemma Craven, They're Playing Our Song;
     Denis Quilley, Sweeney Todd

DIRECTOR
1976 Jonathan Miller, The Three Sisters
1977 Clifford Williams, Wild Oats
1978 Terry Hands, Henry VI
1979 Michael Bogdanov, Taming of the Shrew
1980 Trevor Nunn and John Caird, Nicholas Nickleby

DESIGNER
1976 Farrah, Henry V/IV
1977 John Napier, King Lear
1978 Ralph Koltai, Brand
1979 William Dudley, Undiscovered Country
1980 John Napier and Dermot Hayes, Nicholas
     Nickleby

COMEDY PERFORMANCE
1976 Penelope Keith, Donkey's Years
1977 Denis Quilley, Privates on Parade
1978 Ian McKellen, The Alchemist
1979 Barry Humphries, A Night With Dame Edna
1980 Beryl Reid, Born in The Gardens

MOST PROMISING NEWCOMER
Presented by Benson and Hedges.
1980 Edward Duke, for the creation, adaptation
     and performance in 'Jeeves Takes Charge'

OUTSTANDING OPERA ACHIEVEMENT
1977 Glyndebourne Festival, Don Giovanni
1978 English National Opera
1979 Royal Opera, Rake's Progress
1980 English National Opera, Cosi Fan Tutte

OUTSTANDING BALLET ACHIEVEMENT
1977 London Festival Ballet's Romeo and Juliet
1978 Robert Cohan, London Contemporary Dance
     Theatre
1979 Festival Ballet, La Sylphide (Peter Schaufuss)
1980 The Royal Ballet, Gloria

OUTSTANDING OPERA PRODUCTION
1978 Lohengrin, Covent Garden

OUTSTANDING BALLET PRODUCTION
1978 A Month In the Country

OUTSTANDING FIRST ACHIEVEMENT IN
OPERA OR BALLET
Presented by Benson and Hedges.
1980 Rosalind Plowright, 'The Turn of the Screw'
     (English National Opera)

Above: *Roger Rees as Nicholas Nickleby and David Threlfall as Smike in the award winning* Nicholas Nickleby (Chris Davies). Below: *Jennifer Penney and Julian Hosking in* Gloria, *1980 'Outstanding Ballet Achievement' award* (Leslie E. Spatt)

SPECIAL AWARD
1976 Save London's Theatres Campaign

TONY AWARDS
The Antoinette Perry Awards were started in 1947 to award excellence in the theatre. They are given annually in the United States by the League of New York Theatres.
The winners since 1970:

BEST PLAY
1970–71 Sleuth
1971–72 Sticks and Bones
1972–73 The Championship Season
1973–74 The River Niger
1974–75 Equus
1975–76 Travesties
1976–77 The Shadow Box
1977–78 Da
1978–79 The Elephant Man
1979–80 Children of a Lesser God
1980–81 Amadeus

OUTSTANDING DIRECTION OF A PLAY
1970–71 Peter Brook, A Midsummer Night's Dream
1971–72 Mike Nichols, The Prisoner of Second Avenue
1972–73 A. J. Antoon, The Championship Season
1973–74 Jose Quintero, Moon for the Misbegotten
1974–75 John Dexter, Equus
1975–76 Ellis Rabb, Royal Family
1976–77 Gordon Davidson, The Shadow Box
1977–78 Melvin Bernhardt, Da
1978–79 Jack Hofsiss, The Elephant Man
1979–80 Vivian Matalon, Morning's at Seven
1980–81 Peter Hall, Amadeus

The Antoinette Perry (Tony) award

BEST MUSICAL
1970–71 Company
1971–72 Two Gentlemen of Verona
1972–73 A Little Night Music
1973–74 Raisin
1974–75 The Wiz
1975–76 Chorus Line
1976–77 Annie
1977–78 Ain't Misbehavin'
1978–79 Sweeney Todd
1979–80 Evita
1980–81 42nd Street

BEST BOOK OF A MUSICAL
1971–72 John Guare and Mel Shapiro, Two Gentlemen of Verona
1973–74 Hugh Wheeler, Candide
1974–75 James Lee Barrett, Shenandoah
1975–76 James Kirkwood, Nicholas Dante, Chorus Line
1977–78 Betty Comden, Adolph Green, On The Twentieth Century
1978–79 Hugh Wheeler, Sweeney Todd
1979–80 Tim Rice, Evita
1980–81 Peter Stone, Woman of the Year

OUTSTANDING DIRECTION/ CHOREOGRAPHY OF A MUSICAL
1970–71 Hal Prince, Company/Donald Saddler, No No Nanette
1971–72 Hal Prince and Michael Bennett, Follies
1972–73 Bob Fosse, Poppin
1973–74 Hal Prince, Candide/Michael Bennett, See Saw
1974–75 Geoffrey Holder, The Wiz/George Faison, The Wiz
1975–76 Michael Bennett, Chorus Line/Bod Avian, M. Bennett, Chorus Line
1976–77 Gene Saks, I Love my Wife/Peter Gennaro, Annie
1977–78 Bob Fosse, Dancin'/Richard Maltby, Ain't Misbehavin'
1978–79 Harold Prince, Sweeney Todd/Michael Bennett, Bob Avian, Ballroom
1979–80 Harold Prince, Evita/Tommy Tune, Thommie Walsh, A Day in Hollywood/A Night in the Ukraine
1980–81 Wilford Leach, The Pirates of Penzance/ Gower Champion, 42nd Street

BEST SCORE OF A MUSICAL: MUSIC AND LYRICS
1970–71 Stephen Sondheim, Company
1971–72 Stephen Sondheim, Follies
1973–74 Frederick Loewe and Alan Lerner, Gigi
1974–75 Charlie Smalls, The Wiz
1975–76 Marvin Hamslisch, Edward Kleban, Chorus Line
1976–77 Charles Strouse, Martin Charnin, Annie
1977–78 Cy Coleman, Betty Camden, Adolph Green, On The Twentieth Century
1978–79 Stephen Sondheim, Sweeney Todd
1979–80 Andrew Lloyd Webber, Tim Rice, Evita
1980–81 John Kander, Fred Ebb, Woman of the Year

OUTSTANDING PERFORMANCE BY AN ACTOR IN A PLAY
1970–71 Brian Bedford, The School for Wives
1971–72 Cliff Gorman, Lenny

1972–73 Alan Bates, Butley
1973–74 Michael Moriarty, Find Your Own Way Home
1974–75 John Kani and Winston Ntshona, Sizwe Banzi is Dead
1975–76 John Wood, Travesties
1976–77 Al Pacino, The Basic Training of Pavlo Hummel
1977–78 Barnard Hughes, Da
1978–79 Tom Conti, Whose Life is it Anyway?
1979–80 John Rubinstein, Children of a Lesser God
1980–81 Ian McKellen, Amadeus

OUTSTANDING PERFORMANCE BY AN ACTRESS IN A PLAY
1970–71 Maureen Stapleton, The Gingerbread Lady
1971–72 Sada Thompson, Twigs
1972–73 Julie Harris, The Last of Mrs. Lincoln
1973–74 Colleen Dewhurst, A Moon for the Misbegotten
1974–75 Ellen Burstyn, Same Time, Next Year
1975–76 Irene Worth, Sweet Bird of Youth
1976–77 Julie Harris, The Belle of Amherst
1977–78 Jessica Tandy, The Gin Game
1978–79 Constance Cummings, Wings
        Carole Shelley, The Elephant Man
1979–80 Phyllis Frelich, Children of a Lesser God
1980–81 Jane Lapotaire, Piaf

OUTSTANDING PERFORMANCE BY A FEATURED ACTOR IN A PLAY
1970–71 Paul Sand, Story Theatre
1971–72 Vincent Gardenia, The Prisoner of Second Avenue
1972–73 John Lithgow, The Changing Room
1973–74 Ed Flanders, A Moon for the Misbegotten
1974–75 Frank Langella, Seascape
1975–76 Edward Herrmann, Mrs Warren's Profession
1976–77 Jonathan Price, Comedians
1977–78 Lester Rawlins, Da
1978–79 Michael Gough, Bedroom Farce
1979–80 David Rounds, Morning's at Seven
1980–81 Brian Backer, The Floating Light Bulb

OUTSTANDING PERFORMANCE BY A FEATURED ACTRESS IN A PLAY
1970–71 Rae Allen, And Mrs Reardon Drinks a Little
1971–72 Elizabeth Wilson, Sticks and Bones
1972–73 Leora Dana, The Last of Mrs. Lincoln
1973–74 Frances Sternhagen, The Good Doctor
1974–75 Rita Moreno, The Ritz
1975–76 Shirley Knight, Kennedy's Children
1976–77 Trazana Beverly, For Coloured Girls Who Have Considered Suicide/When the Rainbow is Enuf
1977–78 Anne Wedgeworth, Chapter Two
1978–79 Joan Hickson, Bedroom Farce
1979–80 Dinah Manoff, I Ought to be in Pictures
1980–81 Swoosie Kurtz, Fifth of July

OUTSTANDING PERFORMANCE BY AN ACTOR IN A MUSICAL
1970–71 Hal Linden, The Rothschilds
1971–72 Phil Silvers, A Funny Thing Happened on the Way to the Forum
1972–73 Ben Vereen, Pippin

1973–74 Christopher Plummer, Cyrano
1974–75 John Cullum, Shenandoah
1975–76 George Rose, My Fair Lady
1976–77 Barry Bostwick, The Robber Bridegroom
1977–78 John Cullum, On the Twentieth Century
1978–79 Len Cariou, Sweeney Todd
1979–80 Jim Dale, Barnum
1980–81 Kevin Kline, The Pirates of Penzance

OUTSTANDING PERFORMANCE BY AN ACTRESS IN A MUSICAL
1970–71 Helen Gallagher, No No Nanette
1971–72 Alexis Smith, Follies
1972–73 Glynis Johns, A Little Night Music
1973–74 Virginia Capers, Raisin
1974–75 Angela Lansbury, Gypsy
1975–76 Donna McKechnie, Chorus Line
1976–77 Dorothy Loudon, Annie
1977–78 Liza Minelli, The Act
1978–79 Angela Lansbury, Sweeney Todd
1979–80 Patti LuPone, Evita
1980–81 Lauren Bacall, Woman of the Year

OUTSTANDING PERFORMANCE BY A FEATURED ACTOR IN A MUSICAL
1970–71 Keene Curtis, The Rothschilds
1971–72 Larry Blyden, A Funny Thing Happened on the Way to the Forum
1972–73 George S. Irving, Irene
1973–74 Tommy Tune, See Saw
1974–75 Ted Ross, The Wiz
1975–76 Sammy Williams, Chorus Line
1976–77 Lenny Baker, I Love my Wife
1977–78 Kelvin Klein, On the Twentieth Century
1978–79 Henderson Forsythe, The Best Little Whorehouse in Texas
1979–80 Mandy Patinkin, Evita
1980–81 Hinton Battle, Sophisticated Ladies

OUTSTANDING PERFORMANCE BY A FEATURED ACTRESS IN A MUSICAL
1970–71 Patsy Kelly, No No Nanette
1971–72 Linda Hopkins, Inner City
1972–73 Patricia Elliot, A Little Night Music
1973–74 Janie Sell, Over There
1974–75 Dee Dee Bridgewater, The Wiz
1975–76 Kelly Bishop, Chorus Line
1976–77 Delores Hall, Your Arms Too Short to Box with God
1977–78 Nell Carter, Ain't Misbehavin'
1978–79 Carlin Glynn, The Best Little Whorehouse in Texas
1979–80 Priscilla Lopez, A Day in Hollywood, A Night in the Ukraine
1980–81 Marilyn Cooper, Woman of the Year

SPECIAL AWARDS
1970–71 No award
1971–72 Richard Rodgers and Ethel Merman
1972–73 John Lindsay
1973–74 Revival of an American Play, A Moon for the Misbegotten Artistic Development of the Musical Theatre, Candide Contribution to the theatre of comedy, Peter Cook and Dudley Moore
        Concert Entertainment, Liza Minelli and Bette Midler

Dorothy Tutin presenting the 1978 John Whiting Award to Vince Foxhall for his play Gestures

1974–75 Overall contribution to the theatre, Neil Simon
1975–76 Mathilde Pincus
Arena Stage
Circle in the Square
Thomas H. Fitzgerald
1976–77 Barry Manilow
Diana Ross
Lily Tomlin
Equity Library Theatre
National Theatre of the Deaf
Mark Taper Forum, Los Angeles
1977–78 Lifetime Achievement, Irving Berlin
1978–79 Henry Fonda
Walter F. Diehl
Eugene O'Neill Theatre Center
American Conservatory Theatre (ACT)
1979–80 Mary Tyler Moore
Actors Theatre of Louisville
Goodspeed Opera House
1980–81 Lena Horne
Trinity Square Repertory Company, Providence, RI

JOHN WHITING AWARD

The John Whiting Award was instituted in 1965 by the Arts Council to commemorate the late John Whiting and his contribution to post-war British theatre. The award is given for work which demonstrates a new and distinctive development in dramatic writing and is particularly relevant to contemporary society. John Whiting was a member of the Arts Council Drama Panel from 1955 until his death in 1963.

1965 Award inaugurated
1966 Awarded jointly to Wole Soyinka for 'The Lion and the Jewel and Trials of Brother Jero', and Tom Stoppard for 'Rosencrantz and Guildenstern are Dead'.
1967 Awarded jointly to Peter Nichols for 'A Day in the Life of Joe Egg' and Peter Terson for 'The Ballad of the Artificial Mash' and 'Zigger Zagger'.
1968 Awarded jointly to Peter Barnes for 'The Ruling Class' and Edward Bond for 'Narrow Road to the Deep North'.
1969 Awarded jointly to Howard Brenton for 'Revenge, Christie in Love', etc. and 'The Freehold Company' director Nancy Meckler, for 'Antigone'
1970 Heathcote Williams for 'AC/DC'
1971 Mustapha Matura for 'As Time Goes By'
1972 Awarded jointly to John Arden and Margaretta D'Arcy
1973 David Rudkin for 'Ashes'
1974 John McGrath, but not accepted on a technicality
1975 David Edgar for 'Destiny'
1976 David Lan for 'The Winter Dancers'
1977 David Halliwell, for 'Prejudice' and Snoo Wilson, for 'The Glad Hand'
1978 Vince Foxall for 'Gestures'
1979 Stephen Bill for 'The Old Order'

Tiddlywinks

ENGLISH NATIONAL CHAMPIONSHIPS
Singles
1971 Alan Dean
1972 Alan Dean
1973 Alan Dean
1974 Keith Seaman
1975 Keith Seaman
1976 Alan Dean
1977 Nigel Knowles
1978 Alan Dean
1979 Jonathan Mapley
1980 Jonathan Mapley

Alan Dean (right) *during the England v USA match, 1978*

Pairs

1972 Jonathan Mapley and Harvey Orrock	1976 Keith Seaman and Jeremy Shepherd
1973 Alan Bolton and Simon Gould	1977 Jonathan Mapley and David Rose
1974 Alan Dean and Jeremy Shepherd	1978 Alan Dean and Keith Seaman
1975 Jonathan Mapley and Harvey Orrock	1979 Alan Dean and Keith Seaman
	1980 Jonathan Mapley and David Rose

Ties

TIE MANUFACTURERS' ASSOCIATION: TOP TIE MEN

Although the Association had previously named certain people as Top Tie Men, it was not until 1973 that the event was placed on a formal footing with a presentation of awards. Throughout the year, by monitoring newspaper and magazine photographs and television, the Association compiles its list. Here are the names: all 10 winners are equal, though their names are listed alphabetically.

1973
Leo Abse, MP
Richard Baker
The Duke of Bedford
John Bentley
Gordon Honeycombe
Kenneth Kendall
Rodney Marsh
Eric Morley
Sir Gerald Nabarro, MP
Derek Nimmo

1974
Malcolm Allison
Kingsley Amis
Michael Barratt
Patrick Cargill
Frank Chapple
Henry Cooper
Norman Lamont, MP
Roy Mason, MP
Leonard Parkin
Peter Woods

1975
The Marquess of Bath
Raymond Baxter
Ronnie Corbett
Dickie Davies
Jimmy Hill
Robert Maxwell
Nicholas Parsons
Paul Raymond
Don Revie
Nicholas Winterton, MP

1976
Reginald Bosanquet
Tony Britton
Eric Deakins, MP
Noel Edmonds
Stuart Hall
Victor Hill
Peter Parker
Geoffrey Pattie, MP
Sir Harold Wilson, MP
John Young

1977
Richard Baker
Nicholas Fairbairn, MP
Bruce Forsyth
Gerald Harper
Gordon Honeycombe
David Jacobs
Kenneth Kendall
Terry Neill
Leonard Parkin
Jimmy Perry

1978
Trevor Bannister
Lionel Blair
Ted Croker
Sir Charles Forte
Denis Healey, MP
Derek Hobson
Reginald Maudling, MP
Michael Smithwick
David Steel, MP
Alan Weeks

1979
Joel Barnett, MP
Frank Bough
Trevor Brooking
James Callaghan, MP
David Chipp
Sir Derek Ezra
Joe Gormley
Sir Geoffrey Howe, MP
Laurie McMenemy
Terry Wogan

1980
John Francome
Clement Freud, MP
Greville Janner
Dick Jeeps
Trevor McDonald
Lance Percival
The Rt. Hon. James Prior, MP
Jimmy Savile
Hugh Scully
Donald Sinden

1981
Norman St John Stevas MP
Tom Pendry MP
Terry Griffiths
Sir Michael Edwardes
George Melly
Sir Robin Day
Denis Thatcher
Edward Fox
John Oaksey
David Owen MP

Toastmasters

THE GUILD OF PROFESSIONAL TOASTMASTERS BEST AFTER DINNER AWARD

This was the idea of Ivor Spencer, President and Founder of the Guild, to give an incentive to speakers to improve the quality of their speeches. The Award has been won by the following people. After their names their reaction on hearing the news for the first time about their Award is mentioned.

1967 Lord Redcliffe-Maud, the former Master of University College Oxford, 'What an honour, you have made my day.'

1968 Sir Harold Wilson, former Prime Minister. Michael Halls, Sir Harold's private secretary, said 'Sir Harold said it is the nicest thing that's happened to him since he became Prime Minister.'

1969 Sheila Hancock, 'I can't believe it, please repeat it.'

1970 Alfred Marks, on hearing the news in his dressing room at the London Palladium, said 'It's about time.'

1971 Graham Hill. 'You couldn't have picked a better speaker. When can I make my speech?'

1972 Clement Freud. 'Thank you, I see you have got good taste.'

1973 Rachel Heyhoe. 'I am thrilled.'

1974 Tommy Trinder. 'You're kidding.'

1975 Marshal of the Royal Air Force Sir Arthur Harris. 'I am delighted to hear the news, and will be coming back especially from South Africa to receive the Award.'

1976 No award.
1977 Commissioner Catherine Bramwell-Booth, 96-year-old grand-daughter of the Founder of the Salvation Army. 'I can't believe it. What odd bedfellows, myself as a non-drinker mixing with fellows who are involved all their lives with toasting and drinking. But I am absolutely thrilled and can't wait to make the speech at the Award Luncheon. God bless you.'
1978 No award.
1979 No award.
1980 No award

Tourism

COME TO BRITAIN TROPHY

The 'Come to Britain' Trophy was first offered by the British Tourist Authority in 1956 to stimulate interest in the provision of new services and amenities for visitors from overseas. The Trophy – Britain's 'Travel Oscar' is an award for tourist enterprise to the company, organisation, local authority or individual judged to have introduced the year's most outstanding new service, facility or amenity for overseas visitors. In addition there are two special awards, one for public enterprise, and one for private enterprise. Previous winners:

1956 Trust Houses Ltd (for modernisation within the hotel group)
1957 *Daily Telegraph* (for Son et Lumiere at Greenwich, London)
1958 'Talk of the Town' (for the 'Talk of the Town' theatre-restaurant in London)
1959 British Transport Commission (for various improvements and innovations in rail, hotel and catering services)
1960 Friends of Norwich Cathedral (for Son et Lumiere at Norwich Cathedral)
1961 Borough of Torquay (for the Princess Gardens Development Scheme)
1962 Chichester Festival Theatre Production Company Ltd (for the Chichester Festival Theatre in Sussex)
1963 Eastbourne Corporation (for the Congress Theatre and Conference Hall)
1964 Directors, Ulster Folk Museum (for the Ulster Folk Museum at Cultra Manor, Craigavad, Belfast)
1965 Isle of Man Harbour Board (for the Sea Terminal at Douglas)
1966 Brecon Beacons National Park Mountain Centre (for the Mountain Centre in mid-Wales)
1967 Aviemore Centre (for the Aviemore Centre in Inverness-shire)
1968 Anchor Hotels and Taverns Ltd (for the development of hotels throughout Britain; for the organisation of package tours; and for the introduction of 'Tourist Entertainment' houses)
1969 The Illuminating Engineering Society (for the installation in Trafalgar Square, London, of Britain's biggest ever floodlighting scheme)
1970 Visitor Centres Ltd (for the 'Landmark' visitor centre at Carrbridge, Inverness-shire)
1971 Medway Queen Co. Ltd (for the Medway Queen Leisure Park, Isle of Wight)

A model of the Tower of London at Thorpe Park, winner of the 1979 'Come to Britain' trophy

1972 Quarry Tours Ltd (for the Llechwedd Slate Caverns, Blaenau Ffestiniog, North Wales)
1973 Ironbridge Gorge Museum Trust (for the Ironbridge Gorge Museum, Shropshire)
1974 Welsh Canal Holiday Craft Ltd (for the Canal Exhibition Centre, Llangollen)
1975 National Railway Museum, York
1976 National Exhibition Centre, Birmingham
1977 Brighton Centre
1978 Brighton Marina
1979 Thorpe Park, Chertsey, Surrey (for a pleasure park entered by Leisure Sports Ltd)
1980 The market at Covent Garden, London

Toys

TOY OF THE YEAR
The National Association of Toy Retailers promotes this annual competition for manufacturers. It began in 1965. Retailers around the country vote for the year's ten most popular toys, selected by the Association. Winners:

1965	007 Aston Martin	1973	Master Mind
1966	Action Man	1974	Lego – Family-size kit
1967	Spirograph	1975	Lego – Basic kit
1968	Sindy doll	1976	Peter Powell Kites
1969	Hot Wheels	1977	Playpeople
1970	Sindy doll	1978	Combine Harvester
1971	Katie Kopycat	1979	Legoland Space
1972	Plasticraft	1980	Rubik's Cube

Andy Gray, Scotland and Wolverhampton football star, endeavouring to solve the Rubik's Cube puzzle, 1980 Toy of the Year

Trampolining

WORLD CHAMPIONSHIPS
World Championships were first held in 1964; there are individual championships for men and women and synchronised events for men and women. There is also a team event awarded on the basis of each nation's individual performances.

INDIVIDUAL CHAMPIONS
MEN
1964 Danny Millman (USA)
1965 George Irwin (USA)
1966 Wayne Miller (USA)
1967 Dave Jacobs (USA)
1968 Dave Jacobs (USA)
1970 Wayne Miller (USA)
1972 Paul Luxon (GB)
1974 Richard Tisson (Fra)
1976 Richard Tisson (Fra)
1978 Tonisch (USSR)
1980 Stewart Matthews (GB)

WOMEN
1964 Judy Wills (USA)
1965 Judy Wills (USA)
1966 Judy Wills (USA)
1967 Judy Wills (USA)
1968 Judy Wills (USA)
1970 Renee Ransom (USA)

Judy Wills (left) *and Janice McGaughey* (Associated Newspapers)

1972 Alexandra Nicholson (USA)
1974 Alexandra Nicholson (USA)
1976 Svetlana Levina (USSR)
1978 Tatyana Anisimova (USSR)
1980 Ruth Keller (Swi)

Volleyball

OLYMPIC CHAMPIONSHIPS
First contested in 1964.

MEN	WOMEN
1964 USSR	1964 Japan

		MEN	WOMEN
1968 USSR	1968 USSR	1949 USSR	1952 USSR
1972 Japan	1972 USSR	1952 USSR	1956 USSR
1976 Poland	1976 Japan	1956 Czechoslovakia	1960 USSR
1980 USSR	1980 USSR	1960 USSR	1962 Japan
		1962 USSR	1966 Japan
		1966 Czechoslovakia	1970 USSR
		1970 GDR	1974 Japan
WORLD CHAMPIONSHIPS		1974 Poland	1978 Cuba
In addition to the Olympic Champions listed		1978 USSR	
above.			

Walking

Olympic Games: See Athletics section for Olympic winners.

LUGANO CUP
The IAAF Walking Team Championship is now contested biennially by national teams for the Lugano Cup, which was first held at Lugano in 1961. Winners:

1961 Great Britain	1973 GDR
1963 Great Britain	1975 USSR
1965 GDR	1977 Mexico
1967 GDR	1979 Mexico
1970 GDR	1981 –

RWA CHAMPIONSHIPS
The Race Walking Association (RWA) hold annual British championships at 10 miles (first held 1947), 20000 metres (1965), 35000 metres (held at 20 miles 1908–77 and 30000 metres 1978), 50000 metres (1930) and 100000 metres (1979). Winners of the most titles (in brackets the winners of the most AAA titles held at 2 miles/3000 metres and 7 miles/10,000 metres) have been:

19 Paul Nihill (8)
 9 Don Thompson (0); Olly Flynn (0)
 8 Laurence Allen (0); Harold Whitlock (0)
 7 Ken Matthews (10).
Roger Mills has won 10 AAA titles (and 5 RWA) and Roland Hardy 8 AAA titles (and 6 RWA).

'Mighty Mouse' Don Thompson nears the Olympic Stadium, Rome 1960 (Central Press Photos)

WOMEN'S NATIONAL ROAD WALKING CHAMPIONSHIP
First held in 1933. Winners since 1977:

1977 Carol Tyson
1978 Carol Tyson
1979 Elaine Cox
1980 Carol Tyson
Most wins: 8 Judy Farr 1962–65, 1968, 1970, 1975–76; 4 Joyce Heath 1947–50; Betty Jenkins 1967, 1969, 1971–72

Water Polo

OLYMPIC CHAMPIONSHIPS
First contested in 1900 although the teams in 1900 and 1904 were club rather than national teams. Winners (men) since 1948:

1948 Italy
1952 Hungary
1956 Hungary
1960 Italy
1964 Hungary
1968 Yugoslavia
1972 USSR
1976 Hungary
1980 USSR

WORLD CHAMPIONSHIPS
First contested 1973. Winners:

1973 Hungary
1975 USSR
1978 Italy

Water Skiing

WORLD CHAMPIONSHIPS

The first world championships were held at

Mike Hazelwood (Daily Telegraph)

Juan Les Pins, France, in 1949. Championships are now contested biennially in three parts – slalom, tricks and jumping, with a separate contest for the best overall performer. Overall men's and women's world champions have been:

MEN
1949 Christian Jourdan (Fra) and
      Guy de Clercq (Bel)
1950 Dick Pope Jr (USA)
1953 Alfredo Mendoza (USA)
1955 Alfredo Mendoza (USA)
1957 Joe Cash (USA)
1959 Chuck Stearns (USA)
1961 Bruno Zaccardi (Ita)
1963 Billy Spencer (USA)
1965 Roland Hillier (USA)
1967 Mike Suyderhoud (USA)
1971 George Athans (Can)
1973 George Athans (Can)

1975 Carlos Suarez (Ven)
1977 Mike Hazelwood (GB)
1979 Joel McClintock (Can)

WOMEN
1949 Willa Worthington (USA)
1950 Willa McGuire (née Worthington) (USA)
1953 Leah Marie Rawls (USA)
1955 Willa McGuire (USA)
1957 Marina Doria (Swi)
1959 Vickie an Hook (USA)
1961 Sylvie Hulsemann (Lux)
1963 Jeanette Brown (USA)
1965 Liz Allan (USA)
1967 Jeanette Stewart-Wood (GB)
1969 Liz Allan (USA)
1971 Christy Weir (USA)
1973 Lisa St John (USA)
1975 Lix Shetter (née Allan) (USA)
1979 Cindy Todd (USA)

Team competition has been won by the USA for the 12 successive world championships from 1957.

Weightlifitng

WORLD AND OLYPMPIC CHAMPIONSHIPS
The first weightlifting world championships were held in 189? and weightlifitng was included in the first modern Olympic Games in 1896.

Vasiliy Alexeev, whose hobby is cooking
(Universal Pictorial Press)

From 1928 to 1972 the recognised lifts (all two-hadnded) were 'clean and press,' 'snatch', and 'clean and jerk'. In 1972 the clean and press was dropped from the international programme. At the world championships medals are awarded both for the individual lifts and for the aggregate total achieved in each weight category. Winners (by total) since 1973 (‘ = Olympic champions):

52 kg

1973	Mohammed Nassiri (Irn)	240.0
1974	Mohammed Nassiri (Irn)	232.5
1975	Zigmunt Smalczerz (Pol)	237.5
1976*	Alexander Voronin (USSR)	242.5
1977	Alexander Voronin (USSR)	247.5
1978	Kanybek Osmonaliev (USSR)	240.0
1980*	Kanybek Osmonaliev (USSR)	245.0

56kg

1973	Atanas Kirov (USSR)	257.5
1974	Atanas Kirov (USSR)	255.00
1975	Atanas Kirov (USSR)	255.0
1976*	Norair Nurikyan (Bul)	262.5
1977	Jiro Hosotani (Jap)	252.5
1978	Daniel Nunez (Cub)	260.0
1979	Anton Kodiabashev (Bul)	267.£
1980*	Daniel Nunez (Cub)	275.0

60 kg

1973	Dito Shanidze (USSR)	272.5
1974	Georgi Todorov (Bul)	28.0
1975	Georgi Todorov (Bul)	285.0
1976*	Nikolai Kolesnikov (USSR)	185.0
1977	Nikolai Kolesnikov (USSR)	280.0
1978	Nikolai Kolesnikov (USSR)	270.0
1979	Marek Seweryn (USSR)	290.0
1980*	Viktor Mazin (USSR)	290.0

67.5 kg

1973	Mukharbi Kirzhinov (USSR)	305.0
1974	Peter Korol (USSR)	305.0
1975	Peter Korol (USSR)	312.5
1976*	Peter Korol (USSR)	305.0
1977	Roberto Urrutia (Cub)	315.0
1978	Yanko Russev (Bul)	310.0
1979	Yanko Russev (Bul)	332.5
1980*	Yanko Russev (Bul)	342.5

75 kg

1973	Nedelcho Kolev (Bul)	337.5
1974	Nedelcho Kolev (Bul)	335.0
1975	Peter Wenzel (GDR)	335.0
1976*	Jordan Mitkov (Bul)	335.0
1977	Yuri Vardanyan (USSR)	345.0
1978	Roberto Urrutia (Cub)	347.5
1979	Roberto Urrutia (Cub)	345.0
1980*	Assen Zlatev (Bul)	360.0

82.5 kg

1973	Vladimir Rizhenkov (USSR)	350.0
1974	Trendafil Stoychev (Bul)	350.0
1975	Valeri Shary (USSR)	357.5
1976*	Valeri Shary (USSR)	365.0
1977	Gennadiy Bessonov (USSR)	352.5
1978	Yuri Vardanyan (USSR)	377.5
1979	Yuri Vardanyan (USSR)	370.0
1980*	Yuri Vardanyan (USSR)	400.0

90 kg

1973	David Rigert (USSR)	365.0
1974	David Rigert (USSR)	387.5
1975	David Rigert (USSR)	377.5
1976*	David Rigert (USSR)	382.5
1977	Sergei Poltoratski (USSR)	375.0
1978	Rolf Milser (Ger)	377.5
1979	Gennadiy Bessonov (USSR)	380.0
1980*	Peter Baczako (Hun)	377.5

100 kg

1973	Not held	
1974	Not held	
1975	Not held	
1976	Not held	
1977	Anatoli Kozlov (USSR)	367.5
1978	David Rigert (USSR)	390.0
1979	Pavel Sirchin (USSR)	385.0
1980	Ota Zaremba (Cze)	395.0

110 kg

1973	Pavel Pervushin (USSR)	385.0
1974	Vladimir Ustyuzhin (USSR)	380.0
1975	Valentin Khristov (Bul)	417.5
1976*	Yuri Saitsev (USSR)	385.0
1977	Valentin Khristov (Bul)	405.0
1978	Yuri Saitsev (USSR)	402.5
1979	Sergei Arakelov (USSR)	410.0
1980*	Leonid Taranenko (USSR)	422.5

+110 kg

1973	Vasili Alexeev (USSR)	402.5
1974	Vasili Alexeev (USSR)	425.0
1975	Vasili Alexeev (USSR)	427.5
1976*	Vasili Alexeev (USSR)	440.0
1977	Vasili Alexeev (USSR)	430.0
1978	Jurgen Heuser (GDR)	417.5
1979	Sultan Rakhmanov (USSR)	430.0
1980*	Sultan Rakhmanov (USSR)	440.0

Wine

THE NEW STANDARD ANGLO-FRENCH WINE TASTING CHALLENGE

This wine tasting contest, started in 1979, between the *Evening Standard* (from 1980, *The New Standard*) and *Le Figaro* teams is an annual event, the winning team receiving the Anglo-French Wine Tasting Trophy. Answers to various questions and tests are awarded marks and the team and individual with the highest number of points wins. Winners:

1979 *Evening Standard* team, whose members took the top four places. The overall winner was 75-year-old Robert Mapley.
1980 *Le Figaro* team. The overall winner was M. Raoul Salama from Paris.

Robert Mapley overall winner of The New Standard *1979 wine challenge*

Wrestling

World championships are held annually except in Olympic years at both Freestyle and Graeco-Roman style. Most world and Olympic titles have been won by:

8 Aleksandr Medved (USSR) Freestyle light-heavy 1964*, 1966; heavy 1967, 1968*; super-heavy 1969, 1970, 1971, 1972*
7 Nikolai Bolboshin (USSR) Graeco-Roman heavy 1973, 1974, 1976*, 1978, 1979; super-heavy 1971, 1977
6 Ali Aliev (USSR) Freestyle fly 1959, 1961, 1962; bantam 1966, 1967, 1968*
6 Abdollah Movahed (Irn) Freestyle light 1965–70 (inc. 1968*)
6 Levan Tediashvili (USSR) Freestyle middle 1971, 1972*; light-heavy 1973–75, 1976*
6 Soslan Andiev (USSR) Freestyle super-heavy 1973, 1975, 1976*, 1977–78, 1980*
5 Viktor Igumenov (USSR) Graeco-Roman welter 1966, 1967, 1969, 1970, 1971
5 Roman Rurua (USSR) Graeco-Roman feather 1966, 1967, 1968*, 1969, 1970
5 Valeriy Rezantyev (USSR) Graeco-Roman light-heavy 1971, 1972*, 1973, 1974, 1976*
5 Yuji Takada (Jap) Freestyle fly 1974–77, 1979

1980 OLYMPIC CHAMPIONSHIPS

The moment of winning his third gold medal for Alexandr Medved (Wm. Baxter)

Weight	Freestyle	Graeco-Roman style
Over 100 kg	Soslan Andiev (USSR)	Aleksandr Kolchinsky (USSR)
100 kg	Ilya Mate (USSR)	Gheorghi Raikov (Bul)
90 kg	Sanasar Oganesyan (USSR)	Norbert Nottny (Hun)

Weight	Freestyle	Graeco-Roman style
82 kg	Ismail Abilov (Bul)	Gennadiy Korban (USSR)
74 kg	Valentin Raitchev (Bul)	Ferenc Kocsis (Hun)
68 kg	Saipulla Absaidov (USSR)	Stefan Rusu (Rom)
62 kg	Magomedgasan Abushev (USSR)	Stilianos Migiakis (Gre)
57 kg	Sergei Beloglazov (USSR)	Shamil Serikov (USSR)
52 kg	Anatoliy Beloglazov (USSR)	Vakhtang Blagidze (USSR)
48 kg	Claudio Pollio (Ita)	Zaksylik Ushkempirov (USSR)

Yachting

AMERICA'S CUP

The America's Cup is an international challenge trophy, named after the schooner *America*, the winner of a race around the Isle of Wight in 1851. All the winning yachts listed here have come from the USA.

1870	*Magic*
1871	*Columbia and Sappho*
1876	*Madelaine*
1881	*Mischief*
1885	*Puritan*
1886	*Mayflower*
1887	*Volunteer*
1893	*Vigilant*
1895	*Defender*
1899	*Columbia*
1901	*Columbia*
1903	*Reliance*
1920	*Resolute*
1930	*Enterprise*

1934	*Rainbow*	1967	*Intrepid*
1937	*Ranger*	1970	*Intrepid*
1958	*Columbia*	1974	*Courageous*
1962	*Weatherly*	1977	*Courageous*
1964	*Constellation*	1980	*Freedom*

ADMIRAL'S CUP

The Admiral's Cup is contested biennially by national 3-yacht teams. The competition comprises four races – a 200-mile Channel race, two inshore races held during Cowes Week, and finally the 605-mile Fastnet race from Cowes to the Fastnet Rock, off Southern Ireland, and back to Plymouth. First held 1957.

1957	Great Britain	1969	USA
1959	Great Britain	1971	Great Britain
1961	USA	1973	W. Germany
1963	Great Britain	1975	Great Britain
1965	Great Britain	1977	Great Britain
1967	Australia	1979	Australia

OLYMPIC CHAMPIONSHIPS

The types of boat specified for Olympic competition have varied considerably over the years since 1900 when yachting was first included in the Olympic Games. Individual winner of most Olympic titles:

4 Paul Elvstrom (Den) *Firefly* 1948, *Finn* 1952, 1956, 1960

SINGLEHANDED TRANS-ATLANTIC CROSSING RACE

Now held every four years, all races, except in 1962, have been the Royal Western/Observer Trans-Atlantic Race. It is now raced from Plymouth to Newport, Rhode Island.

1960 *Gipsy Moth III* – Francis Chichester (GB) 40 days 12 hr 30 min
1962 *Gipsy Moth III* – Francis Chichester (GB) 33 days 15 hr 7 min
1964 *Pen Duick II* – Eric Tabarly (Fra) 27 days 3 hr 56 min
1968 *Sir Thomas Lipton* – Geoffrey Williams (GB) 25 days 20 hr 33 min
1972 *Pen Duick IV* – Alain Colas (Fra) 20 days 13 hr 15 min
1976 *Pen Duick VI* – Eric Tabarly (Fra) 23 days 20 hr 12 min
1980 *Moxie* – Philip Weld (USA) 17 days 23 hr 12 min

WHITBREAD ROUND THE WORLD RACE

1973–74 Raymond Carlin, *Sayula II* (Mex)
1977–78 Cornelius van Rietschoten, *Flyer* (Hol)

33 Export, *one of the contestants in the Whitbread Round the World Race*

Index